# Walking This Path Together

# Walking This Path Together
## Anti-Racist and Anti-Oppressive
## Child Welfare Practice

*Edited by Susan Strega & Sohki Aski Esquao [Jeannine Carrière]*

Fernwood Publishing • Halifax & Winnipeg

Editing and design: Brenda Conroy
Cover art: Seletze [Delmar Johnnie]
Cover design: John van der Woude
Printed and bound in Canada by Hignell Book Printing
Printed on paper containing 100% post-consumer fibre.

Published in Canada by Fernwood Publishing
32 Oceanvista Lane
Black Point, Nova Scotia, B0J 1B0
and #8–222 Osborne Street, Winnipeg, Manitoba, R3L 1Z3
www.fernwoodpublishing.ca


Fernwood Publishing Company Limited gratefully acknowledges the financial support
of the Government of Canada through the Book Publishing Industry Development
Program (BPIDP), the Canada Council for the Arts and the Nova Scotia
Department of Tourism and Culture for our publishing program.

Library and Archives Canada Cataloguing in Publication

Walking this path together : anti-racist and anti-oppressive child welfare practice /
edited by Susan Strega and Sohki Aski Esquao (Jeannine Carrière).

Includes bibliographical references.
ISBN 978-1-55266-292-2

1. Native children--Canada--Social conditions. 2. Native
children--Services for--Canada. 3. Social work with native
peoples--Canada. 4. Racism in social services--Canada. 5. Child
welfare--Canada. I. Strega, Susan II. Esquao, Sohki Aski

HV745.A6W34 2009          362.7089'97071          C2008-907799-7

# Contents

*We dedicate this book to the memories of*
*Richard Cardinal, Phoenix Sinclair,*
*Lester Desjarlais, Sherry Charlie*
*and all the too many other children*
*who have died while in the care*
*of child welfare authorities.*

# Acknowledgments

This book is a collective effort, a true walking together, far beyond being an edited collection. We honour the work of the contributors, who shared the vision with us for many months, and the relationships we developed in the course of our work together. We are grateful for the support, interest and engagement of our colleagues and co-workers in the School of Social Work, University of Victoria, and like-minded colleagues, academics and professionals from across Canada. We thank the children and families we worked with in child welfare, who taught us how to be better social workers and tolerated our fumbles on the road to respectful practice. We acknowledge and appreciate that our family and friends often carried the load while this work absorbed us. We are especially grateful for the contributions of Elizabeth Manning, graduate assistant and copy editor extraordinaire, not only for her vast array of skills but for the patience, respect and grace she brought to every page. We acknowledge the work of Seletze [Delmar Johnnie], the Cowichan artist who allowed his vision of the circle of connection and the fierce protectiveness of mother bear with her cubs to grace the cover. We thank John van der Woude, graphic designer, who was respectful both of Seletze's artistic vision and of our need to see it realized in a particular way. We are grateful for the patient work of the rest of the Fernwood production team: Beverley Rach, Brenda Conroy and Debbie Mathers. We thank the three anonymous reviewers for their contributions to improving the chapters individually and the book as a whole. We owe a particular dept to our publisher, Wayne Antony, for taking the risk to publish a radically different book about child welfare practice, for opening the door to new writers and for challenging us as editors to articulate our vision. Finally we acknowledge those who walked and still walk with us in spirit so that we both survived child welfare and arrived in this place where we might contribute to transforming it.

## About the Cover Artist

Seletze [Delmar Johnnie] is a member of the Khenipsen Band, of the Cowichan Tribes in Duncan, B.C. Delmar was born in 1946 and raised by his grandmother. At the age of five, Seletze was sent to Kuper Island Residential School. Because of his experiences at residential school, Delmar has committed his life to healing and worked as a drug and alcohol counsellor until he decided to dedicate his life to the arts. Seletze is a renowned Coast Salish artist and recently designed the logo for the 2008 North American Indigenous Games. Seletze's magnificent art is visible in many places throughout the Duncan area.

As a young boy, Delmar often sat by the river where he would listen to an old man sing a song. One day Delmar's grandmother heard him sing the song and asked where he had learned it. Delmar told her about the old man at the river. His grandmother was shocked and told him that the old man was her late father, who had been dead for years, and the song was his "thank you" song. Seletze knows the teachings of his grandmother, the ancestors and other Sulxwen (Elders) are a sacred part of his own personal transformation and is willing to share his teachings with others who are seeking their own personal transformation. Seletze believes that healing is a lifelong process and every day we should pray to the Creator to be a better human being tomorrow than we were today. Seletze believes we should always strive to be the best human beings we can possibly be. For those of us who are blessed to know him, we know through his love and laughter that he exemplifies being fully human.

# Introduction

*Susan Strega and Sohki Aski Esquao [Jeannine Carrière]*

We are both grateful to be visitors here on the lands of the Esquimalt, LeKwunget and Songhees peoples. We have been allowed to live, work and play here, and we recognize how deeply blessed we are.

## The Bridge

The Norwood Bridge crosses the Assiniboine River just west of its confluence with the Red River in Winnipeg. The meeting of the rivers marks a traditional and sacred meeting place for Manitoba Indigenous peoples. The bridge marks a division between two realities: to the north lies Main Street, the epicenter of Winnipeg's poverty, violence and despair. To the south, Marion Street is a gateway to working-class neighbourhoods and new middle-class suburban developments. As young women at various times we both lived under that bridge, because it provided shelter and protection when social workers could or would not. Although we didn't know each other back then we shared a connection, as we were both affected by child welfare through foster care and adoption. We shared the experience of wondering which side of the bridge we might end up on — or whether it was even worth continuing. After long and separate journeys, we met in the hallways of the School of Social Work at the University of Victoria. We had survived, and how amazing that we had both become social workers and then teachers of social workers! Our belief is that somehow our ancestors invited us to walk this path together, and it is out of those separate but shared journeys that we came to work together.

We share a sisterhood and a story of resistance and survival that in many ways represents the genesis of this book (and we tell a little of our stories later). We developed this book because we want to make a difference for the young people of today who still sit under that bridge or other places of temporary shelter, looking out and wondering, "Is there any hope for me?" We want to make a difference for the families and communities they have been torn from, saved from or estranged from. We believe there is hope, and we invited our like-minded friends and colleagues to share their hopes for transforming child welfare practice.

## What This Book Is and Who It Is For

This is a collection of original pieces by writers and practitioners from diverse locations who share a belief that anti-racist and anti-oppressive practice is both necessary and possible in child welfare. All of them are fundamentally committed to the notion that we can best help those with whom we work when we are willing to work together across difference — when we can walk the path together. The writers in this book share information about strategies and concrete skills that may help in this journey. They offer students and practitioners alike the opportunity to explore a range of ideas and personal visions that can create positive possibilities for children, their families and communities. As editors we are honoured to present these voices. Across their diversity every contributor shares a passionate commitment to the transformation of child welfare through socially just practices.

Walking this path together is the theme, intention and foundation of this book. Most social work students enter their studies and most social workers enter the field because they are interested in working together with people facing challenges. Over the course of social work education a great deal is taught about why working together is necessary not only to assist clients with making changes they desire but to address the context of domination and subordination that shapes their lives and struggles. Students learn that anti-racist and anti-oppressive strategies are essential to bring about the reduction and elimination of structural inequalities and the racism, colonialism, misogyny, ableism and other justifying belief systems that lie at their root. Yet most students can recount a story of entering their practicum placement or first job and being told, "Forget all that useless stuff you learned in school – now we are going to teach you how to practice in the 'real world.'" Inevitably that "real world" perspective involves individualizing and pathologizing practices and perspectives that separate workers and clients into two separate and distinct groups – a hierarchy in which the worker is different and better than the client, who is "Other": lesser than in almost every way. The chapters in this book challenge that idea.

This book is also a challenge to the Anglo-American child welfare paradigm that shapes all current Canadian child welfare policy and practice. We use the term "Anglo-American" rather than "White" in recognition that some White countries (for example, Belgium, Netherlands and Germany) operate child welfare systems oriented to collaboration and family preservation (for a discussion of different child welfare paradigms, see Cameron et al. 2007). We centre Indigenous perspectives because these approaches are based in the paradigm of community caring (Cameron et al. 2007) that we consider essential to transforming child welfare. We also foreground Indigenous voices in recognition of the vastly disproportionate over-representation of Indigenous children and families on child welfare caseloads across Canada. This book therefore represents a radical departure from most other child welfare texts, which relegate Indigenous perspectives to a single chapter or subsume them and other non-Anglo-American ideas in a chapter on "cultural competence." Anti-racist and anti-oppressive approaches to child welfare practice require us to understand any differences between ourselves and those we work with not as technical challenges that can be met through understanding the "Other" but as fundamentally related to power and our own positionality. The first three chapters consider these matters in detail.

While all social work encounters are shaped by power and oppression, we contend that this is particularly so in child welfare because child welfare workers are given the right, through their mandate, to investigate, monitor, assess and dispose of cases in ways that have far-reaching impacts on children, families and communities. In anti-oppressive theory, power is understood as widely dispersed rather than only held by one group and wielded over another group. Individual workers therefore have a choice about whether to produce social justice or reproduce social injustice through how they practice. Our encounters with clients must be placed in a specific time and place so that we can understand the meaning of these experiences in terms of prevailing ideologies, social facts and cultural differences. We must be self-reflective, always considering how our values, beliefs and location are affecting our interactions with people we are working with — the intention being to understand these interactions not in psychological terms, but in terms of sociology, history, ethics and politics. We must be committed to transparency; people we work with must know what we are doing and how we are doing it, and have ample opportunity, without fear of consequence, to reflect on and comment on what we are doing and how we are doing it. We must consider who we believe ourselves accountable to, and why. And we must constantly challenge oppression, not only within larger systems, but also in our interactions, in the organization we work for and within ourselves. Within the current child welfare context, this is a challenge indeed!

Over the last few decades standardized procedures such as risk and safety assessments, legal reporting requirements and managerial processes have proliferated in Canadian child welfare, leaving little room for worker discretion. Students and new workers are taught to regard policy manuals and practice standards as child welfare's "bible" and come to expect that careful attention to these prescriptions will produce the child welfare miracle: every situation successfully resolved. Many of us sitting in our offices on a Friday afternoon with six siblings to place in a resource that does not exist have hoped for these miracles. Although child welfare practice can be one of the most rewarding careers in social work, the current context means that child welfare practice is also challenging and sometimes difficult. This book offers a way through those challenges and difficulties that affirms the strengths and wisdom of those with whom we work. While we envision that the primary audience for this book will be social work students, instructors and practitioners connected to child welfare, we believe the content will be useful to human service practitioners in many related disciplines. For example, the chapters that address violence, working with youth, addictions and other critical topics are applicable to a cross section of professional and academic readers. We hope the book will be used by child welfare's collateral partners in various ministries and community social services. Finally, we hope that the book informs decision-makers who may be looking at ways to improve the delivery of services for children and families.

If there is one reason above all others why we put this book together it is because, although so little has changed in child welfare, we believe that it can and must change, both systemically and in practice. The statistics documenting the number of Indigenous children in care haunt us. The larger story of child welfare parallels our own experiences: those who come to the attention of child welfare are disproportionately poor Indigenous women. Although White children and families have always fared better and continue to do so, we know that poor, racialized, disabled and otherwise marginalized children and families are also vulnerable to the child welfare system.

This collection brings together practitioners, researchers and theorists who are committed to transforming child welfare. We believe them to be some of the most significant voices in Canadian child welfare, people who have greatly influenced our own practice and teaching. The chapters in this book share many commonalities, most importantly that they ask us in each moment in practice to "see double." This means that we must understand the situations of the families and children we work with in the context of the larger structural problems they are facing and at the same time understand what we need to do on the ground in the moment. In one way or another each of these chapters also reminds us that we must be continually engaged in the journey from the head to the heart if we are to be effective, compassionate and respectful practitioners. And many writers emphasize that traditional Indigenous childcare methods have worked since time immemorial and thus we must be mindful of Indigenous ways of knowing, always aware that the need for child welfare will only change once issues such as Indigenous sovereignty, reparation to Indigenous peoples, poverty and wealth disparity are dealt with in some significant manner.

## The Context of Practice

State intervention in Canadian families in the name of protecting children has been happening for more than a century. Over this time, child welfare legislation and policies have oscillated between high-intervention/many-apprehension and low-intervention/few-apprehension paradigms (Dumbrill 2006). Periodic concern that the state is too intrusive into the private sphere of the family has alternated with demands for greater state involvement in the wake of high profile child death inquiries. Currently we are in a high intervention cycle, where in Ontario, for example, in the period 1998 to 2004 apprehensions increased by 65 percent (Dumbrill 2006: 12).

Mandatory reporting laws, x-ray technology, which facilitated the diagnosis of physical child abuse, and feminist activism about child sexual abuse and violence against women all contributed to the expansion of definitions of abuse and neglect and the creation of new categories of child maltreatment that are said to require state surveillance, monitoring and intervention (Vine et al. 2006).

As many writers note (see, for example, Blackstock 2008; Lindsey 2003; Roberts 2002; Swift 1995), child welfare does not intervene in every family experiencing problems. The primary determinants of whether or not a family comes to the attention of child welfare authorities are race and poverty. As detailed in the *Royal Commission Report on Aboriginal Peoples*, the child welfare system across Canada has been marked by the consistent over-representation of Indigenous children in care (Government of Canada 1996; Mirwaldt 2004). In Canada today, Indigenous children and families are still vastly over-represented on child welfare caseloads. There are three times as many Indigenous children in care today as there were at the height of the operation of residential schools in the 1940s (Mandell et al. 2007: 117). Although provincial child welfare data vary, it is estimated that across Canada 38 percent of children in care (approximately 25,000 of the 66,000) are Indigenous despite representing only 5 percent of the child population in Canada. A report exploring the numbers of children in care in three sample provinces found that although non-Indigenous children represented over 92 percent of the overall child population in these provinces, only 0.67 percent of non-Indigenous children were in care as of May 2005, compared to 3.31 percent of Métis children and 10.23 percent of Status Indian children (Blackstock et al. 2004).

In an attempt to explain these percentages, Thobani (2007: 119) notes that the "residential school system institutionalized the idea that Aboriginal families were incommensurable with the national ideal and that the welfare of Aboriginal children was in conflict with that of their families and communities, including that of their mothers." In the colonial context Indigenous peoples in Canada have experienced many significant losses, including, to name but a few, land, children, language and spiritual practices (Bellefeuille and Ricks 2003; Scarth 2004; Schouls 2002; Youngblood Henderson 2000). Although the rest of Canadian children were viewed as being dependent upon their families, Indigenous children were denied this right through residential schools and the child welfare system, which "pathologized individual Aboriginal mothers and their families as deficient, further enhancing personalized definitions of this lack" (Thobani 2007: 123). Schouls (2002: 15) explains that

> the ability for Canadians to *justify* the innumerable documented acts of injustice against Aboriginal peoples on the grounds that European culture was more "modern" and thus "superior" stands as a legacy of the distortion still reflected in today's relationship between Aboriginal and non-Aboriginal peoples. (italics in original)

Youngblood Henderson (2000: 17) describes colonialism as an ideology that created a "massive hemorrhage" and a "traumatic legacy" in Indigenous communities in Canada. He asserts that one of the many consequences of colonialism is that the norms of colonized societies were altered, including relationships between adults and children. For example, Bellefeuille and Ricks (2003: 24) discuss the *protection paradigm* in child welfare services as part of a systematic approach utilized in a "practice orientation based on individual deficit," beliefs that stand in opposition to the Indigenous worldview of child development as holistic. They suggest that this approach has been a causal factor in "a model that has caused so much damage to Aboriginal families and communities" (Bellefeuille and Ricks 2003: 24).

Bennett and Shangreaux (2005: 92) note that "non-Aboriginal social workers often do not understand the depth of feelings and the impact that past historical policies and practices have on First Nation peoples today." Alternatively, Indigenous child welfare workers are also challenged to how best work in their own families and communities. Michelle Reid (2005: 30) notes that the Indigenous child and family services practitioners who participated in her research "discussed the 'pressure' and the 'pain' of working under delegated models within their communities where they are dealing with the ongoing 'impacts of colonization' and do not want to be seen as 'perpetrators of colonialism' within their own people." These practitioners are exceptions; those who intervene with poor, Indigenous and otherwise marginalized children and families have always been and still are disproportionately White and middle class. The differences between workers and clients are remarkable. The most recent extant survey reveals that workers are 94 percent White; 80 percent female; 97 percent with English as their primary language; 70 percent between the ages of twenty-six to forty-four; and only 2 percent Indigenous (Fallon et al. 2003: 45). Although occupying a socially powerful race and class position does not disqualify someone from child welfare practice, it is essential for practitioners to recognize that hierarchical power relations are always embedded in child welfare encounters and that they must be actively resisted or they will simply be reproduced.

During the 1980s, some provinces attempted to balance support and protection functions in child welfare, but stringent fiscal restraint policies introduced during that decade led to designating family support as discretionary and tied to the availability of funds. The shift to a system almost exclusively concerned with the protection of children rather than with their welfare was accelerated by high profile child death inquiries. These inquiries typically focused on administrative and technical failures and the conduct of individual workers and parents while ignoring important contextual matters such as poverty, lack of resources and supports and the impacts of residential schools and the "sixties scoop." Child welfare legislation enacted in most Canadian provinces in the wake of these inquiries enshrined "best interests of the child" as a foundational principle guiding policy and practice, severing concern for children from concern for their families. With the protection of individual children as its mission, child welfare concerned itself with investigating, documenting and intervening with parental failure and inadequacy, while the provision of support and resources to families experiencing difficulties was significantly reduced.

The 1990s saw the rise of the "risk regime" (Parton 1999) in child welfare, which extended child protection categories beyond children who had demonstrably suffered harm to include children that were "likely" to suffer harm. This change contributed to a substantial increase in reports, investigations and court-based interventions (Vine et al. 2006). The development of what Beck (1992) termed the "risk society" occurred in concert with the circulation of the neoliberal discourse of individual responsibility, which conditions us to believe that bad outcomes can be averted by avoiding, reducing or ameliorating risks and that the responsibility for doing so is a personal one. Risk ideology is effective in transforming social problems into individual problems. What it means in child welfare is that workers are indoctrinated into the idea that harm to children can be prevented if risk is properly assessed, reduced or eliminated. Thus the state has become more intrusive at the same time that family supports have been eroded through the shredding of the social safety net, marked by several social policy changes: welfare rates reduced and further restrictions imposed on who may receive welfare and how long they may receive it (Mosher 2008); increased surveillance and threatening of welfare recipients and the creation of welfare snitch lines (Chan and Mirchandani 2007); reduction in the availability of subsidized childcare spaces everywhere in Canada except Quebec; reduction in the availability of social housing; and a general reduction in most child welfare-related support services. In other words, the state increased risks for poor and otherwise marginalized children by withdrawing, restricting or reducing benefits and entitlements at the same time that risk assessment procedures made eliminating risk an individual responsibility. Workers were no longer able to consider "environmental factors" and "lack of supports" when assessing families (Dumbrill 2006: 11) even though changes in social policies increased the influence of these factors. As Chen (2005: 143) notes, the "risk assessment model embodies the paradigm shift from considering certain aspects of reality to be social problems to considering them to be risk factors." Risk assessment models keep the child welfare focus narrow, emphasizing individual issues rather than the structural ones that underlie poverty, violence and homelessness (Barter 2005).

Neglect has contributed greatly to the increase in reported child maltreatment in Canada, as demonstrated by the comparison of Canadian data between 1998 and 2003. During this five-year period, the number of substantiated neglect cases almost doubled (Trocmé et al. 2005). As the Canadian Incidence Study (CIS) demonstrates, neglect is closely intertwined with poverty. In the CIS-2003, 24 percent of all children experiencing substantiated maltreatment were reported to live in families relying on benefits, employment insurance or social assistance; only 41 percent of those experiencing neglect lived in homes where a caregiver had full-time employment (Trocmé et al. 2005). As in 1998, in the CIS-2003, children who experienced substantiated maltreatment of any kind were more frequently reported to reside in a home with a lone parent at the time of the investigation (39 percent lone female, 4 percent lone male) (Trocmé et al. 2005). Census data collected in 2001 indicate that 18 percent of Canadian families were led by a lone female parent while two parents led 78 percent of families (Statistics Canada 2001). Most single mother-led families are poor; in 2001, 42.4 percent of these families had incomes below the poverty line (Silver 2007). While the general poverty rate is about the same now as it was in 1980, child poverty has increased and the poverty rate for Indigenous children (40 percent) is twice that for non-Indigenous children (Silver 2007).

Blackstock (2008: 9) points out that over 60 percent of cases of child welfare involvement for Indigenous children are due to neglect that is directly related to poverty. Other racialized groups (not white in colour or non-Caucasian in race) also have a much higher likelihood of being poor; the incidence of poverty for members of these groups is double that for the Canadian population at large (Galabuzi 2006, cited in Silver 2007). While poverty is increasing among the marginalized (Indigenous people, single mothers, immigrants, members of racialized groups), the rich are getting richer. Earnings among the richest fifth of Canadians grew 16.4 percent between 1980 and 2005, while the poorest fifth of the population saw earnings tumble 20.6 percent over this time period (Statistics Canada 2006).

In the early twenty-first century much of what began in the 1990s continues in the wake of more child death inquiries. Public reviews and media accounts of sensational child death cases invariably find individual parents (most often mothers) and individual social workers ("state mothers") to blame. The blaming of individual social workers is ironic because often they are following the policy priority, set in the 1980s, of least intrusive measures (Swift 2001: 66) and because few resources exist to support families. Since the mid-1980s high profile child death inquiries have served as the focal point for examining and reforming child welfare legislation, policies and practices in Canada in a particular direction: towards a more forensic approach to investigating, assessing and documenting the individual failures and inadequacies of individual parents. These alleged failures and inadequacies are responded to primarily through surveillance and threat of sanction (the temporary or permanent loss of children to state care) rather than with compassion, support and resources. This is not to say that individual workers do not care about and attempt to assist the families with whom they work — instances of anti-racist, anti-oppressive, respectful engagement with children and parents are a regular and daily occurrence in child welfare. But when risk assessment and related managerial procedures define abuse and neglect as brought about solely through the actions or inactions of individual "bad" parents, and there is no space on required forms for other interpretations, it is very difficult for individual workers to resist these ways of thinking and talking. Workers understand that they too are under constant surveillance through compulsory audit and review procedures, practising amidst what Rose (1996: 18) calls "a plethora of practices of blame."

Child welfare's devolution into child protection is not the way it has to be. The practices and policies that evolved over the last few decades do not represent better and more progressive practice, though they do "exemplify the privatization of citizenship and individualization of responsibility" (Chen 2005: 146). Risk management is the predominant technology of current Anglo-American child welfare systems, and most other practices flow from and are oriented around it. For example, while 92 percent of workers in the CIS had been trained in risk assessment, only 32 percent had training in family preservation interventions (Fallon et al. 2003). Applying risk technologies serves to simultaneously enact hierarchical power relations and render them invisible. While resisting and transforming child welfare practices at the micro-level are important and necessary, this is not enough.

Pleas for government to attend to the matters of race, class, gender and ability disparity implicated in almost all child welfare difficulties have been numerous and well-articulated (see, for example, Callahan 1993; Cameron et al. 2007; Lindsey 2003; Roberts 2002; Swift 1995). Yet in the years since Pelton (1978) exposed the myth of classlessness in child abuse and neglect, little positive change has taken place in Anglo-American child welfare. Once provinces and territories took over responsibility for Indigenous child welfare at the end of the residential school era, the number of Indigenous children in care skyrocketed and has stayed at those high levels. The federal government was responsible for instituting and administering residential schools yet continues to ignore its obligation to restore Indigenous families and communities through adequate resource allocations for Indigenous child and family services. Present efforts to support Indigenous child welfare agencies are doomed to failure because the policy context is one of continuing to control and monitor Indigenous populations through funding formulas that privilege child protection over prevention, family preservation and support. For example, federal funding formulas for First Nations and Indigenous agencies primarily provide funding solely for the apprehension of children rather than supportive or preventative work with families (Blackstock 2005). Although differential or alternative response models that use interventions like family group conferencing, mediation and alternative dispute resolution are being developed and implemented in some jurisdictions (Trocmé et al. 2003), workers are discouraged from pursuing these for all but the most benign situations. Indigenous approaches to child welfare that emphasize the involvement of community, Elders and extended family hold promise but even in situations where Indigenous people have assumed authority for child welfare services these services are delivered under the auspices of existing legislation, resulting in "the lack of a cultural fit between child welfare, ideology, law and services delivered" (Mandell et al. 2007: 152).

These examples could suggest that child welfare cannot be reformed and that child welfare workers can only practise oppressively. Yet we know from research with child welfare clients that anti-racist and anti-oppressive practice can and does happen even within the strictures of an oppressive system (Callahan et al. 1998; de Boer and Coady 2007; Dumbrill 2006). While we must advocate for socially just child welfare and social policies to enhance the climate for socially just practice, we can and must ensure that we engage in this way of practising now. This book is a contribution to that possibility.

## Walking This Path Together: Our Stories

Because we realize that engaging in anti-racist, anti-oppressive and respectful practice in child welfare, especially given the context we have outlined, is extremely challenging, we would like to share a little more of our stories so that readers know how our own commitment to anti-racist and anti-oppressive practice came to be. We present this in the form of the conversation between us.

*Susan: I entered child welfare with a great deal of knowledge about social justice and a commitment to practise in socially just ways but persistently found my attempts thwarted. I worked initially in northern Manitoba in Cree and Saulteaux communities, and it was very clear to me that problems I saw were fundamentally related to displacement from traditional lands and lives. All the families I worked with had been devastated by residential schools and loss of traditional territories, yet all that I had learned about social justice really didn't help me much to figure out how to be in practice.*

*I believe that anti-oppressive practice is equally possible when children are taken into care and when they are left at home, in part because I was a child who needed to be apprehended. When I did go home briefly at age fifteen, my worker talked about it as if it was a punishment and I experienced it as a punishment. I wanted to stay in care and didn't understand why it was so difficult for the system to find me a safe and caring place to be. While I was in care I still had lots of contact with my family, with my brother and sister, grandparents, aunts and uncles, but I didn't have to live at home with my father and stepmother, where it was really dangerous. I don't remember the social worker making efforts to maintain these relationships but I remember everyone in my family making an effort to stay in touch with me while I was in care. In many ways being in care really worked for me and perhaps it was not so difficult because I still had connection to my family.*

*From my present perspective I understand that because I am White, workers did not see a need to separate me from my connections because I did not need to be assimilated. Perhaps my workers even thought I needed to stay in touch with the better parts of my family to successfully become a nice White middle-class girl. Most of the girls I was in care with, in the home for girls and on the street, were Indigenous. Because I was White it was easier for me to "look promising," which I know increased the efforts social workers made on my behalf and my access to resources.*

*Sohki Aski Esquao [Jeannine]: It seems that the agenda was different for each of us. Susan lived in kinship arrangements and yet this did not seem possible for Aboriginal kids. Being White made you look promising and you have such a leg up being viewed as one of the kids who "made it" (finished school, held off on having children despite the odds). It's much harder to look promising if you are Indigenous. This relates to the policies of the time where Indigenous children were viewed as "illegitimate, un-adoptable, unworthy" of having a caring family.*

*Social workers had a lot of power in our lives and it seemed important to be grateful. I remember that my original reason for being a social worker was because I thought I could do a much better job than the models I had.*

*Susan: My understanding of how to engage in socially just practice has been a long time coming and is still under construction. Some of the Indigenous teachings that I have been given and exposed to along with anti-oppressive practice ideas helped me figure out how to put social justice into practice. My experiences working in child protection were a study in contrasts. In the North I worked only with Indigenous peoples and then I worked in a part of the B.C. interior which had once been densely populated with Indigenous people but there was not a single Indigenous person left. So I went from thinking that child welfare was all about race to thinking that child welfare was all about poverty. Now I know that it is those two things together that make the perfect child welfare storm. If you are poor and not White and have children you are almost certain to have child welfare show up at your door sooner or later. Until anti-oppressive practice came along I didn't really understand how to braid together that kind of analysis with my professional practice even though I learned much about respectful, strengths-based engagement from my B.C. child welfare colleagues. Since I came to live in the Coast Salish and Nuu-chah-nulth territories and had the opportunity to work in Indigenous communities, I feel that who I am and what I do is much more open to examination and that is a good thing. This is not information I received in my social work education or as a registered social worker. What I received from Indigenous teachings was that I had to live and work what I said I believed in.*

*One of my first experiences in research involved interviewing young women in care – young women like me and like the girls I was with on the street. What they told me about their experiences in child welfare saddened me because it was clear that not much of any significance has changed. I think particularly about one young Indigenous woman who came to her interview with a whole file of clippings about colonization, residential schools and the sixties scoop because she thought she needed to prove to me that Indigenous people came to involvement with child welfare for these reasons. This experience fuelled my commitment to changing child welfare and my recognition that for Indigenous peoples it has to change within the context of a history of child welfare trying to destroy Indigenous peoples.*

*Sohki Aski Esquao [Jeannine]: I remember working in foster care and removing kids from what was documented as the most deplorable conditions; however, these kids wanted to go home. That was their first choice and I knew that for the most part, these kids were never going home. We spoke of permanency planning while Elders cautioned us that nothing is permanent.*

*I was fortunate that some of my early teachers were Elders and that I was able to take these teachings and combine them in social work practice when it was a very new concept to include spirituality in practice. I found that working with young people from those teachings as well as an anti-oppressive lens was making a difference in how these young people perceived hope in their lives. I also learned much from some of my predecessors in Indigenous child welfare, such as First Nation agency directors from the 1970s (Blackfoot Tribal Services — now Siksika Nation Child and Family Services Agreement, in Alberta and the Dakota Ojibway Tribal Council in Manitoba) and how they were the forerunners in taking back the administration of child and family services in our own communities and with our own ways of caring for children. It wasn't long before Métis agencies were also set up to deliver services from a Métis perspective.*

*I became convinced that extended families had as much and more to give our children than strangers and that with support they could become the preferred arrangement for Indigenous kids in need of protection. I always felt that I was accountable to my community as well or maybe more so than my employer if I was working for a ministry. This was a tough balancing act but one that was worth the risk. At the end of the day, I wanted to be the type of social worker who did not give up on those important community and cultural connections for Indigenous children. If I ever forgot, I knew that someone from the Indigenous community would come and remind me of who I was and where I came from. You cannot separate your personal location from your professional work as an Indigenous social worker in whatever community you work.*

*Those kids I worked with for the most part did not have regular contact or didn't know what happened to their families, and they had fears, anxiety and some fantasies about what was going on in their family. It seemed to be such an effort to first of all know who their extended family was and where they were, to maintain connections with them and facilitate those connections, because drivers were expensive and cultural resources were scarce.*

*For a few years I was involved in special case reviews of Indigenous children who died in ministry foster care and community agency care. Those were troubled times in my career as I cautiously reviewed files, case notes and interview notes with the workers involved. I took my role very seriously as the voice for the children who had passed to another world. I was reminded of how important recordkeeping is and how children and their families are portrayed in case notes. My heart also reached toward social workers who felt they had done what they could and carried a burden of guilt for not having done more. For me, the heart of this book is those children, who inspire me to this day.*

*My life has come full circle. I came into this world as a Métis child adopted into a non-Métis family. My adoption story has been woven into my professional life to remind me of some important teachings I wish to uphold. Now I am in an academic position conducting research on cultural planning and adoption of Indigenous children. I don't believe in coincidence — I believe in possibilities. My life could have been very different, and I am grateful that the possibilities that lay before me include an exploration of this important work, guided by my ancestors and all those who are my mentors in this world and the next. There is no resting place away from the world of child welfare until every Indigenous child is confident in their place of family, community and ancestral knowledge and until there is non-judgmental help freely available for every family that is struggling, whatever the reason. Although we both said we would never work in child welfare, we have both found our place of work.*

*Thus, we extend this invitation to all who might read this book.*

### The Invitation — Oriah Mountain Dreamer

It doesn't interest me what you do for a living.

I want to know what you ache for, and if you dare to dream of meeting your heart's longing.

It doesn't interest me how old you are. I want to know if you will risk looking like a fool for love, for your dream, for the adventure of being alive.

It doesn't interest me what planets are squaring your moon. I want to know if you have touched the centre of your own sorrow, if you have been opened by life's betrayals or have become shriveled and closed from fear of further pain. I want to know if you can sit with pain, mine or your own without moving to hide it or face it or fix it.

I want to know if you can be with joy, mine or your own, if you can dance with wildness and let the ecstasy fill you to the tips of your fingers and toes without cautioning us to be careful, to be realistic, to remember the limitations of being human.

It doesn't interest me if the story you are telling me is true. I want to know if you can disappoint another to be true to yourself; if you can bear the accusation of betrayal and not betray your own soul; if you can be faithless and therefore trustworthy.

I want to know if you can see beauty, even when it's not pretty, every day, and if you can source your own life from its presence.

I want to know if you can live with failure, yours and mine, and still stand on the edge of the lake and shout to the silver of the full moon, "Yes!"

### References

Barter, K. 2005. *Working Conditions for Social Workers and Linkages to Client Outcomes in Child Welfare: A Literature Review.* Ottawa: Canadian Association of Social Workers.

Beck, U. 1992. *Risk Society: Towards a New Modernity.* London: Sage.

Bellefeuille, G.L., and F. Ricks. 2003. "A Pathway to Restoration: From Child Protection to Community Wellness." *Native Social Work Journal* 5 (November).

Bennett, M., and C. Shangreaux. 2005. "Applying Maslow's Theory." *First Peoples Child and Family Review* 2, 1.

Blackstock, C. 2005. "The Occasional Evil of Angels: Learning from the Experiences of Aboriginal Peoples and Social Work." *Journal of Entrepreneurship, Advancement, Strategy and Education* (Special Edition) "World Indigenous Peoples Congress on Education" 1.

_____. 2008. "The Breath of Life: When Everything Matters in Child Welfare." Paper presented to University of Victoria Aboriginal Child Welfare Research Symposium, Victoria, B.C., February 15.

Blackstock, C., S, Clarke, J. Cullen, J. D'Hondt, and J. Formsma. 2004. *Keeping the Promise: The Convention on the Rights of the Child and the Lived Experience of First Nations Children and Youth.* First Nations Child and Family Caring Society of Canada, Ottawa.

Callahan, M. 1993. "Feminist Approaches: Women Recreate Child Welfare." In B. Wharf (ed.), *Rethinking Child Welfare.* Don Mills: Oxford University Press.

Callahan, M., B. Field, C. Hubberstey and B. Wharf. 1998. *Best Practice in Child Welfare: Perspectives from Parents, Social Workers and Community Partners.* Victoria: University of

Victoria, School of Social Work

Cameron, G., N. Freymond, D. Cornfield, and S. Palmer. 2007. "Positive Possibilities for Child and Family Welfare: Expanding the Anglo-American Child Protection Paradigm." In G. Cameron, N. Coady, and G. Adams (eds.), *Moving Toward Positive Systems of Child and Family Welfare*. Waterloo: Wilfrid Laurier Press.

Mirchandani, K. and W. Chan. 2007. *Criminalizing Race, Criminalizing Poverty: Welfare Fraud Enforcement in Canada*. Halifax: Fernwood.

Chen, X. 2005. *Tending the Gardens of Citizenship: Child Saving in Toronto, 1880s–1920s*. Toronto: University of Toronto Press.

de Boer, C. and N. Coady. 2007. "Good Helping Relationships in Child Welfare: Learning from Stories of Success." *Child and Family Social Work* 12.

Dumbrill, G. 2006. "Parental Experience of Child Protection Intervention: A Qualitative Study." *Child Abuse and Neglect* 30.

Fallon, B., B. MacLaurin, N. Trocmé, and C. Felstiner. 2003. "The Canadian Incidence Study of Child Abuse and Neglect: A Profile of a National Sample of Child Protection Workers." In K. Kufeldt and B. MacKenzie (eds.), *Child Welfare: Connecting Research, Policy and Practice*. Waterloo, ON: Wilfred Laurier University Press.

Farris-Manning, C., and M. Zandstra. 2003. *Children in Care in Canada: A Summary of Current Issues and Trends with Recommendations for Future Research*. Ottawa: Child Welfare League of Canada for the National Children's Alliance.

Government of Canada. 1996. *Royal Commission Report on Aboriginal Peoples*. Ottawa, ON: Royal Commission on Aboriginal Peoples.

Kufeldt, K., and B. McKenzie. 2003. *Child Welfare: Connecting Research, Policy and Practice*. Waterloo: Wilfrid Laurier University Press.

Lindsey, D. 2003. *The Welfare of Children* (Second Edition). New York: Oxford University Press.

Mandell, D., J. Clouston Carlson, M. Fine, and C. Blackstock. 2007. "Aboriginal Child Welfare." In G. Cameron, N. Coady and G. Adams (eds.), *Moving toward Positive Systems of Child and Family Welfare*. Waterloo: Wilfrid Laurier Press.

Mirwaldt, J. 2004. "Permanency Planning: Trend Analysis and Recommendations." Report of the Western Provinces' Children's Advocates Working Group. Presented by Canadian Council of Provincial and Child Youth Advocates at Building Lifelong Connections: Permanency Options for Children and Families. New Brunswick. September.

Mosher, J. 2008. "Welfare Fraudsters and Tax Evaders: The State's Selective Invocation of Criminality." In C. Brooks and B. Schissel (eds.), *Marginality and Condemnation: An Introduction to Criminology*. Halifax: Fernwood.

Mountain Dreamer, O. 1999. *The Invitation*. San Francisco: Harper.

Parton, N. 1999. "Reconfiguring Child Welfare Practices: Risk, Advanced Liberalism, and the Government of Freedom." In A. Chambon, A. Irving and L. Epstein (eds.), *Reading Foucault for Social Work*. New York: Columbia University Press.

Pelton, L. 1978. "Child Abuse and Neglect: The Myth of Classlessness." *American Journal of Orthopsychiatry* 48, 4.

Reid, M. 2005. "First Nation Women Speak, Write and Research Back: Child Welfare and Decolonizing Stories." *First Peoples Child and Family Review* 2, 1.

Roberts, D. 2002. *Shattered Bonds: The Color of Child Welfare*. New York: Basic Books.

Rose, N. 1996. "Psychiatry as a Political Science: Advanced Liberalism and the Administration of Risk." *History of the Human Sciences* 9, 2.

Scarth, S. 2004. *Straight Talk about Aboriginal Children and Adoption*. Ottawa: Adoption Council of Canada. Available at <www.adoption.ca> (accessed on July 13, 2005).

Schouls, T. 2002. "The Basic Dilemma: Sovereignty or Assimilation." In J. Bird, L. Land and M. Macadam (eds.), *Nation to Nation: Aboriginal Sovereignty and the Future of Canada.* Toronto: Irwin.

Silver, J. 2007. "Persistent Poverty and the Promise of Community Solutions." In L. Samuelson and W. Antony (eds.), *Power and Resistance: Critical Thinking about Canadian Social Issues.* Halifax: Fernwood.

Statistics Canada. 2001. *Census of Canada 2001: Age Groups of Children at Home and Family Structure for Census Families in Private Households for Census Divisions and Subdivisions.* Ottawa: Statistics Canada.

_____. 2006. *Earnings and Incomes of Canadians over the Past Quarter Century.* Ottawa: Statistics Canada.

Swift, K. 1995. *Manufacturing 'Bad Mothers:' A Critical Perspective on Child Neglect.* Toronto: University of Toronto Press.

_____. 2001. "The Case for Opposition: An Examination of Contemporary Child Welfare Policy Directions." *Canadian Review of Social Policy* 47.

Thobani, S. 2007. *Exalted Subjects: Studies in Making of Race and Nation in Canada.* Toronto: University of Toronto Press.

Trocmé, N., B. Fallon, B. MacLaurin, J. Daciuk, C. Felstiner and T. Black. 2005. *Canadian Incidence Study of Reported Child Abuse and Neglect — 2003: Major Findings.* Ottawa, ON: Minister of Public Works and Government Services Canada.

Trocmé, N., D. Knoke, and C. Roy (eds.). 2003. *Community Collaboration and Differential Response: Canadian and International Research and Emerging Models of Practice.* Ottawa: Centre of Excellence for Child Welfare.

Vine, C., N. Trocmé, and J. Finlay. 2006. "Children Abused, Neglected and Living with Violence: An Overview." In R. Alaggia and C. Vine (eds.), Cruel but Not Unusual: Violence in Canadian Families. A Sourcebook of History, Theory and Practice. Waterloo: Wilfrid Laurier University Press.

Youngblood Henderson, J.S. 2000. *Postcolonial Ghost Dancing: Diagnosing European Colonialism.* In M. Battiste (ed.), *Reclaiming Indigenous Voice and Vision.* Vancouver: University of British Columbia Press.

# Chapter 1

# Children in the Centre

## Indigenous Perspectives on Anti-Oppressive Child Welfare Practice

*Kundouqk [Jacquie Green] & Qwul'sih'yah'maht [Robina Thomas]*

This chapter focuses on the key elements of anti-oppressive practice. As Indigenous scholars who teach and analyze anti-oppressive theories, knowledge and praxis, we illustrate similarities of anti-oppressive practice to what we call anti-oppressive living, which is a Way of Life. Anti-oppressive living is rooted in our sacred and traditional teachings. We utilize the teachings of the Medicine Wheel to illustrate our examination of anti-oppressive practice within the paradigm of child welfare. Although there have been significant changes to legislation and polices in child welfare, colonial attitudes continue to manifest. Child welfare attitudes and beliefs must shift; hence the importance of anti-oppressive practice in child welfare. We provide an analysis using the four directions of the Medicine Wheel to undo colonial practice in child welfare.

Questions Addressed in This Chapter

1. The authors speak to aspects of anti-oppressive practice within the four directions of the Medicine Wheel. What are ways these aspects could be adapted to your practice wherever you are?
2. The authors define anti-oppressive practice as anti-oppressive living. What does anti-oppressive living mean for you? What do Indigenous traditional teachings look like for you in practice?

The United Nations *Convention on the Rights of the Child*… sets out… minimum standards for the respect, nurturing, well-being, participation and protection of all children and young people. But in fact… around the world, in countries both rich and poor, Indigenous children are severely marginalized. Their rights under the UNCRC and other human rights treaties are routinely violated, unimplemented, and ignored to a degree not often experienced by other children. This systemic discrimination and disadvantage must end. (Rae 2006: 5)

Throughout Canada, but particularly in British Columbia, child welfare is undergoing drastic change. The B.C. Ministry of Children and Family Development has recruited a deputy minister from South Africa, Lesley du Toit, to assist this transformation. The child welfare system as a whole is failing but it is even more evident with Indigenous children and families. In B.C., 85 percent of the children in care are Indigenous. As this tragic realization unfolds, many Indigenous communities are taking over the responsibility of protecting our children and families. This is a huge task, but one we are prepared to take on. We know our children are sacred; we know our children are our future. After numerous shifts, the government has realized the essence of Indigenous child welfare and has initiated strategies for Indigenous people to protect their children the ways the *Sulxwen* (Elders) want.

As this transformation in child welfare progresses, we wonder, what is best practice for Indigenous children and families? What would anti-oppressive child welfare practice look like? How would we know if someone was practising anti-oppressively?

Key elements of anti-oppressive practice (AOP) include, but are not limited to, the following:

- AOP is necessarily complicated and uncomfortable because as social workers in child welfare, we are forced to enter people's lives. In most cases, the children and families do not know us, but are required to share their intimate and personal history. How we take up their stories is critical. We must learn to respect and honour those stories and not leave children and families more damaged than before they entered the child welfare system;
- AOP, at its core, must include an analysis of power and strive to work across differences; and
- AOP forces us to critically examine how we know what we know and to explore our assumptions not only about helping, but about all living things. AOP invites us to connect our subjective lived experiences to our knowledges —— that is, what we know may be connected to who we are.

Using these key elements, we discuss our collective perspectives of anti-oppressive practice. We focus on practice with Indigenous children and families — as we know they are our future. Many people are seeking a definition of anti-oppressive practice; in this chapter, we demonstrate that, for us, AOP is A Way of Life, one that values the sacred and traditional teachings of Indigenous cultures. We utilize the teachings of the Medicine Wheel to frame and discuss our AOP perspectives.

## The Medicine Wheel

The Medicine Wheel is an ancient teaching tool. It has no beginning and no end and teaches us that all things are interrelated. The Wheel is comprised of quadrants that represent all living things (see Figure 1-1). The Medicine Wheel has many different teachings and principles, but our teachings come from our Anishnabe friend and mentor, Gale Cyr, from the east of Turtle Island — Quebec, Canada.

It is critical to remember that each quadrant of the Wheel is interrelated and that no quadrant is worth more than any other quadrant; all aspects of our being and place are of equal importance and are positioned in balance and harmony with one another. For example, as human beings, we have spiritual, emotional, physical and mental aspects, which connectively make us who we are. Another important teaching of the Medicine Wheel is that once you have journeyed around the Wheel, you have the opportunity to learn from your experiences and to journey around the Wheel again, this time learning from your mistakes. The Wheel teaches us to be conscious of our previous journey so that our next journey can be different and more effective. Starting at the East and working clockwise around the Wheel, we have the four aspects of all human beings — the spiritual, emotional, physical and mental (Bopp et al. 1984: 12; Saulis 2003: 294). The Wheel also has four colours to represent all the races of Mother Earth — red, yellow, black and white. It also provides us the four stages of the lifecycle — infant, youth, adult and elder, as well as the four seasons — spring, summer, fall and winter (Hart 2002: 40). Each of these representations has particular meanings for both life and anti-oppressive practice with Indigenous children and families.

We have been taught to always begin in the East because this is the direction of spirituality, the colour red, the life stage of the infant, springtime and

### Figure 1-1 Medicine Wheel

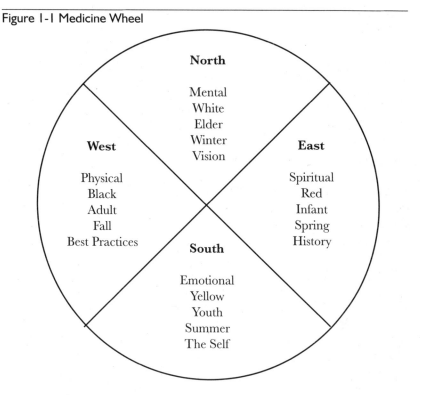

the beginning of all things. This is the direction of daybreak and sunrise. We will begin in the eastern direction and examine the history of Indigenous child welfare in Canada. It is vital to understand the history of Indigenous people in Canada if we are to work successfully with Indigenous children and families.

The South is the direction of our emotional being, the colour yellow and the life stage of youth. This is the direction of summer, a time for lots of activity. For youth, this is a time in their life when they are learning much. The southern direction is also the place where we recognize and honour teachings of our Elders and spiritual leaders. In this direction, our chapter will look at the Self and how we know what we know. We challenge social workers to examine their socialization and "unlearn" some of the ways they may see the world.

In the West, we have the direction of our physical being, the colour black, the life stage of the adult and the fall or autumn season. In this direction we look at best practice with Indigenous children and families. The Western direction is where social workers share their knowledge and work within our communities to help strengthen our children and families. In this direction, we focus on the particular skills that AOP requires: we identify that an historical analysis of Indigenous people in Canada is a necessary skill for anti-oppressive practice. We also assert that critical self-examination is another necessary skill and demonstrate why this skill is so vital for anti-oppressive practice.

The North is the direction of our mental being, the colour white, the life stage of an Elder and wintertime. When we reach the North, we are reminded to reflect on our work. This is the time to focus on what changes we need to make to our lives, a time to re-think and re-evaluate our actions and behaviours. For child welfare practice in Indigenous communities, this is the direction of vision. This is the time to dream. We dream that none of our children are in care; there is no child welfare system. We dream of anti-oppressive living. We dream of a time when our language, culture and tradition are revived and become a part of our day-to-day lives.

## History of Indigenous Child Welfare in Canada

In pre-contact times, Indigenous communities were responsible for their own child welfare. There was the recognition that children are sacred and precious gifts to community. The entire community played a role in raising children with different people having different roles. Among Indigenous communities it was common practice for entire families, including extended families, to be involved in childcare and uncommon for individual families to make important decisions about their children without consulting their larger family — child welfare decisions were made collectively. As a result, if someone was unable or unwilling to look after a child, there was a whole community infrastructure that stepped in and made alternate plans to share the responsibility (Ormiston 2002).

The role of Indigenous families and their communities began to shift during contact with European settlers. While the *Royal Proclamation* sought to protect Aboriginal people from corrupt settlers, other policies, such as the *Gradual*

*Enfranchisement Act*, the treaties and the *Indian Act*,[1] were used to "civilize," control and assimilate the Aboriginal people of this land. Indigenous nations were deemed to be inferior and uncivilized. Nowhere was this more evident than in the creation of residential schools, which solidified the federal government's role of "protecting the child."

Beginning in the late 1800s, attempts were made through Canada's residential school system to strip Indigenous peoples of their culture and identity. Children were separated from their families and communities, prohibited from speaking their native language or practising traditions, and forced to learn European ways. Harold Cardinal (1969: 18) believes:

> These schools were nothing less than state sponsored programs of cultural genocide aimed at Indian First Nations. They were an integral component of a systematic, intergenerational, state planned program of brainwashing aimed at removing the "Indian" from the minds and souls of Indian children.

In 1920, the *Indian Act* was amended to make residential school attendance mandatory for Status Indian[2] children. First Nations children were now legislated to leave their families and communities. The Department of Indian Affairs policy of assimilation, or more accurately cultural genocide, began a path of cultural destruction and devastation for First Nations people (Thomas 2000: 7). The last residential school in Canada — Gordon Residential School in Saskatchewan — closed in 1996.

Even though the federal government started to phase out the residential school system in the 1960s and 1970s, provinces continued the policy of assimilation. Provinces were given jurisdiction to provide child welfare services on reserves in 1951, when revisions to Section 88 of the *Indian Act* extended provincial laws of general application to Indians and lands belonging to Indians (Ormiston 2002). This revision opened up reserve lands to provincial child welfare activities. Without Section 88, provincial legislation would not apply to Indians because Canada's constitution gives the federal government the exclusive power to legislate for Indians and lands reserved for Indians.

Once provinces were given jurisdiction to provide child welfare on reserves, children were apprehended from our communities and adopted out at such alarming rates that this period of time became known as the sixties scoop. Sinclair (2007: 66) asserts:

> The term, "sixties scoop," was appropriate because, first Johnston observed in the statistics that adoption as the mechanism to address problematic child welfare issues had resulted in a notable increase in Aboriginal child apprehensions in the decade of the 1960s. Secondly, in many instances, Aboriginal children were literally apprehended from their homes and communities without the knowledge or consent of families and bands.

Many parents who had returned from residential schools were traumatized and deprived of opportunities to develop positive parenting skills. The government continued to view First Nations parents as incompetent and unable to raise their own children, who were deemed to be in social need. This was the government's justification for bringing these children into provincial care.

Taiaiake Alfred (2004: 89) argues that colonialism "is the fundamental denial of our freedom to be Indigenous in a meaningful way and the unjust occupation of the physical, social and political spaces we need in order to survive as Indigenous peoples." This articulation encapsulates the depth and breadth of the impact and effects of colonialism. In order to subjugate and oppress Indigenous people, the Canadian settler state required the creation and maintenance of violence (Hodge 1990: 93); this violence took on a complex and intricate web aimed at destroying the mind, body, spirit and humanity of our peoples. Colonial violence took on different manifestations, including, but not limited to, the *Indian Act*[2] in its assorted manifestations; biological and germ warfare; theft of cultures, knowledges, traditions, languages and identity; residential school policy; child welfare policies; and various treaty processes. The effect of these policies was to degrade the Indigenous people of Canada and to position them in the lowest strata of society (Aboriginal Healing Foundation 2005: 43–44). Although there have since been amendments to the *Indian Act* and other policies that directly affect Indigenous peoples, child welfare practices, in essence, took over where residential schools left off. As previously stated, there continues to be an increase in the amount of our children in the care of the state. Not only does this significant percentage illustrate that legislation continues to be violent, these alarming statistics reveal that child welfare practices must shift! Child welfare workers must consider the horrific history of Indigenous communities, policies that are violent, and shift their practice to provide families with a vision of hope.

## Anti-Oppressive Practice

In many Indigenous languages, there is no word or phrase that translates to "anti-oppressive practice." Furthermore, there is no word or phrase in many Indigenous languages that references removal of children (child protection). However, there are phrases in our languages that identify A Way Of Life[3] and communal living among Indigenous families. For example, terms such as *Snuw'uy'ul*[4] and *Nuuyum*[5] roughly translate into "sacred teachings" — our ways of knowing and being, our governing structures, our culture, our tradition, our language, our sacred bathing holes, hunting, fishing and gathering rights, our family, our community and our relationship with Mother Earth and Father Sky. Through the banning of the potlatch (and other traditional ceremonies) the government specifically and purposefully attacked and attempted to rupture Our Way of Life (Lawrence 2002: 23–24). Indigenous scholar Lee Maracle (1996: 93) captures the spectrum of these ruptures:

The aims of the colonizer are to break up communities and families, and to destroy the sense of nationhood and the spirit of co-operation among the colonized. A sense of powerlessness is the legacy handed down to the colonized people. Loss of power — the negation of choice, as well as legal and cultural victimization — is the hoped-for result.

Child welfare practitioners must ensure they have studied and learned what their role is within the state. Although there have been shifts in policy and legislation, the attitudes of colonialism remains in the minds and hearts of many Canadians. Many Canadians, and child welfare workers, are not familiar with how much historical colonial policies continue to manifest in the lives of Indigenous peoples today.

Having our ways of knowing and being targeted for destruction and being forced to assimilate into Western knowledge systems has had significant psychological impact on our people. As a result of Eurocentric educational indoctrination, Indigenous people began to forego their ways of life in order to be more like the "superior" others. For many, it was safer and easier to assimilate white values than fight to have the dominant society accept Our Way of Life.

Anti-oppressive practice with Indigenous people requires an intimate understanding of the colonial history of Canada. Colonization of the lands, resources, psyches and hearts of Indigenous peoples was an integral part of colonizing processes. Indian Tribes of Manitoba (1971: ii) remind us of the significance of linking history to the present and to the future: "to deny the past and to refuse to recognize its implications is to distort the present; to distort the present is to take risks with the future that are blatantly irresponsible." As social workers, we must understand the impact these policies have had and continue to have on the day-to-day lives of the Indigenous children and families we work with. It is critical for child welfare workers to ask themselves: What have the experiences of the Indigenous children and families been? Did they, their parents and/or grandparents attend residential schools? Have they been involved in the child welfare system and how might they feel about social workers? What is their history with social work? What are their fears? We must always take these questions into account when we work with Indigenous children and families. We must always situate the present context with the past and continuously query how the families we support have come to know what they know.

## Self

Anti-oppressive *practice* is not enough. We cannot decide when or when not to practice in a good way; it must be about living — anti-oppressive living. Anti-oppressive social work, in essence, is A Way of Life. In her book *killing rage: Ending Racism*, bell hooks (1995: 263) discusses Martin Luther King's image "of a *beloved community* where race would be transcended, forgotten, where no one would see skin color." We too dream of a *beloved community* where a hundred percent of our children are raised in our communities with our families. How can we as social workers engage with this dream? For sure it has something to do with how we practice — or live — our values and beliefs.

Taiaiake Alfred (2005: 51) encourages us to become warriors again — those who carry the burden to peace. He believes that behaving "indigenously" is a personal attribute that is observable. He also states that we need to "recreate a life worth living and principles worth dying for" (25). For us, this is also about A Way of Life — how we are and want to be in the world.

We believe that the same is true for anti-oppression — we must live it. Our *beloved community* would foster anti-racist/anti-oppressive living. But the question becomes: What do we need to do to get there? How do we get to living anti-oppression? Every Indigenous culture and tradition have teachings on how to live a good life. For the Hul'qumi'num speaking people, we have teachings of *kwum kwum skwuluwun* — to have a strong mind and spirit. If we work from a place of honouring the teachings of walking with a strong mind and spirit, we honour all living things. *Kwum kwum skwuluwun* teaches us that all human beings are important — but especially the babies and the old ones — they are closest in spirit to each other. The old ones hold the sacred knowledge and the babies are sacred gifts — both are to be protected at all times.

hooks (1995: 271) says: "to live in anti-racist society we must collectively renew our commitment to a democratic vision of racial justice and equality." And, Dominelli (1988: 16) believes that "to become fully human and live in egalitarian harmony with black people, White people have to become anti-racist. Anti-racism is a state of mind, feeling, political commitment and action." hooks' and Dominelli's statements on anti-racism holds true for anti-oppressive living — we must be committed to justice and equality in all aspects of our lives and be willing to do something about it. Cindy Blackstock, Executive Director of First Nations Child and Family Caring Society of Canada, is a fine example of this. Every time Cindy speaks, she asks the audience, "Now you know the dismal state of Indigenous child welfare in Canada? What are you going to do about it?" Cindy believes that it is not enough to merely recognize that inequalities and injustices exist; we must take action. As social workers, if we are committed to the principles of *kwum kwum skwuluwun*, we too must do something about the inequalities and injustices that exist.

In order to strive for social justice, we must begin this process by asking ourselves how we know what we know. Rarely do we have the opportunity to turn inward and look into our life and critique how we have been socialized and what we have internalized from our socialization. We believe the best helpers are those who know themselves best. Dominelli (1988: 14) believes that by "getting rid of the injustice perpetrated by racism we will begin reclaiming our own humanity and establishing egalitarian relationships between black and white people." If anti-oppression is about living, then reclaiming and politicizing our humanity must be a starting point. Seletze, also known by his English name Delmar Johnnie, believes that healing is life long and that every day we can strive to be a better person than we were the day before and a better person the next day than we were today. Yes, we can all heal and become more fully human. Bopp et al. (1984: 75) in *The Sacred Tree: Reflections on Native American Spirituality* include a code of ethics. The first ethic states:

> Each morning upon rising, and each evening before sleeping, give thanks for the life within you and for all life, for the good things the Creator has given you and others and for the opportunity to grow a little more each day. Consider your thoughts and actions of the past day and seek for the courage and strength to be a better person. Seek for the things that will benefit everyone.

We believe that if helpers thought critically every day about their ways of living, then we would be a step closer towards committing to anti-oppressive living and a step closer to keeping our children in our communities and out of the child welfare system.

Indeed, being committed to living anti-oppressively requires that we not only examine our values and beliefs, but live them out as well. As social workers, we must believe that we are good helpers or we would not be in this field of work. But we need to question our intentions and motivations and ask ourselves: Are we good helpers? Do we truly value all human beings? Do we value parents who neglect their children? Do we care about the poorest and the homeless people? Do we value the gay, lesbian, bi-sexual, transgender and queer communities? These are tough questions, but they must be examined. Exploring our values and beliefs is very difficult, but a commitment to anti-oppressive living requires that we do just this. The eighth code of ethic from *The Sacred Tree* states: "All the races and tribes in the world are like the different coloured flowers of one meadow. All are beautiful. Children of the Creator must all be respected" (80). A commitment to continuously examining our values and beliefs can be instrumental in living anti-oppression, which in turn, informs how we will practice social work. We must never forget the Children of the Creator — they are our responsibility to protect and nurture.

## Practice

For social work with Indigenous children and families, we believe that praxis, which is practice based on knowledge and action, must include knowledge of Indigenous histories. Paulo Freire (2000: 87) identifies praxis as action and reflection to speak a true word to transform the world. Similarly Graveline (1998: 191) states: "Traditionalists believe that we learn, grow and change through actively using our thoughts, desires and feelings as vital components in the realization of our visions." We understand that praxis must include a continuous reflection of self. A research study on best practices in Indigenous communities identified the importance of knowing self in practice:

> One worker talked about always having to remember where she was from and why she was doing this work. It was the personal commitment to her

community that kept her strong and wanting to do social work, but also remembering that she was, at the same time, a social worker and a First Nations person. She always had to remember the historical issues that have impacted our people while at the same time remember our traditional ways. (Green and Thomas 2005: 10)

For child welfare practitioners, a necessary skill is the continual examination of assumptions. For example, there are assumptions about Indigenous people living on or off the reserve system. Non-Indigenous peoples at times assume those who live on reserve are cultural and traditional. However, the reserve system is in fact a colonial regime set up to isolate our people from dominant society. Simultaneously, our children were being removed from our reserves to be assimilated into dominant society through residential school and child welfare policies. The result is that there is spectrum of culture and tradition that varies from person to person. Some people who live on reserve are traditional and follow the teachings of their culture. Others do not. It is critical as social workers that we do not make assumptions about people based on where they live and always remember the range of diversity that is a part of our histories. Child welfare practitioners must examine their assumptions about Indigenous children and families prior to engaging in relationships with them. Workers must know the history of the child and the family. Have they lived on or off reserve? What is the child's history with the child welfare system? Has the child lived in foster care? Does the child or family know their Indigenous family and/or community? Does the child or family want to know their Indigenous family and/or community? There are many possible questions for a worker to ask. It is up to the child welfare worker to do their own historical analysis of the child, family and community in order to provide appropriate care plans to prevent further harm to the child's heart. And for child welfare workers to do these task effectively, they must include the child, parents, family and other community members in planning for the present and the future.

Child welfare workers must have a fundamental understanding of colonialism and colonial relations. Green and Thomas (2005) found that the social workers they interviewed believed *all* social workers must have sound knowledge of the history of Aboriginal peoples. As well, these workers suggested social workers pay particular attention to the history of the geographical area where they are working (Green and Thomas 2005: 8). By attending to and understanding our histories and lives, social workers will come to understand that, in contrast to colonial policies, traditional teachings are rooted in understanding our connections to Mother Earth and Father Sky. It is through traditional ceremonies that we understand our identities and our cultures — no matter where we live[6] — and these ceremonies are important to our social, political and economic knowledges. Cajete (2000: 183) goes on to say it is the intimate relationship that people establish with place and with the environment and with all things that makes them or gives them life.

Thus, skills of reflection and locating our histories are integral to unravelling assumptions we make of Indigenous peoples and the lives we live. A key aspect to unravelling complex Indigenous histories is the skill of learning to listen and learning to hear the stories of families we work with. As practitioners we often assume we are to "fix" the children and families we work with. Definitely, some families need support. However, Indigenous families need to be given an opportunity to share their story of oppression and colonization and work collaboratively with their worker to deconstruct or demystify their experiences.

Often assumptions made about Indigenous peoples are based on racist stereotypes and attitudes. Sinclair (2004: 53) states that even in the new millennium social work education and practice continues to be based on dominant mainstream worldviews and ways of knowing and being. Helpers must recognize that for Indigenous people our worldview and ways of knowing and being are very complex and different. Mainstream worldviews tend to be more individualistic and focus on protection of an individual child or children. Subsequently, when mainstream workers see the need to protect the child, they discount the collective role of the child's family and community. This oversight has resulted in multi-generational trauma. This has led many to misuse substances to numb historical pain. It is critical that helpers understand our unique history and see how we can work together to heal from our past. By engaging in child welfare practice that is anti-oppressive, the worker then must not only protect the child, but indeed protect the entire family — or at least work with the entire family.

To help Indigenous people heal our historical pain, it is important to work from a strength- and resiliency-based model. When working with families we should search for their strengths (rather than always exerting energy on "fixing" a person). This shift opens up the opportunity for families to use their own strengths and abilities to share their stories and create their own solutions. We believe social workers must be open to changing their beliefs about what helping is rather than only believing that helping means "fixing clients." Anti-oppressive child welfare workers often relate to families they work with as families or people. Mainstream child welfare workers often refer to the individuals they work with as "clients," "cases" or "files." Strength-based practice includes transparent relationships with families, which provides families with dignity and pride. In order to shift from "fixing," it is essential to build and nurture relationships between worker and family. Working with families from a strength-based model requires a commitment to valuing and honouring relationships.

We know and believe children are the heart of communities, and they must be central to how we look at practice, particularly in the child welfare system. Because children are gifts from our Creator, they must be at the centre of love and nurturing from a circle of extended family and community members. More importantly, in practice we must remember how children historically have been traumatized by colonial practices and racism. We know how policies, legislation and other laws have harmed Our Way of Being. For many helpers we have seen how stereotypes and assumptions have harmed Indigenous families and resulted in the removal of children from our families and communities. In contrast, mainstream worldviews have utilized the notion of "best interest of the child" to validate the removal of children from their families and communities. Child welfare workers need to examine for themselves how Indigenous communities define children as gifts, which is quite different than how legislation defines best interest of the child.

Building and maintaining relationships with children is especially important in child welfare. Children are precious and must continue to be cared for by our families and extended families. Indigenous people believe children are precious because they represent our collective future. Anderson (2000: 159) reminds us that children are not considered possessions of the biological parents; rather, they are understood to be gifts on loan from the Creator. As helpers it is important to maintain relationships with the children and families we work with to the best of our abilities, most particularly those children who are in child protection. In child welfare it is critical that relationships with the child/ren in care are nurtured. We must believe that these relationships are lifelong because then we invest whole-heartedly in maintaining them in strong and healthy ways. In child welfare, best practices are enhanced when lifelong relationships with children and families are central to workers. When we take time to reflect on our traditional teachings, we see there were many people involved with children in our communities; these were lifelong relationships, which in turn, impacted on the Way of Life for children. In our practice, we must remember that children receive many teachings and form a variety of strong, important lifelong relationships. The relationships we forge with children will affect how they "become" an adult. We must also remember that the children will remember what we do and say as they grow into adulthood.

Mainstream social work education and training stresses the importance of being "objective." We learn that there are certain standards by which to communicate and document what relationships are like between social workers and their "clients." We also learn how to report *on* the lives of children and families. For anti-oppressive practice, the questions become: How do we act and write in a way that is resilient and supportive for children? Can we do this ethically? How do our traditional teachings inform how we work within government practice standards?

We want to emphasize that to practice in a way that benefits children and who they are as human beings, we as practitioners must journey from our head to our heart. Elders and traditional teachers have taught us that this is the longest journey anyone makes. When we practice from our heart, we feel all the pain and hurt the children and families we work with have felt. We then engage from the place of love and responsibility to protect these children and families. What does this mean for practice? And how do we do this? This head to heart journey is important because social workers are directly involved in and influence relationships with families. It is our responsibility to live our values and beliefs and remember all our relations. Thomas King (cited in Sinclair 2004: 54) speaks to this responsibility:

"All my relations" is a first reminder of who we are and of our relationship with both our family and our relatives. It also reminds us of the extended relationship we share with all human beings. But the relationships that Native people see go further, the web of kinship extending to the animals, to the birds, to the fish, to the plants, to all the animate and inanimate forms that can be seen or imagined. More than that, "all my relations" is an encouragement for us to accept the responsibilities we have within this universal family by living our lives in a harmonious and moral manner.

## Vision

The northern direction always reminds us of vision. How do we want our lives to be? We remember the ancestors and old ones and how they fought for everything that we have today. We remember our teachings and how they have the ability to show us how to live a good life. And, we remember the strength and resiliency of our grandparents, ancestors and children who have been warriors throughout history — because we too hope to be remembered in a similar way. Despite the imposition of racist polices such as residential schools and child welfare, our people have survived. Indigenous people continue to re-claim our traditional teachings and regenerate our culture, language and ceremonies.

One of the teachings from the book *The Sacred Tree: Reflections on Native American Spirituality* is that the only thing we can count on is that there will always be change. We are in a generation of immense change in our child welfare practice. We know how policies and practice have affected the lives of so many Indigenous children. Today, we want to recreate polices and practices that ensure our children are protected. We dream of the day when all of our children are raised in their home communities. Our teachings tell us the children are sacred, so as practitioners we must include and centre our traditional ways to uphold that teaching.

Graveline (1998: 43) believes "resistance is essential to our survival." We agree, Indigenous peoples have resisted assimilating and have survived. We must continue to resist, because we know that what we do today will affect the next seven generations.

> We know historically, culture and tradition were instrumental to healthy communities. Acknowledging and recognizing that, although our lives, our lessons and our students are seeped in colonial mentality, we still must accept responsibility to teach, and we can rely on traditional forms to do so. I stand strong in my ability and my willingness to accept personal responsibility for understanding power and relationships and to share what I have learned through my own experiences and voice. (Graveline 1998: 48)

Our buddy, Gord Bruyere, always told his students, "I teach because I do not want to see any more of our children harmed." Gord's words resonate in our work today. We as well do not want to see any more of our children hurt.

We have reflected and shared with you aspects of child welfare practice through the framework of the Medicine Wheel to provide you with tools and skills of what child welfare could look like today in your practice. A hundred years of legislation and policies have not worked for Indigenous children. We ask that you as child welfare workers collaborate with Indigenous helpers to break the cycle of colonialism. We all have an opportunity to create change for the next seven generations. As child welfare workers this is our responsibility.

We believe practice that is rooted in teachings is A Way of Life. We have watched as our children continue to be apprehended in alarming rates. We must be the warriors to protect them. The Mohawk people believe that a warrior is one who bears the burden of peace. If we are to bear the burden of peace, we must live our culture and tradition. We must never forget the children, the Elders, those that have gone on before us and those coming up after us. They are our Vision. All My Relations!

## Suggestions for Further Readings

Graveline, F.J. 1998. *Circle Works: Transforming Eurocentric Consciousness.* Halifax: Fernwood.

Foster, L.T., and B. Wharf (eds.). 2007. *People, Politics, and Child Welfare in British Columbia.* Vancouver: UBC Press.

Dominelli, L. (ed.). 2007. *Revitalising Communities in a Globalising World.* Aldershot, U.K.: Ashgate.

*First Peoples Child and Family Review* <http://www.fncfcs.com/pubs/onlineJournal.html>

## About the Authors

Qwul'sih'yah'maht [Robina Thomas] is Lyackson of the Coast Salish Nation and an assistant professor in the School of Social Work, University of Victoria. Qwul'sih'yah'maht holds a BSW and MSW and is a PhD candidate in Indigenous Governance. She is committed to Indigenous education, and her research interests include storytelling, residential schools, Indigenous women, Indigenous children and families, and Uy'skwuluwun: On Being Indigenous. She is committed to understanding anti-racism and anti-oppression and how these can be "lived."

Kundoque [Jacquie Green] is from the Haisla Nation. She is an assistant professor in the School of Social Work, University of Victoria and holds a BSW, MPA and is a PhD candidate in Indigenous Governance. She is committed to centring Indigenous philosophies and decolonizing pedagogies for cultural regeneration. Her research interests involve strategizing programs and policies that incorporate Indigenous stories, practices and analysis. Her current research is on reclaiming Haisla ways through Oolichan fishing processes.

## Notes

1.  The *Indian Act* is an enforced colonialist, paternalistic legislation that has governed and classified every aspect of the lives of Indigenous peoples in Canada for well over a hundred years. This broad, sweeping *Act* continues to govern, control, classify, regulate and dictate our identity, our movements and the economic, social and political lives of our people today (Lawrence 2003: 4).

2.  A person defined as an Indian by the *Indian Act.*
3.  We capitalize Our or A Way of Life to demonstrate the significance of Indigenous relationships to all living things as A Way Of Life. Moreover, we speak to Our Way of Life, which holds differing translations of cultural and traditional practices among our diverse Indigenous peoples.
4.  A Hul'qumi'num Mustimuhw term.
5.  A Haisla term.
6.  If we speak in the context of the *Indian Act*, we say on and off reserve. For purposes of this chapter we speak in terms of reclaiming our place and say traditional territories, which are inclusive of on or off reserve lands.

## References

Aboriginal Healing Foundation. 2005. *Reclaiming Connections: Understanding Residential School Trauma among Aboriginal People.* Ottawa. Available at <http://firstnationspedagogy. com/healing&trauma.pdf> (accessed on August 5, 2006).

Alfred, T. 2004. "Warrior Scholarship: Seeing the University as a Ground of Contention." In D. Mihesuah and A. Wilson (eds.), *Indigenizing the Academy: Transforming Scholarship and Empowering Communities.* Lincoln: University of Nebraska Press.

_____. 2005. *Wasase: Indigenous Pathways of Action and Freedom.* Peterborough, ON: Broadway.

Anderson, K. 2000. *Recognition of Being: Reconstructing Native Womanhood.* Toronto, ON: Second Story.

Bopp, J., M. Bopp, L. Brown and P. Lane. 1984. *The Sacred Tree: Reflections on Native American Spirituality.* Twin Lakes, WI: Lotus Light.

Cardinal, H. 1969. *The Unjust Society: The Tragedy of Canada's Indians.* Edmonton, AB: M.G. Hurtig.

Cajete, G. 2000. "Indigenous Knowledge: The Pueblo Metaphor of Indigenous Education." In M. Battiste (ed.), *Reclaiming Indigenous Voice and Vision.* Vancouver: UBC Press.

Dominelli, L. 1988. *Anti-Racist Social Work.* London: British Association of Social Workers.

Freire, P. 2000. *Pedagogy of the Oppressed.* New York: Continuum.

Graveline, J. 1998. *Circle Works: Transforming Euro-Centric Consciousness.* Halifax: Fernwood.

Green, J., and R. Thomas. 2005. "Learning through Our Children, Healing for Our Children: Best Practice in First Nations Communities." In L. Dominelli (ed.), *Communities in a Globalising World: Theory and Practice for Community Empowerment.* Aldershot, U.K.: Ashgate.

Hart, M. 2002. *Seeking Mino-Pimatisiwin: An Aboriginal Approach to Helping.* Halifax: Fernwood.

Hodge, J.L. 1990. "Equality: Beyond Dualism and Oppression." In D.T. Goldberg (ed.), *Anatomy of Racism.* Minneapolis: University of Minnesota Press.

hooks, b. 1995. *killing rage: ENDING RACISM.* New York: Henry Holt.

Indian Tribes of Manitoba. 1971. *Wahbung our Tomorrows.* A Policy Paper issued by the four Manitoba Indian Tribes (Cree, Ojibway, Chipewyan and Sioux). Winnipeg, MB.

Lawrence, B. 2003. "Rewriting Histories of the Land: Colonization and Indigenous Resistance in Eastern Canada." In S. Razack (ed.), *Race, Space, and the Law: Unmapping a White Settler Society.* Toronto: Between the Lines.

Maracle, L. 1996. *I Am Woman: A Native Perspective on Sociology and Feminism.* Vancouver:

Press Gang.

Ormiston, T. 2002. "Aboriginal Child and Family Service Agencies: A First Nations Analysis of Delegated Services." Unpublished paper for 598 Management report. Master of Public Administration, University of Victoria, Victoria, BC, Canada.

Rae, J. 2006. *Indigenous Children: Rights and Reality*. A Report on Indigenous Children and the U.N. Convention on the Rights of the Child. Ottawa: First Nations Children and Family Caring Society of Canada.

Saulis, M. 2003. "Program and Policy Development from a Holistic Aboriginal Perspective." In A. Westhues (ed.), *Canadian Social Policy: Issues and Perspective* (Third Edition). Waterloo: Wilfrid Laurier Press.

Sinclair, R. 2004. "Aboriginal Social Work Education in Canada: Decolonizing Pedagogy for the Seventh Generation." *First Peoples Child and Family Review: A Journal on Innovation and Best Practices in Aboriginal Child Welfare, Administration, Research, Policy and Practice* 1, 1 (September).

_____. 2007. "Identity Lost and Found: Lessons from the Sixties Scoop." *First Peoples Child and Family Review* 3, 1.

Thomas, R. 2000. "Storytelling in the Spirit of Wise Woman: Experiences of Kuper Island Residential School." Unpublished thesis for Master of Social Work, University of Victoria, Victoria, BC.

# Chapter 2

# Meeting Here and Now
## Reflections on Racial and Cultural Difference in Social Work Encounters

*Donna Jeffery*

This chapter explores three approaches in social work education and practice — cultural competence, anti-racist social work and anti-oppressive practice — to the challenges posed by racial and cultural difference and the meanings these make in both workers' and clients' lives. Following a discussion of each approach, their application is considered in the context of a basic social work skill — developing relationships. Utilizing Sara Ahmed's (2000) postcolonial work on ethical encounters with "strangers," the chapter explores her critical question, "What are the conditions of possibility for us meeting here and now?" and suggests the need for a contextualized, historically specific understanding of social work encounters, how they are produced, what they mean and how difference comes to matter at all.

Questions Addressed in This Chapter
1. What are the challenges to developing anti-oppressive approaches to child welfare knowledge and practice?
2. What are the links between conceptualizations of whiteness and the ways in which we think about "good social work practice"?
3. Ahmed (2000) tells us that face-to-face encounters are "affected by broader social processes." What does she mean by this?

> In one way or another, we are attached to the idea that if our lives, our organizations, our social theories or our societies, were "properly ordered" then all would be well. And we take it that such ordering is possible, at least some of the time. So when we encounter complexity we tend to treat it as distraction. We treat it as a sign of the limits to order. Or we think of it as evidence of failure. (Law 1994: 4–5)

The point that John Law is making in this opening quotation is that the social world is highly complex and its problems are resistant to simplistic solutions. Yet in a modern liberal context, we seek ever better ways to tame this complexity by developing solutions and practices that promise to contain the seemingly endless diversity we face. Nowhere is this more evident than in the field of child welfare (for example, see Dumbrill 2003: Ch. 6). Child welfare, as a particular branch of social work, is rife with forms of managerialism and doing things in an ordered and properly procedural way. Indeed, this holds true for children and families and for the social workers themselves. For example, the parents must comply with procedures such as risk reduction in order to keep their children or have them returned; workers follow a series of ordered assessment steps in determining whether to remove or return children to parents who come to the attention of child welfare authorities.

So why, we might ask, begin a chapter on anti-oppressive and anti-racist approaches to social work encounters with a discussion of complexity, order and "messiness?" My answer to this is because social work, as Payne (2005: 15) notes, "is a product of *modernism*" (italics in original). By this Payne means that social work is founded on the idea that the social world and its problems can be studied and understood, resulting in rational solutions that simply need to be followed through. In the pursuit of knowledge and skills that facilitate the sorts of managerial practices that constitute professional practice, Parton (1996: 7) explains that "the emergence of modern forms of social regulation was an integral part of the development of modernity" and, as an emerging modern profession, social work was closely aligned with the development of these new forms of social regulation. Indeed, by the turn of the twentieth century, numerous Canadian women's reform organizations (precursors to professional social workers) were active. Comprised of a collection of interest groups, women's involvement in social reform covered a wide range of organizations — missions, settlement houses, day nurseries, prohibition, YWCA, fresh air camps and children's institutions. Though disparate in their focus, all shared a unifying theme of concern for the proper way to live, raise a family and participate in a morally strong society. Thus the mission and practices of the profession evolved out of a history of elites "helping" marginalized groups of people. Early social reform work served to shape social work's precursory understandings of social difference, hierarchy and systems of marginality and its legacy continues today. The profession has a profound investment in modern notions of knowing and managing people and their behaviour, and such investments continue to shape contemporary definitions of service provision. Social work's historical and ideological foundations have particular significance in light of charges that social workers have not adequately addressed issues of social difference, in particular racism and racial inequality.

Modernity represents a worldview that has been, and continues to be, extremely influential in the Western world. Central to modernity are notions of what counts as knowledge and whose knowledge counts. Knowledge is understood as the property of powerful social groups, including professions such as social work. Those positioned outside the dominant group have been excluded from this process and are often represented and judged against the "normal" or dominant standard. However this worldview has come under critique, and its authority has been challenged for the ways that it reinforces hierarchies among people. Further, it has been challenged by the very groups about whom knowledge has been produced. This has created a crisis for professions like social work and has led the profession, with varying degrees of success, to seek new approaches to practice.

One of the most significant challenges that the profession has grappled with is how to address the complexities of social difference or, as it is sometimes referred to, the "problem" of diversity. Responses to this so-called problem reveal something about the tensions described by Law in the opening quotation. In social work practice, we focus on honing our skills. At the same time, we have become accustomed to the critique that skills cannot be divorced from the social contexts in which they are practised. A sense of uncertainty has crept in to muddy professional desires for clear-cut practice strategies. Uncertainty has arisen within a context of increased diversity amongst the recipients of social work services. The crisis presented by the "problem" of diversity has led social work educators and practitioners to revisit what it is they do and how they do it. One of the key questions asked has been this: What is to be done in the wake of allegations of exclusionary practices that have been levelled at a profession that seeks to help? There are no easy answers. In fact, any sort of formulaic recipe of how to "do" difference is antithetical to the argument I make here. What we can and must do, however, is become better equipped to ask ourselves the right questions about what we think, from where such knowledge originates and how we benefit (or not) from accepting and acting on this knowledge.

In this chapter I map out three of the profession's responses to practising with and across social difference: cultural competence models, anti-racist social work, anti-oppressive practice. These represent the main approaches that have been articulated as a means to taking on, in more relevant, timely and ethical ways, the complex contexts in which social workers, including child welfare practitioners, are engaged. While definitions and understandings of each of these may differ amongst educators and practitioners, each suggests a different way of approaching a professional practice that is alert to ways in which inequality and social hierarchy are organized. Following a description of each of these approaches, I turn to a brief exploration of what these conceptualizations of cultural and racial difference offer us in practical, everyday ways. I do this by considering the ways in which we conceptualize what it is to build relationships with those with whom we work.

Many would argue that, at the core of social work are the relationships we develop with clients. Indeed, social work students are often advised that in the absence of certainty and sure-fire prescriptions, or when paralyzed by the sense that our knowledge base is simply insufficient, we fall back on the relationship. Building relationships is thus positioned as the one skill upon which we can rely. Yet a focus on relationship can divert our attention from the context of domination and subordination in which these relationships occur and from active engagement in addressing this context. The ways in which we conceptualize the qualities and impact of social differences such as race and culture, to name only two, shape the ways in which we organize our practice and the expectations we have in our professional relationships.

What are the stories we tell ourselves in social work about social differences such as race, culture and ethnicity? Demographic changes attributable to recent Canadian immigration do not represent the profession's first encounters with understanding and intervening with the Other. "Other" is a term often used to refer to that which is foreign to us, for example, in terms of culture, race or ethnicity, that is, someone *other* than who we are and what we know. In this sense it does not refer to other people who are different from us in a benign way. Rather, it references a worldview where, in relations of comparison with the Other on a global scale, "the Other always comes off as somehow lacking or not quite up to an unmarked standard," thus authorizing "a sense of entitlement and an obligation to intervene for the 'betterment' of the Other wherever he or she resides" (Heron 2007: 7).

Social work has a long history of intervention in the lives of Indigenous people and poor people in this country. For example, social workers were active participants in the implementation of policies of assimilation that led to the radical disruption of Indigenous families. Indigenous people have been pathologized and perceived as social problems, a stereotype rampant in Canadian society to which those in the profession have not been immune (Hudson and Tayor-Henley 1995). Another example of the profession's legacy of intervening in the lives of racialized populations is provided by Canadian social work educator Wanda Thomas Bernard (Bernard et al. 1993: 257), whose work focuses on the relationship between the profession of social work and Black Nova Scotians. She notes that Black people have a long and vibrant history in Nova Scotia and have lived there, either as slaves or as free people, since 1604. Bernard and Thomas (1991: 238) contend that, when asked about the impediments interfering with adequate social service delivery to Black families in the area, Black people claim racism "as the primary barrier experienced… in their attempts to gain access to appropriate social services." In her study of the destruction of the Black enclave known as Africville, Nova Scotia, Nelson (2008) demonstrates how social workers were instrumental in the pathologizing and relocation of Black Canadians from their homes. These examples dispute the idea of racial diversity as a "new problem" and illustrate how social work's management of difference has also been complicit with and essential to colonial or racist practices.

## Cultural Competence Models

In confronting the issues that are generated by a racially and culturally diverse population, one approach has been to create professionals who are culturally competent or cross-culturally sensitive. In general, this approach asks social work and health care professionals to become more aware of, and sensitive to, the norms and nuances that are specific to a wide range of cultural and ethnic groups. The goal is to recognize that some behaviours, ways of speaking and so on may be inappropriate to the cultural mores of the person or family with whom the worker is engaged. Developing heightened sensitivity to these specific types of needs is seen to be beneficial to the working relationship and result in more suitable service delivery.

Elsewhere I (Jeffery 2002) have traced the history of debate around the inclusion of multicultural and anti-oppression content in curricula for Canadian schools of social work with a focus on the place of anti-racism. The cultural competence model was the orthodox means of addressing difference in professional social work contexts in the 1980s and 1990s, and it remains common in some sectors. In this approach, packaged and oversimplified forms of ethnographic knowledge were taught to social work students because these were seen to offer a way to manage the differences embodied in their clients. The term "culture," in this sense, referenced a specifically Western liberal perspective that was quite removed from other worldviews, for example, Indigenous perspectives, where culture reflects a more holistic and integrated notion of collective identity. Within the cultural competence mode, the people who are culturally and racially outside of the dominant group were conceptualized as having a set of attributes to be catalogued, evaluated and managed. The Other was someone to be known rather than understood, and was then acted upon by a neutral and dispassionate social worker. In other words, this approach has typically framed the problem of diversity as one that lies with those other people, our clients. As Sherene Razack (1998:10) puts it, difficulties in communicating and helping across differences are due to *their* cultural practices, *their* racial background. It's about *them.* Thus in social work we can attain the knowledge to know *them* and act accordingly, but our basic mission, knowledge base and approaches to practice are not at issue.

The major problem with cultural competence, within a modern Western multicultural context, is that it reproduced enduring assumptions about the Other that were not far removed from the paternalism, imperialism and racism of early social work (Jeffery 2002; Jeffery and Nelson forthcoming). The model has come under considerable critique from those who charge that it puts forth and applies simplistic and deeply flawed notions of ethnic and racial differences. What is interesting despite such critique is the persistence and evident appeal of the cultural competence approach for professionals who seek to understand clients who are different from themselves in that they come from racially and culturally different backgrounds. Such appeal might be due to the belief that a cultural analysis is able to provide clear indicators of what a population is like, thus leading to tools and strategies for understanding and dealing with them.

Cultural competence (or cross-cultural practice) is seen to encourage openness to differences, expertise in the use of cultural resources and respect for cultural integrity. However, as many theorists have noted, culture often comes to be viewed as a blueprint for human behaviour, values and beliefs. This can be especially appealing to social welfare and health professionals as it offers concrete tools and methods for practice, allowing a sense of competence and being skilled. However, it often does so through the application of overly general, simplified depictions of non-dominant, immigrant, racialized and Indigenous communities, simply reinforcing stereotypes and creating for students and workers a sense of professional anxiety over obtaining and applying information correctly. It also leads to problems with access and equity in social services being attributed to cultural differences, rather than the social, economic or political factors that hold systemic inequalities in place. So, for example, cultural competence models conceptually remove power imbalances. Racism, then, becomes defined as merely a matter of individual prejudice, and "cultural barriers" are positioned as the cause for unequal treatment.

While racism attributed to biological or genetic difference has become less acceptable, similar sentiments are now often expressed through the language of cultural inferiority, where hierarchies are couched in language that claims that it is cultural practices that make some people less civilized and, therefore, inferior or backward (Essed 1991; Razack 1998). Importantly, cultural and other models have developed against a backdrop of racist public discourse that commonly frames the "diversity problem" in terms of multitudes of immigrant and refugee bodies with strange and exotic needs, calling up images of "floods" that threaten to swamp and reconfigure our familiar cultural landscape (Razack 2000; Schick and St. Denis 2005). The mid-twentieth century saw the proliferation of theories about "cultures of poverty" (Banfield 1970; Lewis 1966; Moynihan 1967), which posited an unrelenting apathy and resignation passed down through generations, effectively suggesting that poor and racialized groups were responsible for their own plight and their cultures inherently dysfunctional. More recently, we have seen racist discourses based on cultural inferiority gain ground with the rise of anti-Muslim/anti-Arab sentiment in the West (Razack 2004). Given these criticisms, there are good reasons to be alarmed about the potential of cultural competence approaches to reinforce dominance and marginality.

A critique of these approaches is that they are limited because of their tendency to overlook power differences in the creation and maintenance of social hierarchy and marginalization. Cross-cultural approaches to service delivery and education in the West are seen to provide predominantly white social service professionals with a better capacity to communicate with non-dominant groups. Nestel and Razack (2006: 2) sum up the approach this way:

> The cultural competence approach proceeds on the assumption that what is mainly wrong in the encounter between lawyers, educators, physicians and other health care providers, and their non-white, non-Western clients, patients, or students is that the professionals lack the knowledge of how to manage these populations, and thus cannot adequately serve them.

Social work has historically viewed itself as a profession that respects and works with social difference, and one that advocates for the disenfranchised. Most workers enter the profession out of a sincere desire to help others. Yet, when viewed in a historical context that considers projects of colonization, the encounter between social work and its diverse Others has always involved engagements that are deeply racialized, classed and gendered. From the profession's earliest days, social workers, guided by state policies, professional judgment and expertise as well as by common social values of the time, have been empowered to make distinctions between the deserving and the undeserving and to pass judgment concerning the reform and assimilation of the lower classes and marginalized of society (Jeffery 2002).

For example, child welfare social workers were the Canadian state's hand-maidens in the case of both residential schools and the sixties scoop of Indigenous children (Fournier and Crey 1998). Mohawk scholar Patricia Monture-Angus (1995) cites statistical data that demonstrates the degree to which Indigenous children were over-represented in the child welfare system, while Indigenous adults experience grossly disproportionate involvement in the criminal justice process. In light of these documented inequities, Monture-Angus contends that piece-meal reforms cannot alter the systemic abuse which is devastating Indigenous communities. All individuals who are employed in the child welfare–criminal justice systems continuum must be educated and exposed to the racism inherent in both systems. According to Monture-Angus (1995: 196) "racism (perhaps colonialism better expresses the problem) is woven into our legal system" and not surprisingly, distrust of systems such as child welfare is profound as "it has effectively assisted in robbing us of our children and of our future" (199).

Such collusion is neither surprising nor unique, yet is part of a troubled professional history in "helping" fields that is often difficult to acknowledge for those invested in improving the lives of their clients. Some social work scholars have, however, initiated and responded to critical internal and external views of this troubled history in various ways. Despite its limitations as an explanatory framework, culture's place as an integral part of some identities and practices cannot be simply dismissed. Indigenous communities, for instance, have warranted much attention because their situation demands an understanding of colonial history and how both racism and culture are lived in its wake (Fiske and Browne 2006; Hagey 2000; Dei and Calliste 2000). We might best proceed from an understanding of culture as a dynamic process "lived within and among groups of people, and therefore as deeply enmeshed in power relations and in economic, political and historical contexts" (Browne 2005: 64–65). While narrow understandings of culture and culturalist discourses create an array of problems in the relationships between social service providers and Indigenous people, cultural revitalization has, at the same time, provided a powerful response to the institutional and structural devastation of colonialism. In other words, culture itself is a complex and fraught terrain and the key is how, for whom and by whom the term is applied. There are ways to think about clients' identities and professional practices that make use of culture in complex ways that do not reduce it to a simplistic and essentializing body of knowledge about groups of people.

Social work programs in Canada have become more aware of problems with de-historicized and stereotyped approaches to conceptualizing social difference in general, and cross-cultural practices specifically. More critical and nuanced perspectives, which address the limitations of cross-cultural models, include anti-racist and anti-oppressive approaches to practice. Both of these approaches, with varying degrees of success, seek to transcend the kinds of managerialism that pervade less critical cultural competence models of practice. Definitions and implementation vary but both can be seen to be critical responses to the inadequacies that models based on sensitivity and tolerance have been charged with.

## Anti-Racist Models

Anti-racist social work, as is clear from its name, centres issues related to race and racism in its approach to understanding and working with social problems. In this way, it goes beyond a recognition of individualized racist incidents to address the systemic forms of racism that are rooted in wider societal institutions and structures.

Anti-racist social work takes as its starting point a critical perspective on racial hierarchy as a fundamental aspect of social inequality. It is important here to pause and clarify what is meant by a critical perspective on race and racism. Race is a complex concept whose meaning has gone through many changes but continues to be a fundamental principle of social organization and identity formation. Race is widely regarded as a political and social construction rather than a biological fact. Although no longer valued as a scientific concept, the idea of race continues to be used as a marker of human difference with sometimes devastating consequences (Johnston et al. 2000). There is no single common definition of racism, but in recent years there have been significant shifts in the way that race can be thought about. Feminist anthropologist Ann Stoler (1995: 204) suggests that talking about racism is problematic "because racisms are not, and never have been, about race alone." They are complex and multilayered, invoking multiple discourses to do with identity, nationalism and economics. Self-evident, "common sense" understandings of race and racism have been challenged and opened to critique, demonstrating the ways that normalized sets of assumptions are powerful precisely because of their insidious pervasiveness.

Forms of racism that are conceptualized as a matter of "personal prejudice" share an individualist orientation. By that I mean that they permit a focus on an individual's "bad" words or actions, leaving the insidious and pervasive ramifications of racial hierarchy unexplored. However, we need a broader understanding that can encompass individualist expressions while focusing on systemic racism. To do so we can draw on critical race theory, which interrogates "colourblind" or "raceneutral" policies, practices and beliefs that actually entrench the inequitable treatment of white and non-white groups in society. Critical race theory proposes that racism is "normal" and endemic in social institutions rather than aberrant and that whiteness and white dominance are the norms against which the attributes and positions of other groups are defined. Systemic racism, the more hidden but systematic ways that racism is built into institutional policies and practices, is marked by its structure and its consequences in peoples' lives. This points to how racism is embedded in social systems and allows us to account for forms of discrimination that are not necessarily visible to those working within institutions and that are not consciously enacted. Racialization is a relatively new term (1970s) whose analytical purpose is to refer to a process or situation where the concept of race is introduced to define and give meaning to a particular population, its characteristics and actions. It brings a sense of the fluid and changing nature of something that we often see as static or fixed — the idea of racial thinking and racism as processes and practices that are continually being re-made. This concept permits questions about the parameters within which social workers, and other professionals, frame the impact of racialization on their lives and on the lives and opportunities of their clients. In child welfare it creates a venue for us to notice that it is the children of poor, racialized and Indigenous mothers that overwhelmingly come to the attention of child welfare authorities — and to begin to grapple with what to do about that both systemically and in our individual encounters.

Goldberg (1993: 87) maintains that, whatever the contextually and historically specific meanings assigned to race,

> race basically serves — sometimes explicitly and assertively, at other times silently and subtly — to define capacity for self-ownership and self-direction. It has established who can be imported and who exported, who are immigrants and who are indigenous, who may be property and who citizens, and among the latter who get to vote and who do not, who are protected by the law and who are its objects, who are employable and who are not, who have access and privilege and who are (to be) marginalized.

Race is too often seen not as the social and political relation that it is but as a cultural or biological property of a non-white population. Race resides in those "other" bodies.

If we are to try and make sense of the ways in which racial thinking permeates the social work profession and its knowledge base, it is imperative that we explore the notion of whiteness and its accompanying practices of normalization and domination. Whiteness refers to a set of locations that are historically, socially, politically and culturally produced and are fundamentally linked to relations of domination. There has been a growing recognition that it is important to look at the ways in which all of us, not just those who are not white, live lives that are shaped by race and racial hierarchies (Frankenberg 1993). Like other racial categories, whiteness is a social construction that, beyond referencing white people, refers to a set of social meanings and privileges that have an enormous, and insidious, impact on our social systems and people's lives. Whiteness can be described as a subjectivity, or way of being in the world, and a social system that is naturalized and taken-for-granted so as to be invisible to those of us who live it. Frankenberg (1993: 236–37) sums up the meanings of white subjectivity succinctly when she writes, "the term 'whiteness' signals the production and reproduction of dominance rather than subordination, normativity rather than marginality, and privilege rather than disadvantage." Lack of consciousness or awareness of our racial identity limits our capacity to see how it is that the way in which we create our sense of self, occurs within relations of dominance. By this I mean that white identity is secured in relation to the Other, and it is this relational aspect of whiteness that helps to illuminate the dynamics underlying the social worker–client relationship, both in theory and practice. Dyer's (1997: 1) writing on whiteness clarifies this point: "As long as race is something only applied to non-white peoples, as long as white people are not racially seen and named, they/we function as a human norm. Other people are raced, we are just people." The impact of this is that those of us who are white cannot see the things that account for our positions of privilege and power.

Yee and Dumbrill (2003: 100–101) note that to unpack the concept of whiteness is to "unmask the way the dominant culture shapes the norms and values of Canadian society and reproduces various forms of oppression." Perhaps the most remarkable feature that characterizes whiteness is its unmarked, apparently content-free quality. Whiteness is about being inconspicuous to the point of invisibility, and yet racially dominant. Notably, whiteness is not defined as a "colour," but rather as an implicit and universal norm against which "people of colour" are defined and evaluated. This is not to say that enactments of dominance are intentionally malicious or deliberate. However, the power and accompanying privileges that whiteness discourse generates reproduces itself regardless of intention or goodwill because of the fact that it just appears to be "normal." The term normal is often used in a commonsense way to distinguish between that which is good or proper and that which is seen to be deviant or substandard. Normalization refers to the processes by which particular sets of behaviour and values come to be accepted and acted upon as good, acceptable and correct. Normalization, along with surveillance, is a compelling and potent instrument of power in classifying, measuring and ranking differences against a particular standard (Brock 2003: 333).

Day-to-day practices on which the profession rests and that sustain the profession reproduce whiteness (Jeffery 2005). In addition to its characterization as unmarked, universal and "normal," perhaps its most powerful qualities that hold particular resonance for the helping professions are those of innocence and goodness. Critiques of whiteness, whether implicit or explicit, call into question the desirable identity of oneself as a good person, a caring and altruistic helping professional (see Heron 2007, for example, for a discussion of desire and helping imperatives in the international development context). The challenge is to tease out and expose the specificity of this ideology, which only appears benign in its guise of neutrality and "genericness." An anti-racist social work approach requires us to make visible the ways in which racism insidiously and systematically permeates the social world in which we work. More specifically, we have to address the ways in which the ideology of whiteness serves as a deeply embedded organizing principle in social and cultural relations.

## Anti-Oppressive Social Work Practice

More recently, anti-oppressive approaches to practice have been invaluable in exposing the serious ideological and political problems with practice models that dwell on cultural differences. Anti-oppressive practice (AOP) doesn't represent a single or unitary perspective on social work practice, but rather includes a disparate and multidisciplinary variety of perspectives taken from feminist, anti-racist and other critical philosophies and social movements. As Baines (2007) notes, this eclectic, interdisciplinary approach "does not claim to be, nor does it wish to become, an exclusive and authoritative model containing every answer to every social problem" (19). Rather, its strength is the capacity to "continually evolve to analyze and address constantly changing social conditions and challenges" (20). However, many students and practitioners find that anti-oppressive approaches, like anti-racist approaches, are less readily "operationalized" in interactions with clients where an understanding of difference is required, or in the policies, bureaucracies and discourses that give substance to social work at large. While AOP provides a critical counterpoint to cultural competence, it does not easily translate into practice and can seem more abstract and less appealing than the more formulaic applications of cultural competence skills to static, culturally different people.

And yet if we are to make a commitment to addressing the multiple ways in which racism, sexism, classism, ableism and other forms of oppression are manifest in people's lives, then it is incumbent upon us, according to educational theorist Kevin Kumashiro (2000), to do two things: understand the dynamics of oppression *and* articulate ways to work against it. Although writing in a context of education to an audience comprised, primarily, of teachers, Kumashiro's map of the four main approaches to anti-oppressive practice is equally appropriate for those of us in social work. While I cannot fully describe each of the four here, the overlapping but distinct avenues he identifies are 1. education *for* the Other; 2. education *about* the Other; 3. education that is *critical* of privileging and Othering; and 4. education that *changes* students and society. His point is not to claim that one of these anti-oppressive approaches is right and others are wrong. Rather, he argues that each has its strengths and weaknesses and the work for each of us is to be aware of which approach we are engaged in, what is being accomplished and what we are missing. This is the challenge that AOP sets for us.

## Linking Theory to Practice

In this final section of the chapter, I speak to the relevance and application of the preceding discussion of difference and its analysis. By referencing social work as a series of encounters between workers and clients I am flagging the linkages between theory and practice. Thus far, the discussion has focused on the conceptual — the strengths and perils of various analyses of racial and cultural difference. The task now is to consider the application of these concepts within the social work encounter. The rewards for doing so are great and, I would argue, the consequences of not pursuing such a critical examination can be dire.

For example, child and adolescent development models are typically drawn from research on the ages and stages that white, middle-class children pass through. Deviations from these models are too easily ascribed to failures of culture or ability in "other" families. Workers who have applied simplistic and stereotypical versions of culture have not always intervened when they needed to, at times for fear of interfering with what were seen as cultural norms, resulting in serious consequences for children and their families (see, for example, the U.K. case of Victoria Climbie, in Garrett 2006). Narrow (i.e., white, middle-class) interpretations of "attachment" and "best interests of the child" have resulted in children being separated from family, community and, in the case of Indigenous children, nation (Kline 1992). What these examples demonstrate is that the refusal to critically take up difference in the context of child welfare has meant that we both fail to intervene when we need to and, at other times, intervene too zealously when we should stay out.

Making relationship a fundamental skill in professional social work practice provides a fertile site to consider the consequences of how we think about and act upon notions of cultural and racial difference. This is not to say that building a relationship is the solution to overcoming the sometimes difficult terrain of working across difference. However, if we see our work as a series of encounters with often marginalized and vulnerable people, then relationship-building seems a useful place to begin. I was reminded of the centrality of the skill of building relationships in social work practice from a study of front-line child protection workers (Gomez 2008). The author asked a small sample of workers to talk about their front-line practice in order to better understand examples of good and failed interactions with clients from the workers' perspectives and, in general, to see power at work in child welfare practice. One of the conclusions that she drew from her findings was that in a context where the results of our actions as social workers are very often neither certain nor predictable, participants agreed that effective practice comes down to the relationship. In other words, investment in the quality and humanity of the relationship between worker and client is all that a worker can rely on with any degree of certainty. This is not to say that these interview subjects were rejecting or overlooking the importance of social and institutional factors in their interactions with clients. However, they did specifically speak to the one-on-one relationship as fundamental to their work.

In a similar vein, a colleague and I interviewed social workers about their perspectives on cultural and racial difference as these concepts applied to their practice with racialized clients (Jeffery and Nelson 2007). We found a similar emphasis on relationships. In examining the practice philosophies and approaches workers employed, we found that older practice models based on cultural knowledge were sometimes drawn on in their interactions with clients and later resisted for the ways that these practitioners found themselves over-generalizing these same clients. A common alternative was a reliance on notions of relationship and communication as foundational to their practice. Such approaches, in many cases, treated clients simply as infinitely varied individuals and ignored hierarchies and systems of domination and subordination. The results also presented some poignant examples of how workers grappled with their own discomfort around practising across differences and their own fears of confronting what might be racist views within themselves.

This finding of the centrality of the skill of relationship formation echoes a point made by Strega (2007). Anti-oppressive child welfare practice, she notes, can and should be built on respectful relationships between social workers and clients, and "like all relationships, helping relationships are social, political, cultural and economic relationships within specific geographies and historical situations in which we can enact or resist relations of domination and marginalization (or do both simultaneously)" (74). But what does this mean and how might such relationships be pursued? In light of the complexity of social difference and its impact on social work knowledge and practice, it seems safe to assume that making relationship is neither a simple nor straightforward endeavour.

So how might we think about the sorts of interactions that we wish to create and foster? What would it take to move beyond encounters where differences are simply recognized to those where power relations are unpacked, examined, analyzed and integrated into practice? Barbara Heron (2005) takes up these questions in her work on self-reflection and anti-oppressive practice. Self-reflection, the practice of asserting the social and cultural variables that make up our identity, is a common teaching strategy in social work classrooms. As Heron notes, reflecting on our sites of privilege and oppression as a self-location exercise is considered to be a cornerstone of anti-oppressive practice. However, she is troubled by the usage of self-location because of its tendency to turn something that is fluid and complex — one's sense of self as a subject — into something that is fixed or frozen: for example, my social location as a [race], [class] and [gender] had an impact on the relationships I developed. The problem arises when we suggest that our social location had a positive or negative impact in an encounter without examining the relations and effects of power, the "so what?" of the exchange.

This is not to say that there are not benefits to self-location as a starting point — not the end-point — of analysis. But listing our sites of privilege, for example, in the absence of a deeper analysis of social differences and their interplay, cannot move us beyond simplistic and potentially harmful approaches to our professional interactions. Sara Ahmed (2000), a professor of women's studies in the U.K., tells us that ethical engagement across difference requires us to rethink and complicate the very notion of being face to face with someone and to pay attention to the complexities of such encounters. In order to do this, she suggests that we need to discuss "the temporal and spatial dislocations that are implicated in the very possibility of being faced by this other" (144). Ahmed explains that

> this is partly about locating the encounter in time and space: *what are the conditions of possibility for us meeting here and now?*... So, for example, rather than thinking of gender and race as something that this other *has*... we can consider how such differences are determined at the level of the encounter,

insofar as the immediacy of the face to face is affected by broader social processes, that also operate elsewhere, and in other times, rather than simply in the present (though this is where they may be presented or faced). (144–45, emphasis in original)

This quote from Ahmed underscores the challenge that social workers face as we sort out the details of what it means to approach relationship-building in a critical and ethical way. What she is saying is that we can only understand the face-to-face meeting within a context of its broader social processes. In other words, we have to shift our thinking to see that difference and its meaning in any situation are being produced in the encounter itself. This is in contrast to seeing difference as something that is located in the body of the Other, as a fact brought about by the Other's "strangeness" relative to a dominant norm. Contrast Ahmed's idea, that the meaning attributed to difference is dynamic and fluid, with other approaches that seek to identify difference as something fixed within a person's culture or knowable based on their appearance. It is useful to envision the helping encounter as a microcosm of the broader social and political forces that underpin it, and to see the profound need for socially and historically informed considerations of power relations as they shape our professional practices.

## Troubling Our Practice

I began the chapter with a discussion of the tensions between our desire for certainty — knowing what to do — and the inevitable challenges of complexity that require us to live with uncertainty, leaving us little firm ground on which to stand. Cultural competence, anti-racist social work and anti-oppressive practice represent the profession's attempts to acknowledge, understand and respond to social difference and to the role that racial and cultural differences play in people's lives and identities. None of the three perspectives offers a simple answer to the question of how to work with difference. Cultural competence provides a recipe for cross-cultural practice, but the nature of the knowledge it serves up often creates more problems than it solves. Anti-racist social work and anti-oppressive practice are far more analytical about the politics of diversity in social work, but both can, at times, seem better at transforming the consciousness of the social worker than they are in translating into improved actual practice in the field. Emphasizing the quality of the worker's relationship with the client, regardless of racial and cultural differences, allows us to explore the dynamics of the interaction. But focusing on the relationship can encourage a view of the professional encounter that dismisses or diminishes difference, and the social and political implications that attend on social work in the modern world that cannot be, in good conscience, ignored.

So where does that leave us as people interested in practising effective, just and compassionate social work in a diverse and ever-changing world? Cultural competence, despite its flaws, does have the virtue of paying attention to the need to put our understandings of racial and cultural difference into practice. Anti-racist social work and anti-oppressive practice offer a critically sophisticated analysis of difference and whiteness that is lacking in cultural competence approaches. And last, bringing relationship into focus reminds us that we are more than the sum of our differences. Focusing on relationships allows us to see racial and cultural identities not as obstacles but as opportunities to deepen and enrich our personal and professional connections with others.

The answer to the challenge of encountering racial and cultural diversity, notably given that modernity has shaped social work in such a way as to encourage a debilitating "managerial" approach to difference, perhaps lies in keeping all factors in tension. Social workers need forms of knowledge about difference, including their own, that support a deeply thoughtful appreciation of difference in a way that is historically and contextually accountable; that seek opportunities to translate that knowledge into effective and sometimes radical forms of practice; and that don't overlook the complex nature of the relationship between worker and client. Ahmed's suggestion that difference is not fixed or immutable, but is created in the moment of encounter, gives us hope. If difference is created in the professional encounter, then arguably issues relating to racial and cultural difference in social work that seem to be entrenched, fraught and sometimes difficult, can also be seen as fluid, changeable and capable of meaningful progress.

I conclude with questions you might ask yourself as you consider the relevance and significance of cultural and racial differences in your own life and the lives of the children and families with whom you work:

1. What assumptions do I make about culture? About race? About how these play out in my interactions?
2. Where does my knowledge about people who are culturally and racially different from me come from? Do I trust it? If so, why?
3. How might the professional relationship I have with clients help me to ground and evaluate the ways in which racial and cultural differences factor into my current and future social work practice?

## Suggestions for Further Reading

Brock, D. (ed.). 2003. *Making Normal: Social Regulation in Canada*. Toronto: Thomson-Nelson.

Heron, B. 2007. *Desire for Development: Whiteness, Gender, and the Helping Imperative*. Waterloo: Wilfrid Laurier Press

Jeffery, D. 2007. "Radical Problems and Liberal Selves: Professional Subjectivity in the Anti-Oppressive Social Work Classroom." *Canadian Social Work Review* 24, 2.

## About the Author

Donna Jeffery is an associate professor in the School of Social Work at the University of Victoria, Canada. Her research focuses on processes of racialization, knowledge and subjectivity formation and social work education.

# References

Ahmed, S. 2000. *Strange Encounters: Embodied Others in Post-Coloniality*. London: Routledge.

Baines, D. 2007. "Anti-Oppressive Social Work Practice: Fighting for Space, Fighting for Change." In D. Baines (ed.), *Doing Anti-Oppressive Practice: Building Transformative Politicized Social Work*. Halifax: Fernwood.

Banfield, E. 1970. *Unheavenly City: The Nature and Future of Our Urban Crisis*. Boston: Little, Brown.

Bernard, W.T., L. Lucas-White and D. Moore. 1993. "Triple Jeopardy: Assessing Life Experiences of Black Nova Scotian Women from a Social Work Perspective." *Canadian Social Work Review* 10, 2.

Bernard, W.T., and G. Thomas. 1991. "Social Service Sensitivity Training Program: Developing a Program to Sensitize Social Workers Working With Black Clients." *Canadian Social Work Review* 8, 2.

Brock, D. (ed.). 2003. *Making Normal: Social Regulation in Canada*. Toronto: Nelson Thomson

Browne, A. 2005. "Discourses Influencing Nurses' Perceptions of First Nations Patients." *Canadian Journal of Nursing Research* 37, 4.

Dei, G.S., and A. Calliste (eds.). 2000. *Power, Knowledge and Anti-Racism Education: A Critical Reader*. Halifax: Fernwood.

Dumbrill, G. 2003. "Child Welfare: AOP's Nemesis?" In W. Shera (ed.), *Emerging Perspectives on Anti-Oppressive Practice*. Toronto: Canadian Scholars' Press.

Dyer, R. 1997. *White*. London: Routledge.

Essed, P. 1991. *Understanding Everyday Racism: An Interdisciplinary Theory*. Newbury Park, NJ: Sage.

Fiske, J., and A. Browne. 2006. "Aboriginal Citizen, Discredited Medical Subject: Paradoxical Constructions of Aboriginal Women's Subjectivity in Canadian Health Care Policies." *Policy Sciences* 39.

Fournier, S., and E. Crey. 1998. *Stolen from Our Embrace: The Abduction of First Nations Children and the Restoration of Aboriginal Communities*." Vancouver: Douglas and McIntyre.

Frankenberg, R. 1993. *The Social Construction of Whiteness: White Women, Race Matters*. Minneapolis: University of Minnesota Press.

Garrett, P. 2006. "Protecting Children in a Globalized World: 'Race' and 'Place' in the Laming Report on the Death of Victoria Climbié." *Journal of Social Work* 6, 3.

Goldberg, D.T. 1993. *Racist Culture: Philosophy and the Politics of Meaning*. Cambridge: Blackwell.

Gomez, Y. 2008. "Daily Practice Narratives of Child Protection Social Workers: The Power of the Frontline." MSW thesis, University of Victoria.

Hagey, R. 2000. "Cultural Safety: Honoring Traditional Ways." *Alternative and Complementary Therapies* 6, 4.

Heron, B. 2005. "Self-Reflection in Critical Social Work Practice: Subjectivity and the Possibilities of Resistance." *Journal of Reflective Practice* 6, 3.

_____. 2007. *Desire for Development: Whiteness, Gender, and the Helping Imperative*. Waterloo: Wilfrid Laurier Press

Hudson, P., and S. Taylor-Henley. 1995. "First Nations Child and Family Services, 1982–1992." *Canadian Social Work Review* 12, 1.

Jeffery, D. 2002. "A Terrain of Struggle: Reading Race in Social Work Education." Unpublished PhD dissertation, OISE/University of Toronto.

_____. 2005. "'What Good is Anti-Racist Social Work if You Can't Master It? Exploring a Paradox in Social Work Education." *Race, Ethnicity and Education* 8, 4.

Jeffery, D., and J. Nelson. 2007. "Encounters with Racial and Cultural Difference in Professional Practice." Seventh Annual Critical Race Studies Conference, Toronto, May.

_____. Forthcoming. "The More Things Change…: The Endurance of 'Culturalism' in Social Work and Healthcare." In C. Schick, J. McNinch and L. Comeau (eds.), *The Race/Culture Divide in Education, Law and the Helping Professions*. Regina, SK: University of Regina: Canadian Plains Research Centre.

Johnston, R.J., et al. (eds.). 2000. *Dictionary of Human Geography* (fourth ed.). Oxford: Blackwell.

Kline, M. 1992. "Child Welfare Law, 'Best Interests of the Child' Ideology, and First Nations." *Osgoode Hall Law Journal* 30, 2.

Kumashiro, K. 2000. "Toward a Theory of Anti-Oppressive Education." *Review of Educational Research* 70, 1.

Law, J. 1994. *Organizing Modernity*. Oxford, U.K., and Cambridge, MA: Blackwell.

Lewis, O. 1966. *La Vida: A Puerto Rican Family in the Culture of Poverty — San Juan and New York*. New York: Random House.

Monture-Angus, P. 1995. *Thunder in My Soul: A Mohawk Woman Speaks*. Halifax: Fernwood.

Moynihan, D.P. 1967. "The Negro Family: The Case for National Action." In L. Rainwater and W. Yancey (eds.), *The Moynihan Report and the Politics of Controversy*. Boston, MA: M.I.T. Press.

Nelson, J. 2008. *Razing Africville: A Geography of Racism*. Toronto: University of Toronto Press.

Nestel, S., and S. Razack. 2006 "Wrestling with the 'Ghost of Anthropology Past:' Cultural Competency Approaches in Medical Education." Unpublished manuscript, OISE/University of Toronto.

Parton, N. 1996. "Introduction." In N. Parton (ed.), *Social Theory, Social Change, and Social Work*. London: Routledge.

Payne, M. 2005. *Modern Social Work Theory* (Third Edition). Chicago: Lyceum.

Razack, S. 1998. *Looking White People in the Eye: Gender, Race, and Culture in Courtrooms and Classrooms*. Toronto: University of Toronto Press.

_____. 2000. "'Simple Logic:' Race, the Identity Documents Rule and the Story of a Nation Besieged and Betrayed." *Journal of Law and Social Policy* 15.

_____. 2004. "Imperiled Muslim Women, Dangerous Muslim Men and Civilised Europeans: Legal and Social Responses to Forced Marriages." *Feminist Legal Studies* 12.

Schick, C., and V. St. Denis. 2005. "Troubling National Discourses in Anti-Racist Curricular Planning." *Canadian Journal of Education* 28, 3.

Stoler, A.L. 1995. *Race and the Education of Desire: Foucault's History of Sexuality and the Colonial Order of Things*. Durham: Duke University Press.

Strega, S. 2007. "Anti-Oppressive Practice in Child Welfare." In D. Baines (ed.), *Doing Anti-Oppressive Practice: Building Transformative Politicized Social Work*. Halifax: Fernwood.

Yee, J., and G. Dumbrill. 2003. "Whiteout: Looking for Race in Canadian Social Work Practice." In A. Al-Krenawi and J. Graham (eds.), *Multicultural Social Work in Canada: Working with Diverse Ethno-Racial Communities*. Don Mills: Oxford University Press.

# Chapter 3

# Race Matters
## Social Justice not Assimilation
## ~~or Cultural Competence~~

*Sarah Maiter*

Child welfare practice with members of diverse ethno-racial backgrounds (often referred to as "visible minorities") poses particular challenges for social workers. Stereotypical and generalized thinking and a lack of understanding of the lived experiences of these families can result in biased and oppressive practice. Worker fears of being biased, however, can also leave children in harmful situations while needed services are not provided to families. This chapter[1] draws on the author's child welfare practice experience, research with clients, theoretical explorations of racism and experience as a child welfare trainer and social work educator to explore the complexities involved in services for members of diverse ethno-racial groups. The imbalance of power between child welfare institutions and service recipients is considered, and suggestions for practice are made that include ways to develop worker-client relationships that emphasize certain core values such as a commitment to social justice and anti-oppressive approaches to practice, assessment of agency policies and procedures, advocacy for clients, accessing services that address the unique needs of immigrant and refugee families, and working with clients to help them to build supportive networks.

Questions Addressed in This Chapter
1. What are the stereotypical and generalized thinking in child welfare practice about members of diverse ethno racial groups?
2. What are the experiences of racism for minority families that can impact services?
3. What are the imbalances of power in child welfare settings and how do they impact worker-client relationships?
4. What are the areas to target to ensure anti-oppressive and anti-racist child welfare service provision?

Increasingly, social workers are urged to practice from a social justice and anti-oppressive perspective (Lundy 2004).[2] The *Code of Ethics* of the Canadian Association of Social Workers as well as the mission statements of many schools of social work support this approach to social work practice. Specific attention is being paid to social justice and human rights issues because of the recognition that past approaches to practice tended to blame individuals for problems that they experienced. Traditionally, our attention in practice was to establish order in society through the social control of individuals and families rather than consideration of the human rights of people. Structural inequalities based on class, gender, race, sexual orientation, age, ability and geographical region were ignored, and intervention focused on changing the behaviour of individuals (Hicks 2006; Fook 1993). Despite the greater focus on structural issues that contribute to people's problems, social workers still tend to neglect this kind of assessment; typical intervention continues to require individuals to change. Social workers thus struggle to include an anti-oppressive approach to practice. This struggle is heightened in child welfare work because, understandably, workers feel the burden of upholding the legal protection mandate and are also afraid of leaving children in harmful situations. The current residual approach to child welfare work — a focus on investigation with limited resources for supports for families — inevitably results in blaming workers if harm comes to a child subsequent to a report of abuse or neglect. Within such a context, power differences between worker and client are heightened, with a potential for overuse or abuse of power (Maiter, Palmer and Manji 2006). Thus, the challenge of working anti-oppressively with people from diverse ethno-racial backgrounds is infinitely increased.

## Connecting History to Current Practice

An understanding of history, both general and that of social work, is essential when learning social work practice, as history contributes to who we are, what we see and how we interact with people.[3] Even when we struggle to abide by core social work values of being non-judgmental and giving people the right to self-determination, we are constantly challenged by what we have absorbed about people from diverse ethno-racial backgrounds. We internalize information from the media, schools, society, the community and our families. This information is a remnant of thinking from the early days of colonization by Europeans of countries/continents of people of colour, including Africa, Asia and South and North America. In order to make the colonization palatable, the people of these places had to be viewed as inferior in all aspects of life, with the flipside of the colonizers being declared as superior. This type of thinking continues and permeates all aspects of life today, with the inevitable negative consequences for people of colour.

Although Canada has always been a multi-racial country, the presence of diverse ethno-racial groups has been omitted from both official and popular histories (Christensen 2003), thereby erasing their contributions to Canada and rendering them invisible. As is known, Indigenous people lived in Canada prior to the arrival of the Europeans, but what is less well known is that Africans were brought to work as slaves during the 1600s, while Asians were brought to work on the railways and also migrated to Canada in the mid-1800s (Henry, Tator,

Mattis and Rees 2000). People of colour and other non-Europeans who came to Canada or were brought to Canada experienced considerable hardship because of blatant social and political racism.

In the early years, there were African slaves in Nova Scotia, New Brunswick, Quebec and Ontario, while many Blacks later also came from the U.S. colonies, initially escaping slavery using the underground railroad movement and later, in 1783, in exchange for supporting the British during the Revolutionary War (Walker 1976, cited in Christensen 2003). Christensen notes: "In the Canadian colonies, government-supported social policies ensured that Blacks remained unequal, living in segregated communities and occupying a caste-like status outside of the opportunity structure" (77). Further, they experienced race riots and destruction of their homes and were denied land ownership, fair wages, employment opportunities and food rations during Nova Scotia's famine in 1789.

Early Asian settlers (Japanese, Chinese and South Asian) experienced similar problems. The Chinese and Japanese who came to the West Coast were labelled the "yellow peril," were expected to return home and experienced extreme harassment and oppression from both the general public and the provincial and federal governments. Chinese men were not allowed to sponsor their wives, they filled menial jobs, and they were barred from voting or entering certain professions (Christensen 2003). During World War II the federal government removed Japanese Canadians from their homes to internment camps. They were forced to do road and farm work in Alberta, Ontario and B.C., losing both human rights as well as property. South Asians had similar exclusionary, discriminatory and oppressive experiences. They were exploited as cheap farm labourers and were barred from voting in 1907, only regaining this right in 1947. Racist immigration policies, including the head tax for the Chinese and the infamous 1908 "Continuous Passage" federal law, which required Indians to come to Canada via a direct passage — an impossibility at the time — were put into effect to keep Canada "white." As noted by Jakubowski (2006), racist immigration and refugee practices continue in Canada today.

## From Assimilation to Cultural Competence

Canada's colonial legacy of the appropriation of Indigenous lands and ignorant and racist attitudes toward Indigenous people not only contributed to an erosion and, in some cases, the destruction of Indigenous social, spiritual and economic traditions, but also resulted in the exclusion of these traditions from the history of Canada's social welfare system (Pollock 1994). Similarly, social work did not benefit from the traditions of people of non-European backgrounds living in Canada. Interestingly, current textbooks that contain chapters on the history of social work in Canada (for example Hicks 2006) are written as though it applies uniformly to all people. But this written history is about the Europeans in Canada, and such writing effectively results in the erasure of the histories of diverse ethno-racial groups and Indigenous people. Although social work texts sometimes include chapters at the end on diverse groups, this information becomes relegated as a less significant add-on.

Social work's earlier approaches to diversity favoured assimilation. The assimilationist perspective assumed that newcomers to a country would take on the way of life of the dominant members in the country. Where there was an Indigenous population, assimilation to the newcomer's ways was assumed, indicating that it is not who is first in a country, but rather issues of power and dominance at play (Payne 1997). It was believed that members of diverse groups would relinquish their ways and adopt the customs and lifestyles of their new country or their "superior" colonizers. Assimilationist approaches to social work practice have far-reaching negative consequences for people from diverse ethno-racial backgrounds as diversity is viewed as a problem, while practice remains racist with no efforts to correct inequities in society.

A cultural deficit or cultural deviance approach was also taken, whereby it was believed that certain cultures were both inferior and underdeveloped; thus, their values and behaviour were "abnormal" compared to those of people from European backgrounds. It was also believed that people from diverse cultures did not have the capacity to adjust to their new environment. Social workers had to help newcomers adjust and, in cases when they came into contact with the legal system, provide training and control to help them conform. These ethnocentric and assimilationist approaches have far-reaching consequences for people from diverse ethno-racial backgrounds. Sue, Arrendondo and McDavis (1992: 75) identify these consequences and the concomitant social work theory and practice that emerge:

> The underlying data and research base regarding racial and ethnic minorities have (a) perpetuated a view that minorities are inherently pathological, (b) perpetuated racist research and counselling practices and (c) provided an excuse for counselling professionals not to take social action to rectify inequities in the system.

The ideology of assimilation can be most clearly seen in initial responses to Indigenous children and families (Payne 1997). The culture and ways of the dominant group were considered normative and to be emulated. Indigenous children were removed from their families, placed in residential schools, forbidden to speak their birth languages, banned from participating in their cultural rituals and taught Western ways (Horejsi, Craig and Pablo 1992; Palmer and Cooke 1996).

More recently, attempts are being made to look at the meaning of cultural difference. Several factors contributed to changing our approach to diversity, including the following:

- the increasing diversity of Canada;
- renewed pride in diverse groups' culture and heritage;
- demands by members of diverse racial and ethnic groups for the right to

practise their cultures; and

- increased recognition by the social service system that cultural identification influences problem identification and problem resolution.

These changes resulted in a multicultural approach to diverse ethno-racial people in Canada and other Western nations. With the introduction of the concept of multiculturalism as early as 1971 by Prime Minister Trudeau and the passing of the *Multiculturalism Act* in 1988, a greater focus on cultural diversity as a reality of the Canadian context emerged. A slow shift took place away from blatant assimilationist policies and greater emphasis was placed on valuing diversity. The idea of multiculturalism became very much a part of the institution of social work, including child welfare and child protection. Henry, Tator, Mattis and Rees (1995: 328) describe it as follows:

> Multiculturalism has different meanings. It is a description of the composition of Canada both historically and currently, referring to the cultural and racial diversity of Canadian society. It is an ideology that holds that racial, cultural, religious and linguist diversity is an integral, beneficial, and necessary part of Canadian society and identity. It is a policy operating in various social institutions and levels of government, including the federal government.

With the emergence of multiculturalism came the cultural literacy or cultural competence approach to social work practice (McGoldrick 1982; Hines, Garcia-Preto, McGoldrick, Almeida and Weltman 1992) — the belief that it is necessary to learn about cultural differences. This perspective suggests that there is a need to understand the norms, values and practices of a culture so as to be able to provide services within the framework of the culture. Profiles of different cultures are compiled to allow practitioners to respect cultural values and practices in service provision. McGoldrick (1982) has written on the culture of specific groups in their countries of origin, while others (Furoto, Biswas, Chung, Murase and Ross-Sheriff 1992) have written on specific groups in their new country, including problems these groups may be experiencing. Figure 3-1 captures the idea of the approach, with the person in the centre representing the social worker. The idea is for the social worker to become familiar with the cultures of their clients and apply this cultural knowledge to their practice.

The flourishing literature on diversity has increased the profile of minority groups and highlighted their needs. Theoretically it gives practitioners a framework to respect diversity and to see the client in their cultural context. Practitioners are encouraged to consider that families from diverse cultures function differently and that retention of cultural identity is not problematic. Still, there are problems with this approach.

The sheer number of ethno-racial groups makes it almost impossible for social workers to become familiar with all the hundreds of cultures they come into contact with. Indeed culture is so complex that it may be impossible for social workers to learn enough to confidently interpret how a certain culture works within a family or for an individual (Dyche and Zayas 1995). Moreover, within each culture there is great diversity (Gelfand and Fandetti 1986). For instance, while India is the largest of the South Asian countries, there are numerous languages spoken in India and many religions, traditions and ways of life, which are further complicated by gender, class, sexual orientation, religion, age and urban/rural life. Additionally, learning how culture is internalized for members of a group is impossible as individuals, families and others within the culture interact with cultural messages from their background in unique ways based upon their personality and socio-economic, socio-political and other factors.

Trying to learn about other cultures can lead to oversimplification and devaluing of that which we claim to promote. Aspects of diverse cultures became exotic things to celebrate (Bissoondath 1994). Thus, emphasis is given to specific things such as food, religious festivals and clothing. Although these things are important, practitioners could easily fall into the trap of viewing culture as the only variable for an individual or a group. Simplification can also result when someone is unaware that a group's norms and values are constantly changing, depending on societal changes in both the country of origin and the new country (Gelfand and Fandetti 1986). The complex nature of this emergent ethnicity is

## Figure 3-1 The Cultural Literacy/Competence Approach

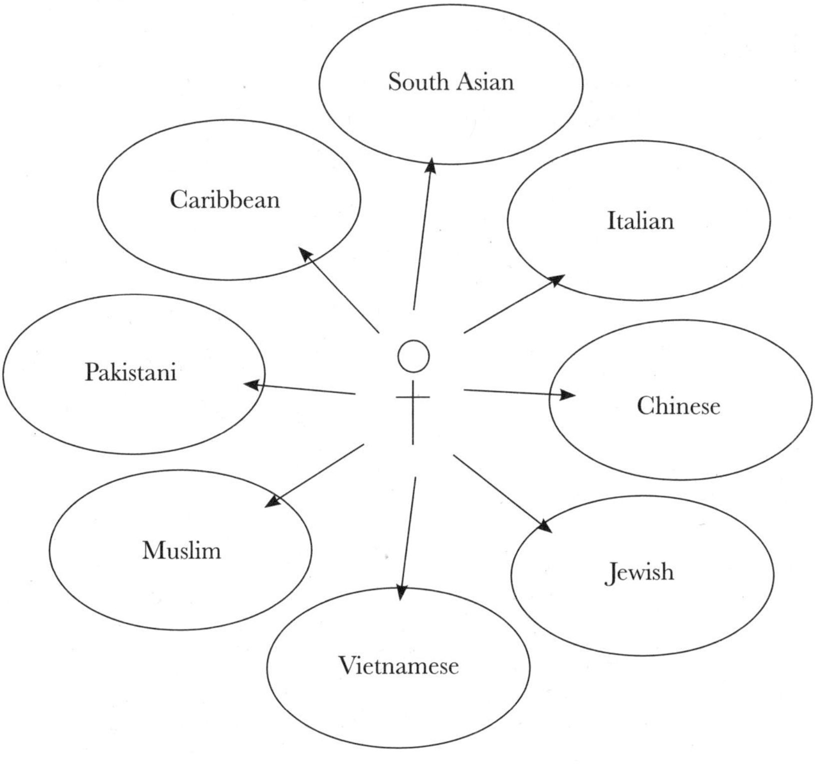

often unrecognized. All too often, identified group characteristics are used to assess a member of the group while the changing nature of culture is ignored.

Learning about cultures may also cause social workers to over-generalize. The study of culture, like the study of any complex relationship, involves simplification; certain aspects or phenomena are chosen and stressed. "A concept as potent as culture is too often reified, lifted from its abstract status and the printed page and perceived as a description of real individuals; that is, clients are seen as their culture, not as themselves" (Dyche and Zayas 1995: 391).

Another more fundamental weakness in the cultural competence approach is the assumption that the worker is "culture free." The way the worker understands clients is not only shaped by the client's culture, it is also shaped by the worker's own culture. In most cases, this is the dominant culture, and even if workers are from a minority culture they operate in the social work context of the dominant culture. In effect they try to view the client in the context of their culture but do that through the lens of their own culture.

### Child Welfare Approaches to Ethno-Racial Diversity

For child welfare practitioner, issues of race, ethnicity and culture have posed considerable dilemmas and struggles. Indigenous populations bore the initial brunt of inappropriate government intervention in the lives of children and families. The residential school system, a church-government partnership for Indigenous education, lasted from the 1840s to late in the twentieth century. The residential school policy of separating children from their families was intended to obliterate Indigenous society and culture through teaching mainstream culture while forbidding anything Indigenous. "This was social welfare, at its worst, and its effects (poverty, family disintegration, poor health, high rates of suicide, high incarceration rates) remain with us today" (Hicks 2006: 227).

Over the last three decades, although there has been increasing attention to the situation of diverse ethno-racial groups who receive services from the child welfare system, problems continue to persist for these groups. There is a lack of research that captures their experiences, but frontline workers realize that these groups face considerable challenges with the system. These range from homogenizing group members (seeing all members of a group as the same), blaming groups for problems in society, failing to provide for the material needs of minority families who come into contact with the system (for example, failure to provide interpreters and the inappropriate use of children as interpreters) and inadequate and inappropriate services to these families (Maiter, Trocmé and Shakir 1999).

Child welfare approaches to ethno-racial diversity emulate social work approaches to diversity in that shifts have occurred from the assimilationist approach to a cultural competence approach. Despite social work's current slow shift to anti-oppressive and structural approaches, within child welfare the dominant approach continues to emphasize cultural competence. This approach, however, has negative consequences for families that come to the attention of the child welfare system. In an effort to be culturally sensitive, child welfare workers try to understand the norms and values of a group, and this understanding is then applied to practice. This approach results in an inevitable comparison with dominant Western culture, a comparison that results in negative judgments. The "other" culture is seen as static while contextual understandings of people's circumstances are disregarded (Miller and Maiter 2008). In comparing "West" with "East," there is necessarily a comparison with "good" and "bad" and "moral" with "immoral" due to the tendency to view our own culture as more enlightened or superior than the other cultures:

> A message of Southern cultural inferiority and dysfunction is so widely disseminated that when we in the North see a veiled woman, we can only retrieve from our store of information that she is a victim of her patriarchal culture or religion. Few alternative images of more complex evaluations are possible. We find it difficult to compare the veil's restrictions of women's movements to the wearing of high heels and tight skirts in the West. (Razack 1998: 7)

Eurocentric analysis of "oppressed women" is too often applied to Third World women:

> Third world women as a group or category are automatically and necessarily defined as: religious (read "not progressive"), family oriented (read "traditional") legal minors (read "they-are-still-not-conscious-of their-rights"), illiterate (read "ignorant") domestic (read "backward") and sometimes revolutionary (read their-country-is-in-a state-of-war; they-must-fight). (Mohanty 1994: 214)

Such comparisons also serve to define the West as developed and progressive. Situations reported to the child welfare system such as parent-teen conflicts tend to be judged through this lens. In such situations with families from the "mainstream," the various factors contributing to the conflict are considered, whereas for families from diverse ethno-racial backgrounds, culture becomes the problem (Alaggia and Maiter 2006). Teenagers who are in conflict with their parents are often thought to be in need of rescue from parents who are seen as oppressive and traditional because it is believed they have not acculturated to Canadian norms and standards. This shortsighted approach is dangerous as serious problems within the family can be missed. For example, I intervened in a situation where a parent reached out to the school social worker about her adolescent's risk taking behaviour and was told that in Canada teenagers were given the freedom to experiment unlike in her home country and that the teen needed to be given this freedom. Further work with the family with a different social worker revealed that the teen's anxiety relating to bullying and her sadness that her racial background resulted in much exclusion by peers in a school that had mostly white students.

Under-involvement with families can also be problematic. As one example, when a mother from a diverse ethno-religious background in Calgary continuously called the police for help with her fourteen-year-old daughter, no help was provided, and the teen's aggressive behaviour in the home was ignored despite the police having been at the home a number of times (Graveland 2007: A11). Severe conflict was present within the family, with the altercations in the home escalating and resulting in the death of the child and the mother being charged for her death. Indeed, this was a refugee family that had come from a war-torn county where each member, including the child, had witnessed many atrocities and now lived with this trauma. The reasons for under-involvement are unclear but it does raise questions about why child welfare and mental health services were not provided to the family.

In child welfare work, our often limited exposure to people from diverse backgrounds has a tendency to lead us to make "common sense" assessments that are based on generalizations about groups (Maiter 2005). For example, some of the stereotyping that is heard in the child welfare setting include:

- "It is their culture to discipline their children harshly…" Note here that the cultural, racial and historical specificity of the mainstream society itself and its institutions is never interrogated and, therefore, does not explain why ethnicity and culture are an issue when dealing with people of colour but not the mainstream society;
- "They believe in arranged marriages… they do not allow women freedom of choice…" Because the cultural, racial and historical roots of mainstream society are not questioned, professionals working in the fields of social services, like child welfare practitioners, do not often question either their own or their institutional values as being culturally, racially and historically defined and thus, perhaps "biased."
- "Why don't they let their daughter go on a date… she is fifteen years old…" Because the cultural, racial and historical "bias" of mainstream workers and institutions is presented as the "norm" in a universal sense, the culturally, racially and historically "different" clients tend to be judged by a "standard" that is outside of their own frame of reference.
- "In their culture they demand obedience from children, therefore, they do not treat children as individuals with rights…" Because people of colour are "ethnicized" and "culturized," any risk factor to the children is linked automatically to "their" culture. While a mainstream parent acts harmfully or not towards his/her child as an individual act, the person of colour is deemed to do so as a representative of his/her culture and race. An individual act becomes a definitive statement for the whole group.
- "It maybe alright in their country… but here it is against the law…" Because people of colour are "ethnic" and "culturally motivated" in their actions and their actions appear to be so "obviously" detrimental to their children's welfare, their culture itself becomes problematic (Maiter, Trocmé and Shakir 1999).

Maiter, Trocmé, and Shakir (1999) note that these stereotypes have the backing of child welfare institutions so that what might be termed as "prejudice" at best and "racism" at worst, gains legal and social legitimacy.

Indeed, the cultural competence approach, in its effort to gain better cultural understanding, may have inadvertently contributed to professionals being trained to expect more abusive behaviour among diverse ethno-racial groups. For example, until recently a child welfare training video and accompanying handbook on cultural sensitivity stated: "Some ethnic or cultural backgrounds may be more likely to condone severe spankings or beatings as a form of discipline" (Crawford 1998: 11). Clearly these kinds of statements lead to the profiling and stereotyping of members of diverse ethno-cultural groups.

## A Discursive Anti-Racist Framework

Given the concerns noted above, the use of a critical anti-racist framework can help to provide equitable services for diverse ethno-racial families who come to the attention of the child welfare system. A critical anti-racist framework can refocus attention away from ethnicity and culture alone to issues of power differences and power maintenance within social and political structures in society. Dei (1996) and others (Calliste 1996; Leah 1991) propose a discursive, integrative, anti-racist framework to study race relations and to address the needs of minority individuals in various social contexts. A discursive rather than a theoretical framework is preferable to avoid focusing on a grand, totalizing foundation (Dei 1996b). It takes into consideration the fact that racism manifests itself differently in different political and social contexts as well as during various historical periods. The advantage of a discursive framework is that it is open to change as the political and social context changes. In addition, a discursive framework allows for analysis of the conditions of minority populations while concomitantly acknowledging that individuals and groups have agency and have drawn on this agency to resist oppressive conditions. Individual and group agency is similar to personal agency when approaching social work from a strengths perspective. It means that we must recognize that people draw on personal strengths and resources to fight and resist oppression in various ways.

Critical race and anti-racism discourse places power relations at the centre of an analysis of race and social difference because proponents of an anti-racist framework are first and foremost committed to social change (Calliste, Dei and Belkhir 1995; Dei 1996b; Leah 1995). An anti-racist framework focuses on power relations in society, notably, on how white power and privilege maintain dominance, which then results in the subjugation of knowledge of people from diverse ethno-racial backgrounds. By interrogating both structural barriers to social change and the social, political and structural practices of addressing diversity, instead of simply acknowledging the material conditions of inequality, these writers question white power and privilege in maintaining dominance. It is necessary to interrogate racism rather than to examine it, as interrogation suggests an explicitly political engagement while examination reduces racism to something containable that can be brought out in pieces for examination (Dei 1996). Dei suggests that this distancing from racism is part of the difficulty in addressing it. The framework questions the marginalization of certain voices as well as the devaluation of knowledge and experience of subordinated groups.

The critical anti-racist framework provides a robust tool to explore services for ethno-racial minorities coming to the attention of child welfare services. The framework moves away from examining issues from only a cultural competence perspective and includes assessment from a structural perspective, one where the reality of race, as it continues to have an impact for racialized populations, is recognized. An example of using a critical anti-racist framework is exploring the social effects of the everyday stress of dealing with issues relating to race and the concomitant racism that is experienced. The uncertainty of knowing whether one is being watched in a store because of one's race or some other reason is a privilege that a person of colour does not have when compared to a white person. The impact of this everyday privilege cannot be emphasized strongly enough as either explicitly or implicitly it will be present in the child welfare encounter with individuals and families from diverse ethno-racial backgrounds (for a more detailed discussion, see McIntosh 2008).

## Practice Implications and Suggestions

First and foremost, it is important to recognize that discussions of history, power relations, dominance and white privilege raise feelings of guilt and anxiety in white people about the deeds of our ancestors even as we continue to benefit from this unearned power and privilege. This sentiment is captured by Bill Gaston:

> Surely no people wish to share in moments which reveal humankind's basest nature. The history of Europe's contact with the North American Natives is strewn with such moments, not the least of which is the opening of the sea chest and handing over, to some thankful people in a wooden canoe, of several blankets. It will never be known for certain whether the sailors knowingly handed over smallpox or if they knew that what these blankets carried would travel hundreds of miles in a very few years and open up so much land to settlers. But so it is suspected. (Gaston 2004: 425)

It is important to acknowledge and confront this sense of guilt so as to be able to move forward from it and examine how we are now going to work with these issues. Engaging with this struggle and learning from it will help us on the journey of social justice that is now the core of social work practice.

Second, we need to resist stereotypical and generalized thinking about people from diverse ethno-racial backgrounds. As with Western culture, people from non-Western backgrounds internalize their culture in a multiplicity of ways (Maiter 2006). Research shows that although there are differences in parenting approaches among cultures, there is great consistency about what is considered to be abuse (Maiter 2004; Maiter, Alaggia and Trocmé 2004). All cultures in fact want to do what is best for their children and want to protect their children from harm. Yet within all cultures some parents behave in harmful ways toward their children for reasons ranging from personal problems to living in harsh neighbourhoods and challenging environments, or what Garbarino (1995) calls "toxic social environments." A client may state that their abusive actions are acceptable behaviours in their culture; however, this statement can be challenged. Such a statement may also be an excuse. The statement sometimes used by child welfare workers that "the behaviour may be fine in their culture but it is still illegal here" is actually racist because it generalizes that certain cultures are more prone to violence than others. Along with understanding that different individuals internalize their culture in unique ways, embracing the idea of cultural difference is also necessary. Differences in worldviews and approaches to life such as an individualistic or collectivist perspective do exist. Our work as child welfare workers is not to impose hegemonic notions of what approach is right or wrong but to help families one at a time to ensure safety for children. We have to resist "cultural hegemony" — the dominance of the beliefs and values of one group over those of others

Third, providing equitable services for families from diverse ethno-racial backgrounds does not mean non-involvement, as this would leave children in harmful situations and families without needed help. Intervening is thus not just a legal issue but also a moral imperative. But intervention must be done sensitively with recognition of the variety of influences that may be impacting the family. Additional services should be accessed to provide optimal support. Organizational and personal changes must be made to meet the needs of the diverse families coming to the attention of child welfare. Here, a critical anti-racist framework can be applied together with the concept of white privilege to build organizational approaches and individual behaviour that are equitable, as specified below.

Fourth, because of changes in immigration policies and despite a continued favouring of those from European and other white nations, many immigrants are members of diverse ethno-racial groups. Given this reality, child welfare workers must consider the barriers that prevent some immigrants and refugees from making transitions into their adopted country. Settlement services can be utilized to assist with transition to the new environment. Additionally, barriers to finding employment, underemployment, loss of supportive networks, financial struggles, struggles with language and mental health struggles because of grief of leaving the home country, war and other traumatic experiences must all be recognized and services accessed for these (Maiter 2003; Maiter, Stalker, and Alaggia in press). In other words, child welfare workers must be knowledgeable about how to access all available immigrant and refugee services.

Fifth, in order to move forward we need to examine specific skills that will assist us to work collaboratively with clients. Maiter, Palmer and Manji (2006) have discussed the issue of power within the client-worker relationship and the challenge of forming collaborative working relationships. When working with minority clients this power differential is heightened because of societal power imbalances based on race and ethnicity. Several factors contribute to the substantial power differential; the child welfare system is state sanctioned, has legal authority, can impose sanctions on a family if suggested services are not accepted and has support from other state agencies, including the police, immigration authorities and the mental health system. Child welfare workers are in a position to coerce clients to change with a threat of sanction if the change is not made. They are empowered through education, knowledge of dominant culture and ability to communicate, and they generally command respect. Child welfare clients on the other hand are generally poor, sometimes people of colour or otherwise marginalized, struggling to meet basic needs such as food, housing and medical care and, if immigrants or refugees, trying to settle and adjust to their new society. Inappropriate actions on the part of the child welfare worker such as impatience, labelling, excessive use of the court system to effect change and disrespect, amongst others, can result in anxiety, fear, anger and distrust on the part of clients, which then feed into further harmful actions by workers (Maiter 2007).

There are practical ways through which we can move away from the assimilationist approaches that initially prevailed in child welfare practice and the more recently predominant cultural competence approach. Both approaches have been and are problematic. The cultural competence approach prevails, which can result in viewing culture as the cause of child abuse and neglect. A critical anti-racist framework holds much more promise for an understanding of the lived reality of the lives of individuals and families from diverse ethno-racial backgrounds. This framework can alert us to the complex and varied social and material consequences of race and help us resist the tendency to overlook strengths and personal and community agency. Providing equitable services does not mean leaving children in harmful situations but rather providing the specific services to meet the unique needs of families. Recognizing power imbalances between families and organizations/practitioners is essential to providing anti-racist, equitable services.

## Suggestions for Further Reading

Maiter, S., C. Stalker and R. Alaggia. In press. "The Experiences of Minority Immigrant Families Receiving Child Welfare Services: Understanding How to Reduce Risk and Increase Protective Factors." *Families in Society: The Journal of Contemporary Social Services.*

_____. 2005. "The Ethics of Child Protection Services for People from Diverse Ethno-Racial Backgrounds." *Journal of the Ontario Association of Social Workers* 32, 1 (February).

Maiter, S., R. Alaggia, and N. Trocmé. 2004. "Perceptions of Child Maltreatment by Parents from the Indian Subcontinent: Challenging Myths about Culturally Based Abusive Parenting Practices." *Child Maltreatment* 9, 3.

## About the Author

Currently teaching in the School of Social Work at York University, Sarah Maiter has taught in the Faculty of Social Work at Wilfrid Laurier University and has extensive child welfare practice experience. Her research focuses on race, culture and ethnicity and child welfare with the aim of improving services for minority families. She is co-author of "Understanding Risk and Protective Factors in Families from Diverse Ethnic/Racial Backgrounds Receiving Child Protection Services" and is co-investigator of a SSHRC-funded CURA that is exploring, developing, piloting and evaluating how best to provide community-based mental health services and supports that are effective for people from culturally diverse backgrounds and a SSHRC study entitled "The Self-Other Issue in the Healing Practices of Racialized Minority Youth."

## Notes

1.  The term *Race Matters* is also the title of a book by Cornel West (2001)
2.  The term "social work practice" is used here broadly to include micro, mezzo and macro practice otherwise also referred to as direct and indirect practice or individual/family/group practice, community practice and social policy (Hicks 2006).
3.  This chapter does not allow for a full exploration of these issues, but they are touched on so as to provide a context.

## References

Alaggia, R., and S. Maiter. 2006. "Domestic Violence and Child Abuse: Issues for Immigrant and Refugee Families." In R. Alaggia and C. Vine (eds.), *Cruel but Not Unusual: Violence in Canadian Families*. Waterloo, ON: Wilfrid Laurier University Press.

Bissoondath, N. 1994. *Selling Illusions: The Cult of Multiculturalism in Canada*. Toronto: Penguin.

Calliste, A. 1996. "Anti-Racism Organizing and Resistance in Nursing: African Canadian Women." *Canadian Review of Sociology and Anthropology* 33, 3.

Calliste, A., G.S. Dei and J.A. Belkhir. 1995. "Canadian Perspectives on Anti-Racism: Intersection of Race, Gender & Class." *Race, Gender and Class* 2, 3.

Christensen, C.A. 2003. "Canadian Society: Social Policy and Ethno-Racial Diversity." In A. Al-Krenawi and J. Graham (eds.), *Cross-Cultural Social Work Practice with Diverse Ethno-Racial Communities in Canada*. Toronto: Oxford University Press.

Crawford, M.G. 1998. *Child Abuse: A Multidisciplinary Approach to Physical Abuse*. Toronto: Canada Law Book.

Dei, G.J.S. 1996. *Anti-Racism Education*. Halifax: Fernwood.

_____. 1996b. "Critical Perspectives in Anti-Racism: An Introduction." *CRSA/RCSA* 33, 3.

Dyche, L., and L.H. Zayas. 1995. "The Value of Curiosity and Naiveté for Cross Cultural Psychotherapists." *Family Process* 34 (December).

Fook, J. 1993. *Radical Casework: A Theory of Practice*. St. Leonard, NSW, Australia: Allen and Unwin.

Furoto, S.M., R. Biswas, D.K. Chung, K. Murase and F. Ross-Sheriff (eds.). 1992. *Social Work Practice with Asian Americans*. Newbury Park: Sage.

Garbarino, J. 1995. *Raising Children in a Socially Toxic Environment*. San Francisco: Jossey-Bass.

Gaston, B. 2004. *Sointula*. Vancouver: Raincoast.

Gelfand, D.E., and D.V. Fandetti. 1986. "The Emergent Nature of Ethnicity: Dilemmas in Assessment." *Social Casework* 67, 9.

Graveland, B. 2007. "Mother Begged for Help with Violent Girl; 'Scared' Woman Called for Police Five Times in Five Weeks, but Support was Never Offered, says Aunt of Slain 14-year-old." *Toronto Star,* March 1.

Henry, F., C. Tator, W. Mattis and T. Rees. 1995. *The Colour of Democracy: Racism in Canadian Society.* Toronto: Harcourt Brace Canada.

_____. 2000. *The Colour of Democracy: Racism in Canadian Society* (Second Edition). Toronto: Harcourt Brace Canada.

Hicks, S. 2006. *Social Work in Canada: An Introduction* (Second Edition). Toronto: Thompson Educational.

Hines, P.M., N. Garcia-Preto, M. McGoldrick, R. Almeida and S. Weltman. 1992. "Intergenerational Relationships across Cultures." *Families in Society: The Journal of Contemporary Human Services* (June).

Horejsi, C., B.H.R. Craig and J. Pablo. 1992. "Reactions by Native American Parents to Child Protection Agencies: Cultural and Community Factors." *Child Welfare* 71.

Jakubowski, L. 2006. "'Managing' Canadian Immigration: Racism, Selectivity, and the Law." In E. Comack (ed.), *Locating Law: Race, Class, Gender, Sexuality Connections* (Second Edition). Halifax: Fernwood.

Leah, R. 1991. "Linking the Struggles: Racism, Sexism and the Union Movement." In Vorst et al. (eds.), *Race, Class and Gender: Bonds and Barriers.* Toronto: Between the Lines.

_____. 1995. "The Emergence of Anti-Racism Studies: An Integrative Paradigm." *Race, Gender and Class* 2, 3.

Lundy, C. 2004. *Social Work and Social Justice: A Structural Approach to Practice.* Peterborough, ON: Broadview.

Maiter, S. 2003. "The Context of Culture: Social Work with South Asian-Canadians." In A. Al-Krenawi and J. Graham (eds.), *Cross-Cultural Social Work Practice with Diverse Ethno-Racial Communities in Canada.* Toronto: Oxford University Press.

_____. 2004. "Considering Context and Culture in Child Protection Services to Ethnically Diverse Families: An Example from Research with Parents from the Indian Sub Continent (South Asians)." *Social Work Research and Evaluation* 5, 1.

_____. 2005. "The Ethics of Child Protection Services for People from Diverse Ethno-Racial Backgrounds." *Journal of the Ontario Association of Social Workers* 32, 1 (February).

_____. 2006. "From Cultural Sensitivity to Anti-Oppressive Practice." In B. Lee and S. Todd (eds.), *A Casebook of Community Practice: Problems and Strategies.* Mississauga, ON: Common Act Press.

_____. 2007. "Working with Diverse Families in Child Protection." Paper presented at the Fifteenth National Conference of the American Professional Society on the Abuse of Children, Boston.

Maiter, S., R. Alaggia and N. Trocmé. 2004. "Perceptions of Child Maltreatment by Parents from the Indian Subcontinent: Challenging Myths about Culturally Based Abusive Parenting Practices." *Child Maltreatment* 9, 3.

Maiter, S., S. Palmer and S. Manji. 2006. "Strengthening Social Worker-Client Relationships in Child Protective Services: Addressing Power Imbalances and 'Ruptured' Relationships." *Qualitative Social Work* 5, 2.

Maiter, S., C. Stalker, and R. Alaggia. In print. "The Experiences of Minority Immigrant Families Receiving Child Welfare Services: Understanding how to Reduce Risk and

Increase Protective Factors." *Families in Society.*

Maiter, S., N. Trocmé and U. Shakir. 1999. "Fabricating Tools of Resistance." Conference Proceeding at Qualitative Analysis Conference: The Interdisciplinary Study of Social Process, St. Thomas University and the University of New Brunswick, Canada.

McGoldrick, M. 1982. "Ethnicity and Family Therapy." In M. McGoldrick, J. Pearce and J. Giordano (eds.), *Ethnicity and Family Therapy.* New York: Guildford.

McIntosh, P. "White Privilege: Unpacking the Invisible Knapsack." Available at <http://www.case.edu/president/aaction/UnpackingTheKnapsack.pdf> (accessed on May 13, 2008).

Miller, W., and S. Maiter. 2008. "Fatherhood and Ethnicity: Moving beyond Cultural Competence." *Journal of Ethnic and Cultural Diversity in Social Work* 17, 3.

Mohanty, C.T. 1994. "Under Western Eyes: Feminist Scholarship and Colonial Discourse." In P. Williams and L. Chrisman (eds.), *Colonial Discourse and Post-Colonial Theory: A Reader.* New York: Columbia University Press.

Palmer, S., and W. Cooke. 1996. "Understanding and Countering Racism with First Nations Children in Out-Of-Home Care." *Child Welfare* LXXV, 6.

Payne, M. 1997. *Modern Social Work Theory.* Chicago: Lyceum.

Pollock, N. 1994. *Critical Choices, Turbulent Times.* Vancouver: School of Social Work, University of British Columbia.

Razack, S. 1998. *Looking White People in the Eye: Gender, Race, and Culture.* Toronto: University of Toronto Press.

Sue, D. W., P. Arrendondo, and R. J. McDavis. 1992. "Multicultural Counseling Competencies and Standards: A Call to the Profession." *Journal of Multicultural Counseling* 20.

West, Cornell. 2001. *Race Matters.* New York: Vintage.

# Chapter 4

# Widening the Circle
## Countering Institutional Racism in Child Welfare

*Joan Pennell*

In Canada and other Eurocentric countries, the child welfare system treats children from Indigenous and non-white families differently than white children. This disparity hurts children's family connections and life opportunities. Changing how decisions are reached is one means of reversing systemic racism. This chapter looks at how child protection workers can use family group conferencing and other restorative practices to engage families in decision-making, disrupt preconceptions of families and create plans reflecting family cultures. I use the case of a Black adolescent to illustrate how a conference widened a family's circle of support and kept the youth in his home and community. A Family Group Protocol is provided to assist students in assessing their own efforts to widen the circle and counter institutional racism.

Questions Addressed in This Chapter
1. What are some practices for countering institutional racism in child welfare?
2. How do these restorative practices affirm culture while safeguarding children and their families?
3. How can we support each other to interrupt preconceived views and create healing alternatives?

Many of us become social workers in order to make our communities and society better places for everyone. Too often our aspirations are stymied by work contexts that reinforce racism, sexism and other forms of oppression; at the same time, these aspirations lead us to reach out to others and collaboratively design empowering approaches. This was my experience as a young child protection worker in Toronto during the mid-1970s. The Children's Aid Society (CAS) was mandated to hold parents accountable for placing their children at risk. In the majority of CAS interventions parents were low-income single mothers and, disproportionately to their numbers in the population, were people of colour. My dual role was to monitor children's safety and support their parents in taking care of them.

In visiting individual families, I was saddened to observe recurring and troubling patterns: isolated and depressed mothers, clinging and bed-wetting youngsters, absent or violent fathers/partners and angry teenagers attacking their mothers. Fortunately, this was not the only story. I was re-invigorated by relatively simple group efforts that widened the circle of supports for families. The "stay at home" mothers and I formed a crafts group; with foster teens, a male worker and I initiated a discussion and activity group. During home visits, I sat around the kitchen table with the parents, children, teenagers, relatives or the neighbour or friend who dropped by. I asked about what was going well and where they wanted to head in their lives. This helped us figure out plans built on their aims and resources. At the time, these kitchen conversations just seemed like a positive and productive way to work together. What I did not realize was that we were also informally practising what I later learned to call "family group conferencing" (FGC).

This chapter examines how we can counter institutional racism in child welfare systems by using FGC and other restorative practices to widen the circle of supports for children and families. Institutional racism, sometimes referred to as systemic racism, refers to "those established laws, customs, and practices which systematically reflect and produce racial inequalities... whether or not the individuals maintaining those practices have racist intentions" (Jones 1972: 131). In child welfare, a prime example is that Indigenous children and children of colour are far more likely than white children to be apprehended into state care (Strega 2007; Wharf 2002). Restorative justice refers to processes involving those who have a stake in the concern "to collectively identify and address harms, needs, and obligations, in order to heal and put things as right as possible" (Zehr 2002: 37). Such restorative processes reverse institutional racism by creating deliberative forums in which participants can draw upon their understandings of how to resolve issues while affirming the human rights of all people.

Families on the whole do not want to lose their young relatives and, when given sufficient information and the chance to make decisions together, base plans on sensible appraisals of their own capacities. This collaborative planning process helps workers have a "realistic sense of the strengths in individual families" (Sherry in press). Family groups creatively apply their own traditions and assets to maintaining familial connections. This may mean keeping children and teens with their parents or placing them with kin or members of their cultural group (Cunning and Bartlett 2006; Glode and Wein 2006).

## Family Group Conferencing

In child welfare, Family Group Conferencing (FGC) is a means of placing children, young people and their families at the centre of the planning process. Typically, the child protection worker is responsible for referring the family to a FGC coordinator, who organizes and convenes the conference but does not take over the role of the worker. At the meeting, the family group, which includes the referred family along with their relatives, friends and other informal supports, come together to make a plan to address the areas of concern. Before the meeting the FGC coordinator invites the family group to take part and engages them in planning their meeting — who to put on the invitation list, where to hold the meeting and how to arrange it so that participants can take part safely and effectively. Preparations are carried out by both the FGC coordinator and family group (Pennell and Anderson 2005).

The conference may open with a ceremony of the family's selection, such as a greeting, ritual or prayer that fits with their particular cultural heritage. Next, the FGC coordinator reviews the purpose, process and ground rules for the meeting so that the participants understand how the meeting is organized. Then the child protection worker and possibly other service providers share background information, with the family group members making their own observations or asking questions. Once the family group has sufficient information for making a plan, all of the service providers including the FGC coordinator leave the room. During their private time, the family group develops a plan. Then they call the child protection worker and FGC coordinator back to review the plan. Prior to the plan going into effect, child protection must approve the action steps in terms of protecting children and authorize the provision of agency resources.

This approach to FGC was first legislated in Aotearoa[1] (New Zealand) for resolving child welfare and youth justice issues and, as is the case with many restorative practices, adapted Indigenous traditions to modern conditions. The *Children, Young Persons and Their Families Act* was enacted in 1989 after a critical review by Maori New Zealanders of Pakeha[2] (European) systems; the Maori saw these systems as undermining Indigenous kinship groupings (Rangihau 1986). The Act mandated FGC in order to advance the family group's responsibilities, children's rights, cultural affirmation and government-community partnerships (Hudson et al. 1996).

Although not framed as restorative justice in the legislation, FGC soon became part of this larger global movement to transform modern institutions (Sullivan and Tift 2006). The model rapidly spread to other countries, including Canada (Burford and Hudson 2000), and with various adaptations was applied in a range of contexts from schools to workplaces to armed conflicts (Adams 2004; Morrison and Ahmed 2006). I was part of an early Newfoundland and Labrador demonstration of its effectiveness in addressing family violence, both spousal abuse and child maltreatment (Pennell and Burford 2000).

Canada is a leader in applying a number of restorative practices in addition to FGC, including circles (Bushie 1997; Pranis, Stuart and Wedge 2003) and victim offender mediation (Galaway and Hudson 1996). Quite justifiably, these approaches have been critically reviewed by Indigenous and women's groups: when restorative practices are imposed on Indigenous communities, they serve as a means of re-colonization in which once again outsiders determine what is permissible (McCaslin 2005); without attention to safety measures, restorative practices re-victimize survivors set again at risk (Strang and Braithwaite 2002). Accordingly, we need to proceed with care in instituting restorative practices.

For this reason, I developed a theory of change called "widening the circle" to serve as a guide to practice and as a way to evaluate our work.

## Widening the Circle

*"Family group conferencing widens the circle by combining the strengths of the family group, community organizations, and public agencies to resolve the issues threatening family members"* (Pennell and Anderson 2005: 5, italics in original). Widening the circle of supports is crucial in addressing child maltreatment and domestic violence. If the immediate family members could have resolved these matters on their own, they would have done so. They need others who care about their family to know what is happening, commit needed resources and collaborate in finding and carrying out solutions. Widening the circle shifts the power dynamics within the family of concern and between the family and the involved protective authorities. For family, the process serves to reaffirm lasting connections across generations, so important to solidifying children's sense of identity and supporting their long-term welfare. For workers, the process interrupts mother blaming, refocuses away from family dysfunction and agency liability, and generates a sense of hope. For relatives, friends and other community members, the process reaffirms their capacities and is a call to socially responsible action. All these changes forward the aims of anti-oppressive social work to counter racism and other forms of marginalization and to restructure social relations.

Based on research in North Carolina (Pennell and Anderson 2005), four pathways to widening the circle were identified:

- community partnerships — a local collaboration in which each partner retains its distinctive role while striving to realize common goals (Pennell 2004: 126);
- cultural safety — a context in which family members can speak in their own language, express their values and use their experiences and traditions to resolve issues (Pennell 2004: 126);
- inclusive planning — a decision-making process that involves different sides of the family in making a plan, incorporates means of sustaining the family group's participation and is authorized and supported by the protective authority (Pennell 2006: 294); and
- family leadership — a relationship in which the family group members are central and their efforts are supported by community organizations and public agencies (Pennell 2004: 126).

A protocol called the *Achievement of FGC Objectives* (see Appendix 4-1 for the questionnaire and Appendix 4-2 for scoring the questionnaire) was developed for assessing the extent to which each pathway was realized.

## Cultural Guidance in Planning the North Carolina FGC Project

On returning from Canada to the United States, I was asked by the North Carolina Division of Social Services to mount an FGC program in the state. They viewed FGC as a "best practice" and wanted to encourage child welfare to adopt this approach. My Canadian experience with FGC had been in a quite different legal, cultural and economic context (and colder climate!) than the southeastern United States. Thus, it was all the more essential to put in place a collaborative process for planning the North Carolina FGC Project. As a newcomer to the state, I needed guidance, but more importantly, state and county participants needed to make FGC their own and identify the distinctive roles that they could play in moving forward FGC.

We used a series of consultative processes to shape the project to local cultures and conditions (Pennell and Weil 2000). At the state level, an advisory council was formed, with families, community organizations, public agencies and universities invited to serve. The advisory council defined the project's philosophy of "building partnerships with and around families" and provided oversight to the development of the FGC policies, training and evaluation. In the participating counties, local advisory groups were formed to guide the development of their programs and offer consultation to the FGC coordinators.

Holding focus groups with different cultural communities (African American, Cherokee and Latino/Hispanic) was particularly crucial because of the region's history of African American enslavement and segregation; the forced removal of the Cherokee, known as the Trail of Tears or more accurately, Nunahi-Duna-Dlo-Hilu-I (Trail Where They Cried); and the current influx of Mexicans and punitive measures against undocumented workers and their families. Although families of colour do not abuse or neglect their children more than white families, African Americans and Native Americans for their numbers in the population are overrepresented on child protection caseloads and in foster care and tend to be treated differently and not as well as white children (Hill 2006). The disproportionate rate of involvement with child welfare not only affects individual families but also undermines communities of colour. As Roberts (2002: 27) cogently argues about predominantly Black neighbourhoods, "Family distintegration leads to community disintegration." A high level of child welfare regulation and child removals in poor, Black communities frays social bonds in families as well as among neighbours.

Focus group participants from the three cultural communities all agreed that FGC was congruent with their traditions and a respectful way for child welfare to engage them in decision-making (Waites et al. 2004). Strong support for the model was also voiced in focus groups with potential service users: men and women in addictions recovery, women who had been abused, men who had abused and women in prison (Pennell and Anderson 2005; Pennell and Francis 2005). Safety measures for carrying out the model were offered by women's advocates and police officers. Their views were reconfirmed by extensive data collected on individual conferences. The main strategy for keeping participants safe was careful preparations, checking on what they thought would help them feel safe before, during and after the meeting. Frequently applied methods were having a support person stay by a person feeling vulnerable, having women's advocates attend the meetings to provide information regarding the impact of abuse on child and adult family members, having the group develop guidelines for their meeting (e.g., listen without interrupting), building a system of monitoring the implementation of the plan and reconvening as necessary to revise the plan.

During interviews and on surveys, family group members, workers and coordinators answered questions on their experience of the process: How well were they prepared for the conference? Were they able to say what they needed to say at the meeting? Did they develop a good plan? Was the plan carried out or modified as necessary? What was the impact of the conference and its plan? All of this feedback led to improvements in implementing the model. Importantly, a sense of pride in the FGC successes helped us to move away from systemic preoccupations with child risk and agency liability to building plans around the hopes and concerns of families. These successes also helped us recognize that the characteristics of individual families should not be the determining factor in holding a conference or holding it off. Instead, we learned about strategic points at which to convene a conference.

A county advisory council identified one of these points. They noted that too often "unmanageable" youth who committed status offences (e.g., truancy, running away)[3] became "gifts of the court" to child welfare. This led to further overloading a foster care system that already struggled to find suitable homes for teens. The advisory council correctly surmised that FGC would be an especially welcomed intervention at this stage by families and workers alike. Frequently, the families had not previously been involved with child protection, and thus, they and their workers were less likely to hold negative views of each other; moreover, both parties wanted help in dealing with acting-out adolescents. This advisory council decision led to a series of conferences for which the referral was made by a juvenile court counsellor rather than the child protection worker.

The following FGC example highlights the four pathways for widening the circle. This conference was held for a teen — Darrian — from an African American family and neighbourhood and shows the process of widening the circle at each stage of the conference.[3] The quotations are from interviews, reflective notes and surveys on the conference. Family group members, FGC coordinators and research observers each completed the Achievement of FGC Objectives.

After reading the example, you may find it helpful to complete the Family Group Protocol (Appendix 4-1) and figure out your own assessment of the extent to which each pathway was realized (Appendix 4-2). Keep in mind that the four pathways should apply across the entire conferencing process, so do not limit your assessment of each pathway to just one phase of conferencing. There is no one right or wrong answer for each item. Instead the Achievement of FGC Objectives is a useful means of learning more about various perceptions of the process.

Darrian was a thirteen-year-old diagnosed with attention deficit and hyper-activity disorder. He excelled in sports but had been missing school, coming home late and hanging out with older youth in his public housing complex. These status offences brought him to the attention of juvenile justice. His mother, Tisha, was clinically depressed and unable to manage her growing son. In the past, Darrian had lived with his father, Taye, but now rarely saw him. A stepfather, Lamarr, had moved into the home and was the father of Darrian's two toddler brothers. Rather than recommending him for foster care, the juvenile court counselor referred his case for an FGC.

## A Family Group Conference in Action

Reflecting back on the referral, the FGC coordinator observed that the court counsellor was "very eager to take this case to conference because she felt like this young man had a lot of potential and had varying degrees of support from his extended family." On meeting Darrian and his family, the FGC coordinator agreed with this assessment but added that "there were some very deep emotions of frustration not only with him, but with his mother." Darrian had learned that "his mother would always get him out of trouble... by not pressing charges, by not reporting his failures with curfews, etc."

The coordinator found that Darrian was "very likeable" and "motivated to avoid leaving his family," and his mother and stepfather likewise wanted to avert a foster or group home placement. Confirming the advisory group's sup-position, the coordinator observed, "The wonderful aspect of receiving a case that early was the freedom from the stigma that many times the family has about meeting with the [child protection service (CPS)] worker. The family seemed to look to the social worker as a viable resource, rather than a threat to the family's cohesiveness."

In this case, the referral for an FGC came from outside of child protection and was supported by the young person, his family and his CPS worker. Each of these parties brought their own reasons for supporting the referral and became partners in moving forward the FGC referral. This early agreement on purpose helped them in preparing for the conference.

### Cultural Safety in Preparing for the Conference

In addition to the youth and his parents and stepfather, Tisha's oldest brother, Uncle Clement, who was quite close to Darrian, accepted the invitation to attend. With Darrian's agreement, Uncle Clement was identified as his nephew's sup-port person and stayed by him at the conference. From the housing project, Ms. Charlotte, a long-term friend of the family and acknowledged community leader, welcomed the opportunity to take part. Tisha noted that Ms. Charlotte was "like a grandmother" to Darrian. Ms. Charlotte's presence, however, did not make up for the two missing grandparents — Tisha's mother and Taye's father.

The family members in attendance later remarked that the grandparents should have been at the conference. Darrian was especially disappointed and wrote on his conference evaluation form, "Grandmother could have been here." Their absence, according to Ms. Charlotte, pointed to a failure in the FGC preparations on the part of the family: "An extra effort should have been put out for both grandparents to be there.... The 'invitation' to them from Tisha was too casual." She explained if the grandparents had attended, the conference "would have had a greater impact" because by not showing up they were "condoning" wrong behaviour.

Nonetheless, at school, Darrian had developed some good supports. Two of his former teachers, both African American, and his school social worker, who was white, volunteered to attend. They joined the two protective authorities at the conference — the child protection worker and the juvenile court counsellor — as well as the FGC coordinator and the research observer (present with the permission of the family); all these attendees were white.

In consultation with Tisha, the FGC coordinator arranged for the conference to be held in the evening, when family members could be present, and at their community centre, which the research observer noted was the "family's turf." The dinner menu, much to his delight, was selected by Darrian. The child protection worker agreed to pay for childcare so that the two young siblings could remain in their apartment, especially given that the conference was scheduled to start at 5:00 p.m. In all, the FGC coordinator estimated that she spent thirty hours in preparing for the meeting, and the child protection worker's estimate was five hours. These preparation times are similar to ones reported for other FGC programs, especially when workers and coordinators are relatively new to the process (Pennell and Anderson 2005: 22).

### Inclusive Planning at the Conference

The conference began an hour late because Darrian's bus was delayed in arriving. Nevertheless, the conference lasted for nearly four hours, an average length for an FGC (Pennell and Anderson 2005: 43). Three sides of the family were present from the beginning: the mother and her brother, the father and the stepfather. They and the service providers chose where they wanted to sit. As described by the research observer, "the room was small and felt a little crowded with everyone there. There were four small round tables set up. Taye, Lamarr and I sat at one table. Tisha, Darrian and Uncle Clement sat at another. The service providers spread themselves among the other two." Ms. Charlotte, arriving even later, pulled up a chair next to Tisha.

When the FGC coordinator asked Tisha how she wished to start the conference, she suggested a prayer. This surprised her brother, Uncle Clement, who had not expected this opening, and on further conferring with Tisha, the prayer was omitted. The coordinator welcomed the group, overviewed the conference process and checked that the group understood and agreed with the purpose of the meeting: "avoid[ing] foster care placement" and "keeping Darrian out of trouble." Next, the group, including Darrian, contributed their ideas on rules for the discussion. Once these ground rules were flipcharted and posted on the wall, the information sharing commenced.

In this case, the father, Taye, led off because he had to leave shortly for his work shift. He "voiced concerns that he doesn't know what Darrian is doing…. Things happen at school and he doesn't find out about it until later." Continuing, Taye observed that Darrian will say, "I'm sorry," when he knows he is in the wrong but then "blames others for his actions." Upset by his father's comments, Darrian in tears ran from the room. Although Uncle Clement was his nephew's designated support person, it was Tisha who immediately followed Darrian to console him. Back in the room, the participants "in reaction to Taye's comments" agreed that Darrian was "brave to be at the conference."

Before leaving, Taye volunteered to spend more time with Darrian, and the teachers gave Taye their phone numbers at school if he had questions on how his son was progressing. Much to everyone's amazement, the stepfather Lamarr offered to drive Taye to work. Up until the conference, Lamarr and Taye had had little to do with each other. The coordinator noted that their connecting with each other "appeared to encourage rather than threaten" Darrian. Not understanding the family and community's culture, the coordinator did not fully appreciate how unusual Lamarr's offer was. Ms. Charlotte, however, did. In an interview a month later, she still recollected clearly this bonding between the two men and emphasized that this was "unheard of" in her community.

After Taye and Lamarr departed, the teachers and the school social worker shared their perceptions on Darrian. They emphasized his academic progress and football prowess, his love for his family and his good fortune in having two loving fathers. Throughout these accounts of his strengths, Darrian glowed with pleasure. Before the protective authorities gave their reports, the two teachers left, with the school social worker remaining. This ensured more privacy for Darrian and the family since the school teachers did not need to hear the issues from the perspective of child protection and the court.

In their reports, the CPS worker and court counsellor summarized what brought Darrian to their attention — the truancy, curfew breaking and unmanageability at home and school — and set forth their expectations that "an adult must know where Darrian is at all times." In addition, they described some services that the family group might wish to consider in making their plan. These options included a mental health assessment, in-home services, parenting classes and wilderness camp. Once they completed their reports, dinner was served. The social workers and the coordinator took their food and moved into another room. Lamarr returned in time for dinner with the family.

### Family Leadership in Making and Carrying Out the Plan

After finishing their meal, the family group, including Ms. Charlotte, began their private deliberations, which lasted over an hour. The length of the private time was disconcerting to the court counsellor, who asked the FGC coordinator "if we should just leave them in there alone, indefinitely" and worried that without facilitation, the family group would "get too far off track." In response, the coordinator reassured the court counsellor and recognized that the counsellor probably required more "coaching on her role" in advance of the conference.

In the conference room, though, there was a natural leader, Ms. Charlotte, who led off the discussion. She emphasized that "Darrian isn't the same person" that he used to be. He "doesn't go to church anymore, walks the sidewalk, wants attention, wants to be grown up, hangs out with an older group, doesn't go where he says he is going." The other family members joined into the "powerful" confrontation and eventually Darrian committed himself to "staying out of trouble."

The main decision-makers during the family's private time were Tisha, Uncle Clement, Lamarr and Ms. Charlotte, and they formulated the plan primarily through democratic means — consensus, inspiring leadership, bargaining and voting. For his part, Darrian saw his amount of say as "just right" and expressed strong support for the group's final decision. After developing their plan, they invited the FGC coordinator, juvenile court counsellor and CPS worker back into the conference room and presented their plan. Once again, according to the FGC coordinator, the court counsellor had some "difficulty with allowing the family to flesh out their own plan."

The plan had ten action steps. These included rules for Darrian on homework, curfews and adult supervision. In recognition of Tisha's difficulties in managing Darrian, the plan stated that she "will be 100 percent for real and put her foot down with Darrian" and that "Uncle Clement will check up on Tisha to see if she following through." In addition to limits, the plan included fun activities: a weekly family night and Lamarr playing ball or lifting weights with Darrian. Only the tenth and final step sought external resources in an area that the family group felt ill equipped to handle: a mental health assessment for Darrian. The plan written in the family group's words was approved by the CPS worker and court counsellor. At the closing, "the final atmosphere… was very positive and upbeat…. Each family member contributed one verbal affirmation of what they were going to commit to the plan."

In interviews about a month later, the family group all agreed that holding the conference had a beneficial impact. Ms. Charlotte reflected, "It opened up some doors… Darrian sitting there saw and felt that love that night. It was something special done for him. No one else in the neighborhood could say that they had that [a meeting] just for them." Tisha acknowledged, "It was something to help me to help my son." The longer-term results were more mixed. In interviews six months to two years later, the youth and his family group agreed that "overall… the conference made the family better off." They still saw just holding the conference was "good therapy" by "having all those people from different fields pulling together." In addition, they reported that the family nights took place and the uncle and two fathers spent more with Darrian. Slippage, however, from the earlier momentum was evident.

Disappointed, Darrian reported, "Some nights when we did go to family nights we were all together. We went to the movies, but now my stepdad works late so we don't go anymore." Taye, frustrated that he only received calls when Darrian was once again breaking his curfews and truant from school, saw matters as becoming worse. Darrian began receiving treatment for his hyperactivity and attention deficit but then refused to continue the sessions. He was charged with assaulting another student and suspended from school. Tisha, though, continued with counselling sessions for herself.

Reflecting on the conference, Taye observed that it "put us in the right direction; the meeting made me think a lot about things I haven't thought about; we need to get together and talk about things before they get worse. There was only one meeting. If we would get together more often, then we could talk about things." For her part, Tisha identified Darrian's continuing behavioural problems but still felt that the conference "helped a lot." She explained, "Helped me get support I needed from friends and family members.... Everybody's staying in contact."

Conferencing certainly did not resolve all the challenges faced by Darrian and his family group. So many of these issues concerned wider societal factors like education, poverty, housing and so forth and were ones that the FGC plan could only partially address. Placing Darrian in foster care away from his family or in residential care with equally troubled and troubling peers, however, were unlikely to be the solution. In all likelihood, Darrian and his family group would have benefited from further conferencing. Nevertheless, the process was one that the family group had no difficulty recollecting. To them, it was a significant because it reconnected them as a family and respected them as decision-makers about their own affairs.

## Countering Institutional Racism

Applying FGC or any model of intervention does not in itself counter institutional racism. What we make of a model in practice is what counts. Provinces need to develop policies and procedures that uphold principled practice (Schmid and Sieben in press); local organizations need to figure out together how to implement an FGC program in their community contexts; and families need to be engaged in planning how their FGC is held. Because of the responsiveness built into FGC, this model, nevertheless, offers the promise of countering institutional racism in child welfare, and the international literature lends support to this conclusion. We turn now to the three questions posed at the outset of this chapter.

*What are some practices for countering institutional racism in child welfare?* Studies of FGC in child welfare repeatedly show that conferencing keeps children and young persons with their families or, if this is unsafe or not feasible, connected to their extended families and cultural communities (Crampton and Pennell in press). This serves to reduce the disproportional removal of children from racialized communities, stabilizes placements and nurtures relationships over the long term. As in the case of Darrian, family groups work hard to figure out ways to hold onto their young relatives and prevent their advancing further into state systems.

*How do these restorative practices affirm culture while safeguarding children and their families?* Too often in child protection, family groups are viewed as a danger to their young relatives. Canadian and other studies show that maintaining kinship ties is not a hazard but instead a way to protect the safety of children (Cunning and Bartlett 2006) and their mothers while strengthening a sense of pride in their family (Pennell 2006; Pennell and Burford 2000). The process in itself re-affirms the family's culture by building their aspirations and resources into the plan. Moreover, as seen in Darrian's family group, FGC unlike so much of child protection work helps to build or re-build connections with fathers, the paternal side of the family and other male relatives (Veneski and Kemp 2000).

*How can we support each other to interrupt preconceived views and create healing alternatives?* Another recurring finding is that families like conferencing and feel respected by the process (Merkel-Holguin 2003). This, in itself, is noteworthy given the often conflictual relationship between families and child protection. More fundamentally, FGC, circles and other restorative practices heal relationships (Bushie 1997; Strang et al. 2006). Speaking of FGC among the Mi'kmaq of Nova Scotia, Glode and Wien (2007) observe that the process "invites consideration of a wider range of options: early intervention, support, customary care and adoption" and in contrast to conventional child protection approaches, leads to "an expanded view of the client" in which the "emotional is legitimate" and the relationships are "less oppositional."

Despite these encouraging findings, FGC or any restorative practice does not in itself assure that disparities are reduced, culture is affirmed, and healing is nurtured. In reflecting on FGC's potential to decrease institutional racism in African American communities, Dorothy Roberts (2007: 7) observes that well-meaning practices that are culturally sensitive may only serve to "regulate minority families more effectively," and thus, "cultural competence must be accompanied by a change in child welfare decision making." Following certain procedures is not what makes FGC culturally competent. Changing how child welfare decisions are made and adapting conferencing to the families' cultural context is what "makes the practice culturally competent" (Roberts 2007: 8). In reaching out to members of racialized groups, the test is not a worker's or agency's level of cultural competence but instead the extent to which people feel safe in expressing their culture and can tap into their traditions to figure out culturally competent solutions.

## Suggestions for Further Reading

Connolly, M. 2004. "A Perspective on the Origins of Family Group Conferencing." Issue Brief. Englewood, CO: American Humane Association. Available at <http://www.americanhumane.org/site/DocServer/fgdm_FGC_Origins_New_Zealand.pdf?docID=1901> accessed Jan 7, 2008.

Pennell, J. 2007. "Safeguarding All Family Members — FGC and Family Violence." *Social Work Now: The Practice Journal of Child, Youth and Family* 37 (May). Available at <http://www.cyf.govt.nz/documents/swn37.pdf> accessed Jan 7, 2008.

Schmid, J. 2007. "The Use of Self in Conference Coordination." Issue Brief. Englewood, CO: American Humane Association. Available at <http://www.americanhumane.org/site/DocServer/FGDM_Brief_13.pdf?docID=6261> accessed Jan 7, 2008.

## About the Author

Joan Pennell is a professor of social work and director of the Center for Family and Community Engagement at North Carolina State University. Her centre has received funding for work on child and family team meetings in child welfare (NC Division of Social Services) and schools (NC Department of Public Instruction). She previously directed the NC Family Group Conferencing Project, funded by the NC Division of Social Services. Before her return to the United States, she was a principal investigator for a Newfoundland and Labrador demonstration of family group conferencing in situations of child maltreatment and domestic violence.

## Notes

1.  The Maori term Aotearoa means the "Land of the Long White Cloud." It is the name that the Maori ancestors gave to what was later called New Zealand.
2.  The Maori term Pakeha has uncertain origins and usually refers to New Zealanders of European ancestry.
3.  Status offence here refers to an act being a crime for a minor while the same act would not be prohibited for an adult.
4.  In order to protect the family members' confidentiality, their identities are masked.

## References

Adams, P. (ed.). 2004. "Restorative Justice and Responsive Regulation." Special issue of *Journal of Sociology and Social Welfare* 31, 1 (March).

Burford, G., and J. Hudson (eds.). 2000. *Family Group Conferences: New Directions in Community-Centered Child and Family Practice.* Hawthorne, NY: Aldine de Gruyter.

Bushie, B. 1997. "A Personal Journey." In *The Four Circles of Hollow Water.* Hull, Quebec: Aboriginal Peoples Collection, Aboriginal Corrections Policy Unit, Supply and Services Canada, JS5-1/15-1997E.

Crampton, D., and J. Pennell. In press. "Family-Involvement Meetings with Older Children in Foster Care: Intuitive Appeal, Promising Practices and the Challenge of Child Welfare Reform." In B. Kerman, A.N. Maluccio and M. Freundlich (eds.), *Achieving Permanence for Older Children and Youth in Foster Care.* New York: Columbia University Press.

Cunning, S., and D. Bartlett. 2006. *Family Group Conferencing: Assessing the Long-term Effectiveness of an Alternative Approach in Child Protection. Final Report: Centre of Excellence for Child Welfare.* Toronto, ON: The George Hull Centre for Children and Families and the Family Group Conferencing Project of Toronto.

Galaway, B., and J. Hudson (eds.). 1996. *Restorative Justice: International Perspectives.* Monsey, NY: Criminal Justice Press.

Glode, J., and F. Wien. 2006. *Evaluating the Family Group Conferencing Approach in a First Nations Context: Some Initial Findings.* Halifax, NS: Mi'kmaq Family and Children's Services and School of Social Work, Dalhousie University.

_____. 2007. "Respecting Aboriginal Families and Communities: Lessons from an Evaluation Research Project on FGDM among the Mi'kmaq of Nova Scotia." Workshop with PowerPoint slides presented at the Annual Conference of the American Humane on Family Group Decision Making, Washington, DC.

Hill, R.B. 2006. "Synthesis of Research on Disproportionality in Child Welfare: An Update." Available at <http://www.racemattersconsortium.org/docs/

BobHillPaper_FINAL.pdf> accessed on December 28, 2007.

Hudson, J., A. Morris, G. Maxwell and B. Galaway (eds.). 1996. *Family Group Conferences: Perspectives on Policy and Practice.* Monsey, NY: Willow Tree.

Jones, J. M. 1972. *Prejudice and Racism.* Reading, MA: Addison-Wesley.

McCaslin, W.D. (ed.). 2005. *Justice as Healing: Indigenous Ways.* St. Paul, MN: Living Justice Press.

Merkel-Holguin, L. (ed.). 2003. "Promising Results, Potential New Directions: International FGDM Research and Evaluation in Child Welfare" Special issue of *Protecting Children* 18, 1 and 2.

Morrison, B., and E. Ahmed (eds.). 2006. "Restorative Justice and Civil Society." Special issue of *Journal of Social Issues* 62, 2.

Pennell, J. 2003. *Achievement of Objectives, Pre and During Conference.* Raleigh, NC: North Carolina State University, Department of Social Work.

_____. 2004. "Family Group Conferencing in Child Welfare: Responsive and Regulatory Interfaces." In P. Adams (ed.), "Restorative Justice and Responsive Regulation." Special issue of *Journal of Sociology and Social Welfare* 31, 1.

_____. 2006. "Stopping Domestic Violence or Protecting Children? Contributions from Restorative Justice." In D. Sullivan and L. Tifft (eds.), *Handbook of Restorative Justice: A Global Perspective.* New York: Routledge.

Pennell, J., and G. Anderson (eds.). 2005. *Widening the Circle: The Practice and Evaluation of Family Group Conferencing with Children, Youths, and Their Families.* Washington, DC: NASW Press.

Pennell, J., and G. Burford. 2000. "Family Group Decision Making: Protecting Children and Women." *Child Welfare* 79, 2.

Pennell, J., and S. Francis. 2005. "Safety Conferencing: Toward a Coordinated and Inclusive Response to Safeguard Women and Children." In J. Ptacek (ed.), Special issue of *Violence Against Women* 11, 5.

Pennell, J., and M. Weil. 2000. "Initiating Conferencing: Community Practice Issues." In G. Burford and J. Hudson (eds.), *Family Group Conferencing: New Directions in Community-Centered Child and Family Practice.* Hawthorne, NY: Aldine de Gruyter.

Pranis, K., B. Stuart and M. Wedge. 2003. *Peacemaking Circles: From Crime to Community.* St. Paul, MN: Living Justice Press.

Rangihau, J. 1986. *Pau-te-Ata-tu (Daybreak): Report of the Ministerial Advisory Committee on a Maori Perspective for the Department of Social Welfare.* Wellington, New Zealand: Department of Social Welfare, Government Printing Office.

Roberts, D. 2002. *Shattered Bonds: The Color of Child Welfare.* New York: Basic.

_____. 2007. "Toward a Community-Based Approach to Racial Disproportionality." *Protecting Children* 22, 1.

Schmid, J., and M. Sieben. In press. "Help or Hindrance: Family Group Conferencing as Alternative Dispute Resolution in Child Welfare. *Protecting Children.*

Sherry, M. In press. "What Have We Learned about Family Group Conferencing and Case Management Practices." *Protecting Children.*

Strang, H., and J. Braithwaite (eds.). 2002. *Restorative Justice and Family Violence.* New York: Cambridge University Press.

Strang, H., L. Sherman, C.M. Angel, D.J. Woods, S. Bennett, D. Newbury-Birch and N. Inkpen. 2006. "Victim Evaluations of Face-to-Face Restorative Justice Conferences: A Quasi-Experimental Analysis." In B. Morrison and E. Ahmed (eds.), "Restorative Justice and Civil Society." Special issue of *Journal of Social Issues* 62, 2.

Strega, S. 2007. "Anti-Oppressive Practice in Child Welfare." In D. Baines (ed.), *Doing*

*Anti-Oppressive Practice: Building Transformative Politicized Social Work.* Halifax, NS: Fernwood.

Sullivan, D., and L. Tifft (eds.). 2006. *Handbook of Restorative Justice: A Global Perspective.* London and New York: Routledge.

Veneski, W., and S. Kemp. 2000. "Families as Resources: The Washington State Family Group Conference Project." In G. Burford and J. Hudson (eds.), *Family Group Conferences: New Directions in Community-Centered Child and Family Practice.* Hawthorne, NY: Aldine de Gruyter.

Waites, C., M.J. Macgowan, J. Pennell, I. Carlton-LaNey and M. Weil. 2004. "Increasing the Cultural Responsiveness of Family Group Conferencing. *Social Work* 49, 2.

Wharf, B. (ed.). 2002. *Community Work Approaches to Child Welfare.* Peterborough, ON: Broadview Press.

Zehr, H. 2002. *The Little Book of Restorative Justice.* Intercourse, PA: Good Books.

## Websites on Family Group Conferencing in Child Welfare

Family Group Decision Making Project, School of Social Work, Memorial University of Newfoundland, St. John's, Newfoundland, Canada A1C 5S7
<http://social.chass.ncsu.edu/jpennell/fgdm/index.htm>

George Hull Center for Children and Families, 600 The East Mall, Third Floor Toronto, Ontario, Canada M9B 4B1
<http://www.georgehullcentre.on.ca/FamilyGroupConferencing>

American Humane Association, National Center on Family Group Decision Making, 63 Inverness Drive East, Englewood, Colorado, United States 80112
<http://www.americanhumane.org/site/PageServer?pagename=pc_fgdm&JServSessionIdr012=okn8urxyw7.app24a>

Center for Family and Community Engagement, North Carolina State University, C.B. 8622, Raleigh, North Carolina, United States 27695-8622
<http://www.Cfface.org>

## Appendix 4-1 Questionnaire for Achievement of FGC Objectives

| Objectives | Strongly Disagree | Disagree | Agree | Strongly Agree | Don't Know | N/A |
|---|---|---|---|---|---|---|
| 1. Each service provider was clear about their role (ex., child protection, counseling). | 1 | 2 | 3 | 4 | 7 | 8 |
| 2. The FGC coordinator was respectful of the family group. | 1 | 2 | 3 | 4 | 7 | 8 |
| 3. The only job of the FGC coordinator was to organize the conference. He/she did *not* have other jobs to do with the family. | 1 | 2 | 3 | 4 | 7 | 8 |
| 4. The family group understood the reasons for holding the conference. | 1 | 2 | 3 | 4 | 7 | 8 |
| 5. The conference was held in a place that felt right to the family group. | 1 | 2 | 3 | 4 | 7 | 8 |
| 6. The conference was held in a way that felt right to the family group (ex., the right food, right time of day). | 1 | 2 | 3 | 4 | 7 | 8 |
| 7. More family group than service providers were invited to the conference. | 1 | 2 | 3 | 4 | 7 | 8 |
| 8. Different sides of the family were invited to the conference (ex., father's and mother's sides of the family). | 1 | 2 | 3 | 4 | 7 | 8 |
| 9. People at the conference were relatives and also people who feel "like family" (ex., old friends, good neighbors). | 1 | 2 | 3 | 4 | 7 | 8 |
| 10. The family group was prepared for the conference (ex., got enough information on what happens at a conference). | 1 | 2 | 3 | 4 | 7 | 8 |
| 11. The service providers were prepared for the conference (ex., got enough information on what happens at a conference). | 1 | 2 | 3 | 4 | 7 | 8 |

*continued on next page...*

| Objectives | Strongly Disagree | Disagree | Agree | Strongly Agree | Don't Know | N/A |
|---|---|---|---|---|---|---|
| 12. The conference had enough supports and protections (ex., support persons). | 1 | 2 | 3 | 4 | 7 | 8 |
| 13. Service providers shared their knowledge but they did not tell the family group how to solve the problems. | 1 | 2 | 3 | 4 | 7 | 8 |
| 14. The family group had private time to make their plan. | 1 | 2 | 3 | 4 | 7 | 8 |
| 15. The plan included ways that the family group will help out. | 1 | 2 | 3 | 4 | 7 | 8 |
| 16. The plan included steps to evaluate if the plan is working and to get the family group back together again if needed. | 1 | 2 | 3 | 4 | 7 | 8 |
| 17. Social Services approved the plans without unnecessary delays. | 1 | 2 | 3 | 4 | 7 | 8 |

N/A = not applicable
*Source: Pennell 2003.*

### Appendix 4-2 Scoring the Questionnaire

**Cultural Safety: Conference held in the right way for family group.**

5. The conference was held in a place that felt right to the family group.
6. The conference was held in a way that felt right to the family group (ex., the right food, right time of day).
9. People at the conference were relatives and also people who feel "like family" (ex., old friends, good neighbors).
12. The conference had enough supports and protections (ex., support persons).

Subtotal divided by 4 (or number of scored items) =

**Community Partnerships: Family group and service providers clear about what doing.**

1. Each service provider was clear about their role (ex., child protection, counselling).
4. The family group understood the reasons for holding the conference.
10. The family group was prepared for the conference (ex., got enough informa-

tion on what happens at a conference).

11. The service providers were prepared for the conference (ex., got enough information on what happens at a conference).

Subtotal divided by 4 (or number of scored items) =

### Family Leadership: Family group empowered to make a plan.

2. The FGC coordinator was respectful of the family group.

3. The only job of the FGC coordinator was to organize the conference. He/she did *not* have other jobs to do with the family.

7. More family group than service providers were invited to the conference.

13. Service providers shared their knowledge but they did not tell the family group how to solve the problems.

14. The family group had private time to make their plan.

Subtotal divided by 5 (or number of scored items) =

### Inclusive Planning: Diverse family participants involved, and continued family-community-state planning supported.

8. Different sides of the family were invited to the conference (ex., father's and mother's sides of the family).

15. The plan included ways that the family group will help out.

16. The plan included steps to evaluate if the plan is working and to get the family group back together again if needed.

17. Social Services approved the plans without unnecessary delays.

Subtotal divided by 4 (or number of scored items) =

# Chapter 5

# The Practice of Child Welfare in Indigenous Communities

## A Perspective for the Non-Indigenous Social Worker

*Christopher Walmsley*

This chapter argues that non-Indigenous social workers need an understanding of Indigenous people's history, an ability to see themselves as ongoing learners and a critical awareness of the parenting values and practices of their own cultures[1] in order to engage successfully with Indigenous children, families and communities. Key to successful anti-oppressive child protection practice is recognizing the dual powers of child protection — the power invested in the role and the social worker's own power to practise respectfully in ways that engage extended families and communities.

Questions Addressed in This Chapter
1. How have education and child welfare programs been oppressive to Indigenous peoples?
2. What does a social worker need to know and be able to do to practise child protection in Indigenous communities anti-oppressively?
3. How might the power invested in the position of child protection social worker be shared with Indigenous families and communities?

Child protection is fundamentally about assessing whether a child is safe to be with their parents or grandparents and whether they can be entrusted to care adequately for their children. Like a flashlight peering into the darkness of the relationship between parents and children, it illuminates a private world. However, when a non-Indigenous social worker shines an investigative light on an Indigenous family, does the "seeing" need to be different? Do different questions need to be asked when assessing a child's safety across cultures and when practising across a cultural divide? What does the worker need to consider beyond the policies, procedures and assessment tools provided by an employer? I argue in this chapter that to be an effective child protection practitioner in Indigenous communities the worker needs an understanding of history, a vision of herself as an ongoing learner, a recognition of herself as a cultural product and an ability to see her power as a person and as a practitioner. A less oppressive and more collaborative practice will then be possible.

## Understanding Indigenous People's History

Indigenous people understand child protection as the forced separation of children from their families and communities by state social workers:

> *They just filled the bus right up and took the kids out and just about every one of my relatives have been in foster care and I was very traumatized as a child, I never did forget my first cousin and her brothers, my first cousin was sitting on my grandmother's knee and Mrs. __ came in and I think there was another social worker with her or the police, I'm not sure, but literally dragged my cousin off of my grandmother and she was just kicking and screaming and didn't want to go.*[2]

Known as the sixties scoop, this historical practice features prominently in the understanding Indigenous people have of child protection practice. Each media story that suggests a child has been unjustly removed from parents reinforces this understanding. At the moment a child protection practitioner appears at the door of an Indigenous person's home, an atmosphere of fear, distrust, anger or passive powerlessness can be unleashed. When a child is removed, the forced separation can harden the family's and community's understanding of child protection — even though the circumstances of a particular removal can be accepted and understood.

Deepened by the community's memory of the impact of the residential school era, state intervention in Indigenous families is most often viewed as a colonizing practice. Beginning in the 1870s, the Canadian government's residential school policy was to separate generations of children from their families, suppress their languages and re-socialize them according to the norms of Euro-Canadian society (*Royal Commission on Aboriginal Peoples* 1996a). Informally, residential schools also served as the Canadian government's child welfare service for Indigenous peoples until the 1950s. By 1948, 60 percent of Indigenous children attended federal residential schools (*Royal Commission on Aboriginal Peoples* 1996a: 351). Memories of residential schools are still powerful for the schools' survivors, who remember being called derogatory names by staff, being sexually abused, being given bread and water as punishment for speaking their language, having letters censored, enduring chronic hunger, having their head shaved and being called a heathen (Furniss 1995: 110; Haig-Brown 1988: 76; MacDonald 1993: 13; *Royal Commission on Aboriginal Peoples* 1996b: 35). One B.C. band chief summarizes the effects of the residential school in her community:

> Later when these children returned home, they were aliens. They did not speak their own language, so they could not communicate with anyone other than their own counterparts. Some looked down on their families because of their lack of English, their lifestyle, and some were just plain hostile. They had formed no bonds with their families, and some couldn't survive without the regimentation they had become so accustomed to... Perhaps the greatest tragedy of this background was the unemotional upbringing they had. Not

being brought up in a loving, caring, sharing, nurturing environment, they did not have these skills as they are not inbred but learned through observation, participation, and interaction. Consequently, when these children became parents, and most did at an early age, they had no parenting skills. They did not have the capability to show affection. They sired and bred children, but were unable to relate to them on any level. (Chief Cinderina Williams, Spallumcheen Band, *Royal Commission on Aboriginal Peoples* 1996b: 35)

Although the last residential school closed in 1996, their influence is omnipresent in Indigenous communities today. The residential school experience was the most powerful common issue raised across Canada in presentations to the Royal Commission on Aboriginal Peoples (Furniss 1995: 31).

The sixties scoop, equally powerful as a memory of the forceful separation of children from families, has not been subject to the same extensive media, royal commission and research scrutiny as residential schools. Beginning in the mid-1950s until the early 1970s large numbers of Indigenous children first entered Canadian child welfare systems. For example, in British Columbia, only twenty-nine Indigenous children were in the care of the Superintendent of Child Welfare in 1955, but by 1960, this number had risen to 849 and in 1964 to 1,446. In a period of ten years, Indigenous children shifted from under 1 percent of the total children in care in B.C. to about 32 percent. The rate fluctuated between 36.7 percent and 39.2 percent from 1976 to 1980 (Stanbury 1975: 384; Johnston 1983: 27). Across Canada, particularly in the Western provinces, northern Ontario and the territories, the percentage of Indigenous children in care climbed rapidly during the 1960s and they continue to be the most significant group in Canadian child welfare:

> By 1983, status Indigenous children were vastly overrepresented in the child welfare systems across the country. In Manitoba, about 60 percent of the children in care were Indigenous, while in Alberta they made up about 50 percent of the caseload, and up to 70 percent in Saskatchewan. (Bennet et al. 2005: 19)

However, these numbers provide a conservative account of Indigenous children in care as official statistics rely on children having registered Indian or Inuit status. Many children of Indigenous parents or grandparents do not have this status due to marriage to a non-Indigenous person or a parent's/grandparent's loss of status. If these children were included, the official percentage of Indigenous children in care would be even higher.

Explaining the rapid increase in the proportion of Indigenous children in care needs to take into account the federal policy of integration, the extension of child welfare laws to reserves and the liberalization of liquor laws that occurred in the early 1950s. In 1951, a number of amendments were made to the *Indian Act* following the 1948 *Report of the Special Joint Committee of the Senate and the House of Commons on the Indian Act*. Education was the major focus of the Special

Joint Committee's work, and integration of Indigenous people into mainstream society became the thrust of Canadian government policy. Educating Indigenous children "for citizenship" with children from different backgrounds in common classrooms became the priority, rather than racially segregating children in separate schools. Indigenous children were integrated into provincial schools in or close to their home communities and came increasingly within the orbit of provincial law. As this occurred, residential schools assumed a residual function as residences for children from isolated communities attending provincial schools and as the child welfare placement resource for the Department of Indian Affairs. The 1951 amendments to the *Indian Act* also included a new Section 88, which provided the legal authority, according to Indian Affairs officials, to extend child welfare services to Indigenous children in the provinces, including those on reserves (MacDonald 1993: 19).

Between 1951 and 1956, the discriminatory provisions of the *Indian Act* about the possession, purchase and consumption of alcohol by Indigenous peoples were removed. This liberalization, argued on the grounds of social equality and non-discrimination, was based in a belief that "Indians should be permitted to drink in the open." By 1955, an amendment to the *Indian Act* was passed to permit Indigenous people to drink off reserve if permitted by the laws of the province. In 1956, the federal government granted full liquor rights to Indigenous people on the same basis as other Canadians (Hawthorn et al. 1958: 378). For the first time people could drink at home, in restaurants and at social gatherings without fear of legal consequences. But the removal, in a few years, of a century's worth of restrictions had dramatic effects. Hawthorn argued that in the previous prohibition period, a social pattern of "wild and secretive" drinking had been established, but with secrecy no longer required, drinking to excess came out into the open (Hawthorn et al. 1958: 381). A member of the Spallumcheen Band, in a study for the *Royal Commission on Aboriginal Peoples*, observed that:

> These changes in liquor policies of governments encouraged and led to excessive drinking among our Band members, both on the reserve and in the adjoining towns of Enderby and Armstrong. Our Elder Romeo Edwards recalls the period of the next ten years as a time when "everything went crazy" and when "drinking affected every household." He notes that people began drinking who had never touched liquor before in their lives. It became a regular social activity and way of life affecting both the old and the young. It led to many deaths from violence, suicides, accidents and impaired health... [and] caused Band members to lose respect for themselves and one another... [and created] a weakened sense of responsibility for the care of children and family members. (MacDonald 1993: 18–19)

As noted above, during the late 1950s and early 1960s, the integration of Indigenous children into provincial child welfare services occurred at an alarming velocity. The period, is referred to as the sixties scoop because provincial social workers would, quite literally, scoop children from reserves on the slightest pretext, because they believed that what they were doing was in the best interests of the child... They felt that the apprehension of Indian children from reserves would save them from the effects of crushing poverty, unsanitary health conditions, poor housing, and malnutrition. (Johnston 1983: 23)

While some social workers from the 1960s demonstrated the ability to think and act critically with respect to provincial social welfare policy (Moran 1992), there is little evidence that social workers questioned or resisted provincial child welfare policy that removed Indigenous children from families and communities. One of those children, now an adult, remembers:

The first memory I actually have is of living in a white foster home. Curiously enough, my first memory is of this dirt road and I was sitting in a little red wagon, maybe a push wagon. I was in the wagon and Thomas and Mary (who I assumed were my brother and sister) were playing with me. We were running down the road, or they were running down the road and one of them was pulling me in the red wagon, and the reason I remember that incident is because my finger got stuck in the handle and of course it really hurt, and I remember screaming bloody murder because of it.... At the time I had no idea that they weren't my brother and sister and that in fact they were White foster kids. And my real brother Raymond was also with me at the time, living like this. He and I and these two other kids were living on a horse farm... I guess Mary and Thomas treated me as brothers — my brother and me — and they stuck pretty close to us, but we didn't think this would last too long.

About two years after I got to school, probably in grade three, I think, the next great memory I have is of Mary and Thomas being taken away. I remember wondering why they'd been taken away. I can remember when we got back from school they were gone....

The real kids of the foster family, a brother and a sister, did not treat any of the foster kids well. They looked down on us and they used to tease us. When I was on the school bus they used to avoid me whenever possible, and sometimes, if they got bored, they used to tease me about being an Indian kid not worth very much....

The foster parents weren't exactly unaware of how their kids treated us. Or maybe if they did they just assumed it was just more convenient to let it go. I don't remember a time when the foster parents didn't choose their own kids over the foster home kids, nor (a time when they) stopped their own kids from doing other things, such as stealing stuff from us (they did that), so I don't ever remember getting preference over their kids....

Halfway through grade four, I was sitting in the classroom one day and this woman walked in, said a few words to the teacher, and then asked me to go with her. I walked with her and she picked up my brother Raymond at the same time.

I didn't know what it was about but we got back to the farm and my (foster) dad was laying all my belongings in these bags. Then the woman picked up the bags and put them in the car and then just drove away with my brother and me. We didn't know what was going on.

We drove towards Vernon and she said that I was going to have a new set of parents. That quite shocked me. Despite the loneliness and feeling on occasion that I didn't like the work, the foster parents were the only ones I had known. (Bruyere 2005: 285–87)

Today, the practice of child protection takes place against the backdrop of the sixties scoop and the residential school era. These legacies surface in day-to-day interactions between social workers and community members. One non-Indigenous social worker describes reaction to her work by community members:

*I even hear it said, "Well you're just like the residential schools, you're trying to tell us what to do," and even when it's not vocalized it is there, you know, that we're an interfering outside agency [that] doesn't share their experience, letting them know how they're supposed to live their lives.*

When an Indigenous social worker returned to her community to begin work in child protection she remembers initial reaction to her work:

*I can recall… going to a home on the reserve and I didn't know that this family was drinking, I walked into the home, they were drinking, and when they seen me coming, they sent the kids to run up the mountains. That was the image they had of social workers.*

Another Indigenous social worker remembers people saying, "Oh, you are one of those baby snatchers," and another chuckles saying, "I'm the black stork, I take children away."

The legacy of the residential school era and the sixties scoop influences today's child protection practice. The non-Indigenous social worker cannot escape this legacy. Instead, she needs to recognize its influence and learn to work with it. A different understanding about child protection can be created based in honesty, openness, reciprocity and integrity, but it may not be reciprocated until a significant level of trust has developed. A non-Indigenous social worker may always be, at some level, a representative of "the white welfare." However, accepting this and understanding it is a first step forward to change it. Generations of Indigenous people have been involved in an historical struggle to preserve families and communities against the oppressive intervention of state education and social service systems. For them to be able to trust that today's practice will be different from the past takes time. At the same time, Indigenous communities have their own ways of protecting children. One Indigenous social worker explains how her grandfather protected her from "child protection" intervention:

*One stability for me when I was growing up, was my grandfather, 'cause my Mom did leave us for about, I think it was about two to three weeks at one time. If it wasn't for my grandfather… me and my brothers and my younger sister would have been apprehended. Yah, and I only found this out later when I was working in… and this person who happened to be there, asks me if I was related to — who was my grandfather. I kind of looked at him and said "Yes. Yes, he is my grandfather." And he said, "You are from —." So he said, "So you must have been one of the grandkids that he wouldn't let me take." And I said, "Well, what do you mean?" And he says, "Well maybe he didn't tell you but a couple of times we got a report that you guys were down there by yourselves and you know that we should go, I was going to go and remove you." Yah, so a couple of times he had gone down there and my grandfather told him, "No, you are not taking my grandkids." So, I didn't know it at the time, it wasn't until later on that I had found this out and I said, "Well this is, you know, my grandfather was the one who had a lot of influence on, on where I am today, because of that." I felt that if I had gone into the system I don't know where I would be right now… So we kind of took care of all the younger ones and you know, sometimes it would be between six and ten of us, you know, kind of all keeping each other safe… Like we would have a nurse who would come around and, you know, we wouldn't say anything. We wouldn't say if our parents were gone. I think that is how the report got to the social worker, that one time, is through our nurse, who had gone down there a couple times and didn't see Mom and saw us with our grandfather and he would try and keep us clean, but when you're kids and it is summer time and, you know, back then during summer I didn't wear shoes and it was only when we had to go to school, in September, that we found it really difficult to put our feet in shoes again. During summer we would be running around without shoes, we would live in shorts and what little t-shirts we had and that was it. Like we wouldn't wash them. We would go in the river and they would get washed. That was basically how it was all summer… We were able to run free and enjoy being a child, at the time. Those were good times.*

Today Indigenous communities still protect children from state intervention by non-Indigenous social workers as this grandfather did. Faced with a community's internal means of protecting children, a non-Indigenous social worker needs to position herself as a learner — open to learning about another people's history and her own preconceptions and judgments.

### Ongoing Learning

A social work degree creates a social work professional out of an ordinary university student. Being able to critically analyze social situations and communicate effectively is assumed to be part of the process, but becoming a social work professional also implies expertise in the application of knowledge to practice. Yet without the experience of living or growing up in an Indigenous community, it is not possible to be an expert in child protection intervention with Indigenous children and families. This is one of the contradictions facing today's non-Indigenous child protection social worker. Throughout a social work education, emphasis is given to the acquisition of knowledge, values and skills to become an effective helper. Graduation with a social work degree implies a state of sufficient knowledge and skill to practice. But this knowledge is usually found in textbooks, journal articles and libraries, not the wisdom of Elders, community leaders or others who have lived and worked extensively in Indigenous communities. Until recently, knowledge of Indigenous communities was not regarded as significant or important. Although this is beginning to change, a level of contradiction exists between the scientific knowledge of the university and Indigenous community knowledge. This creates tension for the new non-Indigenous social worker who begins work in an Indigenous community.

To resolve this tension, a new social worker needs a vision of herself as an ongoing learner, as well as an ability to build trust with families and communities so that they become teachers. Being accepted in the community is possible. This non-Indigenous practitioner describes her process of being accepted:

> *I was just patient. You know, you just kind of learned their ways, like you have to be very respectful. You wait for them to ask for your input, like you don't give them your input, you wait for them to ask, and… I would say I was there two and a half months before they saw me as a worker, rather than the white welfare and it was just a really slow, slow process.*

Credibility to practise child protection needs to be constructed with community members to counter the historical legacy. This is less about formal assessments and safety plans and more about building reciprocal helping relationships with members of the community to ensure children's safety. One child protection social worker describes the change in thinking it required:

> *Going into these small isolated communities, you have to develop that relationship and that's primary…. It's more of who you are, what you are, and how long are you going to stay…. There was that mistrust, distrust, that occurred… I really had to change gears in looking at how I was going to work with these people and most of what it was, was not per-policy or per-legislation, it was developing a relationship with these people and developing a relationship with the community.*

An Indigenous social worker echoes this difference in approach:

> *One of the keys is the ability to form relationships, build relationships and to, in a sense, have relationships with communities. And to be credible and to be visible in the community.*

Recognizing what you don't know and don't have to know is important. Giving yourself permission to ask questions is part of the process of learning. "It's really important to be honest, so don't pretend to know when you don't and don't say you know what they're going through, when you've never been there." Another worker felt it was really important to ask community members for feedback, such as "what am I doing wrong here" or "what am I missing." Equally important is the ability to be open to learn and change your practice based on the responses.

One way to optimize learning is to choose a "cultural guide," someone who is respected by all, knowledgeable about the community and with whom a non-Indigenous social worker can develop an open trusting relationship. It might be a band social worker, band councillor or Elder with the time and willingness to help you better understand the community. Another way is to recognize the learning that is possible through observation and silence. A family and community reveal the subtleties of their lives in powerful ways to those who take the time to watch and learn. An ongoing learner takes time for reflection and feels free to question herself. Some useful questions might be: Why am I here? What do I have to offer? Am I committed to working through the rough days — and learning from them? What have I learned about child protection practice in Indigenous communities during the past month (or year)? What aspects of my work do I find most difficult? Why? What current practice in Indigenous communities do I find oppressive and how might I work to change it? How might my own practice have been oppressive? Am I able to facilitate healing in this family and community?

Seeing yourself as a learner means accepting you can never come to the place of "knowing it all" or become an expert on Indigenous culture and community. In its place, you can be open to learn and open to revising and changing practice based on learning.

## Knowing Your Own Culture

To be effective with Indigenous peoples, a non-Indigenous child protection practitioner needs an understanding of her own culture. Recognizing and understanding that culture informs the many ways of being a parent and raising children is essential before engaging with parents across cultures. A social work student begins her social work education with ideas and values about good parenting, effective childcare and ways in which children should be taught, guided, supported and disciplined. These are based in her own experience of being parented or being a parent as well as her critical evaluation of those experiences. In other words, her feelings and thoughts about how she was raised or things she liked or didn't like about how others parented their children is a basis to articulate her own beliefs about what is good parenting. These experiences are also part of her larger culture and represent ideas about parenting and childcare.

The term "community standards" is sometimes used to describe the ideas and practices, especially within the dominant culture, that would be considered acceptable parenting and childcare within the community. It refers somewhat indirectly to how others of the same class, "race" and gender might view acceptable ways of caring for children. These views are rarely described, analyzed or looked at critically because they represent what feels "normal," "natural" and "right" to people of that culture. But are they for others? Canadians sometimes say, "I don't have a culture, I am Canadian." However, such a statement simply fails to recognize the values, beliefs and practices inherent in the culture. To begin to develop an awareness of your own culture — the one into which you were born and raised — a questioning eye and ear needs to be tuned towards it. Listening to parents, grandparents, aunts, uncles and family friends talk about parenting and childcare and watching how they practise can begin to shed a light on your own culture. The experience of living in another culture also opens eyes to ideas and practices you take for granted in your culture of origin and can encourage a re-examination of their "truth" and "rightness." At the same time, to understand parenting and childcare in the larger society, going beyond your immediate social world is essential.

Child welfare legislation, policy and standards provide documentary evidence of the dominant culture's ways of protecting children. But the ways in which child welfare professionals think and act in day-to-day life is equally powerful. A government ministry devoted to child protection investigation has a culture of its own — the largely unexamined constellation of beliefs and practices that define how social workers think and act in their day-to-day work.[3] Inherent in this are assumptions about right and wrong (or more effective and less effective) ways to parent and care for children. Informed by legislation and policy, reflective of the larger society and, undoubtedly, an expression of Euro-Canadian parenting, these ways will seem right and self-evident to those who are a part of the culture but may be foreign to those who are not.

To recognize equally acceptable ways of caring for children requires an understanding of the ways the dominant society in Canada thinks about parenting and childcare. It then demands a suspension of judgment to recognize that this is only one way and other possibilities exist. Only when there is openness to other ways of thinking about caring for children can there be willingness to understand the teachings of Indigenous peoples with respect to parenting and recognition that many of these ways have worked for generations. Simultaneously recognizing your own culture and being open to learning about another is an important precondition for effective child protection practice.

The history of social work, education and health care intervention with Indigenous peoples has been one where the culture of the colonizer has been viewed as superior to that of Indigenous peoples. The overall aim is the assimilation of Indigenous peoples into the dominant culture. To minimize oppression in child protection practice, you need to start by recognizing and understanding your own culture. This includes being aware of your strong beliefs about parenting and childcare. It also means being prepared to rethink them as you live, work and learn with Indigenous peoples.

## Power in Child Protection

No decision in child protection symbolizes more clearly the power inherent in the practitioner's role than the decision to remove a child from the family and community. It is a decision often filled with tension, uncertainty, political significance and doubt for the social worker. The decision is clear-cut in only a few cases. In most instances, it is complex and involves balancing a multiplicity of factors. The social worker's power to remove children expresses the larger society's belief that the child protection social worker is capable of judging the adequacy of a parent's care. While numerous tools and supervisory support are usually available to make this decision, less visible are the practice alternatives to removal. These rest not on the power of legislation and policy, but on the power of the social worker to recognize that a different practice approach is possible, and carry it out.

Recognizing your power starts when you work in a community and develop relationships of trust with community members and see these as essential to effective child protection practice. It continues when you recognize moments in which the family or community can be given an opportunity to plan and care for a child:

> *Something that's taken me a while to learn is to not try and deal with a client just by himself but also go to his family, bring a family meeting together or talk to the head of the family. You know I've been scolded for that before, "Why did you just, you know, do this without discussing it with, so and so is the head of our family...."*

At times, trying to balance the organizational culture of a child protection authority, with its legislation, policies and standards, and an Indigenous community's culture and history of colonization and oppression is delicate:

> *I was trying to... get the family to solve their problem and I waited... outside the house and they kept telling me, you know, someone would come out, every once in a while and tell me, swear at me and tell me to get lost and I just said, "No, I am not leaving here until the children are out of this house and into a safe house." "I'll see them into a safe house." And they eventually did, they eventually did come out. I took them to a safe house and the police never did have to attend.*

In this instance, a family was at the beginning of a process to reclaim power to protect their children with the social worker's tacit support. At other times, recognizing that an extended family or community can participate in completing a risk assessment redefines the power relationship in child protection to enable an Indigenous community to reclaim its historical power to protect children. A non-Indigenous social worker explains:

> *We're seeing the community as the parent... everybody in some way feels a connection to the child and it's important that they take part in raising that child and therefore*

*they should take part in the decisions that relate to child protection.... So when we were doing risk assessments, I was very comfortable with [asking] "Who would you like involved with the risk assessment?" When I was talking to parents and a lot of times it would be grandmothers and uncles and aunts and extended family and then we would work together on coming up with a safety plan. It would be a real group effort...*

Relationships within Indigenous communities are complex, and a non-Indigenous social worker can easily become engaged in a "power play" between one family and another or some members of a family who are in conflict with others. The overt use of child protection power in the form of parental discipline or child removal can position the social worker on one side of a community or family conflict and reinforce the culture of oppression in the community. Instead, taking the time to involve the entire family and community can lead to a different result:

*The group got together and we talked about what we can do and the group was all people who were from head families... and it was a mixture of people, age level, like we had Elders, some council members, the chief. We had some of the direct family members involved in the case, they were called in and we had some of the workers.... but each case was screened, based on what the call was and who's related and who isn't. We come together as a group and the case is disclosed and together everyone decides, well this is what I think, then the family has a chance to speak, and they usually say where they're coming from, what they are lacking and plans are made from there.*

Searching for practice alternatives to quick removal is important because the long-term consequence of removing a child are often not recognized or understood. As one non-Indigenous social worker says: "All that's looked at is the front-end problem. That is dealt with and the logistics of the long, ongoing issues that result are kind of ignored." Another social worker states:

*There are a lot of kids that are really resilient and they are better off in situations... that are difficult and [to] be with their family.... But just because a family is in crisis, or just because a family's ability to cope is being really challenged doesn't necessarily mean that the child would be better off somewhere else.*

To summarize, the most overt power that a child protection practitioner has is the power to remove children from the family and community. More subtle is the practitioner's power to develop trusting relationships in order to re-engage the family and community in the work of child protection. This demands the practitioner reject the overt use of power expressed by extensive police involvement, threats to parents or children and use of a "big stick" or demands for compliance. As this Indigenous social worker describes:

*We don't just jump in and say, "You do this, this, this and this in order to get your children back...." We ask them what it is they need because they are the best ones to see where they are at and to know what they need.*

It also demands that practitioners reject an overt reliance on policy, where they are focused on ensuring the child or family complies with the extensive rules and requirements of child protection policy and standards. Instead, practitioners need to recognize their power to practise in a way that engages the extended family and the community in the work of child protection.

Child protection practice is a complex balancing act in which the practitioner's choices and the family's and community's response to intervention interact to influence the nature of intervention. Building trusting relationships with the nuclear family, the extended family and community is essential. Indigenous and non-Indigenous practitioners are aware of disempowering, disrespectful and power-oriented practice. The act that most symbolizes this is the removal of an Indigenous child by a non-Indigenous practitioner who is a stranger to the family and is accompanied by the police. However, when practitioners develop relationships of trust with the family and community, the police are usually unnecessary, and a practice approach that is supportive, empowering and inclusive is possible.

## Suggestions for Further Reading

Haig-Brown, C. 1988. *Resistance and Renewal: Surviving the Indian Residential School.* Vancouver: Tillacum Library.

Scourfield, J. 2003. *Gender and Child Protection.* New York: Palgrave.

Walmsley, C. 2005. *Protecting Aboriginal Children.* Vancouver: UBC Press.

## About the Author

Christopher Walmsley is an associate professor at the School of Social Work and Human Service, Thompson Rivers University, where he has taught social work since 1996. He is the author of *Protecting Aboriginal Children* (UBC Press) and co-editor, with Diane Purvey, of *Child and Family Welfare in British Columbia: A History* (Detselig).

## Notes

1.  The author acknowledges the contribution of Laurel Hunt, Shirley Selski, Lise Tessier and several other Kamloops area social workers whose comments and suggestions greatly improved this chapter. One person can be a composite of several cultures.

2.  The quotations in this chapter, except where otherwise cited, are derived from interviews with Indigenous and non-Indigenous child protection social workers in British Columbia found in Walmsley 2001.

3.  Jonathan Scourfield develops this theme in *Gender and Child Protection*, his ethnographic study of British child protection social work.

## References

Bennett, M., C. Blackstock and R. De La Ronde. 2005. *A Literature Review and Annotated Bibliography on Aspects of Aboriginal Child Welfare in Canada.* Ottawa: The First Nations

Research Site of the Centre of Excellence for Child Welfare and the First Nations Child and Family Caring Society of Canada.

Bruyere, G. 2005. "A Spallumcheen Foster Child." In D. Purvey and C. Walmsley (eds.), *Child and Family Welfare in British Columbia: A History*. Calgary: Detselig.

Furniss, E. 1995. *Victims of Benevolence: The Dark Legacy of the Williams Lake Residential School*. Vancouver: Arsenal Pulp.

Haig-Brown, C. 1988. *Resistance and Renewal: Surviving the Indian Residential School*. Vancouver: Tillacum.

Hawthorn, H., C. Belshaw and S. Jamieson. 1958. *The Indians of British Columbia: A Study of Contemporary Social Adjustment*. Toronto: University of Toronto.

Johnston, P. 1983. *Native Children and the Child Welfare System*. Toronto: James Lorimer and the Canadian Council on Social Development.

MacDonald, J. 1993. *Community Study of the Spallumcheen Band Child Welfare Program: Interim Report*. Enderby, B.C.: Royal Commission on Aboriginal Peoples.

Moran, B. 1992. *A Little Rebellion*. Vancouver: Arsenal Pulp.

Royal Commission on Aboriginal Peoples. 1996a. *Report of the Royal Commission on Indigenous Peoples. Volume 1. Looking Forward, Looking Back*. Ottawa: Minister of Supply and Services Canada.

_____. 1996b. *Report of the Royal Commission on Aboriginal Peoples. Volume 2. Restructuring the Relationship*. Ottawa: Minister of Supply and Services Canada.

Stanbury, W. 1975. *Success and Failure: Indians in Urban Society*. Vancouver: University of British Columbia Press.

Walmsley, C. 2001. "The Social Representations of Child Protection Practice with Aboriginal Children." Unpublished doctoral dissertation, Laval University, Quebec.

# Chapter 6

# Métis Experiences of Social Work Practice

*Kinewesquao [Cathy Richardson]*

> *Sa prend lee famee di Michif chee shoohkschichik kispin la Nation di Michif chee shoohkawk* (We must have strong Métis families in order to have a strong Métis nation)

This chapter presents four issues in working with Métis families within an historical context of Métis land theft by the Canadian government. These include 1. decolonization, 2. dignity, 3. resistance and 4. identity theft/identity recovery. Richardson talks about decolonizing approaches to social work, which involve activating a skill set of decolonization, in contrast to the skill set of colonization, which pathologizes families and constitutes an attack on Métis family integrity. She offers a critique of the "seven steps of child removal," which result in the removal, often unnecessarily, of Métis children from their parents. Richardson invites readers to consider ways of helping Métis children and families to find "home," "belonging" and a sense of cultural identity through supporting reconnection with community. Métis cultural spaces provide an opportunity for Métis people to contest colonial history, to articulate their own experience and to share cultural stories, knowledge and strategies for resisting racism. Métis resistance consists of cultural and safety knowledge that may be construed as "signs of safety" for children and mothers. Conducting social work with Métis families means restoring what has been taken or harmed, such as dignity and children, within the larger "colonial container" of the helping professions in Canada.

Questions Addressed in This Chapter
1. How have Métis history and the history of colonial violence influenced Métis families today?
2. How have Métis people responded to colonialism and racism and protected their culture and identity?
3. How can social workers assist families to strengthen Métis culture and identity for children?
4. How can workers attend to issues of connection and belonging in their work with Métis families?

## Canada versus the Métis

Life for Métis families in Canada was disrupted by colonial violence and the white settlement program in Canada. Much of the damage remains unrepaired today. Most Métis children never received emotional support or social restoration for their trauma; many Métis families could not talk about being Métis or "wear" their cultural identity publicly without fear of racialized violence and economic sanction (Adams 1995; Dumont 1996; LaRoque 2001; Richardson and Seaborn 2002; Welch 1991). Without justice, there are many obstacles to healing. Today, at the University of Alberta, Frank Tough runs a research unit where he and his team document every section of land that was stolen by Canada from the Métis. He is creating an archive that may be helpful in a future land claim, and, when contesting empire, people need all the allies they can get.

My own family and the families of many colleagues had land stolen through the Scrip process. My great grandfather George Flett held Lot 139 in Area 62 of the St. Andrew Parish. My great grandmother Emily Anna Flett Wylie lost her home on the banks of the North Saskatchewan in Edmonton, where the parliament building stands today (what others might call prime "real estate"), due to a sudden increase in taxes and the lack of funds to pay. My colleague Sohki Aski Esquao's [Jeannine Carrière] ancestors held Lot 10 in St. Boniface. The family of Bruce Leslie Poitras, a colleague and writer of the cbc Radio Ideas program "The Wisdom of the Grandmothers," lost Lot 41 in the St. Francois Xavier Parish of the Red River Settlement. Many of the 44,000 plus Métis who reside in British Columbia today would report having land stolen by the federal government, at least if their family histories were not eradicated as well. Achimoona (the Cree word for stories) are living histories that are taken underground when it is no longer safe to speak them. Sometimes they do not emerge until they are unearthed or dreamed again many generations later. State information also tends to go missing during times of imperial take over. If you are a post-1985 adoptee or someone trying to find out the name of your Cree great grandmother, you might be surprised to find how many records have disappeared in Canada. Then again, maybe the history of Indigenous people has never been considered all that important. Indeed, new tenants are not always interested in who lived in their place before them, as long as it is theirs now.

The *Merchant Prince* (O'Keefe and MacDonald 2001) provides a deliciously unselfconscious sample of colonial discourse demonstrating the role of the federal government, elected officials, land companies and bankers in Indigenous dispossession. In fact, the book contains absolutely no account of the Métis or First Nations experience, referring to Indigenous homelands as "silent stretches of the prairies between Winnipeg and the rocky mountains... sparsely populated, a vast rolling grassland in summer and a barren white wasteland in winter" (24). In addition, they say, "this [central Canada] was a large and empty landscape crossed by a single railway line... infertile and of little use to anyone" (240). The authors document the Saskatchewan Land Company, run by capitalists Andrew Davidson (president of the Little Falls Bank in Minnesota) and Alexander MacRae. The following account explains, with pride, how these men facilitated the capitalist take over of First Nations and Métis land in Canada, leaving the Métis largely in dire poverty on road allowances or marginalized in white communities.

> McRae sunk every penny he had into the scheme that in a very short time produced great wealth and a mixture of fame, notoriety, envy and criticism as he made an unbelievable fortune in prairie real estate. The money rolled in so fast and there was so much of it that for the rest of his life, particularly during his political career, McRae was haunted by accusations that there had to be something crooked in the way the sales were handled. Nothing ever came to light, and in a manner that was characteristic of him, McRae always met the suggestions of wrongdoing head on. (70)

Fur trade historians and geographers such as Richard Mackie and Cole Harris tell us that in 1860 the Métis in what would become Manitoba constituted 90 percent of the overall population (Harris 2008; Richard Mackie, personal interview, May 25, 2008.). In 1885, the Canadian government sent an army to attack the Métis at Batoche. There, Canada killed fifty-three Métis, including a First Nations girl who happened to be in the village, while soldiers looted the village and stole the contents of people's lives (Adams 1995; McLean 1985; Payment 1985).

This military attack created the conditions for extreme anti-Métis white racism in the area, sending disenfranchised Métis away from their former communities to live in squats on the road allowances, to move West in search of safety and opportunity, or stay and go "underground" (Campbell 1995; Harris 2004; Payment 1986). This war marked an end to community safety and a sense of belonging on the earth for many Métis people. It marked the shift from extended families living together in community to lone mothers living isolated in non-Métis communities, trying to raise children while facing poverty and uncertainty.

In 1891, Métis land Scrip was issued which entitled the Métis individual to 240 acres or $240 (Goyette 2003: 75) in exchange for relinquishing their lands. Land speculators followed, paying twenty-five cents on the dollar, many of whom worked for the Saskatchewan Land Company. This company consisted of half of the federal cabinet and the brother of the federal land claims commissioner. The company later sent recruiters to Europe following famines, encouraging relocation to Canada to benefit from redistributed Indigenous lands according to the federal *Homesteader's Act*, later selling them adjacent properties for elevated cash values (Morin 1996; Tough 2002; Sprague 1980).

The Métis Scrip process has been called "The Greatest Land Swindle" ever witnessed in Canada (Manitoba Métis Federation n.d.; Goyette 2003; Tough 2002 as cited in Goyette 2003). In a pamphlet entitled "Métis Land Claim Launched," President of the Métis Nation of Saskatchewan Clem Chartier states:

> the divide and conquer technique of the scrip system was a breach of the principles of fair dealings set out in the Royal Proclamation and in other

Government dealings with the Aboriginal peoples. Scrip destroyed, rather than secured, the base of land and resources that Métis culture relied upon and which the Métis needed in order to continue to live as a distinct Aboriginal people. (Manitoba Métis Federation n.d.: no page)

Alongside the issue of land theft, Métis researcher Trish Logan (2001) has documented how the federal government used Métis children as "filler" in the residential school travesty, as a way for school and church administrators to gain more money from Indian Affairs. Jeannine Carrière (2005 and 2007), for example, has studied the issue of the violence against Métis children in child welfare foster and adoptive situations, also resulting in identity theft and attempted assimilation. As a result of these and other forms of state oppression, the Métis became what many now call "the Invisible People." Along with their land and their psychological safety, Métis identity was stolen as well. This history of violence has meant that social work, in order to be helpful, must address not only conditions of social safety but also issues of identity theft and identity restoration. The fact that much historical violence against the Métis has remained unaddressed has resulted in large numbers of Métis children and their families coming into contact with child welfare social workers in Canada.

## Key Ingredients of Social Work Practice with Métis Families

The following four issues are critical in working with Métis children and families: 1) decolonization; 2) dignity; 3) resistance; and 4) identity theft/identity recovery. Whether we as social work practitioners provide services in a Métis or non-Métis agency, it is important to orient ourselves to a framework for decolonization, to restore balance individually and collectively in terms of the historical violence against the Métis. Just as colonizers and their capitalist associates had a master plan and strategies of social engineering for Canada, so must we have a vision for a decolonized society, based on renewed commitments to social justice and honouring original responsibilities to protect Indigenous peoples against the interest of "the nation state" of Canada. Boldt reminds us that "the national interest" is an artificial construct used by the Canadian establishment "for asserting its political, economic, and social hegemony over the Canadian nation" (1993: 267). He notes that section 91(24) of the *British North America Act*, 1867, created "special federal government legislative authority over Indians and lands reserved for Indians… to protect Indians from provincial and private exploitation" (167). He then asks:

If the primary rationale for section 91 (24) was to protect Indians, why did the Canadian government use its authority under this section to cede large areas of Indian land to provinces and private enterprises without Indian consent, and far below their market value? (167)

Under section 91 of the Constitution, the Canadian government is declared to be the sole trustee of Indians and lands reserved for Indians, with the legal and moral obligation to act in the best interest of Indian peoples (268). As of 1983, this responsibility extends to Métis and Inuit peoples as well. Clearly this responsibility has not been enacted, and Indigenous populations continue to suffer due to federal abuse and neglect. This situation was made worse by two particular acts in recent history. In 1981, Pierre Trudeau "finally enticed nine of Canada's premiers to support a patriation package, and in order to make the deal he agreed to rip a positive assertion of Aboriginal and treaty rights from the Charter of Rights and Freedoms" (Morisset 1983 as cited in Hall 1986: 81) and later added that the government would support only "existing" rights, at the insistence of several premiers and in contrast to the earlier commitment entrenched in section 91 of the *British North America Act* (Hall 1986: 81). Then, in 1985, Brian Mulroney used his power "to advance some of the premiers' designs in order to diminish the minimal level of constitutional protection currently afforded to Native people" (Hall 1986: 80). When considering the question of stealing and dividing the spoils, it is important to remember that most of the labels used to divide and define the First Nations, Métis and Inuit have been imposed for the purposes of wresting land and rights away from all Native peoples. In reality, Indigenous people tend to be all related to each other or connected through a worldview and spiritual beliefs, despite particular cultural differences.

In order to envision a decolonized Canada, a first step might be to honour pre-existing diplomatic agreements, such as those signed in 1867 and the treaties signed by our Indigenous grandparents, as well as to acknowledge unceded, sovereign lands in British Columbia. The next step could be to create a new social contract, perhaps in line with "The Council of All Beings," in which the wellbeing of humans, animals and all living creatures as well as Earth herself are considered and respected.

Preserving Earth for collective use and stewardship must be part of the decolonial or post-colonial vision, but pre-established land rights must be honoured if non-Native Canadians are going to demonstrate a commitment to social justice. Métis Elder Fred Storey (personal communication, Victoria, B.C., 2005) states that Louis Riel envisioned the Métis prairie homeland (Metisoma) as a place of refuge where dispossessed and oppressed people from around the world would be invited to live with the Métis, in a community of dignity. English anti-imperialist folk singer Leon Rosselson (1981/2004) reminds us that the Earth, indeed, "should be a common treasury for all." Decolonization must be based on a spirit of living together in fairness, with equal access to resources and justice, respect between nations, imposed limits on greed and environmental destruction, and just leadership.

In Canada, a decolonized society means existing governments honouring commitments to Indigenous peoples and imposing limits on corporate capitalism, individual greed and the environmental destruction that tends to wreak havoc on Indigenous communities disproportionately. Andrea Smith (2005) makes the links between violence against Indigenous women and violence against Earth. She documents sexualized violence as a tool of genocide and reminds us of how

1. most mineral resources are situated on Indigenous land; 2. that Indigenous communities bear the brunt of the pollutants linked with resource extraction; and 3. that pollution is leading to increased rates of death, compromised reproductivity and birth defects. Certainly the inhabitants of my mother's community of Fort Chipewyan, Alberta, would concur, while they witness the premature death of community members and never-before-seen cancers and deformities in children. Cree chief Roxanne Marcel has taken this issue to the United Nations and is working to attract global attention to the plight of these dying people. The issue of contaminated water in Aboriginal communities and the toxification of mothers' breast milk also relates to the compromised safety of children. Smith believes that these forms of oppression constitute current forms of genocide.

A 1995 study conducted by Indian and Northern Affairs Canada (INAC) and referenced in a National Aboriginal Health Organization in 2002 reported that 25 percent of the water facilities in Aboriginal communities had the potential to affect (negatively) the health and safety of the community or were in need of repair (NAHO 2002: 3). They reported that those who fell through the cracks were the Métis settlements, the Métis of Labrador and the Inuit (2002: 3). For example, the 268 Métis people who reside in the community of Black Tickle have no clean water or sewage system. In a doctoral thesis, Hanraham documents:

> The local community health nurse points out that flu-like symptoms spread quickly in the community. Participants in the study said that vomiting and diarrhea are common in the community to the point where they are considered "a part of life." (2000: 2)

Decolonization means living in ways that attend to the needs of the most vulnerable first. Indigenous teachings remind us that the honour of one is the honour of all. Our level of civilization and advancement as a society surely depends on how we care for the most vulnerable amongst us, including children, seniors and those who are most marginalized by policies that promote individualism and social inequity.

While we may each have a unique vision for a decolonized society or a postcolonial world where the residue of empire has been transformed into shared resources for living in collective integrity, certain anti-oppressive principles can be identified and applied to social work practice and the helping professions. Like colonization, decolonization involves a particular skill-set that may be drawn upon to guide anti-oppressive, social justice oriented social work (see Figure 6-1). While we cannot undo the past and the brutal history of violence against every evil or selfish act that has been done to Indigenous people, we can make commitments and take steps to avoid repeating or what social justice therapist Vikki Reynolds calls "replicating" dominance (Reynolds 2006).

Attending to human dignity and its indicators can serve as a guide to a best practice with Métis families. Becoming knowledgeable about the signs of dignity and committing as a team or organization to place client dignity in the fore of all interactions will help build a strong foundation to the work. Within the bounds

## Figure 6-1 Skills for Colonization and Decolonization

| The Skill-set of Colonization | The Skill-set of Decolonization |
|---|---|
| Killing | Promoting life |
| Harming | Restoring |
| Stealing/de-resourcing | Giving back/re-resourcing |
| Lying | Working with transparency |
| Telling people what to do | Creating space for people to make their own decisions |
| Undermining | Supporting |
| Instilling fear | Creating safety |
| Isolating | Connecting |
| Ignoring | Attending with compassion |
| Separating | Re-integrating, reconnecting |
| Breaking apart | Making whole |
| Talking at | Listening |
| Humiliating | Esteeming |
| Silencing/hiding | Acknowledging, witnessing, truth-telling |
| Concealing/destroying records | Transparency in record keeping |
| Using courts and laws to facilitate theft against Indigenous people | Use courts in favour of families against the state |

of a "colonial container," the helping professions, guided by European ideology and psychological theory, have served to further marginalize and pathologize Métis children and families. This pathologizing tendency of Western psychology is represented in what Allan Wade calls "the colonial code of relations" (Todd and Wade 1994; Wade 1995; Richardson and Wade chapter 12 in this book). This code is based on assumptions built into mainstream helping as follows:

1.   You are deficient (i.e., heathen, savage, falsely conscious, submissive, passive, internally oppressed, helpless, cognitively distorted and/or afraid).
2.   I am proficient (i.e., critically conscious, expert, professional, closer to god and/or empowered by the state).
3.   Therefore I have the right (duty, sacred obligation and/or authority) to perform certain operations upon you (prescribing, advising, educating, assessing, praying, counselling, legislating and/or apprehending children) for your own good.

Obviously, this way of working humiliates families and undermines dignity, which in turn undermines the helping intervention.

Dignity and decolonization involve many of the same components. People seeking services appreciate that their right to autonomy and sovereignty is entrenched in the services they receive, even if their participation is non-voluntary, such as in the case of most parents involved with child welfare authorities. Coercion of any kind will undermine unequivocally a client's interest in co-operating with the worker and her most eloquent intervention. For example, holding a family's children "hostage" under threat of removal as inducement for the family to "address their issues" within the limited scope of a three-month temporary care order will not lead to success. Richardson and Nelson (2007) document the "Seven Steps to Child Removal" as witnessed by workers in a Métis child and family serving agency. In the context of child protection work, both parents and Métis advocates had very little influence or success in keeping families together once child protection authorities began building a case against the parents. When a worker considers parental resistance against oppression, pre-existing ability and personal knowledge about safety as assets, concepts of safety and risk become more balanced and informative to practice.

From the time child protection workers decided that the parents would not meet the goals outlined in the risk reduction plan, they often began gathering evidence against the family while engaging in concurrent planning, where the social worker plans simultaneously for reuniting the child with the parents and for removal and placement into a foster home. While child removal is a really distasteful option in the context of decolonization, there are ways of working that enhance safety for families while restoring to them some of what has been lost historically (e.g., culture, tradition, stories, identity, relationship with land). One such process is the "Islands of Safety" model for use in cases of violence in Métis and Urban Aboriginal families. This model, developed by Richardson and Wade for Métis Community Services on Vancouver Island, is based on traditional Indigenous teachings, family roles and responsibilities, and collective responsibility for safety that does not blame the mother for risk beyond her control, such as violence against her by others. This process engages extended families in the development of a safety plan for children and mothers where there is violence.

When the safety of those who are most vulnerable or "at-risk" is the central concern, safety plans can be made with family members in facilitated processes (i.e., family meetings, family group conferences, Islands of Safety and traditional processes) that are based on a collaborative approach to planning with a focus on safety. Richardson and Wade (chapter 12 in this book) have documented safety and dignity-restoring processes that are important for child welfare cases involving violence. In this work they are trying to address the inappropriate blaming of mothers in cases of paternal violence.

"Failure to protect" policies have been interpreted inappropriately in social work practice in ways that result in children being removed from mothers due to paternal violence (Strega 2006). Current child welfare practices see many mothers losing children even though they themselves have provided appropriate care to their children. Typically, the mother's resistance and safety practices have not been taken into account as strengths or capacity on risk assessments. Another important point to consider is that much recent research shows that most people who disclose violence and seek help receive negative social responses from friends, families and professionals. These responses tend to result in those people being unlikely to ever report violence again and more likely to become depressed or even suicidal (Brewin, Andrews and Rose 2000).

Social work can be a positive social response when attention is paid to the decolonizing skill-set, to the dignity of the people seeking help and to the reality that people have many strategies for resisting mistreatment and poor practice. A one-time visit may actually mean that the person has fired their worker. Clients who agree with the social worker, or even offer congratulatory praise, may have realized that they will be punished for stating their own views or preferences. As one Métis woman reminds us "being Métis means keeping your mouth shut" (Richardson 2004: 112). Resistance writer Collins (cited in Riessman 1993: 124) points out that many situations do not lend themselves to overt challenges of authority: "Resistance thinking and avoidance strategies do not attack stigma and discrimination directly, but they may be tactically necessary. Open challenge of a dominant ideology is not always possible." There are, for example, dangers in the advice giving for its recipients and there are ways people must move around advice without offending, and without taking it. James Scott (1990: 3), who writes about oppression and resistance, notes:

> The conditions facing the oppressed individual are therefore highly un-predictable. He may be granted long periods of respite from abuse but must remain mindful of the fact that he could be attacked or affronted at any time, and he must shape his public conduct accordingly. Under these conditions, domination and resistance can be said to exist in a "dialectic of surveillance and disguise."

As the Chinese proverb says, "When the grand lord passes, the wise peasant bows deeply and silently farts" (Scott 1990: v). Resistance against violence, oppression and abuses of power is ever-present. Allan Wade (1997) reminds us that "whenever persons are badly treated, they resist" (23). Métis resistance against oppression is essential to the process of identity and self-formation (see Richardson 2006). Surrounded by conditions explained earlier in this chapter, the Métis have had to negotiate and resist cultural attack and ongoing racism or social invisibility, depending on the degree of "Nativeness" in their appearance, as part of daily living.

Dignity is advanced through applying the understanding that humans are sentient beings who respond to events and diverse forms of oppression on a number of levels of their being, in ways that demonstrate pre-existing knowledge, safety awareness and attunement to detail, intelligence and personal values. However, these attributes are often conceived in individualist terms via Western psychology and must be viewed through the lens of a Métis worldview. This

## Figure 6-2 Acts of Métis Resistance

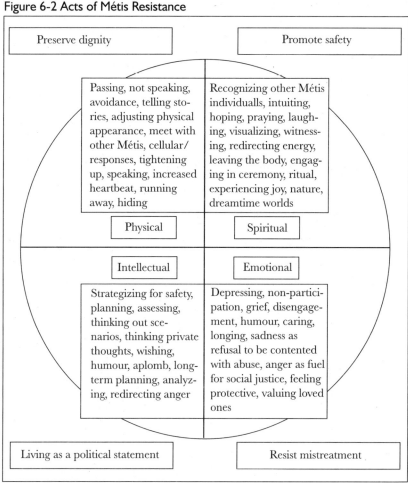

worldview or cosmology involves a strong and resilient spirit within a group or collective arrangement. Qualities such as knowledge, capacity and safety are collective rather than individual, and we understand that they must be provided by the village and the nation, not merely by the women/mothers who have been undermined by violence, patriarchy and misogyny.

Human beings, particularly those who have been most attacked and stigmatized, resist mistreatment through forms of resistance both daring and subtle. While human beings who are victimized cannot be held responsible for stopping violence due to the imbalances in power, they exercise their will and intellect in deciding how they will respond to the violent acts over time. The ways in which people contest or protest violence, often in the form of "small acts of living" (Wade 1997), attempt to preserve their dignity, promote safety and reassert a life force that has been threatened by those who abuse power. As psychologist

Erving Goffman said, "the self is a stance-taking entity" (1961: 320). James Scott documents that, under conditions of oppression, people think thoughts of resistance in what he called "the privacy of the mind" (1990: 2). Keeping important truths "underground" or hidden from the public view, in times when it is not safe to name the violence and oppression, is one form of resistance to oppression. Métis poet Andrea Menard shows us:

> I was born the privileged skin
> and my eyes are bright, bright brown.
> You'd never know there is Métis blood
> raging underground.
> Let me tell you a story about a revelation,
> it's not the colour of a nation that holds a nation's pride
> it's imagination, it's imagination inside. (2001: 32)

## Recovering from Identity Theft

Helping Métis people to recover what has been stolen in terms of their family stories, their cultural identity and their ancestral pride in the wake of white racism is an important aspect of Métis social work practice. The crux of the matter is that after 1885 many Métis families made a choice to go "underground" culturally as a resistance strategy of familial protection. Many Métis left Manitoba to areas where they would be persecuted less and perhaps have the chance of employment; for these reasons many Métis families came to B.C. Living in the coastal province has been a mixed blessing for the Métis. On one hand, because the Métis are not understood or recognized it is easier to live "under the radar" of racism. On the other hand, there is much less understanding of the Métis culture in B.C. than in the prairie provinces.

Whether it is called "passing," "keeping one's head down" or managing identity, Métis families have had to act in ways that protect their children from racism. Too often, reports on discrimination against Aboriginal people, such as in Amnesty International's (2002) "Stolen Sisters," focuses on victims and why they are targeted, rather than the problem of racialized violence, white supremacy and white racism in Canada. While there is a place for both forms of inquiry, it seems less controversial to focus on victims rather than perpetrators, because racism is both an individual and a systemic, political issue in Canada. In fact, the issue of white supremacy or ongoing colonialism is seldom identified as a current issue in Canadian politics. Henry et al. (1995) point out that Canadians are said to value equality and therefore cannot address outstanding issues of racism and oppression against Aboriginal people if it entails treating certain Canadians "unequally." This means that mainstream Canada, under current political conditions, will never accept that Indigenous people have rights that existed before Confederation that are not in the national interest (Boldt 1993) or shared with non-Indigenous Canadians. Indeed much of the violence directed at Indigenous Canadians takes place when Inuit, Métis or First Nations assert traditional rights in relation to land and earth stewardship, particularly when capitalist business interests are challenged, such as in the cases of Batoche, Oka, Gustafson Lake, Burnt Church, Sun Peaks ski development and the Bear Mountain resort in Victoria, B.C. The fact that much of the traditional Red River community lies underneath a shopping mall at "The Forks" in Winnipeg causes spiritual pain for many Métis.

Métis people form/create their sense of self by celebrating what they value and by opposing racism, oppression and exclusion in the dominant culture. While living "underground in Canada" (post-1885), and not able to live openly or speak about their own traditions, the Métis borrowed survival strategies from other cultures. One Métis man spoke of practising "aplomb," which he explained as "keeping calm in situations of danger, to prevent an escalation of danger and promote safety" (Richardson 2004: 145). "Passing," or trying not to stick out in the dominant culture meant living as though one was not Métis, in order to secure greater safety and opportunity for one's family. Métis people frequently hear Anglo Canadians talk about how immigrants should adapt to Euro-Canadian ways, something most non-Indigenous people have never done themselves. Métis people pay attention to levels of animosity and violence in language as a barometer of their psychological freedom. The Métis respond accordingly, adopting resistance tactics to promote safety, survival and optimum wellbeing. Given these conditions, poet Joanne Arnott believes that "passing is one of the very few options for survival of a mixed-race people in a virulently racist society" (1994: 59). She also states: "I am a person of mixed Native and European heritages. Fundamentally what I have inherited is a good deal of information about the various European traditions from which I come, and racist denial of the existence of my Native ancestry" (Arnott 1995: 1). A Métis research participant reports: "Prejudice is such an evil thing, and as Métis we often get it from both sides of the blanket. A feeling of never quite belonging anywhere haunts me" (Richardson 2004: 5).

It is under conditions of adversity and cultural hatred that the Métis must develop their identity. Social workers can serve as allies for people by creating safety and opportunities for Métis families to learn and live according to their cultural values within and outside of the dominant culture. The Métis, along with other Indigenous Canadians, are "at home on foreign soil," as Robert Kroetsch (1995) so eloquently puts it. On this foreign soil, or what I call the "colonial container," the Métis move between the space occupied by the dominant culture and the space occupied by First Nations, often getting lost in the middle and experiencing identity distress or what has been called "fire illness." Fire illness is the name given to Métis people who are grieving the loss of their ancestors, their cultural knowledge and their identity due to colonization and racism. When Métis families seek services from an agency, many do not know why they are grieving or living with feelings of dis-ease, alienation and what Carrière and Richardson (in press) call "a longing to belong."

Post-colonial writers identify a hybrid or "third space," as an opening or third possibility for identification beyond the two parent cultures. Homi Bhabha describes this space as a political and cultural strategy of opening a space of possibility and opportunity, "the application of a third space thinking... quite properly challenges our sense of the historical identity of culture as a homogenizing, unifying force" (1998: 184). Erving Goffman (1963) talks about the importance of oppressed people coming together to strategize and develop ways of challenging dominant or colonial ways of thinking.

Métis people experience an increased sense of wellbeing in a Métis-centred space where they are not in the margins. They experience freedom from being told that they are "not quite this or not quite that." One Métis man asked his brother, "Are you a white man with some Native blood, or are you an Indian with some white blood?" The brother pondered, said he wasn't quite sure and posed the question back to the brother. The interlocutor replied, "I'm neither, I am Métis." This example shows the kind of clarity Métis people experience when they realize that they are a nation, a tribe, that a holistic identity is possible.

Social work takes place within a larger social and political container, "the colonial container." Ojibway social worker and researcher Gord Bruyere states that "decolonization itself is contained within a larger wheel that is grinding the earth to dust" (1999: 177). I believe he is referring to a wheel of global capitalism, militarism, ecological destruction and political corruption. Within such systemic violence and injustice, there are things that individual social workers and their teams can do to assist Métis people in their efforts of strengthening and wellness. However, it is no small task, and decolonizing work often requires stealth and working under the radar of institutional constraints, particularly where services are directed or provided by the same state that continues to destabilize Indigenous people both individually and collectively

The current research on Métis identity and the importance of connection (Carrière 2005, 2007; Richardson and Nelson 2007; Richardson 2004) can guide social workers in their practice. Political issues such as funding and designation of Indigenous agencies to serve their own people are important. However, in terms of daily practice, avoiding the removal of Métis children from their community whenever possible is crucial. This can be done preventatively by supporting families, using strategies of Family Development Response and family support whenever possible. This also means recruiting Métis foster homes and providing Métis families with the resources needed to raise children, recognizing that everyone needs both financial and moral support to raise children today.

Where child removal is inevitable, cultural plans are needed to ensure that the Métis children will always know who they are and can retain or regain cultural practices. While today, social workers are required to "consider" the child's culture in planning, there may be more court challenges in future in regards to this policy. Foster parents may need both incentive and support to maintain cultural connections. Creative solutions are needed to keep children and mothers together wherever possible, such as enabling mothers to live in foster care settings with their children, particularly when the children are young or breastfeeding. Moreover, an enhanced collective responsibility for restoring the damage of colonialism and providing children with connection to land, to Earth, to animals and to cultural practice will help to keep body and spirit alive, as the decolonization wheel revolves. In the meantime, Indigenous scholar Patricia Monture-Agnus has decided that "rather than decolonizing my mind, I think I will opt for revolutioning my thoughts" (1999: 87). Perhaps, as a social work community, that is what we too will need to do in order to address more fully the challenges for Métis children and families.

## The Way Forward

When Métis people realize that they are Métis and that they can find or create Métis cultural spaces, they tend to experience a sense of relief and "coming home." Helping Métis people find their way home should be the main task of social work. This means helping families to find and reconnect with those who have been taken, those lost in the foster care system, those taken to Europe by adoption, those lying in unmarked graves away from home. The integrity of Métis individuals and communities is linked to processes of decolonization that serve to strengthen the nation and the sense of purposeful identity. The Creator gave us all a purpose on Earth. Finding that purpose is preceded by knowing who we are. From this perspective, social work is indeed work that is sacred. Above all, we must remain hopeful. Keeping hope in our hearts for a better world will pull that future towards us; otherwise we will have no map to guide us home. I am inspired by post-colonial Indian writer Arundhati Roy (2003) who reminds us: "Another world is not only possible, she is on her way. On a quiet day, I can hear her breathing."

   *Li Bon Jeu la diresyoon miyinawn, itayha chimiyouitayhtamak, li shmaen chee oushtawy-awk pour la Nawsyoon dee Michif ota dans not Piyee* (Creator provide us with direction and inspiration as we build a road for the Métis Nation in this Country). *Marsee d'twnanan* (Thank you and amen).

## Suggestions for Further Reading

Adams, H. 1995. *A Tortured People: The Politics of Colonization.* Penticton, BC: Theytus.

Graveline, F.J. 1998. *Circle Works: Transforming Eurocentric consciousness.* Halifax: Fernwood.

Lawrence, B. 2004. *"Real" Indians and Others: Mixed-Blood Urban Native Peoples and Indigenous Nationhood.* Vancouver: UBC Press.

Payment, D. 1990. *The Free People — Otipemisiwak. Batoche, Saskatchewan, 1870–* Ottawa: National Historic Parks and Sites Parks Service Environment Canada.

## About the Author

Kinewesquao [Cathy Richardson] is an instructor in the School of Social Work at the University of Victoria, in the Indigenous Specialization. She is a member of the Métis community and a co-founder of the Centre for Response-Based Practice. Her research interests include Métis identity, post-colonial counselling and promoting recovery after violence. She has worked extensively in the north in areas of recovery from residential internment and state-imposed violence on Aboriginal people. She is married, has three children and lives in Cowichan Bay, B.C.

## References

Adams, H. 1995. *A Tortured People: The Politics of Colonization.* Penticton, BC: Theytus.

Amnesty International. 2004. *Stolen Sisters: A Human Rights Response to Discrimination and Violence Against Indigenous Women in Canada.* Available at <http://www.amnesty.ca/stolensisters/amr2000304.pdf> accessed October 7, 2008.

Annett, K. 2002. *Love and Death in the Valley.* Bloomington, IN: Authorhouse.

Arnott, J. 1994. "Mutts' Memoir." In C. Camper (ed.), *Miscegenation Blues: Voices of Mixed-Race Women.* Toronto: Sister Vision.

_____. 1995. *Breasting the Waves: On Writing and Healing.* Vancouver: Press Gang.

Bhabha, H. 1998. "Cultures in Between." In D. Bennet (ed.), *Multicultural States: Rethinking Difference and Identity.* London: Routledge.

Boldt, M. 1993. "Federal Government Policy and the "National Interest." *Surviving As Indians: The Challenge of Self-government.* Toronto: University of Toronto Press.

Brethour, P. 2006. Why is Cancer Sweeping Tiny Fort Chipewyan? Toronto: *Globe and Mail*, May 22.

Brewin, C., B. Andrews and S. Rose. 2000. "Fear, Helplessness, and Horror in Posttraumatic Stress Disorder: Investigating DSM-IV Criterion A2 in Victims of Violent Crime." *Journal of Traumatic Stress* 13, 30.

Bruyere, G. 1999. "The Decolonization Wheel: An Aboriginal Perspective on Social Work Practice with Aboriginal Peoples." In R. Delaney, K. Brownlee and M. Sellick (eds.), *Social Work With Rural and Northern Communities.* Thunder Bay: Lakehead University Centre for Northern Studies.

Campbell, M. 1995. *Stories of the Road Allowance People.* Penticton: Theytus.

Carrière, J. 2005. "Connectedness and Health for First Nation Adoptees." *Paediatrics and Child Health* 10, 9 (November).

_____. 2007. "Promising Practice for Maintaining Identities in First Nation Adoption." *First Peoples Child and Family Review* 3, 1.

Carrière, J., and C. Richardson, C. In press. "A Drop of Longing: Attachment Theory, the *Indian Act* and Indigenous Children in Canada." *Passion for Action.* Regina: Prairie Child Welfare Consortium.

Collins, P.H. 1990. *Black Feminist Thought: Knowledge, Consciousness and the Politics of Empowerment.* Boston: Unwin Hyman.

Dumont, M. 1996. "The Red and White." In C. Camper (ed.), *Miscegenation Blues: Voices of Mixed Race Women.* Toronto: Sister Vision.

Goffman, E. 1961. *Asylums: Essays on the Social Situation of Mental Patients and Other Inmates.* New York: Doubleday.

_____. 1963. *Stigma: Notes on the Management of a Spoiled Identity.* Englewood Cliffs, NJ: Prentice-Hall.

Goyette, L. 2003. "The 'X' Files: By Signing Applications for Land Grants, Were the Prairie Métis Drawn into One of the Largest Property Swindles in Canadian History?" *Canadian Geographic* (March/April).

Hall, T. 1986. "Self-government or Self-delusion? Brian Mulroney and Aboriginal Rights." *The Canadian Journal of Native Studies* vi. Available at <http://www.brandonu.ca/Library/cjns/6.1/hall.pdf> accessed November 24, 2008.

Hanraham, M. 2000. *Brooks, Buckets and Komatiks: The Problem of Water Access in Black*

*Tickle*. St. John's, NL: Division of Community Health, Memorial University of Newfoundland.

Harris, C. 2004. "How Did Colonialism Dispossess? Comments from an Edge of Empire." *Annals of the Association of American Geographers* 94, 1.

_____. 2008. *The Reluctant Land: Society, Space, and Environment in Canada before Confederation.* Vancouver: UBC Press.

Henry, F., C. Tator, W. Matis and T. Rees. 1995. *The Colour of Democracy: Systemic Racism in Canada.* Toronto: Harcourt Brace.

Kelm, M.E. 1998. *Colonizing Bodies: Aboriginal Health and Healing in British Columbia.* Vancouver: UBC Press.

Kroetsch, R. 1995. "Unhiding the Hidden." In B. Ashcroft, G. Griffiths and H. Tiffin (eds.), *The Post-Colonial Studies Reader.* New York: Routledge.

LaRoque, E. 2001. "Native Identity and the Métis: Oteypaymimsuah Peoples." In D. Tara and B. Rasporich (eds.), *A Passion for Identity: An Introduction to Canadian Studies* (Fourth Edition). Toronto: Harcourt Brace/Holt.

Logan, T. 2001. *The Lost Generations: The Silent Métis of the Residential School System.* Winnipeg: Southwest Region Manitoba Métis Federation.

Manitoba Métis Federation. n.d. "Métis Land Claim Launched." Pamphlet. Winnipeg, MB: Manitoba Métis Federation.

McLean, D. 1985. *1885: Métis Rebellion or Government Conspiracy?* Winnipeg: Pemmican.

Menard, A. 2001. "The Halfbreed Blues." *Prairie Fire* 2, 3.

Monture-Agnus, P. 1999. "Considering Colonialism and Oppression: Aboriginal Women, Justice and the Theory of Decolonization." *Native Studies Review* 12, 1.

Morin, G. 1996. *The Manitoba Scrip.* Pawtucket, RI: Quinton.

NAHO (National Aboriginal Health Organization). 2002. "Drinking Water Safety in Aboriginal Communities in Canada." Available at <http://www.naho.ca/english/publications/ReB_water_safety.pdf> accessed May 17, 2008).

Neckoway, R., K. Brownlee and B. Castellan. 2007. "Is Attachment Theory Consistent with Aboriginal Parenting Realities?" *First Peoples Child and Family Review* 3, 20.

O'Keefe, B., and I. MacDonald. 2001. *Merchant Prince: Alexander Duncan McRae.* Victoria, BC: Heritage House.

Payment, D. 1985. "The Métis Homeland: Batoche in 1885." *NeWest Review* 10, 9.

_____. 1986. "Batoche after 1885: A Society in Transition." In F.L. Barron and J.B. Waldram (eds.), *1885 and After: Native Society in Transition.* Regina: University of Regina, Canadian Plains Research Centre.

Reynolds, V. 2006. "Supervision of Solidarity. Notes on the Intersections of Theory/Practice." Presentation in Healing Responses workshop, Victoria, B.C.

Richardson, C. 2004. "Becoming Métis: The Relationship between the Sense of Métis Self and Cultural Stories." Unpublished doctoral dissertation, University of Victoria.

_____. 2006. "Métis Tactical Resistance to Colonization and Oppression." *Variegations* 2.

Richardson, C., and B. Nelson. 2007. "A Change of Residence: Government Schools and Foster Homes as Sites of Forced Aboriginal Assimilation." *First Peoples Child and Family Review* 3, 2.

Richardson, C., and D. Seaborn. 2002. "Working with Métis Children and their Families." *The BC Counsellor* 24, 2.

Riessman, C. 1993. *Narrative Analysis.* Newbury Park: Sage.

Rosselson, L. (1981/2004). "The World Turned Upside Down" [Recorded by L. Rosselson and R. Bailey]. On *Songs of Life from a Dying British Empire* [CD]. Washington, DC: Smithsonian Folkways Recordings/Paredon Records. Lyrics available at <http:www.

bilderberg.org/land/diggers.htm> accessed December 2008.

Roy, A. 2003. "Confronting Empire." Speech presented at the World Social Forum in Porto Alegre, Brazil, January 27.

Scott, J. 1990. *Domination and the Arts of Resistance: Hidden Transcripts*. New Haven: Yale University Press.

Smith, A. 2005. *Conquest: Sexual Violence and American Indian Genocide*. Cambridge, MA: South End Press.

Sprague, N.N. 1980. "Government Lawlessness in the Administration of Manitoba Land Claims, 1870–1887." *Manitoba Law Journal* 10, 4.

Strega, S. 2006. "Failure to Protect? Child Welfare Interventions When Men Beat Mothers." In R. Alaggia and C. Vine (eds.), *Cruel but Not Unusual: Violence in Canadian Families*. Waterloo: Wilfrid Laurier University Press.

Todd, N., and A. Wade. 1994. "Domination, Deficiency and Psychotherapy." *Calgary Participator* Fall.

Tough, F. 2002. "Putting the Métis Back on the Map: An Historical Geography of the Métis Nation 1870–1901." Edmonton: University of Alberta.

Turnbull, P. 2006. "British Anatomists, Phrenologists and the Construction of the Aboriginal Race." *History Compass* 5, 1.

Turnell, A., and S. Edwards. 1999. *Signs of Safety. A Solution and Safety Oriented Approach to Child Protection Casework*. New York: WW Norton.

Wade, A. 1995. "Resistance Knowledges: Therapy with Aboriginal Persons Who Have Experienced Violence." In P. Stephensen, S. Elliott, L. Foster and J. Harris (eds.), *A Persistent Spirit. Canadian Western Geographical Series*, 31.

_____. 1997. "Small Acts of Living: Everyday Resistance to Violence and Other Forms of Oppression." *Contemporary Family Therapy* 19.

Welch, C. 1991. "Voices of the Grandmothers: Reclaiming a Métis Heritage." *Canadian Literature* 131.

## Appendix 6-1 Seven Steps to Removing Aboriginal Children

1. The Aboriginal child is said to be "special needs."

2. The mother/parent is assigned a diagnosis in accordance with the Diagnostic and Statistical Manual of Mental Disorders IV.

3. An expert (psychologist) is called in to develop a report, often out of any cultural or ecological context.

4. The report confirms that because the child is "special needs" s/he requires a caregiver with specialized expertise; because the parent has a diagnosis they are clearly not the one to raise the child.

5. The mother/parent's visits are deemed to cause grief for the child and are thus "attenuated," the relationship with the new caregivers becomes the focus.

6. The diminished connection between the parent and the child is then blamed on the mother.

7. The child is then taken into permanent care of child welfare authorities and placed in a foster residence while adoption is considered; parental rights are terminated.

*Source: Richardson and Nelson 2007.*

# Chapter 7

# What Parents Say

## Service Users' Theory and Anti-Oppressive Child Welfare Practice

*Gary Dumbrill and Winnie Lo*

This chapter shows how service users' theory can enable workers to better understand and collaborate with clients in developing anti-oppressive intervention strategies. Service users' theory reflects the knowledge that clients have about their own needs and about the ways these needs can best be met. We contend that listening to such recommendations is the starting point of anti-oppressive child welfare practice. Drawing on the views of 125 parents who have received Canadian child welfare intervention, recommendations are made for the ways to improve child welfare services. These recommendations include workers learning to hear what parents have to say despite the societal and institutional pressures that attempt to disregard their opinions and perspectives, and also workers learning to respect parents receiving child protection intervention and to consider their opinions not only regarding casework plans but also in relation to the ways child protection services are designed and delivered. As well, the recommendations include a suggestion that child welfare service providers share power with parents by enabling them to develop a service users association or union that speaks on behalf of parents' collective interests as a service user group.

Questions Addressed in This Chapter
1. What is service users' theory and why is it crucial in developing anti-oppressive child welfare services?
2. What causes service users' perspectives, particularly the perspectives of parents receiving child protection intervention, to be ignored by social workers and policymakers?
3. What do parents say social workers should do when delivering child welfare intervention?

Service users' theory emerges from the common knowledge that clients and communities have about the problems they face and about the social work services they receive. There is a slow but growing recognition that service users' knowledge has crucial importance (Beresford 2000, 2001). One of the most significant strides in recognizing this occurred in the U.K. when the disabled peoples movement coined the phrase, "nothing about us without us" (Beresford 2000). This movement made it clear that there was something inherently oppressive about social workers making decisions about people without their participation. There is now a growing recognition in the U.K. that not only disabled people, but other client groups too, must have a say in the way the services that they receive are designed and delivered (Beresford and Croft 2004). Social work in Canada, while not as advanced as the U.K. in this regard, is beginning to pay closer attention to service users' knowledge (Dumbrill 2003, 2006a; Gorlick 1995). The majority of those receiving social work service experience social exclusion, which is a process operating through power inequalities along lines of race, gender, class, physical ability, sexual preference, sexual identity, geography and so on through which groups of people are disenfranchised and denied a voice and life chances. Because social work clients tend to lack voice in society, the starting point for anti-oppressive practice (AOP) is to develop service users' knowledge, through which social work clients can gain a voice in shaping the services they receive (Dumbrill 2003). Indeed, the premise of AOP is that social exclusion causes, or at the very least compounds, the personal troubles faced by the majority of social work clients. As a result it would be contradictory for social workers and policymakers, who are striving to be anti-oppressive, to exclude service users from having a voice in service delivery. Indeed, if lack of voice is a part of the oppression that service users face, then social workers failing to hear their voices can only worsen that oppression.

As well as being vital to hear service users' voice for these structural reasons, it is also important for reasons of efficiency. Clients have an expert understanding of their own needs and they often have lived experience of the programs and social work approaches that attempt to meet these needs. Consequently the most obvious way for social workers to find out how they can be helpful to service users is to pay attention to what they say.

Our research, therefore, gathers the knowledge clients have about their needs and hears their ideas about how those needs can best be met. We then help clients consolidate this knowledge into "service users' theory." We develop service users' theory in the Canadian context. Our work focuses specifically on the views and perspectives of parents receiving child protection intervention. We use the term "parent" to refer to a child's primary caregivers — these can be grandparents, older siblings, friends or family members — anyone defined by a province's child protection legislation as a parent. We realize that the voices of children are not reflected here. Our focus on parents is not because we consider their perspectives to be more important than those of children, but because we believe that where possible the preferred way to serve children is to help their parents. The process of helping parents starts by understanding their perspectives.

The client's voice is important at all levels of intervention and policy development. At the micro level, the child protection worker hearing and understanding the perspective of the parent they are working with is the place where effective intervention begins. At the macro level, hearing the collective voice of parents provides knowledge that is essential in developing effective policies and programs. Yet, despite the benefits of hearing what parents have to say, their voices tend to be missing in much child welfare practice and policy.

## Client Voice: A Needed Perspective

The client's perspective should be the starting point of social work intervention. If we are serving children by helping their parents, this means listening to those parents. This micro starting point can cause ideological tensions for AOP-oriented workers, who see a need to place emphasis on the larger macro issues that contribute to family troubles. Micro practice, with its clinical focus on individual functioning, can easily lose sight of the broader social context and can thereby blame individuals for problems that have a political cause. A competent caseworker, however, will deliver clinical intervention while also identifying the broader political origins of personal troubles. It is important that an AOP-oriented worker have such clinical skills because most parents receiving child protection intervention do not have the luxury of waiting for political remedies to social ills, but instead need immediate strategies to get through the next day safely and with their families intact. In these circumstances parents do not need a worker to explore and explain the ways that they are oppressed — most parents are already very well aware of the inequalities they face — instead they need fast practical and sometimes emotional help to cope with the family and personal consequences of that oppression. The AOP-oriented child protection worker, therefore, must bring a sense of social justice and an astute political analysis to intervention, and must also bring an array of practical micro intervention skills. These micro skills begin with the worker understanding the client's perspective. As workers we must, "understand from our clients' point of view, the troubles and frustrations that bring them to us, what gives them hope, the resources that sustain them" (Pilsecker 1994: 447).

Hearing a parent's perspective shows concern for them and treats them with respect, and it also starts intervention from the place where effective practice begins. Grasping how a parent understands the issues they face is the means through which child protection workers develop congruence between their and the parents' views of the problems that cause the need for intervention. Workers and parents may not be able to develop exactly the same understanding of the problem, but congruence does not refer to identical perspectives, instead it refers to some level of overlap between views (Platt 2007). Of course workers do not need congruence because they have the power to take unilateral action to protect children regardless of a parent's views or wishes. Yet if workers can achieve congruence, this gives them access to the most powerful intervention tool known to social work, the worker-client alliance.

Alliance relies on the development of a shared understanding between the worker and client about the problems intervention needs to address. The power of this alliance cannot be overstated; Marziali (1988) calls it "the glue" that cements constructive casework relationships. In child protection work, alliance and the parent-worker collaboration that flows from it are directly related to children remaining safe (Platt 2007; Trotter 2004). To unlock the power of alliance, the child protection worker must start by understanding the perspective of the parents they are working with (Farmer and Owen 1995).

Just as intervention needs to begin by hearing parents' perspectives, so does intervention on a macro level. Macro social work, with its focus on problems and remedies at societal and political levels, is more closely associated than micro practice with the structural concerns of AOP. Unless workers start macro intervention by hearing client perspectives, they risk imposing their own political agendas on service users. Indeed, child welfare social work has had a long history of imposing oppressive regimes on parents and their children. The residential school system and the sixties scoop (Downey 1999), the ways practice "manufactures bad mothers" by blaming women for abuse and neglect (Swift 1995) and the ways poverty is framed by child protection workers as an individual family problem rather than a social issue (Dumbrill 2003; Lindsey 1994) are all political means through which the child protection system has oppressed families. Of course modern AOP-oriented social workers may claim that they have political insights into the remedies that parents and families need; yet this is the exact claim their predecessors made (Dumbrill 2003). No work can be truly libratory as long as social workers speak for the oppressed rather than with them. As Strega (2007: 68–69) explains by citing Lena Dominelli, "If child welfare is to be transformed so it does not oppress, it is essential to understand how those it oppresses consider it to oppress, and to understand the changes they believe are necessary for it to become anti-oppressive." This work, therefore, begins by hearing service users' perspectives.

Despite the need to hear parents, their voices are rarely heard. On both micro and macro levels the perspectives of parents receive little social work attention (see, for example, Chen 2005; Dumbrill 2003, 2006b; Kellington 2002). At a casework level parents' voices are hardly heard, especially over the past ten years in provinces such as Ontario and B.C., where there has been a growing expectation that workers police parents rather than hear them (Dumbrill 2006b; Parada 2004). At a program and policy level the voices of families receiving child welfare services rarely shape the way help is provided; instead it is directed by the perspectives of expert policymakers who have studied the problems of families. But if the views of parents are so important, why are their perspectives missing?

## Client Voice: A Missing Perspective

Foucault explains that when one form of knowledge is more or less recognized than another, it has less to do with the validity of that knowledge than with power (Foucault 1995). Foucault, who sees power in every construction of reality, considers the production of knowledge to be inextricably linked to the power relations that underlie social and political processes (Foucault 1995). This means that service users' perspectives are ignored not because their knowledge lacks validity, but because service users lack power. The emergence of service users' knowledge in the U.K. is a case in point. During the late 1980s and early 1990s, service users' groups (such as people with disabilities, psychiatric patients and people with HIV/ AIDS) gained a voice not because they convinced social workers and policymakers that their knowledge had value, but because they organized themselves into political movements to gain a say in policy decisions that affect them. It was, however, not just the lobbying of service users that brought this change; it was also because this occurred at a time when the ideological and political climate was open to listening to service users' views (Beresford 2000). In Foucault's (1995) words, this is a "regime of truth," in which the recognition of certain forms of knowledge mirrors the dynamics of power relations within the larger society.

Despite some service user groups gaining a voice, parents who receive child welfare intervention mostly remain unheard. These parents lack the power to be heard not only because, like other service users, they occupy mostly marginalized social locations, but also because being a child protection client brings its own unique brand of marginalization — stigma (Chen 2005; Colton et al. 1997; Swift 1995). The stigmatization of service users has its roots in the Poor Laws, particularly the 1834 *Poor Law Amendment Act*, which introduced the practice of making those receiving social assistance who were not sick or infirm "less eligible" than other members of society through the use of workhouse regimes and other forms of disenfranchisement. Through such measures, Poor Laws deliberately marginalized and stigmatized able-bodied adults receiving aid. This brutish treatment was undertaken in the belief that it would motivate the poor to overcome their "moral failings," which governments, policymakers and the societal elite at the time thought was the root cause of poverty and other social ills (Fraser 1973). These social policies failed service recipients because their need for assistance did not usually result from their personal failings but from social and political failings at structural and economical levels (Fraser 1973). The stigma they created for service recipients by these laws remains, particularly for parents receiving child welfare intervention, who face not only the general stigma of being a social work client, but the additional stigma of receiving intervention as a result of allegedly abusing or neglecting their children (Scholte et al. 1999). Indeed, it is hard to think of a service users' group that faces more stigma than parents who allegedly abuse their children.

Stigma prevents parents from being heard and hinders workers' ability to listen. We tend to think of oppression as a top down relation in which a more powerful party oppresses a less powerful party. But Mullaly (2002) reminds us of a horizontal and more subtle dimension to oppression that is just as potent. Quoting Gil, Mullaly (2002: 27) explains that once oppression is "integrated into a society's institutional order and culture, and into the individual consciousness of its people through socialization, oppressive tendencies come to permeate almost all relations." Likewise the historical social stigma attached to being a service user shapes attitudes and human relations without people even being aware of it — this is because stigma operates on a relational level. In other words, a person or a group of people gets stigmatized not necessarily because they possess specific characteristics, but by the transfer of attitudes and beliefs about the stigmatized group through human interaction (Goffman 1973). Such stigma works like a contagious virus — consequently if one works long enough in a work culture that habitually sees parents in an unfavourable light, one begins to view them through that light as well. The process of stigmatization in the context of child welfare is one in which the perceived deficiency of parents is institutionalized and transacted through human interactions so that it becomes hegemonic, which means that the belief about the deficiency of parents receiving child welfare services becomes an unquestioned norm (Hoare 1990). Under such norms, denying parents basic courtesies of civil human interaction is regarded as "natural," and the suggestion that they should have a significant say in the service they receive appears unnatural.

## Hearing What Service Users Say

Even if workers and policymakers listen to parents, their ability to hear will be constrained by prevailing social attitudes and power relationships. As long as parents who are child welfare users lack power, their views will carry little weight. Attempts to hear what parents have to say must also include attempts to enable them to speak with a collective voice.

Our research examines and attempts to give voice to parents' perspectives.[1] We discuss what parents say from three in-depth studies of the views of parents receiving child protection intervention. In total 125 parents participated in these studies. Of the themes to emerge, we discuss three that we consider to be the most important messages parents give to workers attempting to "walk this path together" with parents and deliver intervention from an AOP perspective: 1) treat us with respect; 2) we need a service users association or union; and 3) we want what is best for our children — but we are not sure if you do.

## Treat us with Respect

What do parents think the most important thing is for child welfare providers to do? It is to treat them with respect. We invited Ontario parents who had considerable experience of receiving child protection services to write from their veteran child protection service users' perspective a guide for parents newly receiving intervention.[2]

The study builds theory and knowledge for the benefit of parents, not for the benefit of service providers. In the process of this research many of the things that parents shared have implications for service providers. The core category to emerge, which links all the themes with relevance to service providers together, was the request by parents to treat them with respect. Simple as that request may seem, it proves to be an important factor for the way child protection services are delivered. Few parents, in this and other studies, report good experiences of intervention. Parents' perceptions of intervention being good or bad did not seem to hinge on the events that took place in a case, such as child removal or attending court, but on whether they perceived their worker treating them with respect through these processes. Respect is, of course, already a core social work principle, but our studies showed that parents felt that this value was missing from the intervention they received. Social work, especially social work from an AOP perspective, cannot be undertaken appropriately without conveying respect to clients.

Parents perceived respect in various forms. These ranged from the worker's attitude, as in parents feeling they were respected as fellow human beings, to workers sharing power, as in parents feeling informed and included in decision-making and planning. Parents perceived a lack of respect in five forms: being judged, being harmed by intervention, being kept in the dark, being misrepresented and having power used arbitrarily over them. A mother described feeling judged and emotionally harmed by intervention:

*[They were] degrading you to a point you feel like you are nothing; I'm a "bad mother"... [The workers] sit there to degrade you and you try to get ahead and to be a better person and they belittle you and it's wrong.*

Another mother described feeling kept in the dark about intervention processes as well as being misrepresented, and on the basis of that misrepresentation having power arbitrarily used over her by workers:

*And where do they [Children Aid Society (CAS)] have the right to make decisions about us... without talking to us? "Oh, we've decided that your partner is not allowed to see your son." What do you guys get this information from? How did you make that decision? By never even talking to him... how do you make that decision?*

These themes capture what parents perceive as a lack of respect: the denial of basic courtesies, treatment and the rights that they are due as human beings. Even if worker believe that they do treat parents with respect, the fact that most parents *do not believe* this to be so demands attention. Additionally, in child welfare, disrespectful acts towards parents can easily go unnoticed and unchallenged because the long standing social stigma attached to child welfare service recipients has created an environment in which it is not unusual to think less of a parent receiving intervention and to deny them basic human courtesy. Given such a climate workers can sometimes show disrespect to a parent without questioning or even realizing it. Perhaps, therefore, the perception by parents that they are not afforded respect by workers is not far off. Either way, the message from parents, "treat us with respect," needs to be heard and responded to in such a manner that this fact or perception is changed.

Equally noteworthy are parents' reactions to feeling that they are not respected. We found three major reactions by parents: negative emotions, such as anger and fear; mistrust; and coping strategies. We consider these emotions to be negative because they are not conducive to honest, open and trusting working relationships and can result in intervention occurring at a predominantly superficial level. Of all the negative emotions, anger was one of the most common:

*I'd agreed [to my child going into care] for a weekend and that weekend turned out to be six months. So you know my anger started right off the bat because I thought I was being manipulated. So, I say it was crazy, crazy.*

Fear was another common negative emotion. A participant explained how fear prevents parents from engaging with intervention:

*Fear kept that [genuine problem solving] from happening. Parents are so worried continually that they never really engage in the process.*

Mistrust refers to parents' cautious and suspicious attitudes towards their workers and child protection agencies. These lead to superficial responses:

*You know not to trust any of them [workers] because they can be all nice to you to try and get you to admit stuff and all of a sudden it comes out against you... with me, it's still the smiley face that I don't trust as far as I can throw them.*

*Basically you just put on a smiley face when they show up and that's all you do. You don't explain nothing to them. "Everything is good." You don't admit nothing to them. "Yup, everything's great." That's what it is, my little happy face.*

*At times you feel like you are manipulating them and not being honest and truthful, but you learned that you have to do that to get them out of your life.*

These three reactions are indications of disengagement. Yatchmenoff (2005: 86) defines engagement as "positive involvement in a helping process," which is consistent with worker-client alliance discussed earlier. Yatchmenoff found that the presence of pervasive negative feeling, of "extreme lack of trust in the intentions of the agency and agency personnel," and compliance behaviours defined as "going through the motion" are indications of disengagement (2005: 86).

It can be seen, therefore, that when parents feel they are treated with disrespect it sets off a series of reactions that prevents engagement and promotes superficiality in the intervention process. For intervention to be effective there is a need for workers to communicate respect to parents, not only for reasons of effectiveness; showing respect is fundamental in any human relationship. Being treated with human dignity does not need to be earned but belongs equally to all by virtue of their very existence as human beings. The request, "treat us with respect," is a message that all child protection workers need to heed.

## We Need a Support Group or Union

The next most striking message to emerge from parents is that they need a service users' association or union.[3] Parents said that they needed help through the intervention process — not necessarily from social workers — but help from other parents who had been through intervention themselves. One mother explained how a friend who had previously received intervention helped her to understand that she needed to make changes in the way she parented. Because this friend had helped her in ways that her worker could not, this mother thought that all parents should have some form of peer support when involved with child protection services:

> You [need] a support system in place, as soon as something happens there should be somebody there for parents. I wouldn't have even gone to counseling unless I had somebody there to say "you're obviously confused."

Parents said that friends and allies were needed not only to help them reflect on the personal changes they may need to make, but also to help them cope with the stress of intervention. Parents explained that the stress of receiving child protection intervention can push a parent into a position of not being able to cope or manage. Recognizing that intervention brings its own stresses, some parents were organizing peer support:

> I've started meetings with me and some other ladies, a parent group and so forth. I've heard this kind of thing before where if you're given some kind of support right away explaining how it works, who can help you, what you need to do, it will go so much more smoothly.

Parents suggested that peer support was so important that its organization should not be left to chance; the child protection system itself should assist parents in establishing an association. Initially these associations could be developed by parents with the help of child protection agencies, but eventually they would operate alongside but independently from them. The message from parents to service providers is:

> We need something that goes with CAS [intervention], a group of people [parents] that have been through it.

Parents also suggested that their association provide peer helpers to attend interviews and investigations with them. As well they suggested that parent representatives meet with agency managers to address concerns that parents have about service delivery on a regular basis — almost like a union meets with managers. Parents began to think of how their service users' association or union would function. They considered associations being organized at each agency with its own elected executive. They also suggested that once established at local agency levels these unions or associations would interconnect to form provincial and national bodies that would represent members at social work conferences and at all levels of government. Although beginning with parents receiving child protection services, the idea of a service users' union could then be taken up by other social work client sectors so that all service users could eventually access a voice through union-like mechanisms.

We have approached a number of child protection agencies with this recommendation and although some are interested, so far none have taken up the idea. We suspect that if we suggested that parents just support each other on a micro-level, the idea might be more readily adopted, but parents accused of child abuse and neglect having an association or a union along with peer support gives them access to collective power and falls outside the boundaries of established child protection practice. The idea, however, is not that radical because it is exactly the same as a foster parents' association. Most child welfare agencies have associations for their foster parents and many allow foster parents being investigated for allegations of abuse to have another foster parent with them to provide support. As well as representing members at a local agency level, by linking with other foster parents' associations, they also represent members at provincial, territorial and national levels. There have even been times when associations have acted like a union by advising members not to take new place-ments as a result of rate or support disputes. If it is appropriate for foster parents to have an association then why not parents? We suggest that the reason this idea is not taken up may have its roots in the stigma and associated attitudes toward parents receiving child protection intervention or perhaps a fear by agencies of sharing power with clients.

There are some concerns that need addressing if service users' groups are to be developed. A number of groups have arisen, mostly on the Internet, rep-resenting or claiming to represent parents who are child protection service users. Some of these groups appear to have broad and active networks of participants who are interested in improving the ways services are delivered, while others appear to be organized around efforts to resist any form of state involvement in family life, including efforts to protect children from abuse and neglect. Can we be sure that if service users' groups are formed, they will be populated by parents wanting to help improve the ways children are protected rather than undermine these efforts? Of course we cannot be sure, but it seems inappropriate to deny people a voice because we fear about how they will use it. In our research, none of the parents we interviewed suggested that child protection services should not be offered to families; most said that child protection agencies do an important job and almost all had constructive ideas they wanted to share about how these services could be improved. A service users' association would provide parents with opportunities to share those ideas.

## We Want the Best for Our Children — but Do You?

The final message comes in two parts. First, parents usually want the best for their children and second, parents are not sure that child protection services want the same. These messages were stated most clearly in a photovoice project we recently undertook with refugee parents.[4] Refugees felt that child protection services did not understand their unique family needs.

In the case of refugees, by bringing their children safely to Canada, these parents had succeeded in a remarkable child protection process of their own. A mother explained, "We did not bring our children to Canada to abuse or neglect them." One mother who escaped a war zone explained, "Do you know how hard it was to bring my child here? And now you think I am going to abuse her?" Such remarks emerged from experiences these parents had of child protection workers questioning their ability and willingness to provide for their children. Parents said that instead of starting with these negative assumptions, workers should begin with the premise that parents care about their children. A mother explained that the starting premise should be: "Parents want the best for their children, even if they fight." Parents said that, beginning with this premise, child protection workers should explain to the parent the worries that have arisen about their children and should then invite the parent to "work with them" to address these concerns. This practice recommendation incorporates the notion of "respect" for parents, which we referred to earlier. This respect and starting point is, of course, characteristic of what is already recognized as good social work practice. Unfortunately many of the parents in our research, not just in our study with refugees but in other studies too, said that they had never experienced this type of practice.

Refugee parents also made it clear that they were not going to stop protecting their children from danger just because they were now in Canada. Parents perceived several risks to their children in Canada; many lived in neighborhoods where drugs, gangs and guns presented significant dangers. Given the track record of refugee parents in protecting their children from significant danger before they arrived in Canada, it is not surprising that they believed that they and other parents in their communities were the best qualified people to protect their children. Of course these parents also recognized that sometimes parents do not know or do what is best for their children; in such instances, parents felt that help should be provided through collaboration between their community and child protection agencies.

Refugee parents, however, were not entirely convinced that social workers always had the best interests of children in mind. Several of the parents said that children in their community had been told by child protection workers that they had the legal right to leave home when they were sixteen years old. Not just refugee parents, but participants in our other studies also made this observation. Parents could not understand how any child could properly care for themselves at this age, especially in some of the dangerous neighbourhoods in which they lived. Refugee parents explained that in their communities there was a tradition and hope that children would remain at home until they had finished university education or had completed some other means of preparing for independence. To parents, social workers telling children that they could, and at times encouraging them, to leave home at sixteen indicated either a profound disregard about that child's wellbeing or an extremely low expectation for that child's future. Parents, therefore, were not convinced that child protection social workers or the systems they worked within always acted or gave advice that was in the best interests of children.

Despite concerns about the ways child protection agencies operated, many of the parents were keen to help these agencies improve their services. The refugee parents involved in this study have already made presentations at undergraduate child welfare classes and are preparing exhibits of their photographs and stories to help policymakers and service providers understand how to work with their communities. As well, these parents helped in the review and preparation of this chapter. These parents (and others like them) are willing to give direct assistance to the child protection agencies serving their communities. Some told of how they offered to become foster parents, particularly for children in their communities. Others had offered to help agencies by delivering training in the cultural competence skills required to work successfully with refugee parents. Indeed, some of the parents in our study, who were community leaders, offered to meet with child protection agencies to develop protocols when working with parents who are refugees. They were prepared to offer an array of supports to workers as well as support and guidance to parents who bump up against child protection services. As yet, few of these offers of assistance have been taken up.

## Service Users and Child Welfare Systems

What are the lessons of these service users' perspectives for the child protection workers who want to "walk with" parents through the intervention process in an anti-oppressive manner? The first lesson is to listen to parents. We have demonstrated how hearing the voice of the service user is not only the beginning point of effective intervention, it is also integral to working anti-oppressively. Most of the parents we work with face problems that are caused or compounded by the marginalized positions they occupy within society. If their lack of voice is integral to the difficulties they face, then our not hearing them makes us a part of the problem rather than the solution.

The next lesson is that service users' voices often go unheard because of the stigma and deep-seated societal attitudes toward service users, particularly child protection service users. Workers, therefore, have to make special efforts to hear their voices and not be prevented from doing so by the dominant discourse comprised of attitudes that stigmatize and silence service users' voices.

Another lesson is that when parents are heard, the ideas they suggest are usually practical and viable. Indeed, the recommendations made by parents in our studies, that they should be treated with respect, that they need a support group and the representation of an association or union and the declaration that intervention should begin with the assumption that parents want the best for their children, are all important ideas that require urgent attention by service providers.

The additional revelation that parents are unsure if child protection agencies truly act in the best interests of children also requires attention. The lesson here is that considerable repair work is needed in the relationship child protection agencies have with the parents of the children they attempt to protect. We contend that when this relationship is improved children will be more effectively protected. To improve this relationship, service providers must pay more attention to service users' perspectives. Indeed, it is only through a dialogue between those providing and receiving service, that workers and clients truly walk through the intervention process together.

## Suggestions for Further Reading

Dumbrill, G.C. 2006. "Ontario's Child Welfare Transformation: Another Swing of the Pendulum?" *The Canadian Social Work Review* 23, 1/2.

Jones, J. 1994. "Child Protection and Anti-Oppressive Practice: The Dynamics of Partnership with Parents Explored." *Early Child Development and Care* 102.

Strega, S. 2007. "Anti-Oppressive Practice in Child Welfare." In D. Baines (ed.), *Doing Anti-Oppressive Practice: Building Transformative Politicized Social Work*. Halifax: Fernwood.

## About the Authors

Gary C. Dumbrill is an associate professor at McMaster University School of Social Work. His teaching and research focus on anti-racism and anti-oppressive social work practice. His research examines the perspectives of service users and develops service users' theory, particularly through the use of participatory action research and photovoice methods. Before moving into academia, Gary worked in the British and Canadian child welfare systems in positions ranging from front-line worker to interim director of services. Before becoming a social worker Gary was a bricklayer.

Winnie Lo is a researcher currently involved in several projects at McMaster University School of Social Work and a project at McMaster Health Sciences. Winnie specializes in qualitative research methods, especially grounded theory, action research and photovoice. She is involved in two of the three research projects mentioned in the chapter. Before becoming a researcher, Winnie worked briefly as a child protection worker but did not fit in because she found it difficult to comply with the dominant discourse of "bad parents" that pervaded the Ontario child protection system at that time.

## Notes

1.  We use grounded theory, which enables theoretical ideas to emerge from the process of undertaking research (Glaser 2002; Miller and Fredericks 1999), to help parents consolidate their knowledge into theory, and participatory action (Park el al. 1993) to help them gain a voice in policy and program development.

2.  This study began in 2004 and is now in its concluding stages. So far ninety-six parents have taken part in fourteen focus groups and eighteen individual interviews. This study is supported by an award from the Canadian Social Sciences and Humanities Research Council.

3.  This finding initially emerged in an earlier SSHRC funded study Gary undertook between November 2000 and August 2001 into the views parents had of intervention. Eighteen parents took part in this study; seventeen from Ontario and one from B.C. (a larger sample from B.C. was planned but was abandoned due to logistic and recruitment problems).

4.  Beginning in mid-2007 we met with eleven refugee parents in a focus group. They had direct or indirect (through close relatives and friends) experience of Canadian child welfare services. Nine were women and two were men; eight came from West Africa and three from Southwest to Central Asia. Three arrived in Canada as landed

immigrants, but the process they followed in leaving their former homelands caused them to regard themselves as refugees. We asked participants to describe in words and photographs the parenting issues they face in Canada, the ways they bump up against child protection services and the information that child protection service providers need to better understand about them to improve service delivery.

## References

Beresford, P. 2000. "Service Users' Knowledges and Social Work Theory: Conflict or Collaboration?" *British Journal of Social Work* 30.

_____. 2001. "Service Users, Social Policy and the Future of Welfare." *Critical Social Policy* 21, 4.

Beresford, P., and S. Croft. 2004. "Service Users and Practitioners Reunited: The Key Component for Social Work Reform." *British Journal of Social Work* 34.

Chen, X. 2005. *Tending the Garden of Citizenship: Child Saving in Toronto, 1880s–1920s.* Toronto: University of Toronto Press.

Colton, M., M. Drakeford, S. Roberts, E. Scholte, F. Casa and M. Williams. 1997. "Social Workers, Parents, and Stigma." *Child and Family Social Work* 2.

Downey, M. 1999. "Canada's 'Genocide.'" *Maclean's,* April 26.

Dumbrill, G. C. 2003. "Child Welfare: AOP's Nemesis?" In W. Shera (ed.), *Emerging Perspectives on Anti-Oppressive Practice.* Toronto: Canadian Scholars'.

_____. 2006a. "Parental Experience of Child Protection Intervention: A Qualitative Study." *Child Abuse and Neglect: The International Journal* 30, 1.

_____. 2006b. "Ontario's Child Welfare Transformation: Another Swing of the Pendulum?" *The Canadian Social Work Review* 23, 1/2.

Farmer, E., and M. Owen. 1995. *Child Protection Practice: Private Risks and Public Remedies: Decision Making, Intervention and Outcome in Child Protection Work.* London, U.K.: HMSO.

Foucault, M. 1995. "Strategies of Power." In W.T. Anderson (ed.), *The Truth About the Truth: De-Confusing and Re-Constructing the Postmodern World.* New York: G.P. Putnam's Son.

Fraser, D. 1973. *The Evolution of the British Welfare State: A History of Social Policy Since the Industrial Revolution.* London: Macmillan.

Glaser, B. 2002. "Conceptualization: On Theory and Theorizing Grounded Theory." *International Journal of Qualitative Methods* 1, 2.

Goffman, E. 1973. *Stigma: Notes on the Management of Spoiled Identity.* New York: Jason Aronson.

Gorlick, C.A. 1995. "Listening to Low-Income Children and Single Mothers: Policy Implications Related to Child Welfare." In J. Hudson and B. Galaway (eds.), *Child Welfare in Canada: Research and Policy Implications.* Toronto: Thompson.

Hoare, Quintin (ed.). 1990. *Selections from Political Writings (1921–1926): With Additional Texts by Other Italian Communist Leaders / Antonio Gramsci, 1891–1937* (Q. Hoare, trans.). Minneapolis: University of Minnesota Press.

Kellington, S. 2002. "'Missing Voices:' Mothers at Risk for or Experiencing Apprehension in the Child Welfare System in B.C." Report Prepared for the National Action Committee on the Status of Women, B.C. Region.

Lindsey, D. 1994. *The Welfare of Children.* New York: Oxford University Press.

Marziali, E. 1988. "The First Session: An Interpersonal Encounter." *Social Casework* 69, 1.

Miller, S.I., and M. Fredericks. 1999. "How Does Grounded Theory Explain?" *Qualitative Health Research* 9, 4.

Mullaly, B. 2002. *Challenging Oppression: A Critical Social Work Approach*. Toronto, ON: Oxford University Press.

Parada, H. 2004. "Social Work Practices within the Restructured Child Welfare System in Ontario." *Canadian Social Work Review* 21, 1.

Park, P., M. Brydon-Miller, B. Hall and T. Jackson (eds.). 1993. *Voices of Change: Participatory Research in the United States and Canada*. Toronto: OISE.

Pilsecker, C. 1994. "Starting Where the Client Is." *Families in Society* 75, 7.

Platt, D. 2007. "Congruence and Co-Operation in Social Workers' Assessments of Children in Need." *Child and Family Social Work* 12, 4.

Scholte, E.M., M. Colton, F. Casas, M. Drakeford, S. Roberts and M. Williams. 1999. "Perceptions of Stigma and User Involvement in Child Welfare Services." *British Journal of Social Work* 29.

Strega, S. 2007. "Anti-Oppressive Practice in Child Welfare." In D. Baines (ed.), *Doing Anti-Oppressive Practice: Building Transformative Politicized Social Work*. Halifax: Fernwood.

Swift. 1995. *Manufacturing "Bad Mothers:" A Critical Perspective on Child Neglect*. Toronto: University of Toronto Press.

Trotter, C. 2004. *Helping Abused Children and Their Families*. Thousand Oaks: Sage.

Yatchmenoff, D.K. 2005. "Measuring Client Engagement from the Client's Perspective in Non-Voluntary Child Protective Services." *Research on Social Work Practice* 15, 2 (March).

# Chapter 8

# Anti-Oppressive Approaches to Assessment, Risk Assessment and File Recording

*Susan Strega*

This chapter critiques current practices in assessment and risk assessment in child welfare and describes alternative, anti-oppressive approaches. The ways in which traditional approaches to assessment mask social problems and structural inequalities is explored, with particular attention paid to risk assessment and risk ideology. Anti-oppressive approaches to assessment that emphasize conducting assessments **with** children and families rather than **about** them are described in detail, including questioning strategies for eliciting full and accurate information. Suggestions are offered for including contextual matters such as poverty in assessment processes. The chapter includes concrete suggestions for applying anti-oppressive ideas to case notes and file documentation.

Questions Addressed in This Chapter
1. What are some of the problems associated with currently dominant approaches to assessment and how might these be avoided?
2. How can anti-oppressive theory be applied throughout all child welfare assessment procedures?
3. What can anti-oppressive assessment approaches contribute to developing positive helping relationships with child welfare clients?

### Current Approaches to Child Welfare Assessment

Traditional approaches to social work assessment, including those in child welfare, usually focus narrowly on individuals or individual families, ignore contextual factors and are oriented towards identifying problems and deficits and understanding how they came to be (Graybeal 2001). These approaches to assessment purport to be neutral and objective. Research, however, tells us that they are strongly influenced by socio-political attitudes and personal and professional biases, and that workers are uncritical of new information that supports their view and sceptical about information that challenges it (Munro 1999; Reder and Duncan 1995). Reich (2005) and Holland (2000) found that most child welfare workers expect parents to agree with their perception of both problems and solutions and are quick to label parents who disagree "hostile" or "uncooperative." Reich (2005) also found that that a mother's willingness to defer to the worker's perspective and power made it more likely that she would be able to keep her children.

Child protection assessments often fall short of "best practice" guidelines (Budd et al. 2002; Conley 2003) and are frequently based on a kind of one-shot data collection, with information drawn from only one or two sources. Assessments rarely include an evaluation of environmental and structural influences on the family and often omit direct observations of parent-child interactions even though these are essential to a comprehensive assessment (Harnett 2007). Historically, child welfare has focused on mothers and assessment has been directed at their moral character, maternal behaviour and housekeeping standards (Krane and Davis 1999; Swift 1995). Fathers or other involved men are minor players if they are considered at all (Strega et al. 2008). In making assessments, workers tend to draw on dominant mainstream constructions of motherhood, which are specific to particular societies and historical periods and change over time. For example, at present Anglo-American culture is in the grip of an "intensive mothering" mode, which requires that children be the primary or sole focus of a mother's life; mothers make sacrifices to ensure the wellbeing and protection of their children; mothers are knowledgeable about dominant ideas of attachment and child development; good mothering is possible regardless of contextual factors such as poverty; and single mother-led families are inherently deficient or pathological (Arendell 2000).

Class and racial biases also influence assessments. Poor, Indigenous, immigrant and racialized families are more likely to come to the attention of child welfare authorities because they are more visible. They are more visible because they are more likely to need and use public social services rather than private and to live in social housing or crowded, poor neighbourhoods rather than in single family homes separated from neighbours. These families also suffer from what Harris and Hackett (2008: 202) call "referent bias" — referrals made to child welfare services because of class or racial bias. For example, they note that although white mothers and African-American mothers are equally likely to test positive for drugs, African-American mothers are ten times more likely to be reported to child welfare authorities after delivery. Boyd (1999) documents a similar situation for Indigenous and other women of colour and poor women in Canada.

Assessment in child welfare is always framed by legislation and government policies, and over the last few decades standardized assessment forms and procedures, especially those related to risk assessment, have become commonplace. These direct worker attention away from social problems such as poverty or lack of safe, affordable housing towards individual responsibility for these factors. Policies and forms also impose dominant ideas and standards about attachment, child development and acceptable childrearing practices. Current child welfare legislation in most Canadian jurisdictions enshrines the notion that the "best interests" of the child are the worker's paramount consideration. Application of this principle can lead workers to consider the child's best interests as though these were completely separate from the interests of the child's family, extended family or community, a view that particularly affects Indigenous children (see chapters 1, 2 and 3 in this book; also Kline 1992). This approach to assessment contributes to a revolving-door phenomenon: cases are opened and children taken into care when children are in serious danger, returned when matters resolve temporarily and come back into care when matters once again worsen — as they almost inevitably do because families cannot access the resources and supports that would help them change their situation in any significant or material way.

## Risk Assessment

Given that we are living in what Beck (1992) termed the "risk society," one in which there is considerable pre-occupation with risk and risk management, it is not surprising that many child welfare jurisdictions require workers to complete risk or safety assessments as part of the assessment process. Risk ideology arose in concert with the neoliberal emphasis on personal responsibility and severe reductions in social spending (Parton 1998). Talk about risk and risk management conditions all of us to think that negative outcomes can be avoided by eliminating, reducing or ameliorating risks and that the responsibility for doing is an individual one. Because risk seems like a scientific concept, it leads to thinking that the "world can be measured, controlled and predicted" (Gillingham 2006: 87). As a result, social work in general and child welfare in particular have shifted from providing services to those in need to assessing the risk that individuals in need pose to themselves or others and recommending action to reduce these risks. Managerialism and standardized, bureaucratic procedures result in an over-emphasis on investigation and disposition of "cases" and a decreased emphasis on longer term processes of helping, healing and change. What this shift means for child welfare is that workers are indoctrinated into the idea that harm to children can be entirely prevented if risk is properly assessed and addressed. It also reinforces the idea that the proper task of child welfare is protection rather than support.

Measuring risk and assigning cases to particular risk categories extracts families from the contexts in which they live. The concept of risk serves to transform social and structural problems such as the scarcity of safe, affordable housing into individual problems because it is difficult, if not impossible, to "insert the social" onto risk assessment forms. For example, frequent moves supposedly indicate risk, but forms do not allow workers to note that a family may need to move frequently because of inadequate housing, harassment by a landlord or because they are fleeing an abusive partner. When context disappears the worker's gaze becomes fixed firmly on individual failures of individual parents.

Ayre's (1998) U.K. study found that 90 percent of completed risk assessments had a predominantly negative focus, emphasizing deficits and problems. Parton (1998) noted that worker evaluations of risk predominantly focused on the moral character of the mother, her maternal behaviour (even if the father was present, his parenting was not assessed) and the physical state of the house. These findings demonstrate that risk assessment as it is usually applied is about collecting evidence with a view to making a case *against* parents, rather than developing a plan for, about or with them. Blaming individuals in this way serves a larger agenda of preserving the existing social order and directing attention away from the context in which harm and neglect occur — matters such as extreme poverty, gendered, racial and other inequalities and the legacies of colonization and colonialism.

When risk ideology is applied in practice through risk assessment and risk reduction processes, the worker-client relationship becomes inquisitorial and disciplinary rather than about helping, and both mothers and workers suffer in this culture of blame (Brown 2006). Parents are regulated through one threat of sanction (loss of children) while worker conducted is regulated through another (being found at fault if "things go wrong"). Guilt and anxiety are activated for both parties: parents fear they are not "measuring up" and workers fear they might be accused of "not following correct procedures." But as Callahan et al. (1998) point out, families and workers can work together to navigate through these fears.

Swift and Callahan (2003) note that high-profile child death inquiries ignore structural and contextual factors and position "bad" mothers and weak, untrained or incompetent workers as at fault. In their discussion of risk, Hollis and Howe (1987, as cited in MacDonald and MacDonald 1999: 23) graphically describe the situation of child protection workers under the risk regime:

> Think of [the worker] as deciding in which of two categories the child belongs. Category A comprises children so much at risk that they should all be removed to a place of safety; Category B comprises those who will be safe if left at home. The child's death proves that it belongs in Category A. Must she not have been incompetent in assigning it to Category B?

In this climate, as Scourfield and Welsh (2003: 400) note, "it is not the right decision that is important, but the defensible one."

Critiques of risk assessment point out that there are significant problems with an actuarial approach to decision-making in child welfare, problems that lead to dangers being both missed and erroneously found (Munro 1999) and resources wasted on unwarranted interventions. Because risk assessment focuses on parents rather than children, workers who rely on risk assessment fail to consider how particular children are faring in particular situations. Risk assessment presents risk factors as causing or likely to cause behaviour when the true relationship between these factors and behaviour is at best one of association or correlation. The idea that future behaviour is caused by past behaviour or the past behaviour of other people in the parent's life has been popularized into the notion that there is an intergenerational transmission of abuse. But a review of several studies that attempted to directly measure the relationship found that "transmission" rates hovered between 25–33 percent (Kaufman and Ziegler 1987). Any worker inclined to accept the notion of intergenerational transmission must ask: Do I believe I will parent like my parents? Do I believe that my adult relationships are similar to my parents' relationship? Do I believe that I have any choice or agency in this? For the purposes of risk assessment, it is essential to ask parents their perspective on how their parenting and relationships are similar to or differ from their childhood experiences rather than accepting or assuming a certain relationship.

Risk assessment continues to be popular even though parents do not find it useful (Brown 2006: Dumbrill 2006; Krane and Davis 1999) and it has been extensively and thoroughly critiqued as being of little use in child protection (Gillingham 2006; Parada 2004; Parton 1998; Rycus and Hughes 2003; Swift and Callahan in press). This may be because this type of assessment procedure is successful at masking structural inequalities and power relations by making difficulties appear as matters of individual "choice" and responsibility. Child welfare workers must familiarize themselves with the critiques and recommended strategies for making risk or safety assessment as anti-oppressive as possible. For example, as with all assessments, risk assessments must be done *with* clients, workers must attend carefully to client perceptions and clients must be made aware of the meanings ascribed to various responses. The potential for risk in any situation is likely to be reduced if children are well-connected within the extended family and/or within wider social networks. Risk assessment must therefore be socially and not just individually situated.

Workers may also better understand how to challenge risk assessment if they "test drive" risk assessment measures on themselves and their own families. In the longer term workers must be prepared to challenge within their agencies and organizations the utility and applicability of standardized measures like risk assessment. It is essential to keep in mind that the deficit focus engendered by current risk assessment procedures is not the way that child welfare has to be. For example, when Khoo, Hyvönen and Nygren (2003) compared decision-making by Swedish and Canadian child welfare workers, they found that Swedish workers focused on assessment, family preservation and providing resources, while Canadian workers focused on protection and procedures and offered little in the way of services or resources. A shift in focus can begin with approaching assessment anti-oppressively.

## Anti-Oppressive Assessment in Child Welfare

Assessment in child welfare involves various assessments conducted at particular points in the family-child welfare system relationship, including initial assessments of child safety, formal risk assessments, ongoing assessments about the match between services and needs, parenting capacity assessments and assessments conducted at case transfer or closure. The overarching aim of all child welfare assessments is the determination of whether parents have the minimal capacity necessary to protect the safety and wellbeing of their children and, if they do not, whether they can achieve this with available resources and supports. Assessments result in decisions about whether children can remain with their parents or must be removed and, if they have been removed, when and if they might be reunified. Assessment is not a stand alone process that must be completed before a decision is made or intervention takes place. Rather, assessment is itself an intervention process as well as the foundation for future interventions (Fook 1993; Graybeal 2001). Identifying needs and helping families make connections to resources and services, whether these are formal or informal, are key to the assessment process.

It is critical to keep in mind that at every stage of involvement workers are not only assessing but also building relationships with parents and children. Given that the first contact that most families have with child welfare involves the investigation of allegations that parents are neglecting or abusing their child, developing a positive and collaborative relationship is challenging. While under the terms of their legislated mandate workers must gather information, the way in which they do so significantly impacts how the relationship between worker and family unfolds (Oppenheim 1992). It is often useful for workers to start by offering information rather than asking for it, including the fullest description possible of who the worker is, why s/he is there, what s/he needs to do and why. Sharing information, so long as it does not break confidentiality or endanger children, contributes to respectful engagement with families. Encouraging parents and children to ask questions right from the outset affirms their right to do so and may lead to more open dialogue between family and worker.

In the first interview, a worker has three main tasks: assessing safety, gathering information and developing relationship. These tasks occur in a cyclical rather than linear fashion. A worker's mandated or statutory obligation means s/he must see the children and assess safety and risk factors immediately present in order to determine whether children are in need of protection as defined by the relevant legislation. This involves gathering information from both children and parents, including an explanation of events surrounding the complaint or incident in question and information about the family. In some situations, an interview with the child will take place prior to contact with the parents, for example, when the parents cannot be located or when there are reasonable grounds to believe that contacting the parent might endanger the child. The initial contact is where the foundation is laid for a future helping alliance (Dore and Alexander 1996), so it is critical to involve the parents and, if they are old enough, the children in a collaborative attempt to understand what may have happened and what, if anything, needs to be done. The development and maintenance of a collaborative and respectful relationship between worker and family is in the child's best interests.

Given the current dominance of risk assessment, child welfare workers must usually enumerate safety and risk factors as part of their assessment. An anti-oppressive approach requires that workers also look for strengths, protective factors, contextual factors and the family's desired outcome. It is important from the beginning to work at understanding the family's point of view including differences in perception among family members. As with all phases of assessment, in discussions with parents workers must make every effort to gather information *with* the parents rather than *from* the parents. Workers must keep in mind that most clients are participating in assessment processes when they are struggling and afraid. How workers ask questions and what they ask about can confirm parents' worst fears and reinforce shame and guilt or can assist families to clarify their situations and to appreciate their strength and resilience. A sensitive rather than accusatory exploration of issues that on the surface appear to be evidence of neglect or abuse increases the possibility of getting full and accurate information and therefore developing a full and accurate assessment. Workers must constantly clarify information to ensure that families and workers share the same understanding (de Boer and Coady 2007). Exploring and clarifying decrease the likelihood of "othering" parents and increase the likelihood of seeing them as experiencing understandable challenges.

All assessments, including initial safety plans, should emphasize facts rather than opinions and include clear and concrete steps for enhancing safety and protective factors and reducing risks. A child's Indigenous status should also be discussed and confirmed during initial contacts, and it is critical that workers not rely on assumptions in this matter. Workers must consider, given that the family home is the preferred environment, not just whether the children can be maintained safely in the home, but *how* they can be maintained safely in the home. The intention is that worker and parents come to an agreement about what actions, if any, must be taken to ensure the safety of the children. Can the worker or parents mobilize extended family or community resources so that the children can remain in the home? If there is agreement that services or resources that can be provided will assist the family, a rationale for each service should be stated and the plan should designate responsibility for initiating services. Strengths, protective factors and resources that might maintain the children in the home must be confirmed. Clients value workers who can provide concrete help (de Boer and Coady 2007), so workers must be knowledgeable about resources and how to access them.

During the initial safety assessment as well as in later assessments of parenting capacity, the focus of discussion needs to be on the parent's capabilities and challenges as a parent and on the parent-child relationship. In both processes workers must ensure that assessments are inclusive of all involved adults and that the children are also interviewed. Although it is a matter of policy in most jurisdictions to interview all family members, workers tend to focus on mothers and exclude fathers (Strega et al. 2008) and sometimes exclude extended family members (Callahan et al. 2004). Unless doing so would endanger children, later stages of assessment must include direct observations of parent-child interaction. Budd (2005) studied assessment for child welfare purposes and provides some ideas about what to look for in these interactions and how to look. It is critical that workers be knowledgeable about how to assess for various types of abuse and neglect. For example, as Levenson and Morin (2006) note, sexual abuse situations present unique and ambiguous indicators and therefore pose particular challenges for assessment because indicators and dynamics of sexual abuse differ considerably from those associated with physical abuse or neglect. As well, perpetrators are often able to present themselves as "intelligent, middle class, non-addicted and generally well-adjusted" (Levenson and Morin 2006: 65) and therefore outside of class and racial biases held by workers.

It may be useful to use the "exception question" to help identify strengths and protective factors. This involves asking the parents and children when a challenge or difficulty was not present and then exploring what was different at that time. Finally, workers must remember to focus on *impact* as much as on *incident*, which can be challenging given the complaint-driven nature of current practice. Because ongoing neglect and abuse are more damaging than single incidents a more accurate picture is developed when assessment takes place over time — the worker is looking for a movie rather than a snapshot of the child's and family's life.

Workers must always apply a minimal rather than optimal parenting standard in assessment processes, asking "What is the lowest threshold of parenting skills necessary to protect and care for these children, given the protective factors, strengths and risks in the family (including extended and involved family) and the community (including supports that you can put in place)?" Some of the specific skills associated with the successful completion of assessments in child welfare include the following:

- ability to establish and maintain an empathic connection with parents, children and extended family members
- ability to manage your internal process, i.e., emotional reactivity to clients, especially blaming and shaming responses;
- ability to convey information in a non-threatening way;
- ability to validate client perspectives;
- willingness to validate client scepticism about agency and worker; and
- knowledge of cultural, class and other biases held by the worker and the agency.

The three possible outcomes of a child protection assessment are 1) the child does not need protection and no further contact is required at this time; 2) the child needs protection and the child's parents, extended family and community are able and willing to care for and protect the child, with available support services if necessary; or 3) the child is in need of protection and steps must be taken to ensure the child's safety and wellbeing. The child will be safest and the family most supported when there is agreement between worker and family about the results of the assessment. As Dumbrill (2006) describes, workers are using "power with" when worker and client mutually agree on objectives and strategize about how they can work together to achieve these and "power over" when workers encourage, manipulate or force a client to comply with or conform to worker instructions, goals or agenda. When workers take a "power with" approach to assessment it becomes possible to collaborate with families in order to figure out what is going on, whether anything needs to change and how it might best be changed. It is essential to remember that anti-oppressive practice is possible to achieve whether children are removed from or remain in their home.

From an anti-oppressive perspective it is especially important to understand how structural factors such as poverty and race exacerbate personal challenges. Workers must have in the foreground of their thinking the probability that a family's difficulties and therefore its needs are fundamentally related to environmental and structural problems (such as poverty and inadequate housing, or being sequestered in dangerous neighbourhoods on account of race) rather than a lack of parenting skill and/or knowledge. Contextual factors can be discussed with parents in ways that make clear that they are not being held responsible for them. Workers are advised to clearly differentiate between individual and contextual or structural factors and understand how each exacerbates aspects of the difficulties that are being experienced. Recognizing that many social work clients are involuntary, Graybeal (2001: 236) invites workers to challenge existing definitions and language around "clients" and encourages workers to redefine client "resistance" as a positive rather than negative attribute.

## Self-Location, Reflexivity and Dominant Ideologies

In assessing child-parent interactions as well as all other assessment information it is essential to maintain an awareness of your own social location and that of the agency and how these positionalities may be affecting your perceptions. Discrimination and bias in child welfare both systemically and on the part of individual workers is extensive, well-documented and positively reinforced by what Scourfield (2003) has called the "occupational discourse" of child welfare. How these play out in child welfare policy and practice has been documented and discussed by many writers.[1] Given these biases, it is critical that workers approach their own perceptions, previous file recordings and information from family members and other professionals (often known as "collaterals" in child welfare parlance) with caution and reflexivity.

The Anglo-American ideology that the "best" family is one in which mother is the primary caregiver while father's role is primarily that of financial support is reflected on the standardized assessment forms that have become common in child welfare. This ideology fails to account for cultural variations in childrearing practices and family forms. In many cultures around the globe, childrearing may be shared amongst many of the child's relatives or amongst all the women in a community. In most Indigenous cultures raising children is seen as a community responsibility, with different groups in the community (such as Elders) having specific duties and various relatives having other responsibilities. For example, grandparents in Indigenous communities usually have significant roles in the lives of children. In the African-American community there is a tradition of blood mothers and "other mothers" (Hill Collins 1993), a phenomenon that occurs to a certain extent in African-Canadian communities. In Jamaican communities and therefore probably in many Jamaican-Canadian communities, all mothers, grandmothers and aunties have a right to intervene with any children including those to whom they are not related (Leo-Rhynie 1997).

Standardized approaches also fail to account for class differences in caring for children. For example, McMahon (1995) found that poor and working-class women were pre-occupied with providing for the material needs of their children, while the middle-class mothers that she interviewed rarely mentioned these aspects of childrearing because they had the privilege of not needing to think about them. She also found that poor and working-class women were much more likely to share child-care responsibilities with a network of friends and relatives than were middle-class women, who tended to use (and be able to afford) professional child minders. Shor (2000) found that differences in childrearing practices between middle-income and low-income parents related significantly to the need for low-income parents to more closely monitor and control their children's behaviour due to the dangerousness of their neighbourhoods. These findings make clear that workers must understand that white middle-class ideas about parenting do not necessarily represent the best or most appropriate standard against which all parenting should be assessed.

The imposition of dominant values is particularly problematic when these ideas are uncritically applied to assessing attachment and the achievement of developmental milestones, as in attachment theory (see Soo See Yeo 2003). Child welfare standards incorporate dominant attachment and child development models without considering how or whether these models apply to different cultural groups (Neckoway et al. 2007). In order to assess these areas anti-oppressively it is important to keep in mind that they are social constructs rather than representative of universal truths. For example, Soo See Yeo (2003: 300) notes that "exploration, autonomy and efficacy are valued in the West and competence defined in this way would be biased against childrearing practices that value and nurture interdependence."

The anti-oppressive alternative to imposing dominant ideas is to ask parents, extended family and involved community members for their perceptions about the attachment and development of particular children. Workers must encourage families to share and explain their own perceptions of the quality of the parent-child relationship rather than evaluating this through a dominant culture lens. This is not a recommendation for a cultural competence approach but a recognition that parents have knowledge and expertise that must be factored into the assessment. Cropper (1997: 39) notes:

> It is imperative that individuals are allowed to speak their narrative… Listening carefully to the narratives of clients may help workers to gain insight into the individual's experiences in a way that can guard against their being influenced by assumptions and stereotypes.

## File Documentation and Case Notes

Most social workers are expected to keep case notes, write reports and maintain files. The exact nature of these expectations and the rules that govern recordkeeping and reports vary from employer to employer, but there are few areas of social work practice where notes and reports are not a regular requirement. Even social workers in private practice are governed by case-note and recordkeeping guidelines of their licensing body. File documentation and case notes are particularly critical processes in child welfare for a number of reasons: child welfare more frequently than other area of social work practice may involve court proceedings; children and families transfer frequently between different parts of the system or different workers; and high turnover among child welfare workers means information is often shared through files rather than face-to-face contacts.

There are many good reasons to keep notes. Social workers often work with many people at the same time and sometimes with many complex situations, and it can be useful to have factual information (name, contact information, age, reason for involvement) about each client organized in some fashion. It is useful for both clients and workers to have some chronology of events including interventions and referrals as well as to record details of any agreements made between client and worker, such as agreements to engage in a particular intervention or participate in an assessment process. A record of client strengths and progress may be helpful to refer to when challenges start to reappear. Social workers who work in contentious areas like child welfare or custody and access need to make particularly detailed notes about interventions, referrals and recommendations. Social work notes are not considered privileged like medical file recordings and can be subpoenaed in relation to legal proceedings.

For a worker committed to anti-oppressive practice, documentation requirements can sometimes be challenging. An anti-oppressive orientation requires that workers analyze and critically reflect on the tensions, dilemmas, values and assumptions that underlay the selection and presentation of information about those with whom we work. Workers must always keep in mind that files and records perform ideological work — clients are sorted, categorized and classified according to dominant cultural standards of what is acceptable and/or "normal" behaviour (de Montigny 1995). Failure to meet dominant standards has serious consequences including loss of children and being kept under state surveillance. Moral judgments that come to define client identities masquerade as the result of neutral, objective and professional judgment: bad mother, non-compliant client, substance abuser. Further, clients are offered or denied access to resources and services on the basis of what social workers write and say about them.

As Alexander (2000) notes, social work's recordkeeping practices are tied to its desire to be seen as a high status profession, and social work has therefore emulated the documentation practices of high status, historically male-dominated professions such as medicine, law and psychology, which purport to be professional, objective and neutral in their recordkeeping. In these professional accounts, the location and perspective of the writer is made invisible and s/he is not required to account for or explain the social, political or cultural influences that inform the ideas reflected in case notes, reports or assessments. The roles of gathering, evaluating and assessing information and through those processes controlling access to services and resources are part of what defines a professional as a professional. Thus it is not surprising that a social worker's account of events comes to be the legitimate account while client experiences, perceptions and opinions are invisible, invalidated or marginalized.

As both Alexander (2000) and Swift (1995) note, standard social work file documentation and recording practices individualize problems while making systemic issues such as sexism, poverty and racism disappear. The increased use of standardized forms makes it even more difficult to insert context into assessments and reports. Nonetheless, it is both possible and necessary to document contextual issues and structural inequalities in notes and reports, including information about how social policies are impacting on clients. It is also possible to not only include but center client perceptions and experiences in notes and reports, including in investigative reports.

The foundation for an anti-oppressive approach to recordkeeping can be laid in initial contacts with clients, during which agency policies about client files, records and reports should be discussed. Clients should be aware of any limitations on confidentiality before they offer information and should be fully informed of any rights they have to access their file. Workers must be prepared to assist clients with any bureaucratic procedures involved in obtaining access to files as well as with challenges related to literacy, language or ability. In situations where clients are not allowed access to files, workers should determine how this policy might be challenged and in the interim provide clients with information about complaint procedures or advocacy resources.

Families (including children old enough to comprehend) need to know about what case notes, records, reports and other file documentation must be kept in order to satisfy statutory and legal requirements. Workers should ask for and listen to client input about how they would like such records to be kept. Case notes should be written *with* clients rather than *about* clients. In many situations it can be useful to record the words of clients, with their consent, as direct quotations in notes, assessments and reports. If it is possible to do so without breaching agency regulations, offer clients space in case notes, reports and file recordings to record their perceptions, opinions and experiences. It is especially important to record how and why clients agree or disagree with workers.

Always clearly distinguish in your recordkeeping between concrete facts and matters of opinion, keeping in mind that many diagnoses and assessments from other professionals, including psychiatric diagnoses, are matters of opinion rather than matters of fact. Systemic barriers that clients may be encountering should be documented, including lack of services or resources and social, economic and historical factors that impact client experiences. When forms such as risk assessment forms do not have space for contextual factors ensure that these are clearly and extensively documented elsewhere in the file.

## In Summary

Parents and children involved with child welfare are most likely to positively improve their situations when they are able to identify, recognize and appreciate their strengths and resources and the strengths and resources available to them in their extended family and community. In an anti-oppressive approach to assessment, strengths are as important as problems and challenges, and it is essential to develop a picture of strengths and challenges with clients rather than about them. When workers "develop an understanding of clients in the context of their social environment and life history" (de Boer and Coady 2007: 38) they can avoid attributing problems solely to individual pathology or deficit. Families have a better chance for success when they come to understand the structural forces they are contending with and that they are not personally responsible for, especially if they appreciate the ways in which they are already resisting those forces.

## Suggestions for Further Reading

Budd, K. 2005. "Assessing Parenting Capacity in a Child Welfare Context." *Children and Youth Services Review* 27, 4.

Brown, D. 2006. "Working the System: Re-Thinking the Institutionally Organized Role of Mothers and the Reduction of 'Risk' in Child Protection Work." *Social Problems* 53, 3.

Dumbrill, G. 2006. "Parental Experience of Child Protection Intervention: A Qualitative Study." *Child Abuse and Neglect* 30.

## About the Author

Susan Strega teaches social work at the University of Victoria. She has practised in many areas of social work including child protection, mental health and alcohol and drug treatment. Her research interests include child welfare, sex work, social policy and violence against women, and she is the co-editor, with Leslie Brown, of *Research as Resistance* (2005).

## Notes

This chapter benefited from the practice, wisdom and editorial support of Michele Fairbairn, whose work proves that anti-oppressive practice is possible in child welfare. I am grateful for her contributions.

1.   See, for example, discussions of gender, race and class biases in Swift (1995) and Reich (2005); race and class biases in Harris and Hackett (2008); gender bias in Krane (2003), Scourfield (2003) and Strega et al. (2008); and bias against Indigenous peoples in Kline (1992) and Fournier and Crey (1998).

## References

Alexander, R. 2000. "Tales of Wayward Girls and Immoral Women: Case Records and the Professionalization of Social Work." (Book review). *Law and History Review* 18, 3.

Arendell, T. 2000. "Conceiving and Investigating Motherhood: The Decade's Scholarship." *Journal of Marriage and the Family* 62, 4.

Ayre, P. 1998. "Significant Harm: Making Professional Judgments." *Child Abuse Review* 7, 5.

Beck, U. 1992. *Risk Society: Towards a New Modernity*. London: Sage

Boyd, S. 1999. *Mothers and Illicit Drugs: Transcending the Myths*. Toronto: University of Toronto Press.

Brown, D. 2006. "Working the System: Re-thinking the Institutionally Organized Role of Mothers and the Reduction of 'Risk' in Child Protection Work." *Social Problems* 53, 3.

Budd, K. 2005. "Assessing Parenting Capacity in a Child Welfare Context." *Children and Youth Services Review* 27, 4, 429-444.

Budd, K., E. Felix, L. Poindexter, A. Naik-Polan and C. Sloss. 2002. "Clinical Assessment of Children in Child Protection Cases: An Empirical Analysis." *Professional Psychology: Research and Practice* 33.

Callahan, M., L. Brown, P. MacKenzie and B. Whittington. 2004. "Catch as Catch Can: Grandmothers Raising Their Grandchildren and Kinship Care Policies." *Canadian Review of Social Policy* 54.

Callahan, M., B. Field, C. Hubberstey and B. Wharf. 1998. *Best Practice in Child Welfare: Perspectives from Parents, Social Workers and Community Partners*. Victoria: University of Victoria, School of Social Work.

Cash, S., and M. Berry. 2002. "Family Characteristics and Child Welfare Services: Does the Assessment Drive Service Provision?" *Families in Society* 83, 5/6.

Conley, C. 2003. "A Review of Parenting Capacity Assessment Reports." *Ontario Association of Children's Aid Societies Journal* 47.

Cropper, A. 1997. "Rethinking Practice: A Black Feminist Perspective." In J. Bates, R. Pugh and N. Thompson (eds.), *Protecting Children: Challenges and Change*. Hants: Arena Publishing.

de Boer, C., and N. Coady. 2007. "Good Helping Relationships in Child Welfare: Learning from Stories of Success." *Child and Family Social Work* 12.

de Montigny, G. 1995. "The Power of Being Professional." In M. Campbell and A. Manicom (eds.), *Knowledge, Experience and Ruling Relations*. Toronto: University of Toronto Press.

Dore, M., and L. Alexander. 1996. "Preserving Families at Risk of Child Abuse and Neglect: The Role of the Helping Alliance." *Child Abuse and Neglect* 20, 4.

Dumbrill, G. 2006. "Parental Experience of Child Protection Intervention: A Qualitative Study." *Child Abuse and Neglect* 30.

Fook, J. 1993. *Radical Casework: A Theory of Practice*. Sydney: Allen and Unwin.

Fournier, S., and E. Crey. 1998. *Stolen from Our Embrace: The Abduction of First Nations Children and the Restoration of Aboriginal Communities*. Vancouver: Douglas and McIntyre.

Gillingham, P. 2006. "Risk Assessment in Child Protection: Problem Rather than Solution?" *Australian Social Work* 59, 1.

Gonzalez-Mena, J. 2001. "Cross-Cultural Infant Care and Issues of Equity and Social Justice." *Contemporary Issues in Early Childhood* 2, 3.

Graybeal, C. 2001. "Strengths-Based Social Work Assessment: Transforming the Dominant Paradigm." *Families in Society* 82, 3.

Harnett, P. 2007. "A Procedure for Assessing Parents' Capacity for Change in Child Protection Cases." *Children and Youth Services Review* 29.

Harris, M., and W. Hackett. 2008. "Decision Points in Child Welfare: An Action Research Model to Address Disproportionality." *Children and Youth Services Review* 30.

Hill Collins, P. 1993. "The Meaning of Motherhood in Black Culture and Black Mother–

Daughter Relationships." In P. Bell-Scott et al. (eds.), *Double Stitch: Black Women Write about Mothers and Daughters.* New York: Harper Perennial.

Holland, S. 2000. "The Assessment Relationship: Interactions between Social Workers and Parents in Child Protection Assessments." *British Journal of Social Work* 30, 2.

Kaufman, J., and E. Ziegler. 1987. "Do Abused Children Become Abusive Parents?" *American Journal of Orthopsychiatry* 57, 2.

Khoo, E., U. Hyvönen and L. Nygren. 2003. "Gatekeeping in Child Welfare: A Comparative Study of Intake Decision-Making by Social Workers in Canada and Sweden." *Child Welfare* 82, 5.

Kline, M. 1992. "Child Welfare Law, 'Best Interests of the Child' Ideology, and First Nations." *Osgood Hall Law Journal* 30, 2.

Krane, J. 2003. *What's Mother Got to Do with It? Protecting Children from Sexual Abuse.* Toronto: University of Toronto Press.

Krane, J., and L. Davies. 1999. "Mothering and Child Protection Practice: Rethinking Risk Assessment." *Child and Family Social Work* 5, 1.

Leo-Rhynie, E. 1997. "Class, Race, and Gender Issues in Child Rearing in the Caribbean." In J. L. Rooparine and J. Brown (eds.), *Caribbean Families: Diversity among Ethnic Groups.* Greenwich, CT: Ablex.

Levenson, J., and J. Morin. 2006. "Risk Assessment in Child Sexual Abuse Cases." *Child Welfare* 85, 1.

MacDonald, K., and G. MacDonald. 1999. "Perceptions of Risk." In P. Parsloe (ed.), *Risk Assessment in Social Care and Social Work.* London: Jessica Kingsley.

McMahon, M. 1995. *Engendering Motherhood.* New York: Guilford Press.

Munro, E. 1999. "Common Errors of Reasoning in Child Protection Work." *Child Abuse and Neglect* 23, 8.

Neckoway, R., N. Brownlee and B. Castellan. 2007. "Is Attachment Theory Consistent with Aboriginal Parenting Realities?" *First Peoples Child and Family Review* 3, 1.

Oppenheim, L. 1992. "The First Interview in Child Protection: Social Work Method and Process." *Children and Society* 6, 2.

Parada, H. 2004. "Social Work Practices within the Restructured Child Welfare System in Ontario." *Canadian Social Work Review* 21, 1.

Parton, N. 1998. "Risk, Advanced Liberalism and Child Welfare: The Need to Rediscover Uncertainty and Ambiguity." *British Journal of Social Work* 28.

Parton, N., D. Thorpe and C. Wattam. 1997. *Child Protection: Risk and the Moral Order.* London: Macmillan.

Reder, P., and S. Duncan. 1995. "Closure, Covert Warnings, and Escalating Child Abuse." *Child Abuse and Neglect* 19, 12.

Reich, J. 2005. *Fixing Families: Parents, Power, and the Child Welfare System.* London: Routledge.

Rycus, J.S., and R.C. Hughes. 2003. *Issues in Risk Assessment in Child Protective Services.* Columbus, OH: North American Resource Center for Child Welfare, Center for Child Welfare Policy.

Scourfield, J. 2003. *Gender and Child Protection.* Houndmills, Basingstoke, Hampshire: Palgrave MacMillan.

Scourfield, J., and I. Welsh. 2003. "Risk, Reflexivity and Social Control in Child Protection: New Times or Same Old Story?" *Critical Social Policy* 23, 3.

Shor, R. 2000. "Child Maltreatment: Differences in Perception between Parents in Low Income and Middle Income Neighbourhoods." *British Journal of Social Work* 30.

Strega, S., C. Fleet, L. Brown, L. Dominelli, M. Callahan and C. Walmsley. 2008.

"Connecting Father Absence and Mother Blame in Child Welfare Policies and Practices." *Children and Youth Services Review* 30, 7.

Swift, K. 1995. *Manufacturing 'Bad Mothers': A Critical Perspective on Child Neglect.* Toronto: University of Toronto Press.

Swift, K., and M. Callahan. 2003. *Problems and Potential of Canadian Child Welfare.* Waterloo: Partnerships for Children and Families Project, Wilfrid Laurier University.

_____. In press. *At Risk: Work Practices in Child Protection, Social Work and the Helping Professions.* Toronto: University of Toronto Press.

Yeo, S.S. 2003. "Bonding and Attachment of Australian Aboriginal Children." *Child Abuse Review* 12.

# Chapter 9

# Supporting Youth in Care through Anti-Oppressive Practice

*April Feduniw*

Putting anti-oppressive theory into practice with youth in care can seem like an abstract concept for many child welfare workers. In this chapter, the author reflects on her experience of being a youth in care, her research and practice experiences with other youth in and from care, her experience of being a social worker and her education in anti-oppressive theory to identify significant practice implications. Although the author has personal insight on these issues, it is important to note that the practice strategies are relevant to anyone working with youth in care, regardless of their background or experience. Some of the key practice strategies discussed include developing an understanding of some of the unique challenges that youth in care face, being aware of how systemic issues have a significant impact on individual youth, learning how to work collaboratively and in partnership with youth and their families and taking a strength-based approach.

Questions Addressed in This Chapter
1. What are some of the challenges facing youth in care?
2. What are some of the particular challenges facing Indigenous youth in care?
3. How can I practise anti-oppressively with youth in care?

Supporting youth in care through anti-oppressive practice creates possibilities for youth to make positive choices and overcome obstacles in their journey towards adulthood. In my own experience as a youth in care, I found that the social workers who made the most meaningful impact on my life were the ones who took the time to get to know me and who provided me with information and options that were relevant to who I was and the positive direction in which I was going. However, encounters with other social workers left me feeling disempowered and oppressed. As a former youth worker, researcher and recent BSW graduate, I have had an opportunity to reflect on all these experiences in developing a better understanding of both the challenges and the possibilities of practising anti-oppressively with youth.

In this chapter, I briefly review research about outcomes for youth in care, describe the specific challenges these youth confront and consider how these challenges might especially impact Indigenous and other marginalized youth. I outline some principles for anti-oppressive practice with youth in care and summarize the systemic issues that impact practice. In keeping with an anti-oppressive approach, I have incorporated a youth perspective throughout and reference my own experience as a youth in care and as a youth advocate. For me, this chapter is equally about informing my own practice as it is about helping to inform and inspire others to practise anti-oppressively with youth in care. Now, as a social worker and former youth in care, I feel compelled both personally and professionally to learn more about how I can best support youth in care. This is my journey, and I invite you along.

## Youth in Care

It is difficult to estimate the proportion of Canadian children in care who fall into a "youth" category due to variations in provincial child welfare legislation. For instance, the age of majority in some provinces is eighteen (Alberta and Ontario), while in others it is nineteen (Nova Scotia and British Columbia). It is also difficult to identify the numbers of youth in care as this statistic is rarely documented for the public. The B.C. Ministry of Children and Family Development states that in September 2005 a total of 9041 children and youth were in care (MCFD 2006). Further, the Office of the Provincial Health Officer in B.C. estimates that "roughly one-third of children and youth in care are teens, aged 15–18" (OPHO 2001: 5). Therefore, it is plausible that there are approximately 3,000 youth in care in B.C. alone.

Outcomes for these youth, both while they are in care and after they leave or "age out" of government care, are poor by virtually any measure, including educational attainment, physical, emotional and mental health, substance misuse and involvement with the justice system. For example, approximately 80 percent of youth in care do not graduate from high school (Representative for Children and Youth 2007), and child welfare involvement is significantly related to youth homelessness (Serge et al. 2002). Youth in and from care have been voicing their concerns about these issues for a very long time in many different venues. For instance, the National Youth in Care Network and the Federation of B.C. Youth in Care Networks facilitate numerous opportunities for youth in and from care to collectively share their experiences and voice their perspectives on both the strengths and weaknesses of the child welfare system. National and provincial youth in care networks in Canada regularly prepare and submit reports to all levels of government outlining negative outcomes for youth in care and recommending policy and practice changes likely to improve these outcomes. Youth in and from care have voiced their concerns through participation in research projects (see Callahan et al. 2005; Rutman et al. 2001) and presentations at child welfare conferences as well as in a variety of publications (see Raychaba 1989, 1993; Strega 2000).

To date these efforts have made little significant impact on child welfare policy or practice. My experiences of advocating for systemic changes have had me observing the painstakingly slow process of government change, as well as the ability for government to reverse progressive changes it has already made.

For instance, B.C. implemented a two-year "post-majority" program in 1994 that was education-based and included supports from social workers to former youth in care who had reached the age of nineteen. This program was expanded to a four-year program in 1999, and then reduced to a bursary application process in 2002. Since then, both youth in care and former youth in care have been advocating for more substantial supports to be instituted as one way of improving their outcomes — a change that has yet to happen after many years of relentless advocacy efforts. Youth in care continue to have lifelong negative consequences associated with their in-care experiences. As Dominelli et al. (2005) point out, the state is often inadequate as a substitute parent, yet youth in and from care often show remarkable resiliency.

## Challenges for Youth in Care

In addition to the common developmental hurdles that most youth experience (such as identify formation), many youth in care are forced to deal with additional challenges that are specific to their experiences in the child welfare system. The National Youth In Care Network has reported that the five major challenges that youth in care face are transience, leaving care, stigma, lack of voice and emotional healing (NYICN 2003). In order to be supportive to youth in care we must consider these challenges in relation to critical child abuse and neglect theories, from an anti-oppressive perspective and in the context of the child welfare system.

## Transience

Transience is experienced by youth in care as repeatedly moving from one placement (such as a foster home) to another. For instance, in a survey conducted by the Federation of B.C. Youth in Care Networks, only 22 percent of the youth reported they had lived in fewer than three placements while in care, noting common experiences of instability in foster homes and frequent accessing of emergency shelters (FBCYICN 2004). Another recent B.C. research project found that 38 percent of youth in care had experienced seven or more different placements (Rutman et al. 2005). From my own experiences and observations, placement changes result from a variety of factors, some beyond the youth's control and some to do with youth acting in their own best interests. For example, youth sometimes take the initiative to leave a placement because of abuse or neglect; a study from the Feminist Research Education Development and Action Centre found that 43 percent of foster children experienced violence in their foster home placements (FREDA n.d.). In a review of B.C. youth safe houses, one youth shelter reported that many Indigenous youth who accessed a shelter became homeless after choosing to leave white foster homes, which they experienced as alienating (Ministry of Children and Family Development 2005). Youth also leave because they experience incompatibility with foster families, something that is likely to be a particular issue for youth with different sexual orientations or cultural backgrounds than their foster parents.

Youth are also forced to change placements for systemic and resource-related reasons, including the unavailability of compatible and appropriate caregivers, caregiver (such as a foster parent) request or closure of the placement. Over the years that I worked as a youth advocate and researcher I observed an overall lack of placement options for B.C. youth in care. Like most Canadian provinces, B.C. has for some years faced a critical shortage of foster homes generally, as well as a lack of diversity among available foster homes. Youth in care who are developmentally disabled or medically fragile, Indigenous, ethno-cultural minority, considered to be "high risk" or come from the inner city are especially likely to face placement difficulties (MCFD 1997). Although it is hard to pinpoint exactly why there is significant lack of foster homes for youth, there are several explanations that can be considered. The B.C. Association of Social Workers reported a loss of 800 foster homes provincially between 2000 and 2001 due to government restructuring and budget cuts (BCASW 2006). The B.C. Federation of Foster Parent Associations has reported similar concerns about budget cuts, particularly around cuts to supports for both foster parents and youth in care (BCFFPA 2006). My own experience and observations provide me with another possible explanation, which is the reduction or elimination of group homes for youth in care in some communities. While some explained this as an effort to reduce "institutionalized" living arrangements for youth in care, my own experience was that living in group homes didn't feel institutionalized, nor would I have preferred to be homeless or placed in an overcrowded foster home.

The experience of transience while in care seems to add to challenges that these youth have in relation to their sense of attachment and security. Child abuse and neglect theories suggest that "because of the significant attachment relationships that children have with their parents and siblings before they enter care, many foster youth recall their entry into care as marked by grief, worry, guilt and loss of identity" (Herrick and Piccus 2005: 849). Throughout my own adolescence and early adulthood, I had a hard time building personal and meaningful relationships because I came to expect that all the relationships I would have while in care, including those with foster parents, social workers, youth workers and others, would be only short-term. I have also experienced, and observed many other youth from care experience, a continued pattern of transience in adulthood that results in ongoing movement from one apartment to the next, one city to the next and so on. For me, and I suspect for many other former youth in care, the struggle to create a sense of security reflects the struggle to ground ourselves in both who we are and where we are.

From an anti-oppressive perspective, workers must recognize the power they have in affecting both the youth's experiences and their outcomes when making decisions about where youth in care will live. Youth must be involved as much as possible in these decisions and must also be given information that allows them to understand when placement decisions are beyond the control of their social worker and/or result from flaws in the system. In short, we must help youth understand how these decisions are being made, all the options that are available and what input the youth may have regarding their placement.

## The Transition to Adulthood

Leaving care is not just a transition from adolescence to adulthood. For youth in care it usually involves the transition from youth to adult services that occurs when youth are no longer eligible for child welfare supports. This transition is legally required once youth turn eighteen or nineteen years old, depending on their province or territory of residence. Existing literature points to a variety of reasons why many youth feel unprepared for transitioning to adulthood, including loss of supports and resources (such as their social worker), lack of life skills and difficulty accessing adult services (Rutman et al. 2005). Although legislation sometimes provides for post-majority services, in practice these are often underfunded and therefore not available (Serge et al. 2002). Unfortunately, "there is good reason to suspect that when the transition from foster care is not well supported, youth are at greater risk for homelessness, sexual exploitation, victimization, and involvement in the criminal justice and child welfare systems" (Rutman et al. 2005).

When considering the situation facing youth leaving care, it is important to keep in mind that most children come into care as a result of experiencing abuse and/or neglect. Corby notes that "emotional abuse, while theoretically able to occur by itself, is also almost certain to accompany or to be a consequence of the other forms of abuse" (2006: 98). Child abuse and neglect theories describe long-term consequences resulting from these experiences that include anxiety, low self-esteem, depression, substance misuse and vulnerability to further abuse (Corby 2006). Thus, it is not surprising that one B.C. study reported that by age sixteen, 74 percent of males in care and 47 percent of females in care had been identified as having special needs, primarily relating to intensive behavioural or serious mental health issues (Representative for Children and Youth 2007). Another study found that 51 percent of youth in care research participants reported depression-related symptoms, mental health treatment and/or serious mental health concerns (Rutman et al. 2005). From my experience, it becomes very difficult sometimes to distinguish when mental health issues influence the abuse and/or neglect that cause youth to come into care, and when mental health issues become the result of having been abused and/or neglected. Nonetheless, the fact is that many youth in care face mental health challenges — challenges that carry on into adulthood.

Yet child welfare systems are curiously unprepared for the likelihood that youth in care will need long-term post-majority supports in order to be successful. As one B.C. youth stated, "Age is not an indication of being prepared for something — being ready is different for everyone" (FBCYICN 2002: 7). The National Youth in Care Network (NYICN 2005:1) mirrors this point more bluntly by stating that "youth who are at the age of majority without extended care and maintenance are symbolically and literally dumped out of the system."

Research shows that if a youth in care is connected to at least one stable and supportive person before, during and after their transition, they will experience better outcomes (Rutman et al. 2001). Since social workers stop working with youth once they reach the age of majority, one strategy involves working with youth to identify who this person could be (such as an extended family member, community support person). Social workers could also start preparing youth for transition when youth are in their early teens, for example, by encouraging them to participate in appropriate services such as life skills workshops. Based on my own experience, I believe another important step to ensure a smooth transition to adult services is for workers to encourage youth to initiate the necessary paperwork and relationship building well in advance of leaving care.

Clearly there is a connection between the personal and the political here — a connection between poor personal outcomes and policies that influence those outcomes. Consistent with anti-oppressive theory, work needs to be done on both micro and macro levels by looking beyond individualizing problems facing youth in care and addressing oppression issues on institutional and structural levels. Too often the struggles of youth in care are viewed primarily as a result of individual shortfalls (micro) while the effects of systemic policies and programs (macro) go virtually unnoticed. Social workers can connect the personal (micro) to the political (macro) by encouraging youth to identify if they believe their experience has been that of oppression and to examine the effects of that oppression. Until the struggles of youth in care are acknowledged and addressed on a structural level, many youth will continue to experience poor transitions coupled with poor outcomes when leaving care.

## Stigma and Youth in Care

Stigma is experienced by youth in care as a negative stereotype that influences how others view them. Some B.C. youth in care have been labelled as being a "bad ass" and explain that "youth in care who are judged and discriminated against are hurt; they act out against others, who in turn spread the discrimination and the cycle continues" (FBCYICN 2004: 6). Stigmatization of youth in care influences their sense of identity and self-image, causing them to internalize negative images (real or imagined) that others have of them (Herrick and Piccus 2005). Also, given the paucity of therapeutic resources available to children and youth in care it is likely that some youth who have been abused and/or neglected react to those experiences with inappropriate behaviours and thus inadvertently contribute to negative labels themselves. Youth in care frequently experience multiple and intersecting oppressions (such as those based on gender, sexuality, ability, race, class) and therefore may be experiencing multiple and intersecting stigmas beyond being youth in care.

The anti-oppressive social worker must be aware of these possibilities and prepared to counteract them. For example, workers must be knowledgeable about resources available to marginalized communities and how to access them, and routinely offer this information to the youth with whom they are working.

Workers also have an obligation to educate themselves about how multiple and intersecting oppressions may impact youth in care and incorporate that into their daily practice. For instance, perhaps a youth doesn't want a social worker to meet their teacher because they don't want to be labelled a foster child at school, or perhaps a youth would rather not receive a service because it targets foster youth and they don't, or don't want to, identify as that. It may be hard for social workers to understand why youth sometimes respond to information or opportunity the way they do, so it is important to keep in mind that stigma, or fear of stigma, may be a significant contributing factor.

## Lack of Voice

Lack of voice is experienced by youth in care primarily in relation to the decisions made about their lives. All Canadian child welfare legislation contains provisions for children, youth and families to be consulted about decisions that affect them. In B.C., section 70(c) of the *Child, Family and Community Service Act* (CFCSA) specifies that youth in care have a right "to be consulted and to express their views, according to their abilities, about significant decisions affecting them." Accompanying policy documents suggest that this right is exercised primarily through case planning (MCFD n.d.a). Research with clients suggests that too often workers fail to consult with clients. A survey conducted by the FBCYICN, for example, found that 22 percent of youth respondents did not even know what a plan of care was (2004). A review of B.C. child protection practice found that in 2001 only 45 percent of case plans had been completed according to practice standards (RCY 2007).

It is also important to keep in mind that some youth may be facing challenges that either directly or indirectly affect their ability to fully participate in decision-making or to advocate for themselves. As noted, many youth may not even know they have the right to participate in decisions. Further, there are historical barriers of fear and anxiety rooted in history and oppression that prevent some people from pursuing their rights (Razack 1998). This might be the case for a refugee youth seeking to protect his family's fragile immigration status or for an Indigenous youth working with a white social worker. For instance, it seems possible and also probable that many of these youth have already developed a sense of mistrust for all adults and may not wish to participate in decision-making processes as a result.

Anti-oppressive practice must therefore include putting time and effort into developing partnership relationships with youth through involving youth in decision-making and assessment processes. This requires clearly demonstrating to youth that you have both listened to and considered their perspectives when you are in a position to make decisions that affect them. An anti-oppressive approach could also include empowering youth to advocate for themselves and/or to go through an agency's complaint resolution process when they feel that they have not been heard.

## Emotional Healing

Emotional healing is experienced by youth in care as a way to cope with the emotional consequences of abuse and neglect. In addition to the likelihood that emotional abuse has accompanied other forms of abuse (Corby 2006), virtually all youth in care are susceptible to emotional risks such as anxiety and depression, and a majority report emotional, psychological and/or serious mental health concerns (Rutman et al. 2005). From an anti-oppressive perspective, I worry about the practice implications of this, specifically that social workers find it quicker, easier and cheaper to pass these issues on to the medical profession rather than looking at them holistically and in a social context. I have seen too many youth quickly diagnosed with psychiatric disorders or psychological impairments in place of the acknowledgment that they may instead be reacting "normally" to extremely difficult and complex circumstances beyond their control. The NYICN (2006: 10) cautions that managing a youth's emotional and psychological needs with medications without addressing the trauma they have experienced can create long-lasting consequences for youth in care:

> Masked by the use of medications, the life history of the maltreated, neglected or orphaned youth is ignored, denied or negated, leaving the young person in or from the system with a plethora of psychological and emotional needs that are untended to when they leave (voluntarily or involuntarily) or age out of the system.

I have personally seen the legacy this kind of practice can create including a lifelong dependency on, and in some cases addiction to, substances used to sooth emotional pain.

## Indigenous Youth in Care

The way in which Indigenous youth in care experience their challenges must be analyzed through a lens that considers the history and present situation of Indigenous peoples in Canada. Generally speaking, we must understand Canada's history of colonization and how colonial practices such as residential schools, the *Indian Act* and the sixties scoop continue to influence Indigenous peoples today. That the mainstream child welfare system failed and continues to fail Canadian Indigenous peoples is well-documented (see several chapters in this book, also Anderson 1998). Indigenous children and youth are disproportionately over-represented in state care throughout Canada, a situation that has seen little change since the time of the sixties scoop. For example, an alarming 40 percent of Indigenous children and youth were in foster care in B.C. in 2006, and this is proportionally similar to the situation fifteen years ago (Absolon and MacDonald 2006). Once in care, Indigenous children are rarely placed with Indigenous families or communities. For instance, in 2007, only 15.8 percent of B.C.'s Indigenous children and youth in care were placed with Indigenous caregivers (MCFD n.d.b).

From an anti-oppressive perspective, these statistics can be viewed as the combined result of the dominant society's imposition of its values on Indigenous peoples, while also failing to recognize and respect Indigenous values and traditions. Thus, Indigenous youth in care experience "triple jeopardy," since removal from parents also entails removal from extended family and from their cultural community (Mandell et al. 2007).

In common with most Canadian child welfare law, B.C. legislation contains provisions for protecting and preserving Indigenous cultural identity. Section 4(2) of the CFCSA (1996) states that "if the child is an Aboriginal child, the importance of preserving the child's cultural identity must be considered in determining the child's best interests." Although references to the value of protecting "cultural identity" are scattered throughout the CFCSA, Absolon and MacDonald (2006: 173) note: "Since this Act has been implemented, there has been little shift to fully incorporate cultural identity into social work practice." The failure to incorporate Indigenous values into child welfare practice is illustrated by the fact that a youth's best interests are seen as separate from their family's and community's best interests, a partitioning that is incongruent with Indigenous beliefs (Kline 1992; Mandell et al. 2007). Noting that Indigenous youth are five to six times more likely to commit suicide than non-Indigenous youth, the Child and Youth Officer of B.C. suggested various strategies to address this, all of which centre around viewing Indigenous youth within the context of their families and communities (CYOBC 2006).

## Youth and Their Communities

Viewing *all* youth in care within the context of their community is beneficial. It allows a worker to identify existing or potential community support connections for youth, increases the visibility of youth within their community and helps inform the community about how they can provide long-term meaningful supports. Seeing youth in care in the context of their community not only helps individual youth with their needs but can also contribute to addressing the collective needs of vulnerable youth populations. Community supports help youth in the short-term and can also help build meaningful long-term relationships for youth. Since many youth in care do not have supportive family or extended family, community connections might be the only source of long-term support available. Because relationships with most professionals (such as social workers and youth workers) are severed once a youth legally becomes an adult, having long-term community support can help youth transition successfully out of care and/or make the transition to adult services. Connecting youth to their community not only helps youth get their needs met and the support they need in achieving their goals, it also helps youth create a sense of community for themselves.

My own experience is that referring youth to community resources is a great way to help facilitate a sense of connection. Referrals can be made to meet specific needs, to connect youth with positive peer relationships or to create opportunities for longer term mentorship supports. Youth can also be encouraged to volunteer in the community and to participate in community activities. By offering various methods and different objectives for youth to connect with their community, youth have a greater chance of creating a sense of community for themselves. When youth have a sense of community and participate in community activities and events they increase their visibility, which serves to reduce both their vulnerability and their likelihood of encountering and engaging in risky behaviour. Community connections can provide youth with supports to build on their strengths, develop resiliency and increase their skills and capacity for transitioning to adulthood. At the same time, communities benefit from youth involvement and learning about youth issues from a youth perspective.

Some youth may engage in more formal opportunities for community involvement, such as community development initiatives, city council youth committees, community research projects and community action groups. Bringing youth out of the margins so that they become more visible and vocal in our communities is likely to positively contribute to systemic change. Many social workers may find that the demands and limitations of their job make it difficult to adequately redress power imbalances and address structural inequalities in their day-to-day work. Still, anti-oppressive practice with youth in care is possible if workers are willing to incorporate intentional practice strategies.

Most clients in child welfare are concerned about how social workers use their power (Dumbrill 2006) so it is often useful to have an open dialogue about power and the use of power with youth. In this, it is critical that workers accept and acknowledge the power they hold to affect the lives of the youth with whom they are working. A worker who demonstrates to a youth her/his commitment to being transparent and accountable in this way is much more likely to build a mutual understanding of exactly where both opportunities and limitations exist. From this foundation, worker and youth can develop greater awareness of government and community resources that may offer additional supports — for both worker and youth.

A second strategy involves practising in ways that youth are likely to experience as empowering, including workers taking a youth-centred approach, workers recognizing youth as experts of their own lives and workers focusing on developing partnership-type relationships. Adequate time must be taken to discuss processes and decisions with youth while placing emphasis on understanding their perspective (Callahan et al. 1998; Strega 2007). Social workers must provide youth with a clear understanding of which decisions youth can make on their own, which decisions they will be consulted about and how they will be consulted. Youth also need to understand about decisions that have to do with legal or bureaucratic processes in which even their own social worker might have no input. For example, a social worker in Gómez's (2008) research invited a youth to describe all he wanted in a foster placement with the proviso that she might not be able to find a placement that met all his criteria. Responding to each youth as an individual, identifying their unique strengths and affirming their experiences and challenges are all key practice strategies that help promote positive self-identity (Ragg, Patrick and Ziefert 2006).

Empowering youth also involves encouraging them to utilize their strengths to find their own solutions and their own sources of power (Deitz 2000). Taking a strengths-based approach simply means identifying the strengths a youth may possess, including specific skills or qualities. Workers can help youth in care resist or overcome the consequences of abuse and neglect by promoting their resiliency and resourcefulness (Corby 2006). For instance, social workers need to resist the temptation to encourage youth who are survivors of abuse or neglect to "treat" their feelings with psychiatric medication and instead initiate empowering practices that identify the youth's strengths, address their challenges and struggles, and help them connect or reconnect with positive relationships (Deitz 2000). The NYICN (2006) proposes these strengths-based interventions as a more effective strategy for helping youth in care emotionally heal from their experiences of trauma. Using this approach, social workers can try and cope with systemic shortfalls by encouraging youth to meet their own needs when the worker's resources are limited. For example, youth might connect with non-child welfare resources, develop skills through community programs available to all youth and build alternative support networks.

A third strategy is the practice of systemic advocacy. While social workers may be discouraged by their employers from participating in activities such as public protest and involvement with social change groups, there are still many actions social workers can take. For instance, they can connect youth to existing advocacy resources such as a child welfare advocate or child and youth representative, which are available in most Canadian provinces and territories. Youth can also be supported and encouraged to follow formal complaints processes. Social workers can intentionally make the connection between a youth's experience and systemic issues and then inform and/or participate in community-based interest groups such as the FBCYICN. By practising systemic advocacy, social workers can actively work towards changing systemic limitations.

These practice strategies can be challenging to implement in adequate and meaningful ways given systemic barriers and the oversize caseloads many workers carry. To support and empower youth to make their voices heard in this context is a daunting task, especially if a worker feels limited in her/his ability to respond to what youth are saying (Munro 2001). It is also important to keep in mind that some individual youth may not wish to or be able to participate in these kinds of practices for reasons that include deep-seated mistrust of workers, cognitive impairments, addiction issues or a crisis-driven lifestyle. In order to address these challenges, social workers need to remain as consistent as possible in their practice and consult widely in order to identify creative ways of dealing with them as they arise.

## Self Location

Two important aspects of practising anti-oppressively are self-locating and critical self-reflection. This means acknowledging and understanding our social location, including factors such as gender, class, age, race and sexual orientation as sources of power and privilege or alternatively as sources of marginalization. When working with youth in care, workers must be conscious of how our multiple locations impact our own sense of self and how they impact our helping relationships with youth and their families. A detailed and evolving understanding of our own locations must be intentionally developed so that we can acknowledge power relations and prevent ourselves from re-enacting and recreating dominance and marginalization (Dei 1999).

My own location includes having experienced being an at-risk youth in B.C. and having been a labelled a "street kid," a "teen parent" and a "youth in care." I view my experiences, in particular being in foster care, as marginalizing and of disempowering relationships. Over time I have worked to turn these experiences into a tool for change by supporting other youth both individually and systemically in different volunteer and employment settings. While these experiences provide me with important information and understanding of the youth in care experience, I must ensure that my practice remains anti-oppressive rather than what Jones (1994) has termed "collusive" practice. This means practising critical thinking (such as evaluating both pros and cons, strengths and weaknesses) rather than just being critical.

Practicing anti-oppressively also means that I need to acknowledge that while my experience of having been an at-risk youth may lead me to identify with the youth with whom I work, it may pose a threat for other youth. For instance, my specific current social locations of dominance, power and privilege (being a white, middle-class social worker) may not be well received, and some youth may only see me as a "power-tripping social worker" who is not able to understand what they are experiencing. As workers, especially given that most of us occupy dominant societal positions (white, middle class), we must never assume that we understand what a client is experiencing, even when we have had similar experiences or when we share some aspects of social location.

Critical self-reflection encourages us to be mindful of how we make meaning of other people's words, actions and behaviours. It also encourages us to acknowledge where people are coming from and how they know what they know. We must be mindful of the social locations of those we work with and reflect on the power relations at play in the context of the worker-client relationship. For instance, we must ask ourselves if a youth and/or family is agreeing with our suggestions because they view them as possibilities to create positive and meaningful changes in their lives, or are they agreeing with our suggestions out of fear of what consequence we may have for them if they don't.

Youth, their families and communities have sources of power that need to be recognized and respected, including experiential and cultural knowledge. Because power is relational and reciprocal within relationships (Solas 1996) it is essential for workers to engage in ongoing dialogue about power relations and power sharing with youth and their families. Such partnership building is a key to anti-oppressive practice with youth in care.

## Conclusion

Youth in care face challenges based both in the reasons they entered care and in the experiences they have while in care. In order to practise effectively and anti-oppressively with these youth, work needs to take place on both micro and macro levels. This involves attending to individual needs, while also looking beyond individualizing the challenges youth face so that we might identify and address oppressions on a systemic level. We need to listen to youth and to involve them in decisions affecting their lives and we need to involve them in our communities, not just for their sake but for all of our sakes. This chapter reflects the beginning of my journey towards practicing anti-oppressively with youth in care as a new government social worker. I look forward to the rest of my adventure and the possibility of meeting you along the way.

## Suggestions for Further Reading

Herrick, M., and W. Piccus. 2005. "Sibling Connections: The Importance of Nurturing Sibling Bonds in the Foster Care System." *Children and Youth Services Review* 27, 7.

Palmer, S., and W. Cooke. 1996. "Understanding and Countering Racism with First Nations Children in Out-of-Home Care." *Child Welfare* 75, 6.

Ragg, M., D. Patrick, and M. Ziefert. 2006. "Slamming the Closet Door: Working with Gay and Lesbian Youth in Care." *Child Welfare* 85, 2.

## About the Author

April Feduniw is a recent graduate of the University of Victoria School of Social Work Child Welfare Specialization Program and is currently employed as a B.C. government child protection worker. Her experience includes being a youth in care and working in various social work practice settings in the community with this population over the last ten years. She has worked with two different University of Victoria research projects focused on the outcomes for youth in care and has co-authored several other book chapters based on this research.

## References

Absolon, K., and J. MacDonald. 2006. "Indigenous Self-Determination and Child Protection Law." In D. Turner and M. Uhlemann (eds.), *A Legal Handbook for the Helping Professional*. Victoria: Sedgwick Society.

Anderson, K. 1998. "A Canadian Child Welfare Agency for Urban Natives: The Clients Speak." *Child Welfare* 77, 4.

BCASW (B.C. Association of Social Workers). 2006. Submission to the B.C. Children and Youth Review. Vancouver. Available at <www.bcasw.org/Images/Home%20page/ Submission%20to%20BC%20Children%20and%20Youth%20Review%20Jan%20 2006.pdf> accessed Feb. 15, 2008.

BCFFPA (B.C. Federation of Foster Parent Associations). 2006. *2006 Annual Report*. Burnaby, BC.

Callahan, M., B. Field, C. Hubberstey and B. Wharf. 1998. *Best Practice in Child Welfare: Perspectives from Parents, Social Workers and Community Partners*. Victoria: Child, Family and Community Research Program and the University of Victoria.

Callahan, M., D. Rutman, S. Strega and L. Dominelli. 2005. "Looking Promising:

Contradictions and Challenges for Young Mothers in Care." In D. Gustafson (ed.), *Unbecoming Mothers: Women Living Apart from their Children.* Binghamton, NY: Haworth Press.

Corby, B. 2006. *Child Abuse: Towards a Knowledge Base.* London, U.K.: Open University Press.

CYOBC (Child and Youth Officer of B.C.). 2006. *Sayt K'uulm Goot — Of One Heart: Preventing Indigenous Youth Suicide through Youth and Community Engagement.* Available at <http://www.rcybc.ca/Groups/Special%20Reports/cyo_of_one_heart_web.pdf> accessed November 21, 2007.

Dei, G. 1999. "Knowledge and Politics of Social Change: The Implication of Anti-Racism." *British Journal of Sociology and Education* 20, 3.

Dietz, C. 2000. "Responding to Oppression and Abuse: A Feminist Challenge to Clinical Social Work." *Affilia* 15, 3.

Dominelli, L., S. Strega, M. Callahan and D. Rutman. 2005. "Endangered Children: Experiencing and Surviving the State as Failed Parent and Grandparent." *British Journal of Social Work* 35.

Dumbrill, G. (2006). "Parental Experience of Child Protection Intervention: A Qualitative Study." *Child Abuse and Neglect* 30.

FBCYICN (Federation of B.C. Youth In Care Networks). 2002. *On Our Own: Independent Living Workshop Events Project: A Final Report.* Available at <http://www.fbcyicn.ca/transitions_to_independence> accessed November 21, 2007.

_____. 2004. *Are You Listening? Final Report of the Youth Speak Project.* Available at <http://www.fbcyicn.ca/youthspeak> accessed October 31, 2007.

FREDA (Feminist Research Education Development and Action Centre). n.d. *Violence Prevention and the Girl Child.* Available at <www.harbour.sfu.ca/freda/articles/stat2.htm> accessed November 21, 2007.

Gómez, Y. 2008. "Stories from the Frontline: Perspectives from Child Protection Social Workers." Unpublished master's thesis. University of Victoria.

Herrick, M., and W. Piccus. 2005. "Sibling Connections: The Importance of Nurturing Sibling Bonds in the Foster Care System." *Children and Youth Services Review* 27, 7.

Jones, J. 1994. "Child Protection and Anti-Oppressive Practice: The Dynamics of Partnership with Parents Explore." *Early Child Development and Care* 102.

Kline, M. 1992. "Child Welfare Law, 'Best Interests of the Child' Ideology, and First Nations." *Osgoode Hall Law Journal* 30, 2.

Mandell, D., J. Clouston Carlson, M. Fine and C. Blackstock. 2007. "Indigenous Child Welfare." In G. Cameron and N. Coady (eds.), *Moving Towards Positive Systems of Child and Family Welfare.* Waterloo: Wilfrid Laurier Press.

MCFD (Ministry of Children and Family Development). 1997. *Report of the Task Force on Safeguards for Children and Youth in Foster or Group Home Care.* Victoria.

_____. 2005. *Review of Youth Safe Houses and Emergency Shelters in BC.* Victoria.

_____. 2006. *2006/07–2008/09 Service Plan.* Available at <http://www.bcbudget.gov.bc.ca/2006/sp/cfd/StrategicContext6.htm> accessed November 21, 2007.

_____. n.d.a. *Know Your Rights: A Guide for Young People in Care.* Available at <http://www.mcf.gov.bc.ca/child_family_service_act/know_rights_3.htm> accessed November 21, 2007.

_____. n.d.b. *Youth Agreements.* Available at <http://www.mcf.gov.bc.ca/other_services/yeaf/index.htm> accessed October 31, 2007.

Munro, E. 2001. "Empowering Looked-After Children." *Child and Family Social Work* 6, 2.

NYICN (National Youth In Care Network). 2003. *Primer: Research Report*. Ottawa: NYICN.

_____. 2005. *Current Themes Facing Youth in State Care: Backgrounder Series #2 — Leaving Care.* Available at <http://www.youthincare.ca/emancipation.html> accessed November 21, 2007.

_____. 2006. *The Chemical Management of Canadian Systems Youth.* Ottawa.

Office of the Provincial Health Officer. 2001. *Health Status of Children and Youth in Care in British Columbia: What do the Mortality Data Show?* Victoria: Ministry of Health and Ministry Responsible for Seniors.

Ragg, M., D. Patrick and M. Ziefert. 2006. "Slamming the Closet Door: Working with Gay and Lesbian Youth in Care." *Child Welfare* 85, 2.

Raychaba, B. 1989. "Canadian Youth in Care: Leaving Care to Be on Our Own with No Direction from Home." *Children and Youth Services Review* 11.

_____. 1993. *Pain, Lots of Pain: Violence and Abuse in the Lives of Young People in Care.* Ottawa: National Youth in Care Network.

Razack, S. 1998. "The Cold Game of Equality Staring." *Looking White People in the Eye.* Toronto: University of Toronto Press.

RCY (Representative for Children and Youth). 2007. *Health and Well-Being of Children in Care in British Columbia: Educational Experience and Outcomes.* Available at <http://www.rcybc.ca/Content/Publications/SpecialReports.asp> accessed November 21, 2007.

Rutman, D., A. Barlow, C. Hubberstey, D. Alusik and E. Brown. 2001. *Supporting Young People's Transition from Government Care: Stage 1 Report.* Victoria: University of Victoria.

Rutman, D., C. Hubberstey, A. Barlow and E. Brown. 2005. *When Youth Age Out of Care — A Report on Baseline Findings.* Victoria: University of Victoria.

Serge, L., M. Eberle, M. Goldberg, S. Sullivan and P. Dudding. 2002. *Pilot Study: The Child Welfare System and Homelessness among Canadian Youth.* Ottawa: National Secretariat on Homelessness.

Solas, J. 1996. "The Limits of Empowerment in Human Service Work." *The Australian Journal of Social Work* 31, 2.

Strega, S. 2000. "Efforts at Empowering Youth: Youth-in-Care and the Youth-in-Care Networks in Ontario and Canada." In. M. Callahan and S. Hessle (eds.), *Valuing the Field: Child Welfare in an International Context.* Aldershot, UK: Ashgate

_____. 2007. "Anti-Oppressive Practice in Child Welfare." In D. Baines (ed.), *Doing Anti-Oppressive Practice: Building Transformative Politicized Social Work.* Halifax: Fernwood.

# Chapter 10

# Reconstructing Neglect and Emotional Maltreatment from an Anti-Oppressive Perspective

*Henry Parada*

Anti-oppressive social work may negotiate its space in dealing with issues of neglect and emotional maltreatment by recognizing that these categories are culturally bound and are not universal. These two core child protection categories can be alternatively interpreted by placing particular emphasis on structures, contexts and interactions with families, at the same time recognizing that there are family and individual influences on caregivers that may increase the risk of a child being emotionally "abused" and/or "neglected." This chapter forges a tentative relationship between anti-oppressive practices and child welfare through an analysis of the categories of neglect and emotional maltreatment.

Questions Addressed in This Chapter

1. How can anti-oppressive discourses engage child welfare social work practices, especially in regard to neglect and emotional maltreatment?
2. How does whiteness as invisible norm affect the assessment of neglect and emotional maltreatment?
3. Are concepts of neglect and emotional maltreatment legitimate categories within anti-oppressive child welfare practice?

Child protection and anti-oppressive practice have had a short and often ambivalent relationship. Writers who have considered this question suggest that successful anti-oppressive practice in child welfare requires that we listen to and rely on service users' knowledge (Dumbrill 2003) as well as modifying how child protection work is conceptualized (Strega 2007). Ross et al. (2007) attempt to apply anti-oppressive theory in their research within a mainstream agency serving clients with addictions and mental health needs. In this case, the authors investigated internalized oppression and its effect on LGBT (lesbian, gay, bisexual and transgender) individuals living with depression. Barnoff and Moffatt (2007: 68) indicate that anti-oppressive practices of social work are still relatively new and are "still very much a work in progress" with "many challenges to be worked out both theoretically and [practically]." Given child welfare's current emphasis on risk discourses, managerialism and social control, and the relative newness of anti-oppressive discourses, the question is how to engage in a critical merging of these seemingly oppositional discourses.

Despite efforts to link anti-oppressive discourses to social work practices, there is still ambivalence about the usefulness of anti-oppressive theory, particularly in child welfare. Cameron et al. (2007: 19) argue that those inside the child welfare system still believe that "[analyses of oppression] are not officially a primary concern and are... illegitimate focuses of helping." Anti-oppressive discourses have also been critiqued for lacking clarity and concrete strategies for practice. Gray et al. (2007: 56) argue that "critically constructed anti-oppressive practice theory... remains a theory in search of a practice" because anti-oppressive "ideas are still highly interpretive and beyond the reach of empirical validation."

Many authors use aspects of anti-oppressive theory to study the "contradictory tensions" (Barnoff and Moffatt 2007: 56) experienced by feminist social agencies as they attempt to reduce inequalities between service providers and users. According to Barnoff and Coleman (2007), if feminist agencies are successful, they should engage in the following additional steps: educate other service providers regarding their approach; assist users in navigating the system; engage authentically; and engage in empowerment and capacity building.

In this chapter I discuss some of these approaches, emphasizing the fluidity of concepts, uncertainty and the need to deconstruct taken-for-granted assumptions common to child welfare. I also address the intersectionality of race and gender, class, sexual orientation and whiteness, which influences child protection practices (Todd and Burns 2007). The construction of categories of abuse in mainstream theories and practice has been highly problematic, and although I do not propose to eliminate them as objects of intervention, I argue that they need to be reconstructed through an anti-oppressive framework.

As Butler (1993) maintains, we as practitioners and theorists need to be aware of our power to name certain behaviours as neglect and emotional maltreatment. We need to question who is regularly included within these categories and who is regularly excluded and how this relates to race, gender, ability, class and other social inequalities.

## Anti-Oppressive Practices and Child Welfare

Similar to its current relationship with anti-oppressive perspectives, the relationship between child welfare and radical social work has been ambivalent at best and openly hostile at other times. Arguably the precursor to anti-oppressive social work, radical social work, at one time refused to engage in child welfare work. In contrast, anti-oppressive social work recognizes child welfare and other statutory organizations as legitimate and seeks to develop a critical practice at these sites (Healy 2005a).

Healy (2005b: 221) expresses concern that critical theorists are unable to integrate theory and practice despite "their commitment... to praxis." She further states that "many social workers experience difficulties translating critical theoretical perspectives [including anti-oppression] into practice" (221). This view was expressed by focus group participants in a study of anti-oppressive practice amongst social workers:

> Anti-oppression… sometimes I think it can be so theorized and people can't funnel it down to practice. When it comes to breaking it down, or making alliances with community or government, they [anti-oppression theorists] can put all the words, but putting the theory into practice, that's the work and the challenge. (Barnoff, Parada and Grassau 2005: 25)

It is perhaps because anti-oppressive practice challenges workers to question what they believe about their work and the institutional categories that guide them that make this form of practice seem so complex. Certainly, anti-oppressive approaches complicate the dynamics between clients and social workers, between social workers and their institutions, and between workers and community and government stakeholders. From an anti-oppressive framework, there is no prescriptive approach that can take into account the complexity of service users' lives (Dumbrill 2003).

The following core principles should guide anti-oppressive social work practice: social work practice is a political practice; social workers need to engage in critical reflection of themselves and their practice; workers must critically assess clients' experiences of oppression and strive to facilitate self empowerment of clients; and workers need to work in partnership with clients and practice minimal intervention (Healy 2005a: 178–88). I add to this the importance of acknowledging that, although clients may come from marginalized populations, they use agency in their struggle against the system and routinely engage in resistance. As social workers we should encourage the exercise of that agency and frame resistance positively. The power dynamic involved in social worker–client interactions, though differently felt, is nonetheless a shared dynamic that affects both worker and client. As Healy (2000: 132) argues, there is a need to "destabilize the opposition between the powerful social worker and the powerless client," an idea that is at the core of anti-oppressive practice.

## Traditional Conceptualizations of Neglect and Emotional Maltreatment

There are various perspectives on the role of child welfare workers, the system and the kind of child welfare system that Canada requires. These discussions are generally framed within mainstream conceptualizations of child welfare and do little to radically address inequities inherent in the system. Although there is an abundance of facts about emotional maltreatment, neglect and other forms of child abuse (Dufour et al. 2008; Freymond and Cameron 2006; Kufeldt and McKenzie 2003; Trocmé et al. 2003) these typically perpetuate traditional intervention practices. An anti-oppressive framework challenges conventional forms of practice and the mainstream conceptualizations that underpin them. With regard to child protection work, the process of destabilization begins with acknowledging and deconstructing the often invisible discourses that permeate every aspect of child welfare theory and practice and that have particular power within the categories of neglect and emotional maltreatment.

There has been considerable writing on how mainstream conceptualizations uphold dominant discourses, which are devoid of critical analysis of structural aspects affecting child welfare clients and are often silent on issues such as race, class, gender and ability.[1] For example, Healy (2005b) points out that we need to move beyond dichotomous constructions of mothers (and workers) as good or bad through considering the structural influences that shape social work practice. We must be attuned to the human agency of both clients and social workers when they interact within the child welfare system (Parada 2002, 2004).

The categories of child neglect and emotional maltreatment still lack precise definitions within the child maltreatment literature. The literature refers to the way these concepts had been ignored by researchers and practitioners until recently (Polonko 2006: 260). Emotional abuse is often conceptualized as abuse that affects a child's emotions and related actions, whereas emotional maltreatment is conceptualized as that which impairs the developmental aspects of a child's life, including mental functioning, intelligence, language development and creativity (Daniel et al. 1999). Although some authors differentiate between these two categories of abuse, others use these categories interchangeably (Barnett et al. 1997). What characterizes both forms of abuse is that they are repetitive, atypical and inappropriate responses towards children (O'Hagan 1995).

Professional child welfare knowledge used in the assessment of neglect and emotional maltreatment tends to uphold discourses of dominant mainstream society. Because "whiteness" is neither questioned nor discussed, it operates instead as the invisible standard against which the behaviour of "others" is assessed (King 2004). King's analysis of social work texts revealed that although there are many on child welfare work with different ethnic communities, she could not find a text explicitly addressing social work with mainstream families. King argues that when clients are not identified as belonging to a particular racialized group or other marginalized population (e.g., gay or lesbian, people with disabilities), the taken-for-granted assumptions that operate uphold white, middle-class, heterosexual and able-bodied families as normative. Therefore, when social workers in child protection talk about neglect or emotional maltreatment, they are referring to behaviours that do not meet those White, middle-class, heterosexual family norms and expectations.

## Neglect

Polansky et al.'s definition of neglect has been the one most commonly used by practitioners and researchers. The authors define neglect as the "caretaker failing to meet the needs of a child that [are] deemed essential for physical, intellectual and emotional development" (Polansky et al. 1981: 15). Dufour et al. (2008) further indicate that neglect does not involve direct assault as in situations of physical or sexual abuse but constitutes a failure to provide the care considered to be necessary for the wellbeing of the child. Dufour et al. consider this care to be the most important component of the parents' ability to assume the tasks and responsibility of caring for the child. The four most commonly accepted forms of neglect are: physical neglect — failure to meet the child's basic physical needs; emotional neglect — lack or absence of attention to the emotional needs of the child; medical neglect — failure to provide appropriate and necessary health and medical care; and lack of supervision — failure to adequately or appropriately provide supervision (Polonko 2006; Dufour et al. 2008).

Less commonly accepted forms of neglect are financial neglect — failure to provide for the child's economic wellbeing; and community, collective or societal neglect — the failure of society and community, including schools, to provide basic support for the wellbeing of parents and children (Polonko 2006). Poverty related to conditions such as low levels of education, underemployment, isolation and single parenthood has been associated with the increased possibility of parents neglecting their children (Polonko 2006). Although the relationship between neglect and poverty has been extensively documented, poverty is not fully accepted as justification for parents to neglect their responsibility.

In their Québec study, Mayer et al. (2007: 727) found that the forms of neglect most frequently substantiated by child protection workers were failure to protect from physical injury (28.6 percent) and lack of supervision leading to maladaptive social behaviours (29.6 percent). This study noted that the neglected children were generally younger than those in other categories of substantiated maltreatment, had prior reports of neglect and had previously experienced child protection interventions. In addition, the parents often faced more challenges than parents in other categories, including mental health issues, divorce, less education and no employment income. Most of these characteristics seemed to apply to mothers more frequently than fathers (Mayer et al. 2007; Dufour et al. 2008). Most neglected children had experienced other forms of abuse. The consequences, both immediate and later in the child's development may include aggression, delinquency, substance abuse, adolescent pregnancy and mental health challenges (Polonko 2006; Dufour et al. 2008).

## Emotional Maltreatment

Trocmé et al. (2003) reported an estimated 135,000 investigations of child maltreatment carried out across Canada during 1998. Child protection systems substantiated 45 percent of child maltreatment allegations; 25 percent of substantiated investigations were classified as emotional maltreatment. Assessing emotional maltreatment is difficult because it "often does not involve a specific incident or visible injury" (Trocmé et al. 2001: 36) and the effect is usually only perceived over time. Trocmé et al. (2001) divided emotional maltreatment into four major categories: 1) emotional abuse (mental, emotional or developmental problems caused by hostile, punitive treatment or extreme verbal abuse); 2) non-organic failure to thrive (marked by a noticeable retardation of growth due to physical or emotional neglect); 3) emotional neglect (mental, emotional or developmental problems caused by inadequate nurturance and affection);

and 4) exposure to family violence (child witnessing or being involved with family violence).

Garbarino (1998) suggests that psychological maltreatment hinders a child's development and social abilities and manifests itself in five ways: 1) rejecting (the adult fails to acknowledge the child and fulfill basic emotional needs); 2) isolating (the adult prohibits the experience of social norms, such as friendship building, and begins a pattern that leads the child to feel isolated); 3) ignoring (the adult may be physically present but fails to respond to the child's need for emotional stimulation); 4) terrorizing (the adult verbally abuses the child, frightens the child through bullying and intimidation and creates a world for the child that is terrifying); and 5) corrupting (the adult exposes the child to inappropriate behaviours, reinforces patterns of defiance and makes the child unfit for normal social experience) (Garbarino 1998: 2–3; see also Chamberland et al. 2003). There are two main points of reference commonly used to assess emotional maltreatment: 1) the caregiver directly causing emotional harm and/or the caregiver's response to either emotional harm of the child or the child's risk of emotional harm; and 2) the child being exposed to adult conflict.

According to Garbarino (1998: 2), "We must accommodate cultural and ethnic differences when defining emotional maltreatment." He further suggests that psychological or emotional abuse is a message of rejection or impairment of what has culturally been valued as psychologically important, such as warmth, open communication, autonomy of the child and protection from trauma. At the same time, we must not minimize or ignore cases in which emotional abuse is suspected out of a respect for a particular culture. Although this acknowledges the importance of considering alternative perspectives when assessing child maltreatment, these discourses still focus narrowly on individual parents and the nuclear family as the source of child maltreatment. There are, however, numerous socioeconomic and institutional factors that we need to consider when assessing possible cases of neglect or emotional maltreatment.

Although emotional abuse is difficult to define and detect, it is generally assessed based on societal norms and by professionals who determine whether a particular situation or act is psychologically damaging (Latimer 1998). As Hart (1987, cited in Chamberland et al. 2003: 16) notes, such abuse can be defined as consisting of

> acts of omission and commission which are judged on the basis of a combination of community standards and professional expertise to be psychologically damaging. Such acts are committed by individuals… in a position of power that render the child vulnerable… [affecting] the behavioural, affective, or physical functioning of the child.

Chamberland et al. (2003) found that children who were emotionally maltreated were significantly younger when compared with those who reported other forms of abuse. Blended families more often reported children with emotional abuse, as did children from single-parent households. Other factors influencing reported cases of emotional maltreatment were mental health issues, drug addiction and parents who themselves were abused, neglected or psychologically maltreated. This may in part be due to the stressors associated with these types of difficulties. Perhaps the most common family problem that increased the probability of a child being emotionally maltreated was spousal abuse (Chamberland et al. 2003).

Although all children who witness violence inside and outside their home are emotionally impacted not all of them reach the same level of psychological or emotional negative response. Children who witness violence may expend a considerable amount of energy developing defence mechanisms to cope with the trauma, resulting in developmental delays (Tomison and Tucci 1997; Zuskin 2000). It is critical to keep in mind that, as Magen (1999) notes, many children, including children who witness television violence and children who live in violent communities, show the same "symptoms" (fear, withdrawal, aggressiveness) as children who witness domestic violence. He also draws attention to the fact that fully half of the children in various research studies were not measurably affected by witnessing abuse.

Adults who suffered emotional maltreatment as children may experience psychological difficulties later in life. Young adults who were psychologically mistreated as children tend to suffer more depression, lowered self-esteem and adopt an external attribution style, namely the belief that they lack control of the events that affect them (Barnett et al. 1997). In their study of past emotional maltreatment and quality of current relationships, Varia and Abidin (1999) posit that one psychological consequence from emotional maltreatment as a child is a deflated perception of trust and love that can result in difficulty forming healthy and positive adult relationships (Barnett et al. 1997; Varia and Abidin 1999).

Resilience has been defined as a child's "tendency to spring back, rebound... and involves the capacity to respond and endure, or develop and master in spite of life stressors or adversity" (Mandleco and Peery 2000: 99). Although children and youth may have been subjected to high levels of stress and/or emotional abuse, these events do not automatically translate to emotional or psychological symptoms of distress. Studies that "assess risk and outcomes... have clearly demonstrated that [children] are able to overcome developmental hazards and adversity without apparent negative outcome" (Smith and Carlson 1997: 236). Resilience has been characterized in three major ways: 1) the ability to cope with emotional/psychological maltreatment; 2) the ability to maintain balance internally and externally; and 3) the ability to use resources when facing difficult situations. Resilience is often linked with recovery, the process of overcoming the effects of emotional/psychological maltreatment so as to ameliorate suffering in the long term. The presence of protective factors such as positive relationships with extended family members or engagement in school or community activities contribute to resilience and may protect the child from developing negative outcomes from a number of risk factors (Smith and Carlson 1997).

## Reconceptualizing Neglect and Emotional Maltreatment

Although I discussed in the previous section dominant psychological discourses that purport to explain reasons for neglect and emotional maltreatment, these referred to neglect and emotional maltreatment in a narrow sense, concentrating on the child's parents (i.e., nuclear family) as the only possible source of child maltreatment. There are many other socioeconomic and institutional factors that we need to have in mind when we assess the presence of neglect and emotional maltreatment.

As Swift (1995) and Callahan (1993) note, neglect is a socially constructed category differentially deployed against parents who occupy certain race, class, gender and ability categories without regard to contexts such as poverty, migration and colonization. Mental health labels such as "emotional maltreatment" or "psychological abuse" are perhaps one of the most powerful tools used by what are sometimes called the "psy" disciplines (Dean 1999): psychiatry, psychology and social work. The psychologization and therapization of everyday experience has resulted in the redefinition of normal family life as damaging people's emotions especially for those on the margins. The expression of strong emotions typical for people in everyday struggle with issues of poverty, lack of community support or isolation due to recent immigration are not necessarily emotional maltreatment. Under these pressures, parents may not be as involved with their children as is expected in North American society (Furedi 2004).

Should child welfare dispense with the categories of neglect and emotional maltreatment entirely, as Callahan (1993) suggests about neglect? These categories demonstrably reinforce the oppression of women, racialized people and others who do not meet the dominant image of the North American family. The child welfare system is "re-authorized... to [manage] racialized and gendered populations" (Lewis 2000: 8) through specific institutional practices. Being managed as the "Other" has become central to the experiences of marginalized families. We might argue that eliminating these two categories will help us reconstruct our relationship with clients and move to a new understanding and collaboration.

I take the position that children in certain circumstances are exposed to neglect and emotional maltreatment and we cannot simply dispense with these notions because they are socially constructed and negatively impact marginalized populations. But we must reformulate these concepts in a way that takes into consideration factors other than individual nuclear family benefits and challenges. We can explore with families how they are connected in their communities and to extended family. We can ask questions about whether there is suitable housing, spaces for play, after-school programs, flexible work arrangements, language skills training for those who speak English as a second language and parental support for those who are isolated. We need to consider with parents how poverty has affected their childrearing in an environment that could be considered neglectful before we label the family dynamics emotionally abusive.

## Applying an Anti-Oppressive Perspective

The practical application of anti-oppressive approaches to situations of neglect and emotional maltreatment remains problematic. Some writers suggest we consider the following elements: understand the history of child welfare; resist the tendency to blame mothers; look beyond individual deficiency as an explanation for problems; ground practice in the stories clients tell us about their lives; and understand our own and our client's social locations and how these locations are affected by micro and macro factors (Carter 1999; Krane 2003; Strega 2007: 67–72). Applying these recommendations is likely to benefit social workers who work in the child welfare system — and their clients.

Agencies providing child welfare services need to acknowledge their historical culpability as part of a larger oppressive system. It is important not to continue the history of blaming mothers and other marginalized groups; rather, child welfare should look towards reconciliation with and within those communities most affected. The child welfare system must acknowledge its inherent and historical problems while affected communities must avoid blaming all their problems on the child welfare system: a sense of "responsibility — forgiveness" might ideally ensue (Pon 2007). Communication is crucial if we are to improve relations with communities affected by the system's abuse of power.

How can this be done? First, agencies need to eschew the discourses of psychopathology and trauma that encourage what might be characterized as an identity of victimhood. Instead of concentrating on weakness and problems, agencies might concentrate on resilience and survival skills parents engage in to provide emotional support for their children in difficult circumstances. Second, child welfare systems need to move away from practising rigid control and become more willing to allow social workers to engage with clients in kinship practices, alternative court practices and family conferences. In this way workers and administrators can help create a space where clients can become allies of the system. Ontario is moving in this direction, with workers being allowed to work intensively with families in order to find ways to overcome difficulties and develop alternative interpretations for pathological discourses (Dumbrill 2006). These first steps in the recovery of agency can encourage both workers and clients to engage in positive forms of resistance. By changing discourses and practices social workers enable micro-resistance to institutional practice (Parada 2004).

Regarding micro-practices, I recommend Barnoff and Coleman's (2007) suggestions, namely that workers need to spend time explaining the system to clients, particularly how to navigate a bureaucracy that may be impersonal and convoluted and in which many decisions may have been made without clients' clear understanding. This is especially crucial for those who do not speak English as a first language, those with limited literacy and numeracy skills and those whose intense emotions may affect their decision-making capacities (Barnoff and Coleman 2007: 33–37). There are other conceptual instruments that social workers can use in their efforts to practise anti-oppressively. First, they can take an "informed not-knowing" stance. Knowledge is always partial and is constructed on the understanding and particular interests of the person or persons involved in the process. Social workers assessing neglect or emotional maltreatment must keep in mind that the information collected is partial and is based on individual worker and agency understandings of what constitutes a healthy and good family. Families from non-dominant cultural backgrounds have particular ways of interacting with their children. Some may appear to be distant and cool, others may seem to be intensely involved. These interactions may be healthy or abusive in particular contexts (King 2004). Notions of children, family, healthy interpersonal dynamics and child development are socially and institutionally constructed concepts. When we accept this, we can approach unfamiliar family interactions knowing they may be different from dominant forms of family dynamics but not necessarily unhealthy, abusive or neglectful.

We have partial knowledge because our knowledge is based on localized interpretations within a set of dominant discourses that influence our way of understanding family dynamics. Each action we take as child welfare workers is based on a body of knowledge that we have accepted as "true." If we wish to maintain an anti-oppressive attitude, we need to reconsider the sources of the knowledge we typically use to understand family dynamics of neglect or emotional maltreatment. When we assess family dynamics do we take into consideration context, child development, family background and history, social and community factors? Do traditional psychologies pathologize our client's behaviours? Do we have the energy or courage in our everyday practice to ask whether we should bring other knowledge into our decision-making processes? How do certain policies affect our relations with clients and other professionals? We must keep asking questions until we understand our client's point of view because we need to know how they understand their behaviour when interacting with their children (Healy 2005a; King 2004).

Theorists who endorse anti-oppressive practice recommend critical re-flexivity (Heron 2005), defined as the "continuous process of questioning one's interpretations of experience (of oneself and others) and one's action in the service of effective listening to, questioning and understanding self and other" (King 2004: 545). Acquiring this skill requires humility, as it reminds us that our knowledge is always only partial. We never reach a point of certainty but are constantly in the process of reaching towards a close understanding of our clients' experiences (Todd and Burns 2007).

## Neglect, Maltreatment and "Good" Families

It is difficult to bring anti-oppressive theories to bear on two of most cultur-ally powerful concepts in the practice of child welfare: neglect and emotional maltreatment. Neglect, psychological abuse and trauma have been getting tre-mendous attention lately, and social workers are encouraged to look for signs of these in every child they meet in their work. The traditional understanding of neglect and emotional maltreatment positions them as realities that are taken for granted without questioning how these concepts are constructed socially, institutionally and within the worker. Some theorists argue for the elimination of these concepts as raced, classed and gendered, with dominant white discourses interpreting what constitutes a good or bad family.

I argue that neglect and emotional maltreatment exist. To take these up anti-oppressively we need to reformulate these concepts, moving away from the trauma-based individual pathology discourse that currently shapes the way social workers make their assessments. We must assess for neglect and emotional maltreatment in context, and when we identify structural factors at play, we must advocate for services and supports such as housing, education, employment, daycare and other essentials for reducing family stressors. When supports and resources are available families are much less likely to engage in dynamics that will cause them to come into contact with the child welfare system.

## Suggestions for Further Reading

Sullivan, S., and N. Tuana (eds.). 2007. *Race and Epistemologies of Ignorance.* New York: State University of New York Press. (This book discusses different forms of "ignorance" as social mechanisms used to support white privilege and racism.)

Cameron, G., N. Coady and G. Adams. 2007. *Moving toward Positive Systems of Child and Family Welfare: Current Issues and Future Directions.* Waterloo: Wilfrid Laurier University Press.

## About the Author

Henry Parada has taught social work at Ryerson University in Toronto and at the Autonomous University of Santo Domingo, Dominican Republic. He spent over ten years in direct practice within child protection as front-line social worker and supervisor. His research interests include analysis of institutional practices, social work epistemology and methodology. Henry has published in the area of the governance of workers and clients in child protection, institutional ethnography, the construction of subject locations, community education and Latin American social work. He is presently carrying out an institutional ethnography of the national Child Protection System practices in the Dominican Republic. His projects have received funds from Canadian International Development Agency, Latin America and Caribbean Exchange Grant, Canadian Institutes of Health, UNICEF, the Government of Italy Aid Agency and Ryerson International Initiative Funds.

## Note

1.   See, for example, Barnoff 2001; Barnoff, George and Coleman 2006; Barnoff and Moffatt 2007; Brown 2007; Campbell 2003; Freeman 2007; Jeffery 2007

## References

Barnett, O., C. Miller-Perrin and R. Perrin. 1997. *Family Violence Across the Lifespan.* Thousand Oaks: Sage.

Barnoff, L. 2001. "Moving Beyond Words: Integrating Anti-Oppression Practice into Feminist Social Services." *Canadian Social Work Review* 18.

Barnoff, L., and B. Coleman. 2007. "Strategies for Integrating Anti-Oppressive Principles:

Perspectives from Feminist Agencies." In D. Baines (ed.), *Doing Anti-Oppressive Practice: Building Transformative Politicized Social Work.* Halifax: Fernwood.

Barnoff, L., P. George and B. Coleman. 2006. "Challenges to Implementing Anti-Oppressive Practice in Feminist Social Service Agencies in Toronto." *Canadian Social Work Review* 23, 1/2.

Barnoff, L., and K. Moffatt. 2007. "Contradictory Tensions in Anti-Oppression Practice in Feminist Social Services." *Affilia: Journal of Women and Social Work* 22, 1.

Barnoff, L., H. Parada and P. Grassau. 2005. "Reports on the Findings of Anti-Oppression Conference." Ryerson University, Toronto.

Brown, C. 2007. "Feminist Therapy, Violence, Problem Drinking and Re-Storying Women's Lives: Reconceptualizing Anti-Oppression." In D. Baines (ed.), *Doing Anti-Oppressive Practice: Building Transformative Politicized Social Work.* Halifax: Fernwood.

Butler, J. 1993. *Bodies that Matter: On the Discursive Limits of "Sex."* New York: Routledge.

Callahan, M. 1993. "Feminist Approaches: Women Recreate Child Welfare." In B. Wharf (ed.), *Rethinking Child Welfare in Canada.* Toronto: McLelland and Stewart.

Cameron, G., N. Coady and G. Adams. 2007. *Moving toward Positive Systems of Child and Family Welfare: Current Issues and Future Directions.* Waterloo: Wilfrid Laurier University Press.

Campbell, C. 2003. "Anti-Oppressive Theory and Practice as the Organizing Theme for Social Work Education: The Case in Favour." *Canadian Social Work Review* 20.

Carter, B. 1999. *Who's to Blame? Child Sexual Abuse and Non-Offending Mothers.* Toronto: University of Toronto Press.

Chamberland, C., L. Laporte, C. Lavergne, C. Malo, M. Tourigny, M. Mayer and S. Heli. 2003. "Psychological Maltreatment of Children Reported to Youth Protection Services: Initial Results from the Quebec Incident Study." In K. Kufeldt and B. McKenzie (eds.), *Child Welfare: Connecting Research, Policy and Practice.* Waterloo, ON: Wilfrid Laurier University Press.

Daniel, K., S. Wassell and R. Gilligan. 1999. *Child Development for Child Care and Protection Workers.* London: Jessica Kingsley.

Dean, M. 1999. *Governmentality: Power and Rule in Modern Society.* Thousand Oaks, CA: Sage.

Dufour, S., C. Lavergne, M. Larrivee and N. Trocmé. 2008. "Who Are These Parents Involved in Child Neglect? A Differential Analysis by Parent Gender and Family Structure." *Children and Youth Services Review* 30.

Dumbrill, G. 2003. "Child Welfare: AOP's Nemesis?" In W. Shera (ed.), *Emerging Perspectives on Anti-Oppressive Practice.* Toronto: Canadian Scholars' Press.

_____. 2006. "Ontario's Child Welfare Transformation: Another Swing of the Pendulum?" *Canadian Social Work Review* 23, 1/2.

Freeman, B. 2007. "Indigenous Pathways to Anti-Oppressive Practice." In D. Baines (ed.), *Doing Anti-Oppressive Practice: Building Transformative Politicized Social Work.* Halifax: Fernwood.

Freymond, N., and G. Cameron. 2006. *Towards Positive Systems of Child and Family Welfare: International Comparisons of Child Protection, Family Service, and Community Caring Systems.* Toronto: University of Toronto Press.

Furedi, F. 2004. *Therapy Culture: Cultivating Vulnerability in an Uncertain Age.* London: Routledge.

Garbarino, J. 1998. "Psychological Maltreatment Is Not an Ancillary Issue." *Brown University Child and Adolescent Behaviour Letter* 14, 8.

George, P., B. Coleman and L. Barnoff. 2007. "Beyond 'Providing Services': Voices of Service Users on Structural Social Work Practice in Community Based Social Services Agencies." *Canadian Social Work Review* 24, 1.

Gray, M., J. Coates and T. Hetherington. 2007. "Hearing Indigenous Voices in Mainstream Social Work." *Families in Society: The Journal of Contemporary Social Services* 88, 1.

Hart, S., R. Germain and M. Brassard. 1987. *Psychological Maltreatment of Children and Youth*. New York: Pergamon.

Healy, K. 2000. *Social Work Practices: Contemporary Perspective on Change.* Thousand Oaks: Sage.

_____. 2005a. *Social Work Theories in Context: Creating Frameworks for Practice*. New York: Palgrave Macmillan.

_____. 2005b. "Under Reconstruction: Renewing Critical Social Work Practices" In S. Hick, J. Fook and R. Pozzuto (eds.), *Social Work: A Critical Turn*. Toronto: Thompson Educational.

Heron, B. 2005. "Self-Reflection in Critical Social Work Practice: Subjectivity and the Possibilities of Resistance." *Reflective Practice* 6, 3.

Jeffery, D. 2007. "Professional Subjectivity in the Anti-Oppressive Social Work Classroom." *Canadian Social Work Review* 24, 2.

King, E. 2004. "From Socio-Cultural Categories to Social Located Relations: Using Critical Theory in Social Work Practice." *Families in Society: The Journal of Contemporary Social Services* 85, 4.

Krane, J. 2003. *What's Mother Got to Do with It? Protecting Children from Sexual Abuse*. Toronto: University of Toronto Press.

Kufeldt, K., and B. McKenzie. 2003. *Child Welfare: Connecting Research, Policy and Practice*. Waterloo, ON: Wilfrid Laurier University Press.

Latimer, J. 1998. *The Consequences of Child Maltreatment: Reference Guide for Health Practitioners*. Ottawa: Health Canada.

Lewis, G. 2000. *"Race," Gender, Social Welfare: Encounters in a Postcolonial Society*. Cambridge: Polity.

Magen, R. 1999. "In the Best Interests of Battered Women: Reconceptualizing Allegations of Failure to Protect." *Child Maltreatment* 4, 2.

Mandleco, B., and Peery, G. 2000. "An Organizational Framework for Conceptualizing Resilience in Children." *Journal of Child and Adolescent Psychiatric Nursing* 13, 3.

Mayer, M., C. Lavergne, M. Tourigny and J. Wright. 2007. "Characteristics Differentiating Neglected Children from Other Reported Children." *Journal of Family Violence* 22.

O'Hagan, K. 1995. "Emotional Abuse and Emotional Maltreatment: Problems of Definition." *Child Abuse and Neglect* 19.

Parada, H. 2002. "The Restructuring of the Child Welfare System in Ontario: A Study in the Social Organization of Knowledge." Unpublished PhD. thesis. University of Toronto.

_____. 2004. "Social Work Practice within the Restructured Child Welfare System in Ontario." *Canadian Social Work Review* 21.

Polansky, N., M. Chalmers, E. Buttenwieser and D. Williams. 1981. *The Damaged Parent: An Anatomy of Child Neglect*. Chicago: University of Chicago Press.

Polonko, K. 2006. "Exploring Assumptions about Child Neglect in Relation to the Broader Field of Child Maltreatment." *Journal of Health and Human Services Administration* Winter.

Pon, G. 2007. "Anti-Racism Education and Responsibility." *Canadian Social Work Review* 24, 2.

Ross, L., F. Doctor, A. Dimito, D. Kuehl and S. Armstrong. 2007. "Can Talking about

Oppression Reduce Depression? Modified CBT Group Treatment for LGBT People with Depression." *Journal of Gay and Lesbian Social Services* 19, 1.

Smith, C., and B. Carlson. 1997. "Stress Coping, and Resilience in Children and Youth." *Social Service Review* June.

Strega, S. 2007. "Anti-Oppressive Practice in Child Welfare." In D. Baines (ed.), *Doing Anti-Oppressive Practice: Building Transformative, Politicized Social Work*. Halifax: Fernwood.

Swift, K. 1995. *Manufacturing "Bad Mothers": A Critical Perspective on Child Neglect*. Toronto: University of Toronto Press.

Todd, S., and A. Burns. 2007. "Post-Structural Possibilities: Beyond Structural Practice in Child Protection." *Canadian Social Work Review* 24, 1.

Tomison, A., and J. Tucci. 1997. "Emotional Abuse: The Hidden From of Maltreatment." *Issues in Child Abuse Prevention* 8 (Spring).

Trocmé, N., B. MackLaurin, B. Fallin, J. Daciuk, D. Billingsley, M. Tourigny, M. Mayer, J. Wright, K. Barter, G. Burford, J. Hornick, R. Sullivan and B. McKenzie. 2001. *Canadian Incidence Study of Reported Child Abuse and Neglect*. Ottawa: Ministry of Health.

Trocmé, N., G. Phaneuf, S. Scarth, B. Fallin and B. MacLaurin. 2003. "The Canadian Incidence Study of Reported Child Abuse and Neglect: Methodology and Major Findings." In K. Kufeldt and B. McKenzie (eds.), *Child Welfare: Connecting Research, Policy and Practice*. Waterloo: Wilfrid Laurier University Press.

Varia, R., and R. Abidin. 1999. "The Minimizing Style: Perceptions of Emotional Maltreatment and Quality of Past and Current Relationships." *Child Abuse and Neglect* 23, 11.

Zuskin, R. 2000. "In What Circumstances Is a Child Who Witness Violence Experiencing Psychological Maltreatment?" In H. Dubowitz and D. Depanfilis (eds.), *Handbook for Child Protection Practice*. Thousand Oaks: Sage.

# Chapter 11

# Oppressing Mothers

## Protection Practices in Situations of Child Sexual Abuse

*Julia Krane and Rosemary Carlton*

This chapter considers a critical feminist approach to investigating and responding to concerns regarding child sexual abuse with a particular emphasis on non-offending mothers. Whereas feminist scholars and practitioners were once preoccupied with disrupting maternal blame for setting the conditions for child sexual abuse, changes in provincial legislation and accompanying procedures for practice now compel us to give attention to the more subtle issue of making mothers responsible for protecting children from sexual abuse once it has come to the attention of child protection authorities. In this chapter, we suggest that current child protection practices — dominated by concerns about further risk to children and their immediate safety and driven by efforts to maintain children in the care of their families following investigations — elicit a narrow focus on mothers' abilities to ensure the safety of their children. Reliant largely on idealized understandings of mothers derived from middle-class, Eurocentric norms, typical practices eclipse the multiple facets of women's identities and social locations, obscure the complexities of mothers' experiences at the time of and following disclosure and may well exacerbate their already precarious life circumstances.

Questions Addressed in This Chapter

1. How does child protection practice in situations of child sexual abuse unfold?
2. Upon what set of assumptions do the child welfare legislation, procedures and protocols rest?
3. What theories and ideologies guide your interpretation of your mandate to protect children from sexual abuse?
4. How might facets of identity and social location guide you to engage with mothers of sexually abused children? What challenges might arise?

## Determining Risk and Need of Protection

Child protection is that arena of social work practice concerned with ensuring the safety and wellbeing of children when parental care is deemed to have fallen below a socially and legally accepted minimum standard. While it is conceivable that any family could come to the attention of child protection, Bala (2004: 24) states that "the clients of child welfare agencies are often poorly educated, living in or near poverty, and not infrequently members of a racial minority group and living in a family led by a single parent, usually the mother." In fact, single mother households are highly overrepresented in the child welfare system. As noted by the 2003 Canadian Incidence Study, 39 percent of all substantiated maltreatment cases involved children living in single mother households, 32 percent were headed by two biological parents and 16 percent by blended/ step parents. Moreover, of all substantiated situations of child sexual abuse, 40 percent involved children in lone female-parent households, 34 percent involved two biological parents and 13 percent involved blended/step parent households (Trocmé et al. 2005). In Canada, 36 percent of single-parent families headed by women live below the poverty line and in "less desirable neighbourhoods" (Ambert 2006: 7). Added to the challenges of parenting, often alone and in impoverished conditions, are stressors such as domestic violence, few social supports, mental health issues, maltreatment as a child and drug or alcohol abuse (Trocmé et al. 2005).

While a nexus of precarious conditions, stresses and struggles with children may bring a family to the attention of the child protection system, it treats children as dependents whose healthy development relies on the care, protection and guidance of adults, and assumes that families are the most appropriate and best equipped to raise children (Anglin 2002; Bala 2004; Parton 2006). The painful awareness "that in too many situations children are not safe or well-protected within their families" (Anglin 2002: 238) affirms the right of child protection authorities to officially enter into the private lives of children and their families.

Typically, a child is considered to be in need of protection specific to sexual abuse when s/he has been sexually molested or exploited or is at substantial risk of sexual abuse by the person having charge of the child. On the frontlines of practice, workers are most likely to face instances of child sexual abuse that are perpetrated by relatives (Bolen 2001), with non-parental relatives such as brothers, uncles, grandfathers representing the largest group of perpetrators at about 35 percent (Trocmé et al. 2005). A child is also considered to be in need of protection when the person having charge of the child knew or should have known of the possibility of the sexual abuse and failed to protect the child. This latter condition allows for a child to be in need of protection as a result of the alleged failures of caregivers or parents to protect when they are thought to have known of the sexual abuse. It lays the groundwork for embroiling "non-offending" parents, usually the mothers, in the problem and its resolution.

Interventions into situations of child sexual abuse are guided by protocols designed to ensure consistent and thorough handling of these complex situations. When a complaint of child sexual abuse is made to either the police or child protection, protocols establish reciprocal reporting and joint investigation procedures. Typically, a police detective interviews the child and the alleged offender in order to gather evidence necessary for criminal proceedings. The child protection worker observes the police interview of the child, interviews the non-offending parents and re-interviews the child to ascertain the child's current safety and assess the parents' capacity to prevent the recurrence of sexual abuse. Deeply committed to the truthfulness of children's disclosures of sexual abuse and belief in children's needs for supportive responses to such disclosures, every effort is made to ensure the child's protection by removing the alleged offender from the child's care or immediate proximity. Since child protection workers most often deal with cases of child sexual abuse in which the offender has caregiving responsibilities or is in the immediate proximity of the child, separating the alleged offender to enable the child to remain in the family sets the stage for scrutinizing the capacity of non-offending parents to offer immediate and long-term protection to the child.

The initial aim of investigating any allegations is to determine the degree of risk. If the child is considered to be at risk for further harm, child protection authorities work with the child and family on a voluntary basis. When necessary, child protection authorities involve the court for more intrusive interventions such as an order to supervise the family or temporarily or permanently remove the child. With a growing realization that "too often decisions to remove children from parental care reflected biases of class or race" (Bala 1998: 29) and informed by theories of attachment regarding the emotional damage caused by separating children from long-term caregivers (Bala 1998), fewer children are now removed from parental care. In all substantiated situations of child sexual abuse, only about 6 percent of children are removed from the family environment (Trocmé et al. 2005).

It is not easy to figure out whether or not a child is at risk and in need of protection. Complicating matters is the urgency within which such investigations take place. The procedures dictating child protection responses to such allegations impose tight time frames that require workers to quickly assess risk to the child and intervene. Investigations of this nature are "forensic," meaning that the objectives are to gather evidence that abuse occurred, determine the degree of risk and ensure that immediate steps are taken to protect the child, all within less than a day or two. This type of investigation stands in marked contrast to the comprehensive assessment that we might imagine to be warranted. Conscientious workers strive to minimize the disruptive effects of the disclosure and its aftermath, often by looking to non-offending parents to take protective action so as to keep the child in their family. At the same time, workers may well be fearful of making decisions that could inadvertently result in the repeated sexual abuse of a child.

Current practices arguably rely on transforming women into "mother-protectors." These practices mirror theoretical developments, which over time have seen mothers in cases of child sexual abuse being blamed for having set up the abuse to now being scrutinized for protective capacity.

## The Potential for Mother-Blame

Child sexual abuse has existed throughout centuries, across countries and cultures. It is a problem that has "repeatedly surfaced into public and professional awareness in the past century and a half" (Olafson et al. 1993: 8). According to Bolen (2001: 3), "perhaps the single most influential person in the history of the professional literature on child sexual abuse is Sigmund Freud." In the late 1800s, Freud proposed "seduction theory," in which he posited that the hysterical and neurotic symptoms expressed by his adult female patients derived from their attempts to cope with traumatic experiences of childhood sexual abuse. Freud grew increasingly uneasy with incriminating fathers and came to publicly reject his own theory. Later, Freud recast his patients' distress as resulting not from actual sexual assault but rather from the projection and sometimes acting out of internal sexual fantasy (Olafson et al. 1993).

Well into the 1960s, the dominant explanation of child sexual abuse was influenced by Freud's later works and thus focused on girls' alleged seduction of their fathers (Hooper 1992). This analysis was gradually challenged by a "family systems" approach, wherein all family members were thought to somehow contribute to father-daughter incest. Significantly, the mother was allotted a key role in the development and perpetuation of the abuse. A groundbreaking study undertaken by Lustig and associates in 1966 identified the mother as the "cornerstone" in the "pathological family system"; they proposed that she set up and sanctioned the sexual abuse by consciously or unconsciously relinquishing her spousal obligations and delegating her daughter to "satisfy" the father's "needs" (Lustig et al. 1966).

Although there have been developments in thinking about child sexual abuse in the context of the family since the 1960s, the centrality of mother as villain or victim prevails (Elbow and Mayfield 1991; Krane and Davies 1996). Mother was identified as a colluder or accessory through her physical or emotional absence and inadequacies or through actions that orchestrate, unwittingly or not, the abuse (Krane 2003). Zuelzer and Reposa (1983), for example, describe the mother as "pivotal" in incestuous abuse. Said to be needy, demanding and lacking sufficient psychological investment in their children, mothers in incestuous families may "unconsciously" use illness or absence (or even death) to escape their maternal responsibilities (105). They are thought to ignore or deny "blatantly inappropriate and provocative sexual behavior" or to ignore, deny or react punitively toward girls' attempts to disclose the abuse (Zuelzer and Reposa 1983: 104–105). The incestuous father, on the other hand, is portrayed as a passive recipient of the mother's abdication of her marital and sexual duties. The authors describe the mother as abandoning her sexual responsibility to her husband by "forcing" the daughter "to take over [mother's]... role sexually and [function] as family caretaker" (Zuelzer and Reposa 1983: 105). They offer no consideration of the appropriateness of the husband/father's needs or actions.

Krane's (2003: 70) analysis of this unrelenting focus on mother's role confirms a shift in emphasis from the actions of the abuser to the inadequacies and "in/actions of women as mothers [and wives]," particularly when it comes to having known and having failed to protect. This theme is seen in the still influential *Handbook of Clinical Intervention in Child Sexual Abuse*:

Mothers can perhaps be most generally described as failing to protect the child victim.... Sometimes the mother is physically absent on a regular and predictable basis, thereby affording the opportunity for incest to occur. The classic example of this situation involves a mother who works a night or evening shift. Sometimes mother is psychologically absent, often ignoring overt seductive behavior between the incest participants that she should be curbing and redirecting and setting limits on at a very early stage. Some mothers fail to protect in a very direct fashion by deliberately setting up situations in which the incest participants are encouraged to engage in sexual behavior. (Sgroi, Blick and Porter 1982: 28)

To illustrate mother's culpability, the authors present a case in which a mother regularly sent her husband to her daughters' bedrooms to "cover them up," knowing full well that the fourteen year old slept without clothing. Presented as evidence of mother's encouragement of the sexual abuse, the authors made no mention of the father's "failure to exert sound paternal/parental judgment and self-control: Rather than removing himself from his nude daughter's bedside, he pursues his objectives; hence he is responsible" (Krane 2003: 71). Sgroi et al. (1982: 29) recognized that not all mothers deliberately set the conditions for incest but held firm that "most mothers of incest victims are aware, consciously or unconsciously, that the incest exists." Like other scholars at that time, Sgroi et al. (1982: 29) claimed that mothers frequently responded to their daughters' disclosures with "hostility and disbelief," inaction or ineffectual action. Ultimately, mothers failed to protect. Sgroi et al. (1982: 27) did give some attention to incestuous fathers. Described as dominating and self-absorbed, these men isolated their families from the "hostile" outside world and maintained "sole authority" over all family decisions. Taking into account this portrayal of the perpetrating father, it is virtually impossible to imagine how a mother, observed by Sgroi et al. (1982: 28) to "usually" occupy "a subordinate position" within the incestuous family, might be able to act in a protective manner towards her daughter.

From the 1980s and into the 1990s, efforts were made to broaden family systems approaches by examining the histories and personalities of family members and exploring the couple's intimate relationship (Bolen 2001; Krane 2003). This complexity is seen in *Child Sexual Abuse: New Theory and Research*, wherein David Finkelhor (1984) introduced a framework with four preconditions for understanding how child sexual abuse comes about. The first precondition, motivation to sexually abuse, includes individual factors such as the offender's emotional congruence with a child, sexual arousal to a child or the unavailability of alternative sources of sexual gratification. At the social level, factors include male dominance, child pornography and the sexualization of male needs. The second precondition centres on the factors that might disinhibit the offender such as alcohol, psychosis, impulse disorder and "failure of incest inhibition mechanism in family dynamics" (Finkelhor 1984: 56). Tolerance of sexual interest in children, weak criminal sanctions, beliefs in the patriarchal rights of fathers and "male inability to identify with needs of children" (Finkelhor 1984: 57) operate at the social level. The third and fourth preconditions delineate factors that enable the sexual abuse to occur by overcoming any external constraints and subduing any resistance by the child. Individual factors include an ill, absent, unprotective, distant or dominated mother, social isolation of family, improper child supervision, unusual sleeping conditions, an emotionally insecure or deprived or unusually trusting child, a child who lacks knowledge about sexual abuse and coercion. Social-level factors are lack of social networks and supports for mothers, barriers to women's equality, ideology of family sanctity, social powerlessness and inadequate sexual education for children.

The four preconditions model, still influential today, grasps the multifaceted nature of child sexual abuse perpetrated by family and non-family members against girls or boys. It includes but is not limited to psychodynamics of the offender and family system dynamics. It takes seriously mother's failure to protect and children's vulnerability as potential factors that come into play only after the offender is motivated to abuse and has overcome his own internal constraints. Although due attention is directed at social factors, in child protection practice, individual factors related to both mother and child take precedence as a result of dominant discourses of risk and safety.

On the frontlines of practice, ways of understanding and responding to child sexual abuse continue to be influenced by family systems theory (Bolen 2003; Krane 1994). As Hooper and Humphries (1998: 556) put it, a family systems analysis allows the father's actions to be "perceived as secondary," as a "response to shared problems such as poor communication," leading to the minimization or denial of his responsibility for his own actions. In contrast, "anything mothers (and in some cases children) did until the abuse was stopped implicated them in it. In relation to women, this [mother-blame] applied whether or not they knew about the abuse, and whatever they might have tried to do to stop it" (Hooper and Humphries 1998: 566).

## Shifting the Gaze onto Mothers as Protectors

More recently, feminists have made efforts to better understand mothers' knowledge of and responses to disclosures of child sexual abuse (Alaggia 2001; Johnson 1992; Myer 1985), mothers' experiences of child protection interventions (Bernard 2001; Krane 1994 and 2003), the impact of child welfare and other institutions on mothers of sexually abused children (Carter 1999) and how mothers "survive" their children's disclosures of sexual abuse (Hooper 1992). This research provides more complex understandings of mothers by shaking up assumptions that they knew of or colluded with the sexual abuse.

Myer's (1985) study was one of the first to examine mothers' responses to disclosures. While some women were ambivalent at first, the majority of mothers accepted the allegations, showed empathy to the child, expressed anger about the abuse and toward the abuser and took some form of action. A few mothers denied, were passive and took no action. Myer also described some the mothers as showing more concern for themselves than their children. These women, emotionally and financially dependent on their partners, supported their mates, who dominated, battered and frightened them. None of these women separated from their husband. Myer's research challenged homogeneous assumptions of mothers as collusive and unprotective and made room for maternal ambivalence in the process of coming to terms with a child's disclosure of sexual abuse.

However, there is little room for maternal ambivalence in child protection practice. Krane's (2003) case study of a child protection agency uncovered how and why mother-blame and responsibility are reproduced in situations of sexual abuse by shifting the protection mandate from the agency to women as mothers. This shift was seen in casework practices wherein workers encouraged mothers to express their belief and support for their victimized child. They expected mothers to assume the protection of their children as an immediate priority by denouncing the offender's actions and, if need be, separating from him (Krane 2003). With seemingly ambivalent or unprotective mothers, workers compelled mothers to "choose" between supporting the child or alleged offender. The responsibility for mothers to protect often resulted in their heightened stresses of adhering to the dictates of protection, loss of significant relationships including those with intimate partners, loss of paid employment and/or income, and loss of voice and say. Ultimately, mothers experienced this process as "intrusive, unsettling and costly" (Krane 2003: 186), leading to unintended and unhelpful alienation from their workers. Mothers' protective action was both expected and taken for granted, and yet mothers' ongoing daily work of ensuring protection remained largely invisible (Krane 2003). This is no surprise given dominant ideologies of mothers and mothering.

While ideologies have varied dramatically over time and place,

> at least since the nineteenth century, motherhood has been glorified as women's chief vocation and central definition. The tie between mother and child has been exalted, and traits of nurturance and selflessness have been defined as the essence of the maternal, and hence, of the womanly. (Thorne 1992: 14–15)

Mothers have traditionally been ascribed the social, legal and ideological responsibility for the care and upbringing of children. As Contratto (1986) points out, children are assumed to require full-time maternal care, and mothers are understood to be willingly available and best equipped to provide that care despite any other obligations or conditions. According to this model, the child's needs take precedence over the mother's, and she is expected to be all-knowing, able to anticipate and respond to her child's every need (Krane and Davies 2000).

This construction of mothers as idealized nurturers has been challenged by feminist scholars for making the labour of mothering invisible, ignoring differences between mothers vis-à-vis social location, silencing mothers' struggles and denying the possibilities of partners' or fathers' involvement in the daily care of children. In describing mothering as work, Levine eloquently reminds us, "there are no fixed hours, there is no sick leave, no vacation, no pension, no job security, no collective bargaining and no unionization. Training is considered unnecessary" (1985: 29). Other feminists drew attention to the Eurocentric, middle-class norm upon which the idealized construction of motherhood rests. For example, Braverman's (1991) ethnographic study uncovered a variety of childcare arrangements that included maternal care, shared care and sibling care, and Hill Collins's (1992, 1994) reflections on the history of Black mothering revealed collective forms of mothering that included blood mothers and other mothers. McMahon's (1995) qualitative study found that mothering practices and preoccupations are circumscribed by their socioeconomic contexts. The conception of mothers as idealized nurturers assumes that mothers are the primary or only caregivers for children. It imposes the maternal facet of a woman's identity as her sole character. At the same time, it renders invisible the emotional and material conditions around which mothering occurs. Women's struggles as mothers are thus silenced for it is assumed that "normal mothers cope" (Krane and Davies 2000: 39). These statutory, theoretical and ideological contexts drive most current child welfare practice to focus on mothers. Yet, we can, and must, rethink such practice in situations of child sexual abuse.

## Protecting Emma West

Thirteen-year-old Emma West[1] came to the attention of child protection after her friend told the school counsellor that Emma was being sexually abused by her seventeen-year-old step-brother, Peter. According to Emma's friend, when Peter asked Emma to "suck his penis," she "freaked out." The counsellor also reported that within the last year, Emma's grades had dropped, she skipped classes, she had been caught smoking up at school and was generally argumentative with peers and teachers. The counsellor raised these worries with Emma's mother, Molly, who admitted to having some trouble managing Emma at home. She said that she and her current partner, Don, talked about it, and they thought it was "just hormones; after all, she's a teenager," or maybe it was Emma's feeling that she was no longer number one in her mother's life.

Molly is the mother of Emma and Tyler (ten years old). The children's father has been an inconsistent figure in their lives. With a criminal lifestyle and involvement in drugs, he has been in and out of jail. Molly was recently hired as a full-time housekeeper on rotating shifts in a large downtown hotel. On and off social assistance, over the years she has struggled to support her children. She met Don, a tow-truck driver, about three years ago. A single father, his wife left him and Peter just shortly after Peter was born. In getting to know one another, Don and Molly decided to "give it a shot and see if it works out," that is, for Molly and her children to move in with Don and his son as "a family."

Following the initial complaint, a child protection worker and a police detective set out to interview Emma. She disclosed that the sexual abuse started shortly after the two families began living together. At first, Emma really enjoyed Peter's attention; they confided in each other. "But then he started talking to me about sex and stuff with boys." She said he introduced her to pornography through the Internet to "teach" her "to be sexy and then he started to do it to me — kissing and touching." Emma didn't think that Tyler had experienced anything similar. When asked if anyone knew what was going on, Emma described how "before Don came around, Mom was depressed. Dealing with us was too much for her. She was on her own, Dad was in and out of jail and life sucked." Pressed further, Emma said, "I kept telling Mom that I didn't want to be alone with Peter but she just didn't listen."

The investigation continued with Molly and Don to determine the immediate safety of all children. Molly and Don, shocked and disbelieving, denied any prior knowledge of the sexual abuse. Molly had noticed a change in her daughter's attitude toward Peter, but thought it was related to the troubles she was having at school. They were notified that Peter would now be interviewed by the police and possibly charged under the *Youth Criminal Justice Act*. They were told that Emma is considered to be "at risk" and that they are responsible for keeping Emma and Tyler safe. The child protection worker expressed the hope to work with the family voluntarily. They would need to make sure that the children were not left alone with Peter, participate in individual support groups, go for family counselling, comply with Youth Criminal Justice proceedings and allow ongoing child protection involvement. The worker explained that failure to comply with this "voluntary" plan would result in family court involvement. At this point, Don raised his voice: "You can't tell me what to do. This is bull. I don't need therapy and neither does Peter. My son never got into any trouble before this. Check his school record. You're gonna need a warrant if you want to lay eyes on my kid." He then turned to Molly and blurted out, "I didn't sign up for this. Your daughter's the slut. She's the problem, not my son." Molly, appearing deflated, mumbles, "How am I supposed to keep the children safe? What do you want me to do?"

The sexual exploitation of children is an arguably unconscionable act that provokes a visceral reaction. Imagine the added emotional impact on protection workers who must investigate, assess risk and ensure children's protection when such abuses are perpetrated by someone known, likely trusted and possibly even loved by that child, as appears to be the case with Emma.

We might anticipate that a call from a police detective or child protection worker about the sexual abuse of one's child would be more than distressing. But what follows would surely catapult most parents — usually mothers — into crisis: presenting the child for a forensic interview; subjected to in-depth inquiries about their own knowledge of the abuse and the circumstances of the family environment in which it arose; scrutinized about their belief in and support of the child; and assessed for their immediate protective capacity. Entrenched in the work of investigation and protection, guided by protocols and accustomed to dealing with situations of sexual abuse, authorities are cognizant of and prepared for what is about to occur; mothers and non-offending fathers are not. This glaring imbalance in knowledge and power exists and infiltrates interactions and relationships with mothers and fathers.

As a worker, imagine being called upon to hear children's accounts of sexual abuse, witness their reactions, and understand and manage their concerns during and post disclosure. Listening to Emma's account, the worker begins to gain insights into Emma's changing relationship with Peter. Whereas once he held promise of friendship and big-brotherhood, this promise was lost to betrayal and exploitation. Imagine deeply appreciating Emma's journey to disclosure given her sensitivity to her mother's struggles with depression, single motherhood, economic hardship and a father on whom neither she nor her mother could rely. She also faces the fear that she might instigate the demise of her newfound family by this very disclosure. The child protection worker is propelled into a position of knowing that ensuring Emma's safety might disrupt Emma's family. Emma may even recant her disclosure. Often a typical phase of the disclosure process (Lovett 2004), recantation is understood as a reaction to children's guilty perception of the family disruption, emotional turmoil and chaos triggered by their revelations (Summit 1988). Committed to ending Emma's suffering, and acutely aware of the responsibility to protect Emma from further abuse, the worker errs on the protection of the child over all else, including Emma's possible retraction of her disclosure or her fears of her family's dissolution. Believing that children's needs are best met in their families, particularly during a crisis, the worker typically turns to non-offending mothers to offer support and safety.

Alongside managing the emotional force of children's disclosures, workers are made privy to the results of police interrogations of alleged offenders — often the step-fathers, brothers or uncles of sexually abused children — and are most likely confronted with offenders' denial, minimization, rationalization, anger and on rare occasion feelings of guilt. In this case, Peter will have been interrogated and charges may have been laid. He likely denied any wrongdoing. Depending on the police detective's confirmation of Don's commitment and capacity to prohibit his son's further sexually abusive behavior, Peter may be allowed to return home until a Youth Criminal Justice trial date is set. As a parent in the home, Molly is subject to the same expectation to prohibit Peter's abusive behavior. Don would likely defer to police authority and comply with the conditions of his son's release. Should there be insufficient evidence to pursue Youth Criminal Justice proceedings, and the police investigation is closed, imagine having to explain that this outcome doesn't mean that the sexual abuse did not happen or that Emma is now safe. Typically, the worker encounters Molly's and/or Don's confusion, frustration and maybe even anger as s/he explains the need for continued child protection involvement due to concerns about Emma's safety.

One might imagine the tensions that arise for workers as they witness a range of reactions from non-offending parents while encouraging them to ensure their children's safety. Imagine having to navigate seemingly loving parents' shock and disbelief for the purpose of protection, knowing full well that the last resort is separating Emma from her family. The worker might recognize the implications of Emma's disclosure on Molly and Don as partners and parents, not the least of which are the potential for divided loyalties, finger pointing and the threat of

Don abandoning Molly after her years of struggle or insisting that Molly and her children leave his home. But with the fast pace of decision-making around child safety, there is little time to include understandings of these issues.

The worker also faces Don's anger for the suggestion that his son might be a child sexual abuser, causing him to be implicated in a protection plan that includes monitoring, counselling and compliance. Coupled with his resentment at Emma "the slut" or at Molly for putting him into this position, Don's anger impedes the worker from turning to him as a resource for Emma's safety even though he may not be out of reach as a protector.

An insightful worker can't evade the realization that Molly's world is falling apart. The worker knows that Molly needs time to come to terms with what has happened to her daughter; she expects Molly to vacillate between believing Emma and accepting Don's assertion that Peter is innocent. Child protection practice, however, demands immediate action. While recognizing the impossible position in which Molly finds herself, the worker encourages Molly to put aside certain facets of her identity and social location in the best interests of Emma and demonstrate unwavering belief in and support to her daughter. Should Peter return home, the worker will require a clear commitment that ensures that Peter is never left alone with his stepsiblings. Given Don's seeming unavailability, the worker turns to Molly to fulfill this mandate and explains that all family members must agree to therapy, support groups or counselling. Overwhelmed by the weight of responsibility cast in her direction and afraid that her family will be torn apart, Molly asks "How do you expect me to do all this? Do you expect me to quit work?" Of course the worker does not want Molly to sacrifice her employment, but in the face of Don's anger, the likelihood of Peter's return home and the risk to Emma and Tyler, not to mention the pervasive ideology conferring primary caregiver status to mothers, the responsibility to protect is typically and almost seamlessly shifted to Molly with a domino effect of consequences.

## Rethinking Practice as Usual with Mothers as Protectors

Child protection practice entails assessing harm, determining risk and protecting the child at all costs while at the same time making every effort to cause the least disruption to families and maintain children in their own homes. Such practice is largely accomplished within the privacy of families and, for the most part, by mothers in ways that prioritize maternal responsibilities for protection at the exclusion of a range of facets of women's identities and social locations. These practices take little stock of discrepant positions of power that surely permeate this mandated practice. A practice that aims to thwart the oppression of women as mothers, it seems, ought to begin with opportunities for workers to interrogate their own positions of power and privilege. As Razack (1998: 22) said, "As long as we see ourselves as not implicated in relations of power, as innocent, we cannot begin to walk the path of social justice and to thread our way through the complexities of power relationships."

We propose that workers engage in a process of critical reflection (Heron 2005) concerning their own subject positions and those of their clients within the organizational setting and the power relations that ensue. In protection practice, critical self-reflection also entails unpacking dominant ideologies of children's needs and maternal responsibilities to meet them, the internalization of the mantra to protect at all costs and interrogations of the assumptions around how child sexual abuse comes about, its impact on children and the centrality of mothers as the best protectors.

Beyond a critical reflection that interrogates one's own power and privilege, we suggest routine interactive conversations with mothers. In the emotionally charged arena of mandated practice with situations of sexual abuse, the desire to protect children from harm and further re-victimization allows us to understand that mothers are all too often pressured to protect and can thus be alienated. However, as Ruch (2005: 113) informs us, "given that all social work interventions involve an interpersonal dimension, to a greater or lesser extent, it could be argued that all social work practice is by definition relationship based." Along with critical reflection, this insight is instructive for rethinking practices with mothers in situations of child sexual abuse.

In investigations, when tensions and stakes are high, establishing a relationship is challenging. A worker's recognition of their own power can't remain an intellectual insight. Rather, acknowledging power with clarity and honesty might inspire the beginnings of a relationship-based practice. However, simply stating one's power as a worker may have the potential to be as oppressive as saying nothing at all. The intent behind naming one's power as a child protection authority is to circumvent coercion and offer information instead. We advocate explicitly acknowledging the protection mandate and its shift to women as mothers in families (Krane 2003). In approaching Molly, a worker clearly presents her/his role and mandate, describes the procedures that are about to unfold and familiarizes Molly about the directions to be taken.

With a narrow focus on risk and safety, coupled with beliefs about the needs of children and the responsibilities of parents, particularly mothers, practice as usual has meant taking for granted mothers as protectors; such practice disregards the actual labour involved and the consequences arising as a result of this expectation. In laying out the directions now, a worker might let Molly know that s/he accepts Emma's disclosure, is mandated to ensure Emma's safety and intends to explore ways to protect Emma with a particular consideration of Molly as the primary protector. This approach stands in stark contrast to practice as usual in that the hopes for the mother to protect are made visible rather than concealed by ideologies of expected maternal care and responsibility. But we can't enter into this protection process or understand its consequences without an understanding of Molly *at the same time*. To do so, we turn to intersectionality theorists.

Each of us in the world sits at the intersection of many categories: She is Latina, woman, short, mother, lesbian, daughter, brown-eyed, long-haired, quick-witted, short-tempered, worker, stubborn. At any one moment in time and in space, some of these categories are central to her being and her ability to act in the world. Others matter not at all. (Grillo 1995: 17)

The above quotation describes a single, whole woman. In the context of protection practice, a woman is seen only in parts as a partner or mother, an available protector or full-time paid worker, but not all at once. Her identities are assumed to exist separately and her personhood is fragmented. This fragmentation is, of course, entirely at odds with her concrete life. Grillo's (1995: 22) work might guide us to explore, articulate and include understandings of women's identities and social locations "as closely to their full complexity as possible" such that we refrain from reducing women to mothers, and mothers to "mother protectors" only.

How might workers enter into understanding a woman at a particular moment in time? Grillo (1995) uses the metaphor of a microphone that provides women with opportunities to describe their own identities and social locations. If handed the microphone, Molly might elucidate the relationships of significance in her life now — with Emma, Tyler, Don and Peter — and her experience of moving in together and merging as families. What of her past relationships and struggles to parent alone and under financial strain? Understanding where she came from, how she got to this point in her life and where she is at right now illuminates important facets of her identity as *she* defines them at the crossroads of her current social location. Opening up a dialogue about her emotional, relational and material conditions, and the skills or strengths she draws on to get by, will surely give rise to a deeper understanding of Molly. This conversation also provides insights into Molly's emotional reactions to her daughter's disclosure, the sudden involvement of police and child protection authorities in her life and the consequences of the expectations for protection. Unlike typical practice where maternal ambivalence interferes with protection, understanding Molly allows for the normalization of maternal ambivalence (Parker 1995) and recognizes ambivalence as an expected response to child sexual abuse.

A first encounter with Molly will undoubtedly be driven by the child protection mandate. It would be unreasonable to think that any worker could come to know her in all of her complexity at this time of investigation. However, engaging with Molly in this way provides a forum for developing an immediate protective plan in which she invests. Providing space for Molly's voice can minimize disruption and counteract oppressive expectations hidden behind assertions of least intrusiveness and meeting children's best interests in the context of their families. Gauging Molly's subjective account of her emotions at this time helps the worker and Molly talk about where she is at with respect to protecting Emma. Given the widely accepted understanding that the disclosure of child sexual abuse can bring about significant distress and crisis for mothers (Elliot and Carnes 2001), it would be reasonable for a worker to explore the influence of a mother's emotional reactions upon her capacity to act as a mother protector. Assessing the degree of maternal distress as signifying either protective capacity or inadequacy is not new to child protection interventions. However, attending to mothers' emotional reactions in a non-stigmatizing and non-blaming manner is critical to a sensitive practice that treats mothers as individuals with their own needs and circumstances. Rather than seeing maternal distress as evidence of the mother's inability to protect the victimized child, we suggest engaging mothers in dialogue about emotional reactions so as to ascertain a better understanding of their needs for support, space and time and to enter into a discussion about alternative routes of protection.

Instead of assuming Molly to be the best and only protector for Emma or hearing her emotional distress as evidence of her inadequacy to protect, we suggest looking into the range of possible options to ensure Emma's safety and the potential consequences for Molly and her family of each option. How might the added expectation of mother protection further compound Molly's already precarious circumstances? This approach assumes that the anticipated consequences of protective options comprise information *necessary* for the creation of a feasible immediate protection plan. In this way, Molly's insights are indispensable sources of knowledge alongside the worker's training and expertise.

This attention to mothers' life circumstances suggests accepting uncertainty regarding the best option for any particular protection plan. A "commitment to uncertainty opens up creativity and novel ways of thinking which are in danger of being lost in a climate obsessed with concerns about risk, its assessment, monitoring, and management" (Parton 1998: 23). Uncertainty allows for the possibility that different facets of women's identities take precedence over others at particular moments in time, and that such facets are not static or fixed but rather fluid and flexible (Grillo 1995).

Molly is simultaneously a mother, lover and worker amongst other identities. Emma's disclosure and the ensuing expectations of mother protection will undoubtedly have consequences for a range of facets of her identity. As Massat and Lundy (1998: 378) found, "reporting costs" include "relationship losses, reduced income, increased dependence on government programs, employment disruption, and change of residence." Molly's pleas "How am I supposed to keep the children safe? What do you want me to do?" and her worries about expectations to quit her job to supervise the children and make herself available for counselling and support groups reveal only one area of potential consequences. Certainly, Don's anger following Emma's disclosure could lead to the end of his relationship with Molly. This separation spares Don and Peter from the pressures of child protection involvement and leaves Molly and her children potentially homeless. Awareness of these consequences is essential as Molly and her worker develop an *immediate* protection plan that may not necessarily be regarded as the *forever* protection plan.

Rather than taking for granted Molly as the protector and keeping invisible the consequences of what it actually takes to protect, a worker could engage her to explore possibilities such as separate after-school programs for Emma, Tyler and Peter; the inclusion of trusted extended family members, friends or neighbours for supervision; bearing in mind the potential availability of non-offending fathers as a resource for their children and partners, Don could possibly be included in both the dialogue and the solutions for protection; or placement of Emma for a period to allow Molly, without stigma or judgment, the space needed to think through her emotional and material circumstances while continuing to develop ideas around a longer term plan. None of these pathways to protection are easy to accomplish. Each one is complicated by its own circumstances: funds, transportation, work and school schedules, and the endless coordination of details, personal relationships, confidentiality and guilt, not to mention the unpredictable obstacles of daily life. The intent here is not to produce a list of protection options. Rather, the intent is to encourage the opening up of possibilities and to forecast what is entailed in pursuing these possibilities in ways that engage rather than an alienate mothers in the process of protection.

## Suggestions for Further Reading

Davies, L., J. Krane, S. Collings and S. Wexler. 2007. "Developing Mothering Narratives in Child Protection Practice." *Journal of Social Work Practice* 21, 1.

Krane, J. 2003. *What's Mother Got to Do with It? Protecting Children from Sexual Abuse*. Toronto: University of Toronto Press.

Ruch, G. 2005. "Relationship-Based Practice and Reflective Practice: Holistic Approaches to Contemporary Child Care Social Work." *Child and Family Social Work* 10.

## About the Authors

Julia Krane is an associate professor in the School of Social Work, McGill University. Her longstanding teaching, practice and research endeavours centre on child welfare and violence against women in intimate relationships. Her publications engage in feminist analyses of mainstream and community child welfare practices, examinations of child protection practices that unwittingly reproduce maternal blame and responsibility for protection in cases of child sexual abuse, critical analyses of services to battered women and their children and cautious reflections on the intersection of domestic violence and child protection interventions. Dr. Krane is particularly interested in the contradictory effects of social work practices with vulnerable women and children that emerge when multiple facets of women's identities are relegated to the margins of such practices.

Rosemary Carlton is a PhD candidate at the School of Social Work, McGill University. With substantial front-line practice experience in child protection as well as a hospital-based clinic for sexually abused children, Rosemary is pursuing doctoral research that centres on the varied experiences of mothers and teenaged daughters in the aftermath of sexual abuse disclosures. With particular interest in social work practice that is reflective of and responsive to diversity, Rosemary approaches practice, teaching and research with a commitment to both feminist and anti-oppressive perspectives.

## Note

1. This illustration represents a composite of cases derived from the front-line practices and research activities of the authors.

# References

Alaggia, R. 2001. "Cultural and Religious Influences in Maternal Response to Intrafamilial Child Sexual Abuse: Charting New Territory for Research and Treatment." *Journal of Child Sexual Abuse* 10, 2.

Ambert, A. 2006. "One Parent Families: Characteristics, Causes, Consequences, and Issues." Ottawa: The Vanier Institute of the Family. Available at <http://www.vifamily.ca/library/cft/oneparent.pdf> accessed January 25, 2008.

Anglin, J.P. 2002. "Risk, Well-Being and Paramountcy in Child Protection: The Need for Transformation." *Child and Youth Care Forum* 31, 4.

Bala, N. 1998. "Reforming Child Welfare Policies: Don't Throw the Baby Out with the Bathwater." *Policy Options/Options Politiques* (September).

_____. 2004. "Child Welfare Law in Canada: An Introduction." In N. Bala, M.K. Zapf, R.J. Williams, R. Vogl and J.P. Hornick (eds.), *Canadian Child Welfare Law: Children Families and the State* (Second Edition). Toronto: Thompson Educational.

Bernard, C. 2001. *Constructing Lived Experiences: Representations of Black Mothers in Child Sexual Abuse Discourses.* Aldershot, U.K.: Ashgate.

Bolen, R.M. 2001. *Child Sexual Abuse: Its Scope and our Failure.* New York: Kluwer Academic/Plenum.

_____. 2003. "Nonoffending Mothers of Sexually Abused Children: A Case of Institutionalized Sexism?" *Violence Against Women* 9, 11.

Braverman, L. 1991. "Beyond the Myth of Motherhood." In M. McGoldrick, C. Anderson and F. Walsh (eds.), *Women in Families: A Framework for Family Therapy* New York: W.W. Norton.

Carter, B. 1999. *Who's to Blame? Child Sexual Abuse and Non-Offending Mothers.* Toronto: Toronto University Press.

Contratto, S. 1986. "Child Abuse and the Politics of Care." *Journal of Education* 168, 3.

Davies, L., J. Krane, S. Collings and S. Wexler. 2007. "Developing Mothering Narratives in Child Protection Practice." *Journal of Social Work Practice* 21, 1.

Elbow, M., and J. Mayfield. 1991. "Mothers of Incest Victims: Villains, Victims, or Protectors?" *Families in Society: The Journal of Contemporary Human Services* 72.

Elliot, A.N., and C.N. Carnes. 2001. "Reactions of Nonoffending Parents to the Sexual Abuse of their Child: A Review of the Literature." *Child Maltreatment* 6, 4.

Finkelhor, D. 1984. *Child Sexual Abuse: New Theory and Research.* New York: Free Press.

Grillo, T. 1995. "Anti-essentialism and Intersectionality: Tools to Dismantle the Master's House." *Berkeley Women's Law Journal* 10.

Heron, B. 2005. "Self-Reflection in Critical Social Work Practice: Subjectivity and the Possibilities of Resistance." *Reflective Practice* 6, 3.

Hill Collins, P. 1992. "Black Women and Motherhood." In B. Thorne and M. Yalom (eds.), *Rethinking the Family.* Boston: Northeastern University Press.

_____. 1994. "Shifting the Center: Race, Class, and Feminist Theorizing about Motherhood." In D. Bassin, M. Honey and M. M. Kaplan (eds.), *Representations of Motherhood.* New Haven: Yale University Press.

Hooper, C.A. 1992. *Mothers Surviving Child Sexual Abuse.* London and New York: Tavistock/Routledge.

Hooper, C.A., and C. Humphreys. 1998. "Women Whose Children have been Sexually Abused: Reflections on a Debate." *British Journal of Social Work* 28.

Johnson, J. 1992. *Mothers of Incest Survivors: Another Side of the Story.* Bloomington: Indiana University Press.

Krane, J. 1994. "The Transformation of Women into Mother Protectors: An Examination of Child Protection Practices in Cases of Child Sexual Abuse." Unpublished doctoral dissertation, University of Toronto.

_____. 2003. *What's Mother Got to Do with It? Protecting Children from Sexual Abuse.* Toronto: University of Toronto Press.

Krane, J., and L. Davies. 1996. "Mother-Blame in Child Sexual Abuse: A Look at Dominant Culture, Writings, and Practices." *Textual Studies in Canada* 7.

_____. 2000. "Rethinking Risk Assessment in Mothering and Child Protection Practice." *Child and Family Social Work* 5.

Levine, H. 1985. "The Power Politics of Motherhood." In J. Turner and L. Emery (eds.), *Perspectives on Women in the 1980s.* Winnipeg: University of Manitoba Press.

Lovett, B. 2004. "Child Sexual Abuse Disclosure: Maternal Response and Other Variables Impacting the Victim." *Child and Adolescent Social Work Journal* 21, 4.

Lustig, N., J. Spellman, S. Dresser and T. Murray. 1966. "Incest." *Archives of General Psychiatry* 14.

Massat, C.R., and M. Lundy. 1998. "'Reporting Costs' to Nonoffending Parents in Cases of Intrafamilial Child Sexual Abuse." *Child Welfare* 77, 4.

McMahon, M. 1995. *Engendering Motherhood: Identity and Self-Transformation in Women's Lives.* New York: Guilford.

Myer, M. 1985. "A New Look at Mothers of Incest Victims." *Feminist Perspectives on Social Work and Human Sexuality* 3.

Olafson, E., D.L. Corwin and R. Summit. 1993. "Modern History of Child Sexual Abuse Awareness: Cycles of Discovery and Suppression." *Child Abuse and Neglect* 17, 1.

Parker, R. 1995. *Torn in Two: The Experience of Maternal Ambivalence.* London: Virago.

Parton, N. 1998. "Risk, Advanced Liberalism and Child Welfare: The Need to Rediscover Uncertainty and Ambiguity." *British Journal of Social Work* 28.

_____. 2006. *Safeguarding Childhood: Early Intervention and Surveillance in a Late Modern Society.* Hampshire and New York: Palgrave.

Razack, S. 1998. *Looking White People in the Eye: Gender, Race, and Culture in Courtrooms and Classrooms.* Toronto: University of Toronto Press.

Ruch, G. 2005. "Relationship-Based Practice and Reflective Practice: Holistic Approaches to Contemporary Child Care Social Work." *Child and Family Social Work* 10.

Sgroi, S., L. Blick and F. Porter. 1982. "A Conceptual Framework for Child Sexual Abuse." In S. Sgroi (ed.), *Handbook of Clinical Intervention in Child Sexual Abuse.* Toronto: Lexington Books, D.C. Heath.

Summit, R. 1988. "The Child Sexual Abuse Accommodation Syndrome." *Child Abuse and Neglect* 7.

Thorne, B. 1992. "Feminism and the Family: Two Decades of Thought." In B. Thorne and M. Yalom (eds.), *Rethinking the Family.* Boston: Northeastern University Press.

Trocmé, N., B. Fallon, B. MacLaurin, J. Daciuk, C. Felstiner, T. Black et al. 2005. *Canadian Incidence Study of Reported Child Abuse and Neglect.* Ottawa: National Clearinghouse on Family Violence.

Zuelzer, M., and R. Reposa. 1983. "Mothers in Incestuous Families." *International Journal of Family Treatment* 5, 2.

# Chapter 12

# Taking Resistance Seriously
## A Response-Based Approach to Social Work
## in Cases of Violence against Indigenous Women

*Kinewesquao [Cathy Richardson] and Allan Wade*

*This chapter is dedicated to Lily and Angel.*

In this chapter, the authors present a response-based approach to social work practice in cases of violence, especially as it concerns Indigenous women. The chapter reviews key aspects of a response-based approach, examines the colonial code of relationship that is reflected in representations of the oppressed in the discourse of colonialism and the helping professions, reviews recent research on social responses to victims of violence and considers its implications for social work practice, presents a case example to elucidate one woman's responses and resistance to violence and to a series of negative social responses from human service professionals and briefly describes response-based interviewing and its applications in child protection work. The authors suggest that response-based practices address safety and restore dignity to victims, and allow for the effective use of authority while avoiding the replication of dominance in social work practice.

Questions Addressed in This Chapter
1. How do women respond to and resist violence by their partners?
2. How can exploring women's ever present resistance to violence be used as a basis for safety planning in child protection work?
3. How can social workers contest the blaming and pathologizing of mothers while promoting safety and collaborative planning?

Child protection social work is an orchestrated social response to children who have been harmed or put at risk by one or more forms of violence. It is also the point at which the power of the state meets some of the most oppressed and marginalized members of the community. It follows that careful analysis of violence and oppression, from minor affronts to dignity to extreme and protracted forms of abuse, must be central to the theory and practice of child protection work. Where Indigenous families are concerned, it is particularly important to expose the functional links between the diverse forms of violence and oppression. In Canada, for example, the theft of Indigenous land on the prairies displaced

Indigenous peoples from their territories, disrupted most traditional ways of living and caused the breakdown of local communities. The communities were less able to protect young women, some of whom fled to urban centres to avoid violence and poverty, there to become socially isolated and exposed to further violence. The government and corporations benefitted from the destabilizing of communities to access land and accrue massive wealth (Adams 1989; Harris 2002; O'Keefe and MacDonald 2001). Thus, colonialism is implicated directly in the many current forms of interpersonal violence.

Six of ten Canadian provinces and one territory (Alberta, Saskatchewan, Prince Edward Island, Newfoundland, New Brunswick, Nova Scotia and Northwest Territories) expanded their statutory definition of child abuse to include children who witness or are exposed to "domestic violence." Four Canadian provinces (British Columbia, Manitoba, Ontario and Québec) and two territories (Yukon and Nunavut) do not explicitly define exposure as a separate form of child maltreatment but do include it in their definitions of emotional abuse. The Canadian Incident Study of Reported Child Abuse and Neglect 2003 found that exposure to domestic violence was the second most common form of substantiated child maltreatment in Canada (excluding Québec), with an estimated 50,000 cases of child exposure to domestic violence being substantiated in 203 (Blackstock and Trocmé 2005).

The notion of "children witnessing" is often paired with the view that mothers "fail to protect" their children from witnessing the violence and thus are guilty of child abuse or neglect. "Failure to protect" implies that mothers are not concerned about the violence that they endure, and their children witness, until the state intervenes. In fact, most mothers who are battered do take steps to stop the abuse, often seeking help from several sources (Magen 1999) and to protect and care for their children (Hilton 1992; Schecter and Edleson 1995, 1999). Child welfare authorities consistently overlook these efforts (Edleson et al. 2003). When children are exposed to violence against their mothers, it is mothers who are the primary and usually the sole focus of child welfare intervention, while the perpetrators are ignored, even when they are fathers or father-figures (Strega 2006; Sullivan et al. 2000).

## Response-Based Ideas

Response-based ideas arose from direct service with people who had endured violence, including Indigenous women and men who were violated in the so-called residential schools (Coates, Todd and Wade 2000; Richardson and Nelson 2007; Wade 1997, 2000, 2007). In the course of our clinical work, we (Coates, Todd and Wade 2000, 2003; Todd and Wade 1994; Wade 1997, 2000) noted that victims invariably resist violence and other forms of oppression, overtly or covertly, depending on the circumstances. We found that engaging clients in conversations that elucidated and honoured their resistance could be helpful in addressing a wide variety of concerns (Epston 1986; Kelly 1988; Richardson 2004, 2006; Todd and Wade 1994; Wade 1997, 2000). This required a significant shift in theory and practice, however. Acts of resistance are *responses to* violence, not *effects* or *impacts of* violence. We found that focusing on victims' responses allowed us to better identify and construct accounts of their resistance. Accounts of resistance provide a basis in fact for contesting accounts of pathology and passivity, which are typically used to blame victims.

Todd (2007) extended this line of thought to work with men who use violence against women, and Coates (1996) integrated response-based practice with a program of critical analysis and research on the connection between violence and language (Coates and Wade 2007). Richardson (2003, 2004, 2005) applied response-based ideas to her work on the development of Métis identity and developed the "Medicine Wheel of Resistance" as a framework for understanding Indigenous resistance to colonization, racism and oppression. And, we are currently developing and testing a model of child protection practice that integrates response-based ideas with Richardson's research and direct service work and with other recent work in the field, such as the "signs of safety" approach (Turnell and Edwards 1999).

## The Colonial Code

The European cultures that gave us the prison camps called residential schools and the other mechanisms of colonial domination also gave us the talking cure and the human service professions. Naturally, then, the discourses of colonialism and the helping professions would reflect common lines of thought and action. This is arguably most evident where the problem of violence is concerned. Many of the linguistic devices that make up colonial discourse (e.g., stereotypical images, euphemisms, passive and agentless grammatical forms, mutualizing terms, deterministic metaphors) appear widely in the discourses of the legal and human service professions, and serve similar functions (Coates and Wade 2007). Victims are represented as passive individuals who invite or unconsciously desire the violence they endure, while perpetrators are portrayed as hapless individuals who are compelled to violate others by forces they do not understand and cannot control. Unilateral acts of violence, from genocide to rape to wife-assault, are portrayed as mutual acts for which the victims are substantially to blame (Coates 1996). These misrepresentations promote a host of negative social responses to victims, especially those who already face multiple forms of oppression (Andrews and Brewin 1990; Andrews, Brewin and Rose 2003; Justice Institute of B.C. 2007).

The intimate relationship between colonialism and psychiatry, and by extension the helping professions, is baldly stated by Mannoni, a psychiatrist who worked in Madagascar before and after the French suppressed the rebellion of 1949, killing an estimated 90,000 Malagasies.

> Colonization has always been based upon the existence of need and dependency. Not all people are suitable for being colonized; only those who feel this need are suitable. In almost all cases where Europeans have founded

colonies… we can say that they were expected, and even desired in the unconscious of their subjects. (Mannoni, cited in Macey 2000: 188)

Mannoni uses the psychoanalytic notion of unconscious desire and dependency to define colonization as a mutual, rather than a unilateral, process. The oppressor and the oppressed are presumed to form a kind of symbiotic relationship in which the oppressed need domination and control. The corollary of this view is that women unconsciously want to be dominated, raped and beaten; men simply fill the need.

Similar views found their way into modern studies of oppression and the helping professions through some unexpected routes. For instance, Freire (1970) stated:

The oppressed, who have adapted to the structure of domination in which they are immersed, and have become resigned to it, are inhibited from waging the struggle for freedom so long as they feel incapable of running the risks it requires. (32)

Like Mannoni, Freire (1970) underestimated the resistance of the oppressed. He argued instead that the oppressed feel an "irresistible attraction to the oppressor" (49) and, with this claim, took the definitively colonial position that he could read the unconscious minds of literally millions of oppressed people.

Pence incorporated Freire's views in the Duluth model of batterer treatment (Ellen Pence, interview, November 3, 2007), as did White (1995) in the theory of narrative therapy, with the view that women who were assaulted as girls cannot distinguish violence from love and so do not resist violence by successive men. Similarly, Carniol (1992) and Moreau (1990) asserted that oppression "may seriously impair a client's capacities to accurately construe reality" (54). Blinded by perceptual impairments, the argument goes, the oppressed "develop magical ideologies… that rationalize their passive submission to their own situation of suffering" (60). The worker is to challenge the client's "magical ideologies" and help her develop a "critical consciousness" — that is, the consciousness of the social worker. This model rests on the belief that the oppressed do not resist violence and positions the professional as the primary engine of dissent. It thus reinstates a class distinction between the critically conscious professional and the internally oppressed victim (Rossiter 1994).

The view that victims are socialized into submission is common in the anti-violence field, including in the cycle theory of violence (Walker 1979). Walker described some forms of women's resistance, but then adopted the theory of learned helplessness to explain their alleged passivity.

If she has been through several cycles already, the knowledge that she has traded her physical and psychological safety for this temporary dream state adds to her self-hatred and embarrassment. [S]he is selling herself for brief periods of phase-three behaviour. She becomes an accomplice to her own battering (69). [Battered women's] behaviour is determined by their negative cognitive set, or their perceptions of what they could or could not do, not by what actually existed (48).

This cognitive theory of the psychopathology of battered women does not explain how battered women continue to resist even when they seem to be helpless (Burstow 1992; Kelly 1988), for instance, by denying the offender a pretext for further abuse while waiting for an opportunity to take overt action. And it obscures perpetrator responsibility by portraying violent behaviour as an effect of uncontrollable anger. Following is an example of how the cycle theory is used currently:

> During the first stage [of the cycle].... The woman tries to calm the abuser and often changes her lifestyle to avoid angering the man. This usually sets a precedent of submissiveness by the woman building the gateway to future abuse. The second stage consists of an 'uncontrollable discharge of tensions that have been built up during phase one'.... During the third stage, the abuser acts remorseful and apologetic, usually promising to change. As a result, many women grant abusers multiple opportunities to repent and thereby fall into a cycle of abuse. (Ciraco 2001: 171)

Here, women's presumed submissiveness is presented as the catalyst of the abuse. Women are portrayed as active only to the extent that they invite violence (i.e., they "*build* the gateway" and "*grant* abusers"), while violence by men is portrayed as an effect of forces ("tensions") they cannot control.

Echoing Mannoni, the following passage suggests that wife-assault is a property of a complementary relationship between perpetrator and victim.

> The partners' characteristics hold them together.... As abused partners adapt and become more compliant... the partners' characteristics make them increasingly dependent on one another. After prolonged abuse they develop complementary characteristics: aggressive/passive, demanding/compliant, blaming/accepting guilt. (12)

Just as for Mannoni, the colonizer and colonized complement one another, this passage suggests that women acquire "characteristics" that are the perfect complement to the characteristics of violent men. Violent men and passive women are fused in a "neat binary" (Mardorossian 2002). The victim is the catalyst of the abuse and the perpetrator of her own misfortunes.

Much has been written about the discursive production of the "Other," but the act of representing an other also entails the act of representing one's self (Crapanzano 1980). Representing "the oppressed" is a principal means by which helping professionals represent themselves. The passages we examined here reflect what Todd and Wade (1994) call the colonial code of relationship, which can be expressed as a three-part message:

1. You are deficient (i.e., heathen, savage, falsely conscious, submissive, passive, internally oppressed, helpless, cognitively distorted and afraid).
2. I am proficient (i.e., critically conscious, expert, professional, closer to god, empowered by the state).
3. Therefore I have the right (duty, sacred obligation, authority) to perform certain operations upon you (prescribing, advising, educating, assessing, praying, counselling, legislating, apprehending children)... for your own good.

This code of relationship is most visibly at work in negative social responses to Indigenous people who have endured violence, particularly Indigenous women, who face multiple forms of deprivation and violence that are obscured by public and professional discourse. It is no accident that women's resistance to violence is excluded from the risk assessment tool used by child protection workers in B.C.; that battered women are accused of "failing to protect" their children (Strega 2006); that judges mutualize and eroticize sexualized assaults in Canadian courts (Coates 1996); that high school social studies curriculums omit honest analysis of European violence and administrative domination of Indigenous people; or that training across the legal and human services professions excludes detailed analysis of resistance to violence and oppression.

## Social Responses to Victims of Violent Crimes

The term "social responses" refers to the reactions of others to victims once the violence is exposed. Some social responses are *personal* in that they are directed solely at the individual victim. For instance, friends and professionals might criticize the victim for making poor decisions or lacking personal boundaries, or they might provide a safe haven and reassure her that she is not to blame. Other social responses are *systemic* or *contextual* and directed at many victims. For instance, decisions about what services to fund and how to deliver them are de facto responses to victims as a group, as are decisions that create poverty, isolation, homelessness and other conditions that limit the options available to victims.

Positive social responses restore safety and dignity and help victims recover. However, a majority of victims of sexualized assault and abuse and wife assault report receiving negative social responses from family, friends and professionals (Andrews, Brewin and Rose 2003). Women and members of socially marginalized groups are the most likely to receive negative social responses. Victims who receive negative social responses tend to experience more intense and lasting distress and are more likely to blame themselves for the abuse. They are also more likely receive a diagnosis of mental disorder, even long after the abuse has ended. Women who, as girls, received negative social responses to early disclosures of abuse are less likely to report abuse as adults and more likely to avoid authorities (Andrews, Brewin and Rose 2003; Andrews and Brewin 1990; Fromuth 1986). Following are some examples of *personal* and *contextual* negative social responses.

### Personal Negative Social Responses

- A victim of sexualized assault is interviewed by a police officer who asks, "What were you doing in that part of town?"
- A woman calls the police after being beaten by her husband. The officer enquires, "How long have you had this marriage problem?" She replies sharply, "This is a violence problem, not a marriage problem." Later, when the offender violates the no-contact order, the police officer is slow in responding to the victim.
- A nine-year-old boy tells his mother that he is being sexually abused by his older brother. His mother holds his head under water until he gasps for breath and yells angrily that his brother would not do such a thing.

### Contextual Negative Social Responses

- Sexualized and physical assaults are widely misrepresented in legal and mental health settings (see examples in Coates, Bavelas and Gibson 1994; Coates 1996; Coates and Wade 2007; Ehrlich 2001; O'Neill and Morgan 2001).
- A Canadian Supreme Court ruling gives defence lawyers wide latitude to use the health records of alleged sexual assault victims to attack their credibility.
- Victims' resistance to violence is ignored or recast as problems to be treated (Ridley and Coates 2003; Wade 2000; Kelly 1988). For instance, women who refuse to be content with abuse are recast as clinically depressed.
- Judges, prosecutors and defence counsel ask abused children developmentally inappropriate (i.e., too complex) and even humiliating questions (i.e., those that embed the view that the victim invited or wanted the abuse) (Bala, Lee and McNamara 2001; Park and Renner 1998).

### Contextual Negative Social Responses to Indigenous People

- An Indigenous woman who contacts child protection authorities to help protect her children from her violent partner is told she has "failed to protect" her children, who are then apprehended.
- Indigenous children are apprehended and taken into care in disproportionately high numbers.
- The *Indian Act*, an inherently racist government policy, remains in force in Canada.
- Greater self-governance is associated with lower rates of suicide (Chandler and Lalonde 1998). Yet self-government initiatives are stalled by virtually all levels of Canadian government.
- Hughes (2006) reports that the health, wellbeing and sense of identity of Indigenous children in foster care is highly compromised.

We have found that it is not possible to understand the concerns expressed by victims until the social responses they have received are taken into account. Many people who suffer from complex trauma, who are thought to possess concurrent mental disorders or who are reluctant to cooperate with professionals, have received negative and debilitating social responses, over and above the violence. Indeed, in many cases, victims find negative social responses more distressing than the violence itself. Consequently, we believe the topic of social responses to victims and victims' responses to positive and negative social responses should be raised routinely in child protection and therapeutic work.

## A Study of Dignified Resistance to Violence and Negative Social Responses

Human service workers are privileged to hear sacred accounts of living. The events recounted in Lily's story occurred in a peaceful, mid-sized B.C. city. Lily had no prior involvement with police. She was the sole parent of Angel, then six. Lily initially came to speak with Kinewesquao [Cathy Richardson] about how to deal with chronic pain and strengthen her Métis cultural connections, but soon began to talk about a brutal assault she had endured and a series of negative social responses from various professionals.

*One day Lily was invited to a party by a colleague, Doris. Lily went over her standard safety check before agreeing to attend: "Who would be there? What kind of people were they? How much alcohol would be there? Is it safe to bring my daughter?" She knew that Doris took medication that made her drowsy. She told Doris she did not want to be left on her own with strangers. Doris said she would take the medication only when the evening was winding down. Having done her research, Lily felt it would be safe to attend.*

*The group consisted of Doris, Doris's husband, a friend and a neighbour who came later. They spent the evening was spent talking, eating and laughing. Lily put Angel down to sleep on a bed. Soon after, Doris announced that she was tired and would be going to bed. She invited Lily to spend the night. Lily agreed and was about to go to bed when she started to feel woozy, unsteady and incoherent. Much later, she realized that something had been in her drink. At that point, Doris's partner began to assault Lily. For several hours, he punched, kicked and dragged Lily, leaving her with numerous injuries. Lily still cannot recall a significant period of time and does not know what took place. She wonders: "What did he do to me? Was my daughter safe?"*

*During the assault Lily asked repeatedly, "Please, just let me take my daughter and go home!" Finally, hardly able to walk, she sensed an opening. Broken-boned, bleeding and broken-hearted, Lily collected her daughter, made her way to the jeep, started it up and backed out of the yard. The roads were windy and slippery and made worse by the dark. Despite broken wrists and bloodied vision, Lily drove forward a short distance before crashing into the train tracks at an awkward angle, still in view of the perpetrator. Lily and Angel remained in the car until an ambulance arrived. Between the confusion caused by the "date rape" drug and her injuries, Lily could not recall the sequence of events.*

*Before Lily could piece the events together, she soon found herself in a jail cell.*

*Her requests for information about the welfare of Angel were met with silence and crude remarks. She was called a "drunken squaw" and other derogatory names. Lily was told that she was being charged for impaired driving, although she had not been drinking that evening. She received no medical help for days.*

*Lily remembered the ambulance drivers and police moving her body out of the destroyed vehicle. She told them: "See that man back there, standing in the window (pointing to the perpetrator in the apartment window)? He has just assaulted me!" She told the police that the man had beaten her up and that she needed to get away from him. At the time, she did not realize that she was bruised, bleeding and intoxicated by the date rape drug.*

*Lily was finally offered medical attention but the hospital had been told that she was an Indian who was charged with impaired driving, and she was treated accordingly. Still, Lily decided to treat her helpers with the respect they did not accord her. The man who assaulted her was not arrested.*

*Four days later, Lily was allowed to see her daughter. They cried in each other's arms. Lily was left with her injuries, an impaired driving charge and the indignity she met at virtually every turn. But, she reasoned, at least she had seen her daughter. Angel was not immediately returned, but remained in the foster home for six weeks while Lily was investigated and forced to prove that she was a responsible parent. Lily continued to cooperate and demonstrate great aplomb and presence of mind. She retained her sense of calm hopefulness because she thought the whole mess must be a mistake that would be cleared up soon. This is Canada, after all.*

## Restoring Dignity

We aim to restore dignity to the person wherever possible. Initially, this means building rapport without expecting the client to trust us (DeJong and Berg 2008); asking for the client's best hopes (Dejong and Berg 2008); offering choices whenever possible; asking for permission to raise sensitive topics, especially when required to do so (Turnell and Edwards 1999); being honest and direct about the power we possess; and being curious about the client's perspectives and concerns. With Indigenous clients it also means beginning with ordinary get-to-know-you conversations about daily life, family connections. It is important to make room for extended family.

We typically ask about the client's previous contacts with professionals, to get a sense of what kinds of social responses they have received: "Have you spoken to other professionals about these things? How did that go? What, if anything, has been helpful? How did that help? Have you always felt respected by the folks you've met with?" If the client reports that they have received effective help, we ask for more information about what was helpful and what difference it has made. When the client reports negative social responses, we ask for details and go on to ask about her responses: "So, when you got the sense that the counsellor was siding with your (abusive) husband, how did you respond? You know, how did you handle that — right then?" We can then begin to acknowledge the many ways in which the client preserved her dignity, tried to exert some control in the circumstances, pursued just redress and either let her feelings be known or sagely kept them to herself. These responses tend to reveal the client's values, such as the value she places on respect and dignity, and the various skills she has used in managing adverse circumstances. These skills are often similar to those used in resisting violence and can be readily explored as a basis for safety planning. Lily was terrified and deeply humiliated by the assault and by the negative social responses she received in its aftermath. Despite the most prudent and determined resistance, she was left with the prevailing sense of being *acted upon*, as though she was an object. Because she could not stop the violence or prevent the negative social responses, she felt as though she "let it happen" and did not do enough on her own or Angel's behalf. The trauma of the assault was magnified by the humiliation of the negative social responses, especially by the apprehension of Angel and the suggestion that Lily was an unfit mother.

### Obtaining a Detailed Account of Violence and Resistance

Violent acts are social in that they involve at least two people, a victim and a perpetrator, and occur in specific social settings and social-historical contexts (Coates, Todd and Wade 2000). Consequently, to be complete and accurate, any account of violence must include a description of the actions of both individuals and the social settings and social-historical contexts in which it occurred. Often, clients do not at first recall the many ways in which they resisted the violence, for several reasons. When the client begins to talk about an incident of violence or other adverse event, we generally ask permission to ask further questions: "Would it be okay if I asked you a few questions about that?" We then ask questions about how she responded at the time, moment-by-moment, paying careful attention to small details: "When you noticed that he was becoming aggressive, and you started to feel unsafe, how did you respond? You know, what did you do? How did you ask him to stop? How did you become angry? Then what happened? How did you respond to that? Do you remember what was going through your mind?" These questions elicit micro-level details of the client's responses and resistance, which in turn reveal capacities that can inform the protection risk and safety assessment.

We also focus on what the perpetrator did to suppress the victim's resistance, to highlight the deliberate nature of the violence and sole responsibility of the perpetrator: "Why do you think he blocked the door? If he had really 'lost it' and was 'out of control,' how did he manage to stay so calm until you got home? Why did he present himself at first as a really gentle and peaceful guy? Was he unable to stop or unwilling to stop?" These questions presuppose that the perpetrator anticipated, actually encountered and tried to overcome the victim's resistance.

Lily resisted in many ways. During the assault, she asked the perpetrator to stop, tried to get away and kept herself conscious long enough to escape. She managed to carry Angel outside, start the vehicle and drive it a short dis-

## Figure 12-1 The Medicine Wheel of Responses

Examples of Lily's Responses and Resistance to the Assault

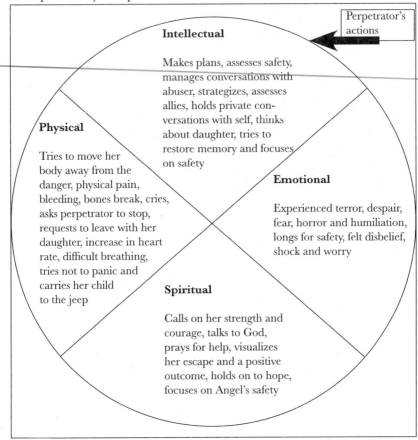

tance. Before accepting the invitation to attend the party, she asked a number of questions to ensure that she and Angel would be safe. Once we obtained an account of these responses, it became clear that Lily already knew a great deal about danger and safety. We have mapped Lily's responses (Figure 12-1) on The Medicine Wheel of Responses to Oppression. *Kakionewagemenuk:* with thanks to those who share traditional teachings and those who came before.

### Summarizing Responses and Introducing the Language of Resistance

We summarize the client's responses, using her own words and introducing the language of resistance. For example, after summarizing her responses, we might say, "You know, it seems that all of these things you've mentioned are different ways of resisting, of fighting back and protecting yourself and Angel. Do you know what I mean?" When there is good rapport, this can be done in a playful manner, to lighten the mood: "Wow, I can see that you don't much like it when other people treat you badly. Is this a chronic problem with you? I mean, have you always been this way?" These comments and questions formulate certain responses as forms of resistance and contest the view that she is oppressing herself internally.

### Contesting Attributions of Passivity and Deficiency

The account of resistance provides a set of facts that can be used to contest attributions of passivity and pathology. Many victims say that they have "no self-esteem" or "poor boundaries" and feel that they "deserved it" because they "didn't stand up" for themselves. Yet the victim's account of her own resistance tends to contradict these attributions. We sometimes directly contest deficiency statements that blame and pathologize the victim. For example:

- "How could anyone possibly suggest that you have poor boundaries when you asserted your boundaries so clearly, even though he overpowered you?"
- "Just because you could not make it stop does not mean you let it happen."
- "Where did you get the idea that you lack self-esteem: I mean, are these the actions of a woman who doesn't esteem herself?"
- "The fact that he did not respect your boundaries does not mean you have none"
- "I can certainly see that you were oppressed and have been very distressed about it, rightly enough. But I don't see how this adds up to depression. What would it mean if you were this badly treated and did not feel incredibly sad."

When contesting these and other diagnoses, it is important to respect the client's orientation to the diagnosis.

### Connective Questions

After introducing the language of judicious resistance and asking the client to consider the validity of the new account, we use connective questions to explore the nature and origins of particularly unique and compelling responses. Connective questions link vital responses and the myriad personal capacities and convictions they reveal, across times and settings:

- "How did you learn so much about safety?"
- "Where did you get the strength to keep fighting back?"
- "How did you manage to remain so calm and focused, even though you were terrified?"
- "How did you keep your hope alive when things were really bleak?"
- "Have you faced other situations like this, where you were isolated and really in danger?"

- "How is it that you knew so clearly that you had done nothing wrong when so many people in power were blaming you?"

These questions are restorative in the sense that they restore cultural and personal knowledge to its rightful place of prominence and acknowledge the relationships in which that knowledge took shape and was passed on. Lily recalled that she learned a great deal about safety from her mother and this was perhaps passed down from her ancestors. In this way, connective questions reveal intergenerational histories of resistance to violence and oppression, and to negative social responses. Clients can then honour their ancestors and cultural knowledges as their own capacities and convictions are revealed more fully. Lily's ability and commitment as a parent stood out clearly in her account of her own resistance.

## Responses to Negative Social Responses

With Angel in the hands of child protection authorities, Lily had little room to maneuver and no margin for error. In response, she held quietly onto what she knew to be true while she acted outwardly as she knew she must: She did what was told, asked politely about her daughter, exercised aplomb, reassured herself, visualized a positive outcome, prayed and refused to treat others as she had been treated. Despite ongoing humiliation, Lily kept her spirit strong. She had many private conversations in which she reasserted what she knew to be true and rehearsed what she knew she would be forced to say. In the longer term, Lily responded by maintaining her faith in goodness. Lily did not openly reject professionals' assessments and complied with their interaction until she got her daughter back. Over the longer term, Lily developed a closer relation to spirit, became more aligned with her inner guide and more conscious of her connection with all that is. She realized that she wanted to become a healer to help others, began meditating and went on to live on her own terms.

## Developing Safety, Reducing Risk

Accurate assessments of safety and risk depend on accurate accounts of the events in question. Accounts that omit mention of the victim's resistance are at least incomplete and often highly misleading. After all, if the victim's resistance is concealed, that the perpetrator acted to suppress that resistance cannot come up for consideration. The perpetrator's responsibility and the level of risk he presents are then obscured. Women's predictions of future violence are more accurate than any formal assessment device (Gondolf 2003). It is crucial, therefore, to learn how the victim responded to and resisted the violence and other forms of adversity. The precise forms of the victim's resistance to violence, and to negative social responses, point to pre-existing abilities that can become the foundation of safety. Careful exploration of Lily's responses revealed that she already knew the skills, awareness and desire to ensure her own and Angel's safety. The process of exploring and acknowledging Lily's responses restored her dignity and her faith in what she already knew to be true.

## Resistance and Wellness

The more barbarous mechanisms of colonialism have been dismantled but the colonial code of relationship is still reflected in the discourse of the human service professions, particularly in the literature on the different forms of violence. As a result, plans for the protection of children and the treatment of victims and perpetrators are too often fashioned in the very terms that obscure the problem. Victims of violence are widely portrayed as perpetrators of their own misfortunes and perpetrators are portrayed as victims of forces they do not understand and cannot control. These stereotypical images reinforce negative social responses that further violate and marginalize victims, embolden perpetrators and impede efforts to protect children. Alternatively, a response-based approach consists of practices that reveal violence, clarify responsibility, elucidate and honour victims' responses and resistance, and contest the blaming and pathologizing of victims. Information drawn from conversations about resistance can be used in the risk and safety assessment process to document a mother's ongoing knowledge and experience of creating safety for children in the midst of danger.

## Suggestions for Further Reading

Burstow, B. 1992. *Radical Feminist Therapy*. Newbury Park, CA: Sage

Logan, T. 2001. The Lost Generations: The Silent Métis of the Residential School System. Winnipeg, MN: Southwest Region Manitoba Métis Federation.

Laerniu, P. 2000. "Processes of Decolonization." In M. Battiste (ed.), *Reclaiming Indigenous Voice and Vision*. Vancouver, BC: UBC Press.

Yazzie, R. 2000. Indigenous Peoples and Postcolonial Colonialism. In M. Battiste (ed.), *Reclaiming Indigenous Voice and Vision*. Vancouver, BC: UBC Press

## About the Authors

Kinewesquao [Cathy Richardson] is Métis mother of three children who lives in Cowichan Bay, BC. She is a family therapist, child welfare advocate and faculty member in the School of Social Work at the University of Victoria. She has taught in various counselling psychology programs, conducts counselling supervision and has worked extensively with Indigenous survivors of violence.

Allan Wade is a family therapist and researcher in private practice, and a neighbour of Kinewesquao [Cathy Richardson]. He has a primary interest in responses and resistance to violence, social responses to victims and perpetrators, the connection between violence and language, and applications of response-based ideas in legal and human service settings. Allan is a co-founder of the Centre for Response-Based Practice, with Linda Coates and Kinewesquao [Cathy Richardson].

## References

Adams, H. 1989. *Prison of Grass: Canada from a Native point of view*. Saskatoon: Fifth House.

Andrews, B., and C.R. Brewin. 1990. "Attributions of Blame for Marital Violence: A Study of Antecedents and Consequences." *Journal of Marriage and the Family* 52.

Andrews, B., C.R. Brewin and S. Rose. 2003. "Gender, Social Support, and PTSD in Victims of Violent Crime." *Journal of Traumatic Stress* 6, 4.

Bala, N., J. Lee and E. McNamara. 2001. "Children as Witnesses: Understanding Their Capacities, Needs and Experiences." *Journal of Social Distress and the Homeless* 10, 1 (January).

Blackstock, C., and N. Trocme. 2005. "Community-Based Children: Supporting Resilience Through Structural Change." Social Policy Journal of New Zealand 24: 12–33.

Burstow, B. 1992. *Radical Feminist Therapy.* Newbury Park, CA: Sage.

Carniol, B. 1992. "Structural Social Work: Maurice Moreau's Challenge to Social Work Practices." *Journal of Progressive Human Services* 3, 1.

Carrière, J. 2006. "Promising Practices for Maintaining Identities in First Nation Adoption." *First Peoples Child and Family Review* 3, 1. Available at <http://64.233.169.132/search?q=cache:M3D-LzdtBr4J:www.fncfcs.com/pubs/vol3num1/Carriere_pp46.pdf+%22Promising+Practices+for+Maintaining+Identities+in+First+Nation+Adoption%22&hl=en&ct=clnk&cd=1&gl=ca> accessed December 2008.

Carrière, J., and C. Richardson. 2007. "From Longing to Belonging." *Passion for Action: Voices From the Prairies*. Regina: University of Regina.

Chandler, M., and C. Lalonde. 1998. "Cultural Continuity as a Hedge Against Suicide in Canada's First Nations." *Transcultural Psychiatry* 35, 2.

Ciraco, V.N. 2001. "Fighting Domestic Violence with Mandatory Arrest, Are We Winning? An Analysis In New Jersey." *Women's Rights Law Reporter* 22, 2 (Spring).

Coates, L. 1996. "The Truth Enslaved: Anomalous Themes in Sexual Assault Trial Judgments." Paper presented at the Psychology Department, University of Birmingham, U.K.

Coates, L., J.B. Bavelas and J. Gibson. 1994. "Anomalous Language in Sexual Assault Trial Judgments." *Discourse and Society* 5, 2.

Coates, L., N. Todd and A. Wade. 2000. "An Interactional and Discursive View of Violence and Resistance." Handout from Spring Institute on Response-Based Practice, Cowichan Bay, B.C.

_____. 2003. "Shifting Terms: An Interactional and Discursive View of Violence and Resistance." *Canadian Review of Social Policy* 52.

Coates, L., and A. Wade, A. 2004. "Telling It Like It Isn't: Obscuring Perpetrator Responsibility for Violent Crime." *Discourse and Society* 15, 5.

_____. 2007. "Language and Violence: Analysis of Four Operations of Discursive Operations." *Journal of Family Violence* 22, 7.

Crapanzano, V. 1980. *Tuhami: Portrait of a Moroccan*. Chicago: University of Chicago Press.

DeJong, P., and I. Berg. 2008. *Interviewing for Solutions* (Third Edition). Pacific Grove, CA: Brooks/Cole.

Edleson, J.L. 1999. "Children's Witnessing of Adult Domestic Violence." Journal of Interpersonal Violence 14 (8): 839–70.

Edleson, J., L.F. Mbilinyi and S. Shetty. 2003. Parenting in the Context of Domestic Violence. San Francisco, CA: Judicial Council of California.

Ehrlich, S. 2001. *Representing Rape: Language and Sexual Consent*. New York: Routledge

Epston, D. 1986. "Writing your History." *Family Therapy Case Studies* 1, 1.

Freire, P. 1970. *Pedagogy of the Oppressed*. New York: Seabury.

Fromuth, M. 1986. "The Relationship of Childhood Sexual Abuse with Later Psychological and Sexual Adjustment in a Sample of College Women." *Child Abuse and Neglect* 4.

Goldolf, E.W. 2003. "Evaluating Batterer Counselling Programs: A Difficult Task Showing

Some Effects and Implications." *Aggression and Violent Behaviour* 9.

Harris, C. 2002. *Making Native Space: Colonialism, Resistance, and Reserves in British Columbia.* Vancouver: UBC Press.

Hilton, N.Z. 1992. "Battered Women's Concerns About their Children Witnessing Wife Assault." Journal of Interpersonal Violence 7: 77–86.

Hughes, E.N. 2006. "B.C. Children and Youth Review: An Independent Review of B.C.'s Child Protection System." Victoria: Ministry of Children and Family Development of B.C.

Justice Institute of British Columbia. 2007. *Final Report: Empowerment of Immigrant and Refugee Women Who Are Victims of Violence in Their Intimate Relationships.* Victoria: Justice Institute of British Columbia.

Kelly, L. 1988. *Surviving Sexual Violence.* Minneapolis: University of Minnesota Press.

Lee, M.Y., J. Sebold and A. Uken. 2003. *Solution-Focused Treatment of Domestic Violence Offenders.* New York: Oxford University Press.

Macey, D. 2000. *Frantz Fanon: A Biography.* London: Granta Books.

Magen, R. 1999. "In the Best Interests of Battered Women: Reconceptualizing Allegations of Failure to Protect." Child Maltreatment 4,2: 127–35.

Mardorossian, C. 2002. "Towards a New Feminist Theory of Rape." *Signs: A Journal of Women in Culture and Society* 27, 3.

Monture-Agnes, P. 2001. *Thunder in my Soul: A Mohawk Woman Speaks.* Halifax: Fernwood.

Moreau, M.T. 1990. "Empowerment through Advocacy and Consciousness Raising: Implications of Structural Approach to Social Work." *Journal of Sociology and Social Welfare* 17, 2.

O'Keefe, B., and I. MacDonald. 2001. *Merchant Prince.* Surrey, B.C.: Heritage House.

O'Neill, D., and M. Morgan. 2001. "Pragmatic Poststructuralism (II): An Outcomes Analysis of a Stopping the Violence Programme." *Journal of Community and Applied Social Psychology* 11.

Park, L., and K.E. Renner. 1998. "The Failure to Acknowledge Differences in Developmental Capabilities Leads to Unjust Outcomes for Child Witnesses in Sexual Assault Cases." *Canadian Journal of Community Mental Health* 17.

Razack, S. 2002. "Gendered Racial Violence and Spatialized Justice: The Murder of Pamela George." In Sherene Razack (ed.), *Race, Space and the Law: Unmapping a White Settler Society.* Toronto: Between the Lines.

Richardson, C. 2003. "Stories that Map the Way Home." *Cultural Reflections* 5, Fall. Victoria, BC: University of Victoria, Anthropology Department, (peer reviewed).

_____. 2004. "Becoming Métis: The Relationship between the Sense of Métis Self and Cultural Stories." Unpublished dissertation, University of Victoria.

_____. 2005. "Steps to Dignity and Decolonization: Family Group Conferencing in Aboriginal Communities." *Restorative Directions* March.

_____. 2005. "Cultural Stories and the Creation of the Self." *Relational Child and Youth Care Practice* 18, 1.

_____. 2006. "Métis Tactical Resistance to Colonization and Oppression." *Variegations* 2.

Richardson, C., and B. Nelson. 2007. "A Change of Residence: From Residential Schools to Foster Homes as Sites of Aboriginal Cultural Assimilation." *First Nations Child and Family Caring Society of Canada* 3, 2.

Richardson, C., and A. Wade. 2007. "Safety in Alternative Dispute Resolution with Aboriginal Families." Forthcoming in *Restorative Directions.*

Ridley, P., and L. Coates. 2003. "Representing Victims of Sexualized Assault: Deficient or Proficient?" Unpublished manuscript, University of Lethbridge.

Rossiter, A. 1994. "Teaching Social Work Skills from a Critical Perspective." Unpublished manuscript, York University, North York, ON.

Schecter, S., and J. Edleson. 1995. "In the Best Interest of Women and Children: A call for Collaboration Between Child Welfare and Domestic Violence Constituencies." Protecting Children 11(3): 6–11.

_____. 1999. Effective Intervention in Domestic Violence and Child Maltreatment Cases: Guidelines for Policy and Practice: Recommendations from the National Council of Juvenile and Family Court Judges Family Violence Department. Reno, NV: The National Council of Juvenile and Family Court Judges.

Sinclair, J., D. Phillips, and N. Bala. 1991. "Aboriginal Child Welfare in Canada." In N. Bala, J.P. Hornick and R. Vogel (eds.), Canadian Child Welfare Law: Children, Families and the State. Toronto: Thompson Educational.

Strega, S. 2006. "Failure to Protect? Child Welfare Interventions when Men Beat Mothers." In R. Alaggia and C. Vine (eds.), Cruel but Not Unusual: Violence in Canadian Families. Waterloo: Wilfrid Laurier University Press.

Sullivan, C.M., J. Juras, D. Bybee, H. Nguyen and N. Allen. 2000. "How Children's Adjustment is Affected by their Relationships to their Mothers' Abusers." Journal of Interpersonal Violence 15 (6): 587–602.

Todd, N. 2007. "An Eye For and I: A Response-Based Approach to Counselling with Perpetrators of Violence and Abuse." Unpublished manuscript, Calgary, Alberta.

Todd, N., and A. Wade. 1994. "Domination, Deficiency and Psychotherapy." Calgary Participator (Fall).

_____. 2003. "Coming to Terms with Violence and Resistance: From a Language of Effects to a Language of Responses." T. Strong and D. Pare (eds.), Furthering Talk: Advances in the Discursive Therapies. New York: Kluwer.

Turnell, A., and S. Edwards. 1999. Signs of Safety. A Solution and Safety Oriented Approach to Child Protection Casework. New York: WW Norton.

Wade, A. 1997. "Small Acts of Living: Everyday Resistance to Violence and Other Forms of Oppression." Journal of Contemporary Family Therapy 19.

_____. 2000. "Resistance to Interpersonal Violence: Implications for the Practice of Therapy." Unpublished PhD dissertation, Department of Psychology, University of Victoria.

_____. 2007. "Hope, Despair, Resistance: Response-Based Therapy with Victims of Violence." In C. Flaskas, I. McCarthy and J. Sheehan (eds.), Hope and Despair in Narrative and Family Therapy: Adversity, Forgiveness and Reconciliation. Hove: Brunner-Routledge.

Walker, L. 1979. The Battered Woman. New York: Van Nostrand Reinhold.

White, M. 1995. Re-Authorizing Lives: Interviews and Essays. Adalaide: Dulwich Centre.

Yukon Family Violence Project. 2002. Public Brochure. Family Violence Unit. Whitehorse.

# Chapter 13

# Healing versus Treatment
## Substance Misuse, Child Welfare and Indigenous Families

*Betty Bastien, Sohki Aski Esquao [Jeannine Carrière] and Susan Strega*

This chapter explores the impacts of substance misuse for children and families involved in child welfare while distinguishing between healing and treatment as a means for Indigenous family restoration. Treatment as described in Western medical models addresses symptoms while Indigenous healing approaches focus on the use of ceremony, kinship and spirituality. Indigenous ways of being in relation to wellness and recovery are discussed, and cultural practices that involve community resources and kinship systems are suggested for anti-oppressive social work practice within the context of substance abuse.

Questions Addressed in This Chapter
1. What are the current challenges for substance misuse and child welfare practice?
2. What are the current challenges for substance misuse and child welfare practice with Indigenous children and families?
3. What models of practice can influence healing for substance misusing Indigenous and non-Indigenous families involved in child welfare?

The past decade has seen increased concern about potential harms to children associated with drug or alcohol misuse by their caregivers (Poole and Dell 2005). The 1998 Canadian Incidence Study (CIS) found substance abuse concerns noted in 34% percent of child welfare investigations and a significant factor in 56 percent of emotional and/or psychological maltreatment cases (MacLaurin et al. 2003). Studies from the U.S. report that between one-third and two-thirds of families involved with child welfare misuse substances in ways that contribute to child maltreatment (Semidei, Radel and Nolan 2001). The Center for Addictions and Substance Use (1998) surveyed over 900 child welfare professionals, 71.6 percent of whom cited substance abuse as one of the top three causes for a dramatic increase in reports. Substance misuse is often strongly linked to neglect (Mayer et al. 2004) though this finding must be viewed with caution. Given the linkages between poverty and child welfare involvement, substance misusing poor parents may lack funds for substitute caregivers or to otherwise ameliorate the effects of their substance misuse, while more advantaged parents have resources that reduce substance misuse impacts.

For substance misusing parents who come to the attention of child welfare, mostly mothers, the most significant factors shaping their interactions with the system are stereotyping and resultant discrimination from workers (Rutman et al. 2000). Workers often add to a mother's burden of guilt and shame through harsh and judgmental treatment and by automatically classifying her as "unfit" (Smith 2006). Indigenous parents carry the additional weight of the "drunken Indian" stereotype, which is both greatly exaggerated and widely circulated within Canadian society (Royal Commission on Aboriginal Peoples 1996). Since Canada's child protection statistics demonstrate an over-representation of Indigenous children, the issue of substance misuse for Indigenous families requires critical exploration. We begin our discussion by examining some of the current statistics on substance misuse for Indigenous peoples in Canada. This is followed by exploring the implications of substance misuse for children and families. We conclude with some models to consider in working anti-oppressively with Indigenous families involved in substance misuse and child welfare.

## Substance Misuse and Indigenous Peoples in Canada

After examining recent statistics, we decided to focus our discussion on three substances — illicit drugs, solvents and alcohol — as these are the prevalent addiction issues that bring Indigenous families to the attention of child welfare authorities. As discussed throughout this chapter, a correlation exists between poverty and substance abuse, and that correlation is particularly strong for Indigenous people.

Substance misuse includes an array of illicit drugs, and studies indicate that Indigenous people in Canada, as a group, experience disproportionately high rates of nonmedical drug abuse (Scott 1997; Framework Sub-committee of the National Native Addictions Partnership Foundation and Thatcher 2000). According to the 2002–03 First Nations Regional Longitudinal Health Survey, although the documented rate of illicit drug use in the past year was low (7.3 percent) among Indigenous people, it was still more than double the rate of the general Canadian population (3.0 percent) (First Nations Centre 2005). The overall morbidity rate from illicit drug use is almost three times higher for Indigenous people than for the general population: 7.0 per 100,000 vs. 2.6 per 100,000 (Scott 1997). The abuse of prescription drugs has also come to the attention of epidemiologists.

A study carried out in Calgary concluded: "Inappropriate prescription medication use was a significant problem among an Aboriginal population that sought addiction treatment, and many of these individuals accessed medication from a prescribing physician" (Wardman, Khan and el-Guebaly 2002: 355). However, a Health Canada report on client safety improvements within the First Nations and Inuit Health Branch (FNIHB) Non-Insured Health Benefits (NIHB) program recognized that the vast majority of NIHB clients use prescription drugs in an appropriate way (Health Canada Non-Insured Health Benefits Program 2007).

Research and practice have uncovered high rates of volatile solvent abuse (VSA) among some Indigenous and Inuit youth living in rural and remote areas of Canada. For example, a 2003 report from Pauingassi First Nation in Manitoba concluded that half the children under eighteen living on reserve abused solvents (O'Brien 2005). The current rate of VSA among Canada's Aboriginal youth as a whole is not known. In some Indigenous communities the use of solvents has been portrayed as a chronic outcome of unemployment and poverty within a context where hope has vanished. But perceptions about the prevalence of this behaviour may be inflated due media coverage, for example, the repeated showings of 1993 and 2004 media clips of Innu youth in Davis Inlet, Labrador getting high on gasoline.

The introduction of alcohol to Indigenous peoples can be framed in a colonial context of attempted genocide, and certainly alcohol remains as a prevalent factor in addictions treatment for Indigenous peoples in Canada (Health Canada 2005). Canadian statistics on patterns of drinking indicate that although Indigenous people have among the highest rates of abstinence from alcohol and drink less often than the general population (17.8 percent vs. 44.0 percent reported drinking weekly), there are high levels of heavy use, such as binge drinking (Framework Sub-committee of the National Native Addictions Partnership Foundation and Thatcher 2000). Drinking patterns were also explored in the 2002–03 First Nations Regional Longitudinal Health Survey, which indicated that Indigenous adults have a higher rate of abstinence from alcohol (65.5 percent) than the general Canadian population. Rates were lower among Indigenous women (61.7 percent) than among men (69.3 percent), and increased with age (First Nations Centre 2005). The survey also concluded that the proportion of heavy drinkers among Indigenous adults was higher than in the general Canadian population (First Nations Centre 2005).

Fetal Alcohol Syndrome (FAS) is estimated to occur at a rate of one or two for every 1,000 live births in Canada, while Fetal Alcohol Spectrum Disorder (FASD) rates are estimated to be higher (Roberts and Nanson 2000). It is also estimated that the incidence of FAS/FASD in some Indigenous communities in Canada is higher than the national rates. It is important to note, however, that studies on drinking during pregnancy have focused disproportionately on Indigenous women and the geographic areas in which they live, and this raises some methodological concerns (Tait 2003). We explore Tait's caution further in the chapter as we discuss approaches that promote healing and wellness for Indigenous families involved in substance misuse. Statistics may not always be an accurate reflection of a community's desire for change within a challenging context. What we do know however is that substance abuse affects children, who, with their parents, often come to the attention of child welfare.

## Substance Misuse and Child Welfare

The relationship between substance misuse and child abuse is uncertain. Some studies say that the risk of abuse and neglect is higher when parents misuse substances (see, for example, Sun et al. 2001; Walsh et al. 2003), but these have been critiqued as failing to take into account social factors such as poverty that increase the likelihood of child welfare involvement (Albert et al. 2000). The focus of neglect related to substance use has been largely targeted at women. A study of women that matched demographic factors such as education, race and marital status, found that those who used drugs during pregnancy were no more at risk of abusing their children than non-drug using mothers (Hobart, Myers and Elswick 2006, cited in Dawe et al. 2006). Bennett and Sadrehashemi (2008: 11) state that "there is a need for enhanced treatment options for mothers experiencing difficulties related to drug or alcohol use and better training for [child welfare] staff about the dynamics of addiction."

Parental substance misuse impacts children and families in three main ways:

- The misuse of alcohol and other drugs reduces parental functioning and parental effectiveness.
- When substance misuse coexists with structural inequalities such as poverty children are more likely to be neglected or otherwise maltreated.
- Substance misuse is often a coping response, a way of self-medicating, for people who have experienced trauma. If the trauma is untreated and the focus remains on the substance misuse, parenting will suffer even when parents remain abstinent (DiLorenzo, Johnson and Bussey 2001). Intersections of Indigeneity, race, gender, ability and class are particularly relevant here. For example, Sun (2000) suggests that women's misuse of substances is often a posttraumatic coping response.

For Indigenous peoples, coping with trauma has been exasperated by their existence within a "colonial container" (Richardson and Wade 2007). As a precursor to discussing effective practice models for working with Indigenous substance misusing families we pause to reflect on the nature of trauma for Indigenous peoples in Canada.

## Lest We Forget…

Structural factors such as inadequate and overcrowded housing, lack of drinking water, poor nutrition, poor education, racism, external community control, unemployment, poor health and lack of culturally appropriate services are sources of continued stress and crisis for Indigenous people who live embedded in poverty and experience an absence of control over their own lives and communities. The systemic and endemic destruction of a way of life and a people (cultural genocide) with economic oppression and institutional racism has been erroneously transformed into an individual and personal, psychological (internal) shortcoming (Chrisjohn et al. 2006: 116). The purpose of creating such an illusion is to enable the system responsible to do the least possible to address these issues while still appearing to do something (Chrisjohn et al. 2006: 117).

These beliefs have guided the evolutionary theory of Western colonial cultures in the "civilizing" and assimilation of Indigenous peoples. The absence of economic sustainability and policies of apartheid justified the practices of the *Indian Act* through institutional racism and stigmatization, processes and politics inherent in genocide. On the surface, the comparison to the Holocaust is accurate although there are many important differences between the Jewish experiences of the 1930s and 1940s and that of Indigenous peoples. The most important is that the losses of Indigenous peoples are not confined to a single catastrophic period but remain ongoing and present (Whitbeck et al. 2004: 120). One of these losses is the loss of culture.

In recent years, cultural continuity/integration theory has come forward as an explanation for variations in levels of illnesses and pathologies for Indigenous peoples. This theoretical view moves research from the individual level to the contextual level. Cultural continuity theory states that contemporary pathologies must also be understood within the context of continuing cultural traditions, not severed ones, and the adaptation of people to new circumstances (Kunitz et al. 1999). This argument is an important one since it recognizes that culture for Indigenous peoples did not cease to be a dominant factor in their lives with the arrival of Europeans or the construction of reserves (Waldram 2004: 174). Cultural discontinuity has been linked to high rates of depression, alcoholism, suicide and violence, all of which have a profound impact on children and youth (Kirmayer et al. 2000: 607). Disconnection from culture, family and community can result in behaviours and events that are viewed as deficits within Indigenous communities.

We believe that we can measure the presence of this persistent sense of loss and begin to understand its prevalence and impact on the physical, emotional, mental, spiritual and psychological wellbeing of Indigenous peoples on a global level. As an empirical question, it must be contextualized in the domain of social justice and retribution for the massive and deliberate onslaught on Indigenous societies across the world. The incidence of substance abuse amongst Indigenous peoples is just one "symptom" of this onslaught. Tait (2008: 29), a Métis health scholar, reminds us:

> Individuals who are mentally ill, distressed or struggling with addictions are among the most vulnerable in any Aboriginal community. However in addressing their needs, Western medical models of diagnosis and treatment marginalize the historical and social context of their suffering, the social inequities that exacerbate their distress, and the inner strengths and reliance of Aboriginal peoples and their cultures to survive despite ongoing adversity.

We assert that symptoms of addiction and substance misuse must be understood at the macro level in order to begin to address the fragmented micro management of populations in the child welfare system. Whose responsibility is this? By now you might be asking yourself, so how can I as an individual practitioner address such a massive challenge? We believe you can begin by deepening your understanding of the context for practice with Indigenous children and their families.

## What Are Indigenous People Healing From?

To understand pain and to be able to alleviate it in the process of healing, we must see its wider context, which includes a person's mental attitudes and expectations, belief systems, emotional supports from family and friends and many other circumstances. Instead of dealing with pain in this comprehensive way, current practice, operating within a narrow biomedical framework, tries to reduce pain to a symptom that can be treated (Capra 1982: 142). Frequently pain is dealt with by denial and suppressed with the help of "pain killers" (143).

Colonialism denies the pain that was inflicted on Indigenous peoples and views the process of assimilation into the dominant culture as a natural and beneficial approach to management and treatment of this pain. Lack of material and cultural resources is perpetuated, any means of economic sustainability is absent and Indigenous knowledge production was disrupted through legislation forcing the residential school system on generations of children. The core aspects for their sense of community and continuity were shattered, with Indigenous people being severed from the essential aspects of humanity that provide social cohesion for a viable and thriving community. Moreover, programs of intervention and treatment targeted at the fallout from colonization are premised on hierarchy, patriarchy, control, rationality and empiricism, which are also tenets of colonialism. These tenets can be found in the structure, content and delivery of child welfare policies and practices (Lafrance and Bastien 2007: 105).

The effects of intergenerational violence against Indigenous peoples must be understood in order to shift existing policies and frameworks to a cultural and humanistic approach that includes relationship building. Trauma expert Judith Lewis Herman (1992: 44) writes that traumatized people who cannot dissociate from the trauma use alcohol and drugs to produce the same numbing effect that dissociation produces. Grinker and Spiegel (1945, cited in Herman 1992) found that uncontrolled drinking increased proportionately to a combat group's losses. They suggested that solders' use of alcohol appeared to be an attempt to obliterate their growing sense of helplessness and terror. Hendin and Has (1991, cited in Herman 1992) note that 85 percent of combat veterans with severe post traumatic stress disorder developed serious drug and alcohol problems although only 7 percent had prior alcohol problems.

Post traumatic stress disorder (PTSD) has been suggested as one way of understanding the impact of 500 years of colonization and genocidal practices on Indigenous peoples (Duran et al. 1998). Substance abuse and dependency may accompany PTSD; the traumatized individual self-medicates to reduce emotional, psychological and spiritual pain. First-degree relatives of survivors with PTSD also manifest a higher prevalence of substance misuse as well as mood and anxiety disorders. Brave Heart (2004: 13) found that suicide attempts among children of substance abusers appear to be more prevalent than among the general U.S. population. She notes that another possible manifestation of intergenerational trauma transfer, childhood sexual abuse, is reported among boarding school survivors and is a significant risk factor for substance abuse as well as depression and anxiety.

Most substance misuse treatment programs and practices are guided by deficiency approaches, which, for Indigenous people, replicate the processes of marginalization that are at the core of their trauma. Consequently, treatment interventions often re-traumatize them. This has been painfully evident for Indigenous mothers involved in child welfare. Cull (2006: 141) states that "the stereotype of Aboriginal women being 'unfit' mothers has a long history and it has, over time, become an entrenched aspect of the Canadian social and state system, with often devastating consequences for Aboriginal women and their communities." Smith (2006) suggests that most substance misusing mothers are "automatically" considered "unfit." But Boyd (1999) notes that poverty is a more salient factor than drug use in child welfare involvement: the poor mothers she interviewed feared child welfare involvement but middle-class mothers did not. Bennett and Sadrehashemi (2008: 110) report that,

> for women who have not previously had drug problems at least in recent years, the apprehension of their children and subsequent [child welfare] involvement can leave them so emotionally drained and depressed that drug and alcohol use feels like the only way of getting a reprieve from the pain — this only further complicates a child protection case.

Those who work with traumatized people must always contend with a tendency to discredit the victim through minimizing, denying, rationalizing or blaming. In the case of Indigenous peoples, these arguments are familiar to most Canadians: residential schools were positive as well as abusive; it all happened a very long time ago; the sixties scoop and residential schools were the best we knew at the time; and in any case that is all in the past and it is time for Indigenous people to get on with their lives. Seeking compensation for past genocidal practices becomes a double-edged sword, as it can feed into a model of individual deficiency and activate these victim-blaming discourses. Further, Indigenous people continue to live out their colonization with the colonizer, within a paradigm that is continually constructing and creating dependencies without contributing to sustainability or stability in their environments. To understand this trauma from an Indigenous perspective requires that practitioners question the ideology and assumptions of white Western ontological perspectives. But Blackstock (2005: 20) notes that "the concept that we [social workers] can do harm or even do evil rarely appears on the optical radar screen of professional training, legislation or practice in anything other than a tangential way through procedural mechanisms such as codes of ethics." Tait (2008: 35) proposes that in health care programs we need to attend to ethics:

> The systematic development of ethical guidelines will result in the success rates for prevention, promotion and treatment programming increasing

because of the added commitment to Aboriginal patients, clients, communities and organizations; potential harm to vulnerable populations will decrease and higher levels of trust between government health ministries and different levels of primary health care in Aboriginal communities most specifically community front line health organizations and workers will be achieved.

## A Framework for Indigenous Healing

Healing must be conceptualized by understanding the impacts of trauma on every part of existence (Herman 1992). For Indigenous peoples, healing approaches, including substance abuse services, must include a strong decolonization component, through which trust and affinity can be fostered. Healing within the Indigenous paradigm is tied to the renewal of the cultural group's ontological responsibilities. Indigenous ontological theory contains a complex system of kinship relationships based on the existential purpose and meaning of communities (Bastien 2004: 84–85). The kinship system provides a framework for the process of reclaiming, renewing and affirming the shattered relationships of family and community. Spirituality is the foundation for the renewal of relationships and the core of existence. The Aboriginal Healing Foundation's *Framework for Understanding Trauma and Healing* (2006) supports healing from historical trauma and includes a decolonization process. The initial phase of such healing involves treatment for PTSD. The goal is to assist traumatized people to move from being haunted and dominated by traumatic events from the past to being able to respond to contemporary situations with their full potential. Archibald (2006: 21) explains:

Healing from historic trauma begins with creating a personally and culturally safe environment where the impacts of history, including the legacy of abuse in residential schools [or soul wound], can be safely explored through a process of remembering and recounting the abuse story, as well as reconnecting with lost traditions and languages, and cultural and spiritual practices. The third stage is mourning — speaking about and grieving personal and collective losses experienced by the present generation, but also those previous generations…. An ongoing engagement with cultural and spiritual practices takes place throughout the healing process. Affirming and rebuilding important relationships within the family and community, developing new relationships, and reaching a stage of freely being able to contribute to the family and community are activities related to the latter stages of healing.

An Indigenous kinship system has the essential components for recovery and renewal. Duran (2006) explains that recovery involves the concept of standing at the centre of the cardinal directions, or standing in the "seventh sacred direction," which is the centre of the universe. Each cultural group has their own language that addresses their own ontological responsibilities of balance. In Blackfoot, it is *ihpo kiitomohpiipotokoi* (collective ontological responsibilities). The collective responsibility of balance and harmony is premised on being in good relation with others and the world in which we live. Traditional knowledge and a kinship framework together provide an approach to child welfare in which children and parents make lives together within a supportive structure and nurturing relationships.

Indigenous languages are necessary for cultural continuity, for survival and for renewal and affirmation. *The language is the connection to the good heart*, to the good path, the red road. It connects us with a world that shapes and guides the processes for maintaining ontological responsibilities. Language guides the human development process, the social relations that orient us toward balance. It contains the meanings ascribed to existence and describes the purpose of relationships, as well as the responsibilities inherent in these connections; it provides a way of making sense of the world (Bastien 2004: 129). Language embodies the connections, relationships, responsibilities and cosmic alliances necessary for balance of Siksikaitsitapi (Blackfoot). An Indigenous worldview provides guidance for health, healing and survival.

## A Framework for Healing Children

Because there is no clear picture in the literature of how substance misuse impacts children (Dawe et al. 2006) and because some children may have more protective factors such as extended family relationships or strong cultural connections than other children, it is necessary for workers to provide children with opportunities to talk about their experiences and express their views. In doing so, workers must understand that many children experience safety, security, care and support even when parental substance misuse is present (Hogan and Higgins 2001). Children may be understandably cautious about speaking given that a family "conspiracy of silence" about parental substance misuse is common (Barnard and Barlow 2002) and because they rightly fear that disclosure could lead to apprehension (Kroll 2004). Displaying genuine compassion and support for both parents and children is likely to enhance the possibility of children disclosing. If children disclose, workers should assist them to connect to healthy extended family members and to age-appropriate community supports.

For Indigenous families, effective interventions need to target parents' capacity to seek and sustain support systems in their family and social networks. Therapeutic interventions that directly address the parents' access to social services and community supports can effectively reduce maltreatment risks and also foster adaptive parenting behaviours (Dawe et al. 2006: viii).

For children to survive in substance using families, they need to feel a sense of connectedness to their school and also to caring, healthy adults within their community and social networks. Connectedness has been described as a spiritual process that enhances our sense of self (Carrière 2005; Burkhardt and Nagai 2002). Carrière (2005) describes connectedness as a feeling of being an integral part of the universe. Burkhardt and Nagai (2002: 283) describe connectedness with our lineage as a "sacred journey." In caring for children we must remember to care for their families to help them develop their sense of connectedness.

## A Framework for Healing Families

When child welfare services and substance abuse services collaborate, outcomes for families with substance abusing parents improve (Drabble 2007). Unfortunately, collaboration is rare as the approaches, values and attitudes of these systems frequently conflict in the following ways:

- Different primary client: Child welfare services define the children as their primary client while substance abuse services focus on the substance misusing parent.
- Different sense of time: Because child welfare is concerned with immediate safety of the child as well as developmental and attachment issues, it wants to see significant change on the part of parents within a fairly short time. Substance abuse services accept that processes of recovery and relapse prevention take time and acknowledge that when clients are Indigenous or otherwise marginalized, a long-term healing approach will be more effective than short-term treatment. Child welfare is concerned with children's developmental timelines, whereas alcohol and drug workers see recovery as a process that might involve relapse and that often must take place in conjunction with other types of healing. This is especially true for Indigenous parents, who often need to reconnect with cultural and spiritual influences that they may have been deprived of.
- Different attitudes towards substance-misusing parents: Child welfare workers may be more blaming and shaming because they see substance misuse as "voluntary" (Akin and Gregoire 1997; Smith 2006), while alcohol and drug services may see substance misuse more contextually or within a disease model and therefore may be more compassionate and supportive.
- Different attitude to relapse: Child welfare workers see relapse as endangering children and indicative of a parent's lack of willingness to change, while alcohol and drug services understand relapse as a normal part of the recovery process.

Although parental substance misuse is seen as problematic, it is often difficult for parents to access appropriate services. Pregnant women and mothers with substance misuse problems face many barriers to accessing treatment (Poole and Dell 2005). Poole and Dell note (2005: 9) that "treatment services supportive of women's role as mothers are very limited in Canada," meaning that mothers who want to maintain custody and attend treatment are often forced to temporarily place their children with child welfare authorities. Services that accept entire families are rare, and facilities where fathers can attend with children are non-existent. It is in this context that Indigenous families may become permanently fractured unless healing is considered paramount in treatment (Red Horse et al. 2000) and kinship ties are maintained and strengthened.

Other Indigenous scholars concur (Littlebear 2000; Henderson 2000). Littlebear (2000: 79) describes kinship as a "spider-web of relations." He explains how extended families are interconnected circles that include social and religious functions, based on wholeness with the strength of providing balance, and that "from the moment of birth, children are the objects of love and kindness from a large circle of relatives and friends" (Littlebear 2000: 81). Within this worldview, kinship extends beyond humans to include kinship with the nature. For example, this ecological view of kinship includes social obligations such as reciprocity in relationship with plants and animals. Henderson (2000: 257) states that within this kinship system, "plants, animals and humans are related, and each is both a producer and a consumer with respect to the other, in an endless cycle."

Among the Blackfoot, there is a story that teaches about the nature of our relationship to each other and the nature of our spirituality. As many of the stories begin, one day old man and old woman were walking along the river making the laws of life. Old man said, "If we throw a buffalo chip in water and it floats, we will die and four days later we come back — cycle of life." Old lady said, "No, if we throw a rock in and it sinks we will not come back." The rock sunk to the bottom. After some time, a discussion ensued to change the law. Old man said, "Through death we will maintain our good relations with each other and have compassion for each other. The nature of the universe is understood to be compassionate and governed by affinity." The story informs the listener about two natural laws: one, the natural course of life is cyclical; and two, compassionate relationships are paramount. These two natural laws embody the health and sustainability of the group. The pervasive dicta for healing and healthy relationships are the development of high levels of trust, respect, gratitude, belonging, safety and purpose.

In the Blackfoot context, relationships are sourced from the ontological responsibilities that form these connections. Identity or self is constructed through an intricate system of collective responsibilities that are all inclusive in their orientation to each other, family, community, nature and the universe. These responsibilities embody the meaning of life, the purpose of existence and the structure and order of the universe. Relationships begin with a good heart and are the measure of health and social functioning. The self is located in place (ecology). The point of harmony with the kinship system of alliances is characterized by affinity and balance. Relationships are timeless and by their nature determine the continuity of life.

Healing is reclaiming and affirming tribal ways of generating the knowledge systems and restoring the ontological responsibilities for strengthening life. These responsibilities are encapsulated through the processes of transferring the group ontological responsibilities for the purposes of health, wellbeing and cultural (group) continuity.

## A Cultural Healing Approach

Healing practices among Indigenous peoples are consistent with their holistic orientation to the universe. This consciousness is located in their traditional knowledge and spiritual practices. Healing is a way of life, not techniques dissociated from their identities and social relations. Through the kinship system another generation of harmony and survival can be created (Bastien et al. 2003). Relatedness and relationship (*isskanaitapsi*) mean that life is purposeful and all-inclusive. This connection with community and the environment provides a network of alliances that are central to the healing process. As an example of practice, a basic ontological responsibility, *ihpo kiitomohpiipotokoi*, is about giving and sharing. The path of the good heart, *Aatsimoyihkanni*, is the concept of maintaining the sacred balance and good relations. *Aatsimoyihkanni* builds the connection to a sacred and harmonious state within a cosmic universe. These basic but powerful ways of being place one in the center of the universe. In the centre of creation, one is neither dysfunctional nor deficient. The balance of this interconnection is the source of identity, wellbeing, security and belonging among Indigenous peoples. This is healing in a profound manner.

The kinship systems of Indigenous peoples are premised on nurturing and generative forces. The experiences of healing are embodied in relationship with the sacred as the basis of their humanity. The consciousness of spirituality and the connections to the generative forces with the source of life (*ihtsipaitapiiyo'pa*) has been their strength and resiliency. These relationships have always been the source for the transformation of Siksikaitsitapi (Blackfoot), with their transformational powers enhanced through ceremony (Bastien 2004). The healing process itself is premised on inclusive decision-making processes, often referred to as "circle work" in contemporary literature. Building on the capacity of Indigenous communities, a holistic approach for substance misusing families supports the strengths and resources they bring with them to the healing process. These resources include Elders, who perform vital mentoring and advisory roles. Tait (2008: 47) promotes the use of community mentoring programs to assist all substance using women and states that mentoring is viewed as a "best practice" within substance misuse interventions with Indigenous clients.

A community-based model of healing requires practice that embraces a tribal worldview. This includes the following:

- Building the capacity of families and their children through protecting and supporting natural family systems and social networks. This is accomplished through a wellness-based assessment and life plan that includes internal and external family resources.
- Strengthening extended family and kinship systems through healing approaches that provide continuity and sustainable relationships. The raising of children in healthy and nurturing environments and communities is a collective and collateral responsibility.
- Promoting traditional healing and problem solving approaches, which are

the strength of Indigenous families and communities. Treatment standards that promote safe and sustainable relationships for families and their children, based on their cultural values and heritage, are predictive of a higher success rate for abstinence and harm reduction.

• Practising holistic healing. This includes the responsibilities and values of Indigenous peoples as identified by their community and cultural competencies for community decision-making processes and interventions.

## Conclusion

Healing from substance abuse requires an all-inclusive approach that includes a cultural orientation to improved health and wellness for children and families. To focus solely on treatment, especially short-term treatment, is to continue with the fragmentation of Indigenous families and may perpetuate existing social ills that result from colonialism. Treatment approaches that purport to "fix" Indigenous families without regard to their collective history of colonial trauma will result in the continuation of cultural genocide. Anti-oppressive child welfare practice with Indigenous substance misusing families begins by centring healing approaches that stem from the foundation of spiritual connectedness and transformation through the use of cultural safety and practices with holistic foundations. We encourage you to be witnesses to the restoration of Indigenous families in Canada.

## Suggestions for Further Reading

Adelson, N. 2005. The Embodiment of Inequality: Health Disparities in Aboriginal Canada. *Canadian Journal of Public Health* 96, 2.

Benoit, C., D. Carroll, and M. Chaudhryc. 2003. In Search of a Healing Place: Aboriginal Women in Vancouver's Downtown Eastside. *Social Science and Medicine* 56, 4.

de Leeuw, S., and M. Greenwood. 2003. *Recognizing Strength, Building Capacity: Addressing Substance Abuse Related Special Needs in First Nations Communities of British Columbia's Hinterlands.* Prince George: Centre of Excellence for Children and Adolescents with Special Needs

Dell, C., and T. Lyons. 2007. *Harm Reduction Policies and Programs for Persons of Aboriginal Descent.* Ottawa: Canadian Centre on Substance Abuse <www.ccsa.ca>.

## About the Authors

Dr. Betty Bastien is a member of the Piikani First Nation and an associate professor in the Faculty of Social Work, University of Calgary. She has been teaching for eighteen years in the areas of Indigenous studies and social work. Her research and publications include writings on Indigenous epistemology, the impact of the colonization and the de-colonization practices of Indigenous peoples, Aboriginal child welfare, intergenerational impact of trauma and indigenous and anti-oppressive social work.

Sohki Aski Esquao [Jeannine Carrière] is Métis, originally from the Red River area of southern Manitoba and teaches at the University of Victoria in the School of Social Work Indigenous Specialization. Her research interests include Indigenous child and family practice and policy, Indigenous ways of knowing, mental health and decolonization for Indigenous people. Sohki Aski Esquao has an extensive background in child welfare services with a range from practice to policy development. Her PhD work in 2005 was entitled *Connectedness and Health for First Nation Adoptees*, where she explored the connection between loss of identity and health outcomes. Dr. Carrière has an extensive list of publications related to Aboriginal child and family services.

Susan Strega teaches social work at the University of Victoria. She has practised in many areas of social work including child protection, mental health and alcohol and drug treatment. Her research interests include child welfare, sex work, social policy and violence against women, and she is the co-editor, with Leslie Brown, of *Research as Resistance* (2005).

## References

Aboriginal Healing Foundation. 2006. "A New Model: Historic Trauma Transmission. Ottawa: Aboriginal Healing Foundation.

Akin, B., and T. Gregoire. 1997. Parents' Views on Child Welfare's Response to Addiction. *Families in Society* 78, 4.

Albert, V., D. Klein, A. Noble, E. Zahand and S. Holtby. 2000. "Identifying Substance Abusing Delivering Women: Consequences for Child Maltreatment Reports." *Child Abuse and Neglect* 24.

Archibald, L. 2006. *Decolonizing and Healing: Indigenous Experiences in the United States, New Zealand, Australia and Greenland*. Ottawa: Aboriginal Healing Foundation. Available at <http://www.ahf.ca/publications/research-series> accessed May 25, 2008.

Barnard, M., and J. Barlow. 2002. "Discovering Parental Drug Dependence: Silence and Disclosure." *Children and Society* 17.

Bastien, B. 2004. *Blackfoot Ways of Knowing*. Calgary: University of Calgary Press.

Bastien, B., J. Kremer, R. Kuokkanen and P. Vickers. 2003. "Healing the Impact of Colonization, Genocide, Missionization, and Racism on Indigenous Populations." In Stanley Krippner and Teresa McIntyre (eds.), *The Impact of War Trauma on Civilian Populations*. Connecticut: Praeger.

Bennett, D., and L. Sadrehashemi. 2008. *Broken Promises: Parents Speak About BC's Child Welfare System*. Vancouver: Pivot Law Society.

Blackstock, C. 2005. "The Occasional Evil of Angels: Learning from the Experiences of Aboriginal Peoples and Social Work." *Journal of Entrepreneurship, Advancement, Strategy and Education* 1 (Special Edition) "World Indigenous Peoples Congress on Education").

Boyd, S. 1999. *Mothers and Illicit Drugs: Transcending the Myths*. Toronto: University of Toronto Press.

Brave Heart, M.Y.H. 2004. "The Historical Trauma Response among Natives and Its Relationship to Substance Abuse: A Lakota Illustration." In E. Nebelkopf and M.P. Healing (eds.), *Health for Native Americans: Speaking in Red*. Toronto: Altamria.

Burkhart, M.A., and M.G. Nagai-Jacobse. 2002. *Spirituality: Living Our Connectedness*. New York: Delmar.

Cajete, G. (2000). *Native Science Natural Laws of Interdependence*. Santa Fe, NM: Clear Light.

Canadian Centre on Substance Abuse National Policy Working Group. 1996. *Harm Reduction: Concepts and Practices. A Policy Discussion Paper*. Ottawa.

Capra, F. 1982. *The Turning Point: Science, Society and the Rising Culture*. Toronto: Bantam.

Carrière, J. 2005. "Connectedness and Health for First Nation Adoptees." Unpublished doctoral dissertation, University of Alberta.

Chrisjohn, R., S. Young and M. Maraum. 2006. *The Circle Game: Shadows and Substance in the Indian Residential School Experience in Canada* (Revised Edition). Penticton, BC: Theytus.

Cull, R. 2006. "Aboriginal Mothering under the State's Gaze." In M. Lavell-Harvard and J. Corbiere Lavell (eds.), *'Until Our Hearts Are on the Ground': Aboriginal Mothering Oppression, Resistance and Rebirth*. Toronto: Demeter.

Dawe, S., S. Frye, D. Best, D. Moss, J. Atkinson, C. Evans, M. Lynch and P. Harnett. 2006. *Drug Use in the Family: Impacts and Implications for Children*. Canberra: Australian National Council on Drugs.

DiLorenzo, P., R. Johnson and M. Bossey. 2001. "The Role of Spirituality in the Recovery Process." *Child Welfare* 80, 2.

Drabble, L. 2007. "Pathways to Collaboration: Exploring Values and Collaborative Practice between Child Welfare and Substance Abuse Treatment Fields." *Child Maltreatment* 12, 1.

Duran, E. 2006. *Healing the Soul Wound: Counseling with American Indians and Other Native Peoples*. New York: Teachers College Press.

Duran, E., B. Duran, M.Y.H. Brave Heart and S.D. Yellow Horse. 1998. "Healing the American Indian Soul Wound." In D. Yael (ed.), *Intergenerational Handbook of Multigenerational Legacies of Trauma*. New York: Plenum.

First Nations and Inuit Health Branch. 2005. *2005 NNADAP Treatment Centre Directory*. Ottawa.

First Nations Centre. 2005. *First Nations Regional Longitudinal Health Survey 2002–2003*. Ottawa.

Framework Sub-committee of the National Native Addictions Partnership Foundation, and R. Thatcher. 2000. *NNADAP Renewal Framework*. Saskatchewan: National Native Addictions Partnership Foundation.

Government of Canada. 2005. *National Framework for Action to Reduce the Harms Associated with Alcohol and Other Drugs and Substances in Canada*. Ottawa: Health Canada. Available at <http://www.nationalframework-cadrenational.ca/index_e.php?orderid_top=2> accessed February 2, 2007.

Health Canada Non-Insured Health Benefits Program. 2007. *Report on Client Safety Improvements*. Ottawa.

Helin, C. 2006. *Dances with Dependency*. Vancouver: Orca Spirit.

Henderson, Youngblood. 2000. "Ayukpachi: Empowering Aboriginal Thought." In M. Battiste (ed.), *Reclaiming Indigenous Voice and Vision*. Vancouver: University of British Columbia Press.

_____. 2000. "Postcolonial Ghost Dancing: Diagnosing European Colonialism." In M. Battiste (ed.), *Reclaiming Indigenous Voice and Vision*. Vancouver, BC: University of British Columbia Press.

Herman, J.L. 1992. *Trauma and Recovery*. New York: Basic Books.

Hogan, D., and L. Higgins. 2001. *When Parents Use Drugs: Key Findings from a Study of Children in the Care of Drug Using Parents*. Dublin: Trinity College.

Indian and Northern Affairs Canada. 1996. *Report of the Royal Commission on Aboriginal Peoples*. Ottawa. Available at http://www.ainc-inac.gc.ca/ch/rcap/sg/sgmm_e.html> accessed September 12, 2006.

Kirmayer, L., G. Brass and C. Tait. 2000. "The Mental Health of Aboriginal Peoples: Transformations of Identity and Community." *Canadian Journal of Psychiatry* 45.

Kroll, B. 2004. "Living with an Elephant: Growing Up with Parental Substance Misuse." *Child and Family Social Work* 9.

Kunitz S.J., K.R. Gabriel, J.E. Levy, E. Henderson, K. Lampert and J. McCloskey. 1999. "Alcohol Dependence and Conduct Disorder among Navajo Indians." *Journal of Studies on Alcohol* 60, 2.

Lafrance, J., and B. Bastien. 2007. "Here Be Dragons! Breaking Down the Iron Cage." Paper presented at Putting a Human Face on Child Welfare: Voices from the Prairies. Prairie Child Welfare Consortium. Regina. Saskatchewan.

Littlebear, L. 2000. "Jagged Worldviews Colliding." In M. Battiste (ed.), *Reclaiming Indigenous Voice and Vision*. Vancouver: University of British Columbia Press.

MacLaurin, B., N. Trocmé and B. Fallon. 2003 "Characteristics of Investigated Children and Families Referred for Out-of-home Placement." In K. Upheld and B. McKenzie (eds.), *Child Welfare: Connecting Research, Policy, and Practice*. Waterloo: Wilfrid Laurier Press.

Mayer, M., C. Lavergne and R. Baraldi. 2004. "Substance Abuse and Child Neglect: Intruders in the Family." CECW Information Sheet #14. Montréal: Université de Montréal. Available at <http://www.cecw-cepb.ca/DocsEng> accessed April 3, 2008.

O'Brien, D. 2005. "Manitoba's Sniff Crisis has given Birth to a Tragic Trend... Babies that Smell like Gas." *Winnipeg Free Press*, August 24: A1–A2. Coverage of the 2003 Pauingassi First Nation Report on Solvent Abuse (Manitoba Office of the Children's Advocate).

Poole, N., and Dell, C. 2005. *Girls, Women and Substance Use*. Ottawa: Canadian Centre on Substance Abuse. Available at <www.ccsa.ca>.

RCAP (Royal Commission on Aboriginal Peoples.) 1996. *Gathering Strength: Report of the Royal Commission on Aboriginal Peoples*. Ottawa. Minister of Supply and Services.

Red Horse, J., C. Martinez, P.A. Day, D. Day, J. Poupart and D. Scharnberg. 2000. *Family Preservation: Concepts in American Indian Communities*. Portland, OR: National Indian Child Welfare Association.

Richardson, C., and A. Wade. 2007. "Understanding that Violence Is Deliberate and Not Accidental." Handout from Responding to Violence: Preserving Dignity and Spirit through Small Acts of Wellness workshop, Victoria, British Columbia, March 12–13.

Roberts, G., and J. Nanson. 2000. *Best Practices. Fetal Alcohol Syndrome/Fetal Alcohol Effects and the Effects of Other Substance Use During Pregnancy*. Ottawa: Government of Canada.

Rutman, D., M. Callahan, A. Lundquist, S. Jackson and B. Field. 2000. *Substance Use and Pregnancy: Conceiving Women in the Policy Making Process*. Ottawa: Status of Women Canada. Available at <http://www.swc-cfc.gc.ca/> accessed June 24, 2008.

Scott, K. 1997. "Indigenous Canadians." In Canadian Centre on Substance Abuse (ed.), *Canadian Profile 1997: Alcohol, Tobacco and Other Drugs*. Ottawa: Canadian Centre on Substance Abuse.

Semidei, J., L. Radel and C. Nolan. 2001. "Substance Abuse and Child Welfare: Clear Linkages and Promising Responses." *Child Welfare* 80, 2.

Smith, N. 2006. "Empowering the 'Unfit' Mother: Increasing Empathy, Redefining the Label." *Affilia* 21, 4.

Sun, A. 2000. "Helping Substance-abusing Mothers in the Child Welfare System: Turning Crisis into Opportunity." *Families in Society* 81.

Sun, A., A. Shillington, M. Hohman and L. Jones. 2001. "Caregiver AOD Use, Case Substantiation, and AOD Treatment: Studies Based on Two Southwestern Counties."

*Child Welfare* 80, 2.

Tait, C. 2003. *Fetal Alcohol Syndrome among Aboriginal People in Canada: Review and Analysis of the Intergenerational Links to Residential Schools.* Ottawa: Aboriginal Healing Foundation

_____. 2008. "Ethical Programming: Toward a Community Centered Approach to Mental Health and Addiction Programming in Aboriginal Communities." *Pimatisiwin: A Journal of Aboriginal and Indigenous Community Health* 6, 1. Available at <http://www.pimatisiwin.com/Articles/6.1B_Ethical_Programming.pdf> accessed December 2008.

Terr, L. 1991. "Childhood Traumas: An Outline and Overview." *American Journal of Psychiatry* 148, 1.

Waldram, J. 2004. *Revenge of the Windigo: The Construction of the Mind and Mental Health of North American Aboriginal Peoples.* University of Toronto Press.

Walsh, C., H. Macmillan and E. Jamieson. 2003. "The Relationship between Parental Substance Abuse and Child Maltreatment: Findings from the Ontario Health Supplement. *Child Abuse and Neglect* 27, 12.

Wardman, D., N. Khan and N. el-Guebaly. 2002. "Prescription Medication Use among an Aboriginal Population Accessing Addiction Treatment." *Canadian Journal of Psychiatry* 47, 4.

Whitbeck, L., G. Adams, D. Hoyt and X. Chen. 2004. "Conceptualizing and Measuring Historical Trauma Among American Indian People." *American Journal of Community Psychology* 33.

# Chapter 14

# Engaging Fathers in Child Welfare Practice

*Leslie Brown, Susan Strega, Lena Dominelli,*
*Christopher Walmsley and Marilyn Callahan*

Despite increased attention to fathering in the popular media, the circulation of professional child development discourses about the importance of the involved father, nationally funded studies on fathering, self-help websites for fathers and research on young fathers, in child protection services most fathers remain absent or invisible. Child protection services fail to engage purposefully with fathers, either as risks or as assets, while continuing to hold mothers responsible for most aspects of family functioning. This chapter explores barriers to engaging fathers and considers what is required to overcome them. In so doing, it also explores the dangers of adopting a practice model that uncritically embraces fathers. From the experiences of fathers and practitioners, strategies for the engagement of fathers are proposed.

Questions Addressed in This Chapter

1. How are fathers rendered invisible in child welfare practice and what are the implications for mothers and children?
2. What are some of the challenges in engaging fathers in child welfare practice and how might they be overcome?
3. What are the dangers of adopting a practice model that might uncritically embrace fathers and how can these be avoided?

> *So you know, it's like these people need to start opening up their eyes a little bit more and looking at our perspective, our point of view instead of always judging the woman.... this old fashioned thinking doesn't get you nowhere but old fashioned thinking. You want to re-fix your nineteen sixties automobile, well great go ahead. You're not going to find no parts for it. (Kyle)*

The child welfare system has historically focused on women and their children, relegating fathers as largely invisible and irrelevant to child welfare practice. As Kyle's words reflect, a new approach that includes fathers and moves away from practices of mother-blame is long overdue. He challenges us to consider the perspective of fathers.

So where are fathers in the practice of child welfare? In previous studies conducted by the authors focusing on the experience of families in child welfare (Rutman et al. 2002; Callahan et al. 2004; Callahan et al. 2005; Strega 2006), the active presence of fathers was evident within the family but unacknowledged by child welfare. Frequently, there were a series of fathers coming and going, absent fathers who nonetheless still played a role in the lives of the women and children and hidden fathers who were scarcely acknowledged by child welfare because mothers would not acknowledge them. In short, fathers *exist* in the lives of women and children in child welfare, and yet they are *rarely seen* by child welfare, even when present.

There are differing uses of the term "father." Eichler and McCall (1993) define the term broadly, suggesting that men become designated as fathers through their association with women who are mothers, through behaving in a parental manner or through a legal or administrative act. Indeed most typologies include biological fathers, stepfathers and "social" fathers, the latter being men who, although unrelated to a child either biologically or legally, demonstrate parental characteristics and take on childrearing roles and responsibilities (see Cabrera et al. 2000; Dubeau 2003; Marks and Palkovitz 2004).

This inclusive approach is not without controversy. During a presentation of our research, for example, the authors were challenged by a biological father offended at being lumped in with men he viewed as having less right to the status of father. The concept of "father" is similarly contested by academic writers. Haney and March (2003) note that while policymakers define "father" in terms of men's connections with family (biological, legal and/or financial), poor mothers instead view men's performance as parents and the quality of the relationship with the children in their definition of "father." These mothers found that money makes men intrusive rather than involved and that requiring men to provide financial support to their children encouraged them to "evaluate, not to participate" (Haney and March 2003: 475). Nonetheless, we use the term "father" in the inclusive sense as it accurately describes the range of fathers and fathering behaviour evident in child welfare.

Our research began by examining the presence of fathers in child welfare. We reviewed a selection of child protection files from a child protection agency in a mid-size Canadian city to see if and how fathers were characterized. These files, dated between 1997 and 2005, included case file recordings, court documents, parenting and risk assessments, social worker logs, referral letters and other documents. The assertion that fathers are largely invisible in the lives of women and children in child welfare was borne out in this review (Strega et al. 2008).

There were 166 of these files that had both documented child protection concerns and at least one identified father. These particular files were then examined more carefully to determine how fathers were characterized by the workers. In making this determination, we examined the language used to describe fathers and assessed the type, purpose and quantity of contacts with fathers, purposefully using a very generous definition of "contact," including actions as modest as sending a letter or leaving a phone message. We then were able to establish whether workers viewed the fathers as assets, risks, a combination of asset and risk, or irrelevant. In 52 percent of the cases, fathers were seen as irrelevant. Contact of any sort was not commonly observed, though when it did occur, it was most often when the father was seen as an asset to the children. In those cases where the fathers were identified as risks to the mothers, social workers only made contact 50 percent of the time, and when they were considered risks to the children, contact was even less frequent (40 percent). We observed, as have other writers (O'Hagan 1997; Trotter 1997), that fathers were rarely considered as placement resources, even when the alternative was permanent guardianship. Fathers who expressed interest in custody were typically told to get a lawyer, and interestingly the few fathers who ended up with custody did so serendipitously rather than through any effort on the part of child welfare.

Subsequent to the file review, we conducted in-depth interviews with eleven fathers of children who had come to the attention of child welfare. We also conducted focus group interviews with child welfare workers, inviting them to comment on our research results and reflect on their own practice in relation to fathers. The results of our study, supported by others (Stanley 1997; Scourfield 2001), suggest that invisible, irrelevant "ghost" fathers are consistently manufactured in the child welfare system through a series of administrative and professional discourses and practices (Brown et al. 2008).

## Why Child Welfare Workers Fail to Engage Fathers

Child welfare has historically, and remains, focused on mothers (O'Hagan and Dillenburger 1995; Swift 1995). From the North American tradition of using a matriarchal filing system[1] to the gendered implementation of "failure to protect,"[2] mothers are manufactured into the targets of our interventions. Even progressive initiatives such as gender neutral language, which substitute terms like caretakers or parents for mothers or fathers, have done little to shift the focus from women to both women and men. The use of "parent" rather than mother and father can lead to shortcuts for busy workers where once a parent is contacted and interviewed there is little incentive to similarly contact other parents, despite legislation and policy requiring workers to do so. Our hegemonic attention on mothers, to the exclusion of fathers, results in seemingly absurd, yet unexamined, practices. For instance, in the risk assessment model widely used in Canada, a descriptor for the highest rating of risk for violence reads, "The parent is pregnant and incidents of physical violence have occurred since becoming pregnant" (Province of British Columbia 1996). Obviously, workers would read "mother" for "parent." Notably there is no requirement in scoring this item to identify the gender or existence of the perpetrator.

As one worker noted, being child centred does not remove one's attention on the mother.

*It's really difficult when all of your training and all of the procedures and everything tell you to go out and be child focused. If you can see damage happening to a child, you look around and you find the handy adult who sat there and is responsible. I mean the mother is responsible. You hold her responsible. (child welfare worker)*

Workers expect little from men, even when they are biological fathers. When not threatening or abusive, and sometimes when they are, men are generally considered irrelevant or rendered invisible, though men who perform even minor childcare tasks are frequently regarded as heroic figures (Daniel and Taylor 1999; Swift 1995). Scourfield (2003) and Swift (1995) have noted the existence of a gendered "occupational discourse" in child welfare that supports absenting men. In this gendered discourse, women are responsible for the effects of their behaviour on children but men are not.

The discourse of "mother-blame" permeates child welfare. McMahon and Pence (1995) offer a constructivist perspective, suggesting that because men are constructed as having rights (to stay in *his* house, to have access to *his* children) and women are constructed as having responsibilities (emotional and physical caretaking of men and children), workers are hesitant to infringe on men's "rights" but quick to expect women to fulfill their "responsibilities." Their idea is confirmed in a recent U.K./Canada study of child welfare cases involving men who beat mothers, where social workers and mothers in both jurisdictions repeatedly constructed men as having rights but did not in a single instance construct mothers in this way (Strega 2004). Indeed, there is evidence that fathers have, throughout the twentieth century, approached child welfare from a rights perspective (Adamoski 2002).[3] Similarly, in our file review, we noted that men who expressed interest in caring for their children were usually told to "get a lawyer." Although fathers have been successful in appropriating and deploying the discourse of "rights" in relation to custody and access disputes in the U.K. (Smart and Neale 1999) and in Canada (Mann 2003), this perspective has yet to significantly impact child protection.

The focus on mothers and mother-blaming is not the only discourse in child welfare that renders fathers invisible. In recent years, child welfare like many government services has embraced the concept of managerialism, founded on the idea that management principles from the private sector can greatly improve public sector functioning (Parada 2002). Managerialism's concern with efficiency and standardization rather than effectiveness and its practice of defining relationships on the basis of money and contracts rather than care and concern, subordinates professional knowledge to managerial knowledge (Tsui and Cheung 2004). Tasks are broken down into specific component parts, assigned to a series of workers and limited by timelines. There is an emphasis on outcome measures such as completing assessments in a timely manner and referring parents to remedial work with contracted agencies, where they can be kept under surveillance in a cost-efficient manner. Under these circumstances, finding and contacting fathers and developing relationships can be viewed as inefficient.

Workload pressures and the need for efficient management of caseloads was seen by both workers and fathers in our study as contributing to the lack of engagement with fathers.

> *It's different when caseloads are smaller because we can be more thorough, but when caseloads are big, which they usually are, we look for outs and [ignoring fathers is] an easy one. (child welfare worker)*

> *They're trying to get through their cases. They're not making good judgment calls because [it's] on to the next case. They're in a rush. And they're devastating the lives of families in the process… it's not all men. There are some women out there that are devastated by child welfare as well but you know in my experience, I mean I really felt they ruined my life. (Henry)*

Our review of child protection files found that even when information relating to fathers was present, most often workers relied on mothers to be the source of this information. Mothers living on the margins have disincentives to identify the fathers of their children. Policies such as welfare provision and social housing make it difficult for women to identify fathers in their households for fear of jeopardizing their and their children's benefits. As one father noted when talking about his girlfriend filling out her form for income assistance, "She put zero, zero, zero" when asked about income and his presence even though he was living in the home and bringing in wages. The intrusive nature of welfare provision means that mothers have to prove that they are not in a spousal relationship in order to maintain their benefits, which may serve to decrease men's helping, support and contact with children. Welfare policies also lack provision for poor non-custodial fathers to maintain adequate space and resources to remain involved with their children, as needs are determined based on children in the home or family unit and children are rarely residing with the father. Mann (2005) notes that that Canadian Indigenous women are reluctant to ascribe paternity if the father does not have status under the *Indian Act* because they and their children are adversely affected by their children's loss of benefits. Between 1985 and 1999 nearly one in five children born to Indigenous women registered under the *Indian Act* did not have their paternity designated (Blackstock et al. 2004). Invisibility in social welfare and social housing systems translates into invisibility in child welfare as well.

Even if workers wanted to engage fathers, the lack of support services for fathers is a barrier. A social worker commenting on this research noted that she wouldn't open up the Pandora's box of the father as she had no resources to offer anyway, while another stated that contacting fathers would amount to doubling her caseload. Other workers said they are frustrated with the lack of means to hold men accountable for utilizing what little services might be available to them.

> *We can monitor, encourage and offer services and look at what's out there, not that there's loads, but if they choose not to…then at that point you have this kind of, "we*

*want you to do this assessment, identify work that you should do as a guy," but he doesn't have to within those proceedings. He can't be compelled to do any assessment for anything. (child welfare worker)*

Child welfare workers seem ill-prepared to work with fathers, which may in part contribute to their reluctance to engage with fathers, and thereby to father invisibility. Our review of undergraduate course syllabi found that fewer than 5 percent of courses related to children and family work had any required readings that mentioned fathers in any way (Walmsley et al. 2006). Yet there is a small but growing literature on fathers in child and family welfare (Daniel and Taylor 2001; Ferguson and Hogan 2004; Scourfield 2003) and a larger pool on fathering in general (see, for example, Ryan 2000) that does not support this exclusion. This point was reaffirmed to us recently when a child welfare supervisor commented that a newly hired social worker must have been taught by one of us as she kept insisting on the inclusion of fathers in her case planning, a highly irregular practice. Our focus groups with workers found that, while some workers appear to be putting more effort into contacting fathers and sense more expectation to do so from some judges and team leaders, fathers are often viewed as demanding of workers, controlling of the women in their lives and difficult to engage or set expectations of a parental role or responsibility for children. The absence of fathers in the preparation of professional social workers is replicated in parenting education (Sunderland 2006) and popular parenting literature. Fleming and Tobin (2005) found that very few of these books (4.2 percent of their sample) make reference to fathers, and further that fathers' roles were characterized as voluntary, negotiable and ancillary to those of mothers.

Child welfare workers often see working with fathers as difficult and challenging.

*Nobody goes anywhere near him. I certainly feel that about social services. We're always working with women. The men are out, in the pub, in the shed, over at their mothers — they're somewhere else, aren't they? So working really hard to engage what are fairly scary blokes, they're not necessarily scary to professionals, but some of them are, and say to them that their behaviour is unacceptable and some work needs to be done is much harder than it sounds, considering that we do that all the time to women. (child welfare worker)*

Failing to engage fathers potentially fails to protect mothers and children. Some fathers are a risk to their families through their violent, sometimes lethal, behaviours. Having the father leave the home is often seen as the treatment option.

*When I think of our more successful cases, the ones the social workers would be pleased with, they tend to be where the woman has been able to actually move and with support then change everything for herself and her children and that tends to mean separating from him. (child welfare worker)*

But men who are cut out of one family involved with child welfare often show up in another family, and also often remain in contact with their old family.

> *Most of them walk away and go off to find new families. There's lots of times I meet the mom and she'll say he did the same thing to his last family. She'll even have a copy of the restraining order that he brought with him from the other relationship. (child welfare worker)*

Leaving the home does not therefore justify a lack of engagement by child welfare. It does not satisfy the obligation to protect mothers and children.

Failing to engage fathers potentially deprives mothers and children of resources, support and connection. Recent research, confirmed by our own, suggests that we can both increase child safety and sometimes better resource mothers and children by engaging fathers (Featherstone 2008; Ferguson and Hogan 2004; Peled 2000).

### Dangers of Uncritically Engaging Fathers

As we have argued, by failing to engage fathers we potentially fail to protect mothers and children, and therefore child welfare workers need to engage with fathers as part of their practice. We are not purporting that all fathers should be included in the lives of their children, but rather that all fathers need to be seen and engaged by workers. The reality is that men, commonly a man with a fathering role in the family, perpetrate the majority of domestic violence to women and children (Lavergne et al. 2003). Yet workers tend to ignore dangerous men when assessing risk and family functioning (Munro 1998; Stanley 1997). The situation of engaging fathers may be further complicated when the perpetrator lives in the same house as the mother and children. These cases suggest a greater complexity that requires more thorough evaluation on the part of the worker around the wisdom and nature of engaging with a father and the impact of that engagement on the safety of the mother and children.

Indeed, the responsibility for monitoring men's behaviour is often downloaded by child welfare to mothers. Workers hold mothers accountable for keeping their children safe from their violent or abusive fathers.

> *It's up to the mom to protect the children. So we talk to her only. We believe it's the mom, the custodial parent, it's up to her to be protective — or frequently he's a step-parent. So it's up to her to protect her children. (child welfare worker)*

Women are expected to socialize their men, to nurture and facilitate father-child relationships and even father-worker relationships. We heard of mothers working hard to have child welfare workers "understand" their partners and at the same time working with their men to help them "get along" with the child welfare workers.

When fathers are known to be violent, engagement must begin with safety and accountability; intervening with men must not place mothers or children at more risk. Batterer intervention programs rarely focus on parenting or the effects of violence on children, and anger management programs rarely focus on violence. Fleck-Henderson (2000, cited in Hartley 2004) suggests that child protection workers must "see double" when dealing with violent men in families, drawing from both child protection and domestic violence perspectives. Child welfare supervision and service plans need to focus primarily on the batterer rather than mothers (Strega 2006), and claims of failure to protect must be substantiated against batterers rather than mothers. Workers need to determine not just whether fathers want to continue relationships with their children but their reasons for doing so. As Goodmark (2004) notes, different intervention strategies must be applied with fathers who care about involvement with their children, fathers who don't care and "unrelated boyfriends." At the same time, encouraging father involvement must not become a substitute for continuing to engage with mothers in supportive and empowering ways.

There are other potential problems to be aware of that can result from including fathers in child welfare practice. Sometimes including fathers can actually reduce the resources available to children and mothers. As discussed earlier, mothers (and fathers) may choose to hide fathers from the system in order to not jeopardize social assistance, social housing or other benefits. There can sometimes be more informal support available to mothers and children when fathers are invisible than when fathers are connected to formal systems like child support enforcement. For child welfare workers it is a delicate balance of risk and asset for children in choosing to "see" fathers. Workers must be cognizant of these factors and tell mothers that they are cognizant as well as whether and how they will act in any given situation. For instance, under what circumstances will the worker make a father's presence known to other agencies such as financial assistance services? It is the worker's responsibility to "lay the fears on the table" and make their practice decisions transparent.

## What Works from the Perspective of Fathers

The fathers interviewed in our research had a myriad of experiences with child welfare, and their stories offer instruction on what works and what doesn't work in engaging them. Bill spoke of his first encounter with a child welfare worker that occurred when he was in jail. The worker made the effort to seek him out when the child was apprehended. The worker asked, *"Like are you going to be a part of your daughter's life when you get out? I said sure."* So the worker kept visiting him. *"While I was in jail, I was doing all this like having visits inside the jail you know with the baby and everything. They'd come once a week."*

At some point, Bill made the decision to really become a father. *"[The child welfare worker] asked me you know, would you be, would you want to be the father. Well I am the father I told her. But would you want to take care of her and stuff like that."* Once he was released from jail, he took custody of the child. *"I had to step up and grow up in a hurry."* Child welfare remained involved *"because I was becoming the father, the*

*caregiver and they wanted to track my stages of how I'm doing and how [child] was doing."*
He appreciated their support. *"You know, without [child welfare] stepping in, they're
helping me but they're not against me. So that's what helped me to become this."*

The first child welfare worker in Bill's life reached out to him in jail and
then continued to work with him in a supportive way. *"She knew that I was a
person who could do it."* They had established a relationship. *"We know each other,
for the last three years with [child], so it's like a relationship, but like nothing involved but
like a relationship."* He felt understood by this worker. *"[She] would understand why
I'm doing the stuff I'm doing."* He also developed a trusting relationship with the
support worker.

> *She's not against me. She's with me. That's the good thing about it. If I sense that you're
> willing to help me instead of trying to be against me well then I'll open up more....
> It's like a relationship there too. She's not against me, she's with me.... That way it's
> caring instead of, business like caring where you have to care. She wants to care.*

A new child welfare worker was assigned and all the rules seemed to change.
Bill and this new worker had no relationship to build from. *"I have to prove to her
what I can do."* He did not feel the support from her that he did with the previous
worker. *"She wants me to fail 'cause she thinks I can't do it."* He perceived a very different style of child welfare practice. *"She doesn't want to work with me; she wants to
work at me."* He did not trust the new worker. *"I don't feel comfortable talking to her. I
figure if I tell her something she writes it all down and then she uses it against me, which the
other one would understand why I'm doing the stuff I'm doing."* His relationship with the
new worker impacted how he saw his relationship with the child welfare system.
*"It's just going to be me going up against them."*

Several of the fathers interviewed spoke of the importance of being offered
concrete resources, support and information. *"I've had a lot of support to become a
different, a better parent"* noted Eddie. He went on to comment that he had to work
to keep this support. *"I've had a lot of support from [child welfare]. They stayed with
me for almost four years and then they left. They said that's it for you. But I got them back
involved. We're re-involved with [child welfare]."* One resource identified by Eddie and
some other fathers as being a huge support was a fathering program. Fathers
who attended such a parenting support group spoke about how critical it was to
have this help in taking responsibility for their behaviours as fathers.

Support also came in small ways. Bob told of how one worker who came
to visit and monitor his parenting, didn't just ask questions, but pitched in while
she was there. *"She takes one baby, maybe I take one baby, to sort of make it easier and
stuff like that."* This was in contrast to another father who told a story of the
worker coming and sitting uncomfortably in his home and asking questions
while he rushed around to care for his children. He felt mistrusted and did not
find that worker supportive. Several fathers also spoke appreciatively of workers
who were transparent in their practice, providing them information about their
children who were in care, the processes of child welfare and the expectations
of their behaviours. Conversely, many also told tales of workers who were not

forthcoming with such information and how that created mistrust and confusion for fathers.

Keeping fathers informed and involved was seen by the fathers as being a part of being in relationship with workers. Brad commented, *"I have a relationship with — like the workers. Like you know they knew me."* Seeing their worker advocate for them when appropriate was also highly valued and nurtured the father-worker relationship. Ken on the other hand had had poor relationships with child welfare workers.

> *I'm scared; I'm scared of this system. I'm scared of social workers and I can't stand the thought of me talking to a social worker because that person, they won't understand where I'm coming from. They'll just shake their head, okay yeah whatever. Then they'll say well, they'll go fill out their papers.*

Without a relationship to build upon, fathers felt judged and mistrusted by child welfare workers. In such situations, they often chose to "fly under the radar" of child welfare thereby making themselves as invisible as possible to the system.

One father in our study had made the choice to cooperate fully with the child welfare worker, regardless of whether or not he agreed with her. He told of being sent to a plethora of programs on instruction of his worker. Anger management classes, a parenting course, Alcoholics Anonymous groups were piled onto expectations of holding down a job. He was collapsing under the weight of expectations.

> *...instead of letting the willow bend you know, you don't have to snap the damn thing in half. You can let it bend and let it go back and it'll swing on forever. You don't have to snap the damn thing to make it work. (Ian)*

Most of the fathers we interviewed in our study were highly visible to child welfare, and in fact many had become the primary parent in their children's lives. We found that in these situations they were often treated like mothers, and the processes of "mother-blame" were replicated. These fathers were expected to keep violent or drug using mothers away from the children, despite their children's strong desires to keep connected to their moms. They were seen to be "good fathers" when they met the expectation of "good mothering."

## Principles and Practice Strategies

Basic principles of anti-oppressive child welfare practice apply to fathers as well as to mothers. But because fathers have been both ignored and demonized in child welfare, there is a need to have certain principles and practice strategies in place to counter dominant occupational discourses. We suggest four principles, with concurrent practice strategies, that are aimed at engaging fathers in child welfare in order to protect children.

### First Principle — Acknowledge their existence
Fathers exist in the lives of children. Whether we approve of these men or not, whether they are part of their children's lives or not, they exist.

### First Practice Strategy — Acknowledge their presence
Fathers do exist in the lives of their children, but too often they are not seen by child welfare. Acknowledging their presence requires that workers reach out to find and contact fathers. Within considerations of the context of the particular family, there are several ways that fathers can be engaged by child welfare workers.

- Include fathers in assessments, such as assessments of children's safety or other risk assessments as well as assessments of parenting or other caregiving. Inclusion of a father does not mean just gathering information about the father from the mother. For example, in the case of a violent father, gather his criminal history and interview him directly as part of any risk or capacity assessment and planning.
- Visit the home when the father will be there. O'Hagan and Dillenburger (1995) found that workers tend to visit the home when men known to be violent are absent, or they avoid meaningful contact with him.
- Include fathers in protection or supervision orders. Indeed, a father should have his own supervision order or be specifically named if the order includes both parents.
- When children are placed in alternate care, consider contact arrangements for both father and mother. Mothers should not be responsible for facilitating or monitoring this contact.
- Include fathers in rehabilitation planning (e.g., parenting courses, even for violent men).
- Include the father's and the mother's extended family in the assessment and planning process. Behind the father may be a grandmother, grandfather, brothers and sisters who can encourage and support the father to take a more active caregiving role with his child.

### Second Principle — Understand there are many different ways to be a father
As Scourfield (2006) notes, the welfare state was premised on a male breadwinner/female caregiver model, and this legacy lives on in child welfare and social policies that continue to primarily focus on men as a source of financial support and therefore fail to nurture the continued involvement of men who are emotionally attached but unable to financially provide for their children/families. Policymakers generally focus on men's connections to their children (biological, institutional, financial) as defining fatherhood, but marginalized mothers, as Haney and March (2003) note in their study of poor African-American mothers, focus on men's performance as parents as defining fatherhood. From the perspective of these mothers the quality of men's relationships with children are more important than any formal ties. For instance, we heard from a father whose

children were in permanent care and yet this father was preparing for the day when his children would "age out of care" and be old enough to return home. Another father told of his commitment to remain drug and alcohol free in the presence of his children. There are many different ways to be a father.

### Second Practice Strategy — Be strengths-focused

The fathers in our study gave endless illustrations of how child welfare workers, when they did acknowledge their existence, saw their deficits as fathers but rarely their strengths or potential. The focus on problems, to the exclusion of strengths, was defeating for many. They knew they had serious issues to work on and they also wanted to be seen as good fathers. Taking a strengths perspective in child welfare practice can enable better fathering. Some things to remember in doing so include:

- Be aware of the need for balance of physical, mental, emotional and spiritual aspects of fathering and nurture those parts that need strengthening while acknowledging those that are strong.
- Recognize that fathering is more than financial support.
- Appreciate that the identity of fatherhood is different than that of motherhood and that parenting by fathers often looks different that parenting by mothers.
- Notice, emphasize and support all positive involvement from fathers.
- Realize that fathering is life long. We know that even when children grow up in care, they often re-establish contact once they age out of care.
- Do what you can to foster a positive relationship between fathers and children, even if it's by phone or postcard and whether infrequent or unreliable.
- Recognize that engaged fathering is a learned process, for which fathers have few role models or knowledgeable peers. Being more than a playmate takes coaching and support to learn how to safely bathe, feed, transport and change a baby or young child.

### Third Principle — Violence does not necessarily eliminate men from being involved as fathers, but it must be taken up directly with them

This principle challenges prevailing practices where "a violent man's parenthood is conceptualized in terms of rights to the child, rather than as a responsibility to heal the harm done by violence" (McMahon and Pence 1995: 199). Violent men are most commonly constructed as perpetrators or offenders, and as Featherstone and Peckover (2007) argue, this limited view of their identity obscures their identity as fathers. Fathers who are violent have to be purposefully engaged with by child welfare as both fathers and as perpetrators of violence.

### Third Practice Strategy — Respectful practice involves holding fathers accountable

When fathers are violent child welfare workers still need to engage with them. The treatment option of "leaving home" does not hold fathers accountable. Workers may have to meet with fathers in jail, at a probation office or at an agency where they are getting services. As part of child welfare practice, workers need to be prepared to actively pursue these fathers and to engage in purposeful interactions that seek to hold fathers responsible and accountable for their violent behaviours. What must be avoided most is holding mothers responsible for managing men's violence and protecting children. As Strega (2006) explains, when men are assaulting mothers we have to stop asking "Why does she stay?" and ask "Why does he hit her?"

Respectful practice acknowledges the multiple identities that people embody. For fathers who are violent, child welfare workers need to directly engage with these men as both fathers and as perpetrators of violence. Some specific practice suggestions include:

- Use language that acknowledges the violence and holds perpetrators responsible. As Todd and Wade (2004: 159) describe, currently most professional and public discourse "conceals violence, mitigates perpetrators' responsibility, conceals victims' resistance, and blames or pathologizes victims."
- Aim to accurately assess the risk men pose to children and mothers. This requires the gathering of the father's history of violence through interviewing the father and others such as the police or other workers (Strega 2006).
- Be knowledgeable about resources for men that deal with men's violence (go beyond anger management programs and seek out resources that deal particularly with violent behaviours).
- Advocate for fathering/parenting programs to address violence and for violence programs to address parenting.
- Recognize that men often resist asking for help, not merely because it would go against his "dominant hegemonic definition of himself as an invulnerable, controlled, coping male, but because it is seen as a real threat and would only add to their problems" (Ferguson and Hogan 2004: 12).
- Be aware of and utilize where appropriate any policies or legislation that allow for orders to keep violent men away (for example, in British Columbia, Section 28 of the *Child Family and Community Services Act*).

### Fourth Principle — Understand the context

One of the fundamental tenets of anti-oppressive practice is to recognize the context of multiple oppressions that construct our social world. As Baines (2007: 20) explains,

> social relations shape, perpetuate and promote social ideas, values and processes that are oppressively organized around notions of superiority, inferiority and various positions between these two polar opposites. These

multiple oppressions, including gender, disability, sexual orientation and race, shape our everyday experience.

Awareness of the structural inequalities, histories and identities that shape our lives and those with whom we work is critical to such a social-justice practice approach.

### Fourth Practice Strategy — Be knowledgeable about structural contexts and how location affects father involvement

Fathers have multiple identities, informed by their gender, sexual orientation, race, class, culture, ability and so on. A father then relates to his family and to his role as father from these locations. Fathers involved with child welfare are embedded in a particular structural system of power, policies and practices. Child welfare workers need to be aware of these contexts and how they impact both fathers and workers. In our study, one Indigenous father told the story of how his parents had gone to residential school, but growing up he had denied his history and culture. *"I was ashamed of what I was. I didn't want to be, I didn't want to be an Aboriginal."* He went on to describe how his children were seen to "belong" to the child welfare system. The colonial and historical context of his fathering, and of the relationship between him and the child welfare worker, must be understood for effective practice to occur. Without such knowledge, workers become complicit in maintaining oppressive structures.

Being knowledgeable about the structural contexts of fathers requires workers to be lifelong and active learners. Knowledge can certainly come from the fathers and their families directly, but it is the responsibility of practitioners to seek out knowledge about history, politics, power and oppression on their own. It is also important for workers to consider how they might "buy in" to dominant Canadian discourses about fathering and mothering based on their own experiences and the culture in which they live. For example, does the conception of dad "helping out" mom with childcare responsibilities that has predominated North American thinking since Dr. Spock's influence in the 1950s result in mothers being viewed as primarily responsible for protecting their children or is this truly seen as a co-parenting task with the father (Carter and McGoldrick 1999)?

While the list of things to include as part of this practice strategy is endless, here are a few beginning suggestions.

- Understand the history of colonization, its past and present impact on Indigenous peoples and their responses to it. (For example, understand the implications of the *Indian Act* for identifying fathers.)
- Be informed about the history of child welfare and its focus on mother-blame and father-absence, and the impact of this on your practice. (For example, are you expecting mothers to manage fathers' behaviours or to manage your communication with fathers?)
- Be aware of contiguous policies (e.g., financial assistance) that may impact fathers and their families.

- Respect the need for some fathers to "fly under the radar." That is, recognize the policy context of child welfare that induces some fathers to remain invisible to the system for the good of their children and families.

## Involving Fathers, Not Oppressing Mothers

Child welfare practice has focused, almost exclusively, on mothers. The mother-blame and father-absence practices of child welfare workers are not in the best interests of children. Child welfare workers need to engage fathers. Any promotion of father involvement however must be accompanied by consideration of context, including violence and resources, as in and of itself it does not lead to better outcomes for children. There is nothing in law or policy preventing workers from taking a more father-inclusive approach to practice, though lack of attention to fathers in social work education, coupled with gendered occupational discourses and practices, makes such a practice shift challenging. But excluding fathers and focusing primarily on mothers, whether fathers are risks or assets, fails to adequately protect and resource children. Workers can redress this through seeking out and engaging with fathers and father figures, including perpetrators, both as risks and as potential assets.

## Suggestions for Further Reading

Ball, J., and R. George. 2006. "Policies and Practices Affecting Aboriginal Fathers' Involvement with Their Children." In J. White, S. Wingert, P. Maxim and D. Beavon (eds.), *Aboriginal Policy Research: Moving Forward, Making a Difference*, Volume 3. Toronto: Thompson Educational.

Daniel, B., and J. Taylor. 2001. *Engaging with Fathers: Practice Issues for Health and Social Care*. London: Jessica Kingsley.

Ferguson, H., and F. Hogan. 2004. *Strengthening Families through Fathers: Developing Policy and Practice in Relation to Vulnerable Fathers and Their Families*. Dublin: Department of Social and Family Affairs. Available at: <http://www.welfare.ie/publications/fathers_fams/contents.html> accessed May 19, 2008.

Peled, E. 2000. "Parenting by Men Who Abuse Women: Issues and Dilemmas." *British Journal of Social Work* 30, 1.

Strega, S. 2006. "Failure to Protect? Child Welfare Interventions When Men Beat Mothers." In R. Alaggia and C. Vine (eds.), *Cruel but Not Unusual: Violence in Canadian Families*. Waterloo, ON: Wilfrid Laurier University Press.

Todd, N., A. Wade and M. Renoux. 2004. "Coming to Terms with Violence and Resistance: From a Language of Effects to a Language of Responses." In T. Strong and D. Pare (eds.), *Furthering Talk: Advances in Discursive Therapies*. New York: Springer.

## About the Authors

Leslie Brown is Associate Dean of Research in the Faculty of Human and Social Development, University of Victoria. Her scholarly interests are critical and Indigenous approaches to research and social work practice. She is co-editor of *Research as Resistance: Critical, Indigenous and Anti-oppressive Approaches*.

Susan Strega is an assistant professor in the School of Social Work at the University of

Victoria. She has published in the areas of social policy, child welfare and sex work. She is co-editor of *Research as Resistance: Critical, Indigenous and Anti-oppressive Approaches*.

Lena Dominelli is a professor of Applied Social Sciences and Academician in the Academy of Learned Societies for Social Sciences, Durham University, U.K. Amongst her most recent books are *Social Work Futures: Transforming Theory and Practice in Social Work* (edited with R. Adams and M. Payne) and *Women and Community Action*.

Christopher Walmsley is an associate professor in the School of Social Work and Human Service, Thompson Rivers University, Kamloops, British Columbia. He is the author of *Protecting Aboriginal Children* and is co-editor of *Child and Family Welfare in British Columbia: A History*.

Marilyn Callahan is professor emeritus at the School of Social Work, University of Victoria, Canada. She has written extensively in the field of child welfare, her most recent works focusing on young mothers using substances, the experiences of grandmothers raising grandchildren, fathering in child welfare and risk assessment.

## Notes

1.   The exception to this is Quebec, where the file is in the child's name.
2.   In the United States, where the notion of "failure to protect" has been most vigorously deployed, researchers did not find a single instance in which a man had ever been prosecuted for his failure to protect his children from an abusive mother (Davidson 1995, cited in Kopels and Sheridan 2002; Fugate 2001).
3.   For example, in the early part of the century a children's home in B.C. reported that 41 percent of all single father families boarded their children at the home as a result of asserting their desire to have their families granted this aid while they still retained rights of guardianship. This occurred for less than 15 percent of all other families.

## References

Adamoski, R. 2002. "The Child — The Citizen — The Nation: The Rhetoric and Experience of Wardship in Early Twentieth Century British Columbia." In R. Adamoski, D. Chunn and R. Menzies (eds.), *Contesting Canadian Citizenship Historical Readings*. Toronto: Broadview.

Baines, D. 2007. "Anti-Oppressive Social Work Practice: Fighting for Space, Fighting for Change." In D. Baines (ed.), *Doing Anti-Oppressive Practice: Building Transformative Politicized Social Work*. Black Point, NS: Fernwood.

Ball, J., and R. George. 2006. "Policies and Practices Affecting Aboriginal Fathers' Involvement with Their Children." In J. White, S. Wingert, P. Maxim and D. Beavon (eds.), *Aboriginal Policy Research: Moving Forward, Making a Difference*, Volume 3. Toronto: Thompson Educational.

Blackstock, C., S. Clarke, J. Cullen, J. D'Hondt and J. Formsma. 2004. *Keeping the Promise: The Convention on the Rights of the Child and the Lived Experience of First Nations Children and Youth*. Ottawa: First Nations Child and Family Caring Society of Canada.

Brown, L., M. Callahan, S. Strega, L. Dominelli and C. Walmsley. 2008. "Manufacturing Ghost Fathers: The Paradox of Father Presence and Absence in Child Welfare." *Child and Family Social Work 14*.

Cabrera, N., C. Tamis-LeMonda, R. Bradley, S. Hofferth and M. Lamb. 2000. "Fatherhood in the 21st Century." *Child Development* 71, 1.

Callahan, M., L. Brown, P. MacKenzie and B. Whittington. 2004. "Catch as Catch Can: Grandmothers Raising Their Grandchildren and Kinship Care Policies." *Canadian Review of Social Policy* 54.

Callahan, M., D. Rutman, S. Strega and L. Dominelli. 2005. "Looking Promising: Contradictions and Challenges for Young Mothers in Care." In D. Gustafson (ed.), *Unbecoming Mothers: Women Living Apart from their Children*. Binghamton, NY: Haworth.

Carter, E., and M. McGoldrick. 1999. *The Expanded Family Life Cycle: Individual, Family, and Social Perspectives* (Third Edition). Boston: Allyn and Bacon.

Daniel, B., and J. Taylor. 1999. "The Rhetoric vs. The Reality: A Critical Perspective on Practice with Fathers in Child Care and Protection Work." *Child and Family Social Work* 4.

_____. 2001. *Engaging with Fathers: Practice Issues for Health and Social Care*. London: Jessica Kingsley.

Dubeau, D. 2003. "Portraits of Fathers." Occasional paper, Vanier Institute of the Family. Ottawa.

Eichler, M., and M. McCall. 1993. "Clarifying the Legal Dimensions of Fatherhood." *Canadian Journal of Family Law* 11, 2.

Featherstone, B. 2008. "Engaging Fathers in Child Welfare Services: Interrogating the Politics." Conference presentation, Gender and Child Welfare Network, Montreal, April 10/11.

Featherstone, B., and S. Peckover. 2007. "Letting Them Get Away with It: Fathers, Domestic Violence and Child Welfare." *Critical Social Policy* 27, 2.

Ferguson, H., and F. Hogan. 2004. "Strengthening Families through Fathers: Developing Policy and Practice in Relation to Vulnerable Fathers and Their Families." Dublin: Department of Social and Family Affairs. Available at <http://www.welfare.ie/publications/fathers_fams/contents.html> accessed May 19, 2008.

Fleming, L., and D. Tobin. 2005. "Popular Child-Rearing Books: Where Is Daddy?" *Psychology of Men and Masculinity* 6, 1.

Fugate, J. 2001. "Who's Failing Whom? A Critical Look at Failure-To-Protect Laws." *New York University Law Review* 76.

Goodmark, L. 2004. "Achieving Batterer Accountability in the Child Protection System." *Kentucky Law Journal* 93, 3.

Haney, L., and M. March. 2003. "Married Fathers and Caring Daddies: Welfare Reform and the Discursive Politics of Paternity." *Social Problems* 50, 4.

Hartley, C. 2004. "Severe Domestic Violence and Child Maltreatment: Considering Child Physical Abuse, Neglect, and Failure to Protect." *Children and Youth Services Review* 26.

Kopels, S., and M. Sheridan. 2002. "Adding Legal Insult to Injury: Battered Women, Their Children, and the Failure to Protect." *Affilia* 17, 1.

Lavergne, C., C. Chamberland, L. Laporte and R. Baraldi. 2003. "Domestic Violence: Protecting Children by Involving Fathers and Helping Mothers." CECW Information Sheet #6E. Montreal, QC: Institut de Recherche pour le Développement Social des Jeunes and Université de Montréal. Available at <http://www.cecw-cepb.ca/DocsEng/DomesticViolence6E.pdf> accessed May 19, 2008.

Mann, M. 2005. *Indian Registration: Unrecognized and Unstated Paternity*. Ottawa: Status of Women.

Mann, R. 2003. "Violence Against Women or Family Violence?" In L. Samuelson and W. Antony (eds.), *Power and Resistance: Critical Thinking About Canadian Social Issues* (Third Edition). Halifax: Fernwood.

Marks, L., and R. Palkovitz. 2004. "American Fatherhood Types: The Good, The Bad, and The Uninterested." *Fathering* 2.

McMahon, M., and E. Pence. 1995. "Doing More Harm Than Good? Some Cautions on Visitation Centres." In E. Peled, P. Jaffe and J. Edleson (eds.), *Ending the Cycle of Violence: Community Responses to Children of Battered Women*. Thousand Oaks, CA: Sage.

Munro, E. 1998. "Improving Social Workers' Knowledge Base in Child Protection Work." *British Journal of Social Work* 28.

O'Hagan, K. 1997. "The Problem of Engaging Men in Child Protection Work." *British Journal of Social Work* 27.

O'Hagan, K., and K. Dillenburger. 1995. *The Abuse of Women within Childcare Work*. Buckingham: Open University Press.

Parada, H. 2002. "The Restructuring of the Child Welfare System in Ontario: A Study in the Social Organization of Knowledge." Unpublished PhD dissertation, OISE, University of Toronto.

Peled, E. 2000. "Parenting by Men Who Abuse Women: Issues and Dilemmas." *British Journal of Social Work* 30, 1.

Province of British Columbia. 1996. *The Risk Assessment Model for Child Protection in British Columbia*. Victoria: Ministry for Children and Families.

Rutman, D., S. Strega, M. Callahan and L. Dominelli. 2002. "'Undeserving' Mothers? Practitioners' Experiences Working with Young Mothers in/from Care." *Child and Family Social Work* 7, 3.

Ryan, M. 2000. *Working with Fathers*. Abingdon, U.K.: Radcliffe Medical Press.

Scourfield, J. 2001. "Constructing Men in Child Protection Work." *Men and Masculinities* 4, 1.

_____. 2003. *Gender and Child Protection*. Houndmills, Basingstoke: Palgrave MacMillan.

_____. 2006. "The Challenge of Engaging Fathers in the Child Protection Process." *Critical Social Policy* 26, 2.

Smart, C., and B. Neale. 1999. *Family Fragments?* Cambridge: Polity.

Stanley, N. 1997. "Domestic Violence and Child Abuse: Developing Social Work Practice." *Child and Family Social Work* 2, 3.

Strega, S. 2004. "The Case of The Invisible Perpetrator: A Cross-National Investigation into Child Protection Policy and Practice in Cases Where Men Beat Mothers." Unpublished PhD dissertation, School of Social Sciences, University of Southampton, U.K.

_____. 2006. "Failure to Protect? Child Welfare Interventions When Men Beat Mothers." In R. Alaggia and C. Vine (eds.), *Cruel but Not Unusual: Violence in Canadian Families*. Waterloo, ON: Wilfrid Laurier University Press.

Strega, S., C. Fleet, L. Brown, M. Callahan, L. Dominelli and C. Walmsley. 2008. "Connecting Father Absence and Mother Blame in Child Welfare Policies and Practice" *Children and Youth Services Review* 30,7.

Sunderland, J. 2006. "'Parenting' or 'Mothering'? The Case of Modern Childcare Magazines." *Discourse and Society* 17, 4.

Swift, K. 1995. *Manufacturing "Bad Mothers:" A Critical Perspective on Child Neglect*. Toronto: University of Toronto Press.

Todd, N., A. Wade and M. Renoux. 2004. "Coming to Terms with Violence and Resistance: From a Language of Effects to a Language of Responses." In T. Strong and D. Pare (eds.), *Furthering Talk: Advances in Discursive Therapies.* New York: Springer.

Trotter, J. 1997. "The Failure of Social Work Researchers, Teachers and Practitioners to Acknowledge or Engage Non-Abusing Fathers: A Preliminary Discussion." *Social Work Education* 16.

Tsui, M., and F. Cheung. 2004. "Gone with the Wind: The Impacts of Managerialism on Human Services." *British Journal of Social Work* 34, 3.

Walmsley, C., L. Brown, M. Callahan, S. Strega and L. Dominelli. 2006. "Where's Waldo? Fathering in the BSW Curriculum." Paper presented at the Canadian Association of Schools of Social Work Conference, Toronto, ON., May.

# Chapter 15

# Considerations for Cultural Planning and Indigenous Adoptions

*Sohki Aski Esquao [Jeannine Carrière] and Raven Sinclair*

This chapter provides an overview of Indigenous adoption in Canada and situates the voices of Indigenous adoptees, scholars and practitioners at the centre of this discussion. Based on two recent studies (Carrière 2005; Sinclair 2007) this chapter sets the context of Indigenous transracial adoption in Canada. The intent of this chapter is to honour the voices of those who have lived adoption experiences and those who have personal testimonies to assist in the deconstruction, reconstruction and critiquing of issues that relate to Indigenous adoption practices in Canada. We contend that respecting Indigenous adoptee rights to information, support and connection to their birth family and community is in line with anti-oppressive child welfare practice methods because such an approach respects and preserves Indigenous culture and identity.

Questions Addressed in This Chapter
1. How can articulating the experiences of Indigenous adoptees with respect to their adoption and post-adoption experiences inform anti-oppressive social work practice?
2. What are the critical components of cultural planning for Indigenous adoptees and what do adoptees recommend for policy and practice related to the adoption of Indigenous children?

## Indigenous Adoption in Canada

The adoption of Indigenous children in Canada between the years of 1960 and the mid-1980s was first coined the "sixties scoop" in a report written by Patrick Johnston (1983), published as *Aboriginal Children and the Child Welfare System* by the federal department of Social Policy Development. The term was applied because, first, Johnston observed in the statistics that adoption as a mechanism to address problematic child welfare issues had resulted in obvious increases in Indigenous child apprehensions in the decade of the 1960s (National Archives of Canada Vol. 6937). Second, in many instances, Indigenous children were apprehended from their homes and communities without the knowledge or consent of families and bands (Johnston 1983; Timpson 1995; RCAP 1996; Saskatchewan Indian 1977). Johnston was provided with the term "scoop" by a B.C. social worker who told him, "with tears in her eyes — that it was common practice in B.C. in the mid-sixties to "scoop" from their mothers on reserves almost all newly born children. She was crying because she realized, 20 years later, what a mistake that had been" (P. Johnston, personal email communication, December 8, 2005, cited in Sinclair 2007).

Across Canada, Indian Affairs (INAC) statistics (the A-list or Adoption List) tell us that over 11,000 First Nations children were apprehended and subsequently adopted, primarily into non-native homes in Canada, the United States, and around the world between the years of 1960 and 1990. This number does not include children who weren't status Indian according to the *Indian Act* or who but were not recorded as such in the interests of promoting their "adoptability" by non-Native families (Sinclair 2007). Indigenous spokespeople place the figure anywhere between 20,000 and 50,000, but until research can uncover more accuracy, the true numbers are unknown.

Why were Indigenous children the targets of a program of transracial adoption? To understand, we must place the program in the context of Canada's historical policy of assimilation of Indigenous peoples. The *Indian Act* obligates governments with fiduciary duty towards First Nation peoples, which, history tells us, has resulted in paternalistic and oppressive measures designed to control First Nation people and lands (Royal Commission Report 1996). Two methods of assimilation, enfranchisement (removal from the Indian Register) and residential schools, proved unsuccessful. Duncan Campbell Scott, Superintendent of Indian Affairs, speaking about the issue of enfranchisement, stated in 1920:

> Our objective is to continue until there is not a single Indian in Canada that has not been absorbed into the body politic, and there is no Indian question, and no Indian department. This is the whole object of this bill. (cited in Jamieson 1978: 120)

Walmsley (2005: 9) describes residential schools as "the cornerstone of the government's assimilation strategy." With the incorporation of "child care and education, this policy aimed to civilize, Christianize and socialize Aboriginal children to work in the wage economy," with an aim "to erase their identities and replace them with the norms of non Aboriginal societies" (RCAP 1996: 1: 333, cited in Walmsley 2005: 9). Rather than assimilation in any significant form, the residential school project led to severe interpersonal, familial and community social problems that interfered with the wellbeing of Indigenous peoples.

For new social workers in the 1960s, who were primarily white, middle class and privileged, exposure to the foreign context of reserve life and encountering the social fall-out of the residential school period resulted in a disastrous mingling of good intentions to rescue Indigenous people from themselves and governmental assimilation-influenced mandates. Removing Indigenous children and placing them into non-Indigenous contexts was likely perceived as an ideal solution to complicated social problems. Unfortunately, the reality was much less stellar. As one B.C. worker noted:

When we discovered a child at risk in his own home, we had no resources to move him into a foster home. Over and over again we played Russian roulette with the lives of the young. In the end, when we removed children from their own homes and put them in foster homes about which we knew next to nothing, no matter how we cloaked our actions in welfare jargon, we were putting those children at risk. (Moran 1992: 86, cited in Fournier and Crey 1997)

Over time stories began to surface about the abuse in some foster and adoptive homes and Indigenous people began to resist removal of their children. Chief Wayne Christian of Splats'in was instrumental in putting a nation-wide stop to the transracial adoption of Native children by implementing a by-law that governs child welfare in their community (Walmsley 2005: 25). Justice Kimmelman (1985) noted that the scooping and subsequent transracial adoption of Indigenous children amounted to genocide, defined as the deliberate destruction of an ethnic group through the forced removal of their children.

After 1985, the transracial adoption of Indigenous children in Canada slowed significantly, with adoption in some provinces only occurring with the full consent of the birth parents and their respective band authorities. In terms of adoption outcomes from the sixties scoop, however, until recently we had to rely on anecdotal evidence in the scant literature available. In the last few years, there has been a resurgence of interest in the topic, and in North America several theses, dissertations and articles have shed light on the experiences of Indigenous adults who were adopted into non-Indigenous homes during the period (Arsenault 2006; Carrière 2005; Kulusic 2005; Nuttgens 2004; Sindelar 2004; Swidrovich 2004). It is indicated that transracial adoptions (TRA) generally (e.g., black/white, Korean/white) are as successful as same-race adoptions, while Indigenous TRA breakdown rates were between 70 and 95 percent by the time the children reached their teenage years (Adams 2002; Fournier and Crey 1997). The key themes to emerge from the collected literature include issues of loss, identity and racism. Adoption stories are fraught with trauma in many instances, and yet in the long term we see glimpses of positive outcomes.

## Loss, Identity and Cultural Connections

The studies upon which this chapter is premised found that the concept of loss was intricately tied to notions of identity, cultural identity and cultural connections. In Carrière (2005) and Sinclair (2007) every adoptee, with perhaps one exception, spoke of loss as a defining concept in their adoptive experiences. For many, these were losses of birth and cultural connections and a loss of individual or cultural identity. Loss was expressed to some degree by each of the adoptees[1] and often manifested in their poor health and wellbeing. One participant described it this way:

*They just took us, shipped us off, put us somewhere else and forgot about us; that's it.*

*I think they should be accountable for that, because — I know there were good adoptions, and a lot of kids probably had good lives, but I would say the majority of the adoptions were, and foster home placements were, not so good. I hear so many stories of things that happened. I hear very few success stories. You know what I mean? I always hear adoptees saying how lost they felt and how disconnected and "Who am I? Who are my people?" Lots of emotional instabilities, like, I put down right here, there's a lot of unrest and I think — I don't know what the government was thinking, what their reason was that they felt they had the right to do this. (Eagle)*

Many adoptees were keenly aware of their sense of isolation and loss:

*I guess I had friends but I was a bit of a loner. I mean I had friends at school but nobody would ah come to my house and I wouldn't go visit people cause we also lived out in the country. So right there I am a little isolated. So when I got to high school, socially I didn't really do much. I was also taking music lessons and I immersed myself in piano so, right there I'm kind of one of those classical weirdos, you know. (Ivy)*

For some, the grief of their losses carried into adulthood:

*It's also the loss of even being able to connect and have close relationships with brothers and sisters from my adopted family. I don't spend Christmas with family, I don't go to family dinners, I don't participate in and I actually don't actually celebrate um any holidays. Valentine, birthdays, Easters, these are all nightmare days for me. Christmas is still a horrible time. I'd far rather be locked in a room and, and send my kids to their father's where they can go and have a Christmas where they can enjoy it. 'Cause I just don't see it, I don't feel it, I don't, I don't relate to it. So that would probably be the worst. (Sam)*

Most of the adoptees, as could be expected, identified with white culture due to their isolation or lack of knowledge of Indigenous culture.

*We certainly didn't consider ourselves Indian kids and I certainly didn't consider myself an Indian kid until probably mid-way through my elementary school life.... I always say that, during the time that I was white, and that was right through my high school years... I mean, bi-culturally I thought, I really thought that I was a white person. (Lacey)*

Over time, as the adoptees were exposed to school and social discrimination and racism, identity became a negative factor and was a painful topic for some to discuss.

*Yep, I don't know... because I didn't know what being Native was... I just knew that I was different and that was bad. (Sally)*

*Well you get the whole Pocahontas and you know the, you know the hand over the mouth kind of thing always. Ah you know you get well meaning adults telling you — well be proud of being Native. I've often wondered you know how do you develop this, this horrible self-image and, and negative stereotype like where does that come from? I don't know. (Ivy)*

Being identified by others as an Indigenous person was difficult for some.

*I really kind of felt ashamed of, of who I was as a person and who I, you know, who like for some particular reason who I was… I was ashamed of some, somebody I didn't even know. (Paul)*

In fact, there was anxiety and fear around being associated as an Indigenous person.

*But I always knew that there was something, there was something somewhere along the way that someone was gonna finally expose me for who I was, and that I would be then lumped in with those two kids who came that were from you know, who were the Indians. (Lacey)*

Many began to recognize that there was a relationship between their ancestry and their social problems.

*I had no idea. Like, to put it bluntly, I had no idea until I got to Ottawa, how Indian I was, and how in the last few years I've had to understand why I was treated the way I was treated all my life. (Randi)*

The process of reconciling Indigenous identity for many adoptees is one that involves a journey of reflection on their adoption experiences, learning about birth cultures, and reconciling the two.

*So I'm not saying that I'm second-guessing my life course or anything but I kind of wonder where this, like how can I balance these two out? Or is there, is there a balance in-between those? Or do I have to make a choice, right? Is it like a conscious choice of basically saying well, identify more with my Native heritage and that's where I decided to go, or do I have to base it or is it more internal and have to balance these two things out? (Paul)*

*Figuring out where, where I came from and ah that changed my perspective on every-thing once I found my parents. I didn't, I found my cousins and uncles and that first you know and ah that changed again you know. So I, I think you go through stages. At least for me I went through stages you know in terms of, of your identity and who you are and, and what role you have to play in life you know. (Mark)*

Many adoptees recognized that learning about themselves as Indigenous people would involve reconnecting with their birth and cultural communities.

*So now I have to go back, I guess like a little kid, go back to my own community and start to re-learn some of those cultural things, those ceremonial things that I think are now the next leg of my journey, is to try to re-connect some of those things for myself and I started to do that, but it's a slow process. (Lacey)*

## Tribal Identities and Adoption Standards

It is important to understand the importance of tribal identity in order to recognize the impact of separation or disconnection from tribal knowledge and cultural connection for Indigenous children. Cajete (2000: 86) explains that relationship is the cornerstone of tribal community, and the nature and expression of community is the foundation of tribal identity. Furthermore he states that, "through community, Indian people come to understand their 'personhood' and their connection to the communal soul of their people."

Kim Anderson illustrates her search for her identity as an Indigenous woman and describes how she struggled while taking university classes and examining Indigenous issues from the voice and writings of others. She proposes a theory of identity formation for Indigenous people that includes the following four steps: (1) resisting definitions of being or rejecting negative stereotypes; (2) reclaiming Indigenous tradition; (3) constructing a positive identity by translating tradition into the contemporary context; and (4) acting (e.g., using one's voice) on a new positive identity (Anderson 2000: 229)

Identity in the Indigenous context, thus, encapsulates community. Kral (2003), for example, discussed identity in terms of meanings of wellbeing in Inuit communities. He notes that Indigenous people have a self-identity that is collective in orientation and that "collective selves see group membership as central to their identity whereas individualistic selves are more autonomous from any particular group and may value individualism quite highly" (Kral 2003: 8).

## Racism

The Canadian ethos has been that Canada is not a racist country, and Canada is sometimes held up on the world stage as a country that protects human rights. People who live on the other side of the colour line in Canada have a different perspective (Frideres and Gadacz 2001). Adoptive parents who believe that racism does not exist may be unable or unwilling to prepare a child to deal with these issues. The child who experiences racism and discrimination in social encounters learns quickly that their experiences do not necessarily match with what they are told or what they have been socialized to anticipate that life will be like. They may believe that they are inherently "different" because they know that their parents and family do not have the same experiences (Kim 1978). Marilyn and Royal Rue astutely recognize the challenge of racism for the adoptee:

Racism, even its non-violent forms, is still pernicious. The difficult thing about racism in our particular situation is that when it is directed at [our adopted son] Carl, he must deal with it alone. He does not have the comfort of knowing that the rest of the family shares in his experience. If we were an entire family of minorities, his situation would be much different in this respect. And since neither of us has ever been the victim of racial prejudice, we are ill-prepared to help him develop the skills useful in combating it. (1984: 249)

An adopted child who experiences racism and discrimination may not share that with their family because it is not part of their family ethos. Many Indigenous adoptees were raised in an environment of privilege, power and status (Sinclair 2007; Nuttgens 2004; Swidrovich 2004). Their economic status was often higher than that of the average Canadian, and yet they were inevitably forced to confront a socially ascribed inferior status associated with their ethnic group (Kim 1978).

Sinclair's (2007) study clearly links the negative outcomes of Indigenous TRA to racism in Canadian society. Her findings indicate that Indigenous adoptees raised to be white and often with privilege are treated as Indigenous people in a racialized social context when they interface more with society as teenagers and young adults. In the adoption milieu, the prevailing myth has been that children, once adopted, become subsumed into their family as if born to them (Thompson 1999). This myth results in a "colour-blind" approach to minority children, which, although well-intentioned, can have disastrous consequences in terms of preparing children to deal with the realities of racism. Adoptees recounted stories of racism, and because racism wasn't part of the family or social ethos, most internalized the pain and, subsequently, engaged in destructive behaviours. They all spoke of racism, and, frighteningly, many adoptees experienced the cruelest aspects of racism within their family systems — directed at them from parents, siblings and extended family members.

For some, this was a shocking reality. Indigenous adoptees' ethnic and cultural identities are wrapped up in cultural stigmatization related to poverty, alcoholism and other negative stereotypes. In a few instances, racism was used as a deterrent and a means to instill fear.

*My adopted father he would, always kind of go out of his way to basically draw focus to the penitentiaries. And because I was struggling with like identity and struggling with my behavioural problems and stuff like that he would always say you know that's where I'm going to end up. That's where Indian's end up when they're bad. (Mark)*

In other instances, it seemed that the adoptive parents used racism to try to protect adoptees from themselves as Indigenous people.

*They felt that as an Indian if they gave me any chances that I would just take advantage of it being a lazy Indian. So they never did help me but they helped all the other kids. They gave them money for university, they gave them, they would go to their house when they had babies move in and help out. But nobody came to help me. So I think my mom realized at that point that they had given everything to the other two, their other children, thinking that if they help me that they were just going to create a stereotype. (Sam)*

In several instances, the adoptees noted that their families had racist attitudes towards Indigenous people but did not direct it at them specifically, almost as if they did not recognize the Indigeneity of their child.

*And ah we'd go and see all the hookers and the bums and the all the street people down there, drive by them and cruise downtown for an hour or so. At the time I didn't realize you know probably what he was trying to do you know, um I guess he was like, oh look at the Native people, look. We drove by the Silver Dollar, well you know what I mean all the hangouts that all the ah places where Aboriginal people would hang out, the street people. (Mark)*

Although these parents may have had positive intentions, the adoptees experienced terrible conflict because they had to reconcile their families' acceptance of racism and racial stereotypes with themselves as Indigenous people. Racism tended to prolong the challenges related to identity re-acculturation and reconnecting with families and communities.

## Resemblance and Belonging

For many adoptees reunion and reconnecting with birth families and cultures was an exciting and euphoric time. For some, discovering people who looked like them, for the first time in their lives, was an overwhelming experience.

*It was finally a relief because I knew that I actually looked like somebody. Because maybe as a kid and teenager and as an adult, I always went, "I don't look like anybody." I mean, people would say, "You sort of look like your adopted mother and brother but upon closer examination you see we don't… (pause)… I don't look like them. Now, I know there are people out there who I look like. (Billy)*

Reconnection with original family members provided a number of adoptees with a sense of belonging that they described as missing from their childhood. Of course, not all reunions were positive, and many, after an initial honeymoon period, deteriorated. Some adoptees have had practically no connection with birth families since their initial reunion.

## Reunion Conflicts

Reunions are not always a positive experience for adoptees, and there are no guidelines to prepare Indigenous adoptees for the myriad dynamics related to reunion. Some described their birth families as dysfunctional or unhealthy, but the urge to maintain ties remains a traumatic bond that is difficult to break. This experience caused deep emotional pain for each adoptee who witnessed this other face of reunion.

*I met my mom. I got to know people in the family and a lot of them don't talk to each other. There's always that fighting going on, which I don't understand, because I can't imagine not ever talking to my kids or my brother for any length of time. Sure, we get mad at each other, but this family, they get, you say something the wrong way, and they won't talk to you. And, my mom has pulled that off on me since I met her. I express myself, I confront, and I share my feelings, and she's the type that thinks that's wrong and then I won't talk to her for two years. (Paris)*

In some instances, reunions involved violence and long-term psychological harm.

*We, we tried to basically salvage some things, like we went up, like long hikes into the mountains, stuff like that, but it wasn't the same like… Like we didn't want to go downtown Eastside. We didn't want to see our mom anymore right? So we get back to Ottawa… and then um I get to back to Ottawa and I just go back to my regular routine. Like people… were like excited to hear my story right? And I couldn't say it, I didn't, I mean I told them it was good and I downplayed it you know. And I couldn't, I couldn't speak about it because it hurt, like I thought my, my entire dream has gone like. It's boom just like that, like and it turned into a nightmare. (Paul)*

Many reunions are unfolding and will continue to evolve over the years. Some adoptees recognize that their adoption experiences profoundly affected their lives and will continue to play a role for the remainder of their lives.

## Positive Outcomes

In spite of the turmoil and trauma intrinsic to the experiences of sixties scoop adoptees, many of them have developed exceedingly strong and well-articulated identities, and many other adoptees are content with their adoptive experiences (Nuttgens 2004; Swidrovich 2004)

Interestingly, many adoptees are, in their adult lives, employed in professional capacities, well educated, lead stable lives and are exceptionally attentive parents to their children. Some report difficulties in dealing with emotional upheavals as adults, and many identify relationship difficulties as a consequence of their adoptive experiences. However, many adoptees also acknowledge having acquired advantages as the result of being adopted. Some of the advantages include being able to traverse both Indigenous and white worlds with ease, a sense of personal efficacy in terms of education and career and economic success. These positive outcomes beckon further inquiry in order to find more balance in the Indigenous adoption discourse.

Indeed, there is no single group identity label or theory that can be applied to all adoptees. Although some personality and identity characteristics are shared as the result of similar experiences, each individual's sense of identity is unique and derived from their own combination of experiences and perspectives (Carrière 2005; Sinclair 2007; Nuttgens 2004). The resilience of the human spirit is evident because, despite the losses and traumas experienced, most adoptees found and created their own cultural and identity niche.

## Practice Recommendations

Adoptees, when given a forum in which to speak, were articulate and comprehensive in their recommendations for changes to Indigenous adoption policy and practice. The recommendations they asserted come from their own words:

- Resources should be directed to family preservation.

  *I want to see more to keep our families together and that there's support offered you know for mothers, fathers, extended family, adoptees, siblings and everybody. Not um, you know not the way um the solutions have been right now, as in to take children away and separate them. You know I'd rather see ah things leaning towards keeping families and communities together. (Abby)*

- Eliminate Indigenous transracial adoption or place children within extended family.

  *Maybe that, maybe let them um instead of taking them out completely maybe just put them into um you know Uncle's and Aunt's you know. (Mark)*

- Educate potential adoptive parents.

  *We need to educate um the adoptive parents. You know because I think maybe they're misinformed you know um and they don't know the consequences of the possible consequences that they could have on, on bringing up an Aboriginal child. Or somebody that is not of their... culture I guess you know. I know my wife's sister has just adopted well she's taking care of, they're foster kids and, and they're, well they're black kids. And I can see that they're you know, that she doesn't know a lot about that culture you know and, and I know that I can see the beginning of, of some problems that might happen you know. I can see it in the kids now that they're not relating well with their parents you know. (Mark)*

- Educate child welfare workers about adoptive parent selection.

  *I think there needs to be some sort of ah I don't know... education process when, when they do adoptions because there needs to be stricter guidelines (for adoptive home approvals) that in terms of who gets to adopt kids. You know a lot stricter policies. (Mark)*

- Recognize that adoption is a privilege.

  *I would like it to be understood that those who adopt those children that it's a privilege that they have, not a right, to raise that child. (Sam)*

- Collaborate with First Nations on behalf of children.

*But if our communities are not in a position to offer the stability in a family then I don't have a problem looking outside as long as there is an understanding and a relationship between the Nation and those families with that have those children. (Sam)*

- Adopt siblings together.

*For me we'll… the best um I still, I'm still with my brothers and sisters. Um I, I think that really helped me a lot you know and I think um I don't know how, I don't know how others ah survived you know. Being alone you know and I look around and you all did that you know and I think that's amazing, that you survived all of that, alone, you know? I thought it was tough and I had two other people you know to confide in you know. Um so I think you know maybe, maybe that was the best that I was adopted out with my siblings. (Mark)*

- Promote ongoing ties between adoptive families and Indigenous cultural resources.

*My recommendations would be at least from my perspective um I believe Native adoptees and their parents should have some sort of connection or availability to the information and the heritage of, of the natural heritage of the Native child. I'm not saying that they should its okay to remove them from the Native environment and, and you know just totally separate them but I think there should always be a tie. If not with the birth parents with their natural identity. I think that should be available. If they want it, fine it's there, if they don't, that's fine too. But that was never available to me and I, and I, and I never had any way to, to connect with it, was just there were no Native people around. I didn't know what Native people were about, I knew nothing about the culture so I guess that would be my recommendation. (Max)*

- Promote openness in order to help maintain birth and cultural knowledge.

*I never really knew until I was eighteen where I was from. I thought I was told that I was Cree, and it wasn't until I was talking with my biological dad one day and he said, "You're not Cree. You're Ojibway. You're from [community] and that's all Ojibway land." I had heard for so many years that I was Cree because that's what I had been told by my adoptive parents and that's what they were told. So, it was a shock, it really was. So, all over the place, I had been learning the Lakota tradition thinking I was Cree, but really Ojibway. (Sierra)*

- Support the child to acculturate and maintain cultural ties.

*I would have liked to learn my language and know more about my tradition. That's what I miss; my language and my tradition that I lost it, and it's hard to get back.*

*I'll probably never get it back and my kids lost it, too. (Mama Bear)*

- Provide elder support.

*His wife actually explained a lot of things to me. I'd had two abortions and you know was really suffering from the guilt from that and don't know how she saw it but she saw it in me and my mother, and you know she said your mother didn't have a chance to change and you do, and those children knew that they weren't coming you know you can't blame yourself for it. And you know just offered me the kindness and that's what I look for now is just the kindness. It's not a big deal you know, it's not a big production or doing lots of things it's just being kind, you know, kind energy. (Sally)*

## Cultural Planning in Adoption

The recommendations from adoptees have been synthesized into a cultural planning framework for policy and practice. The cultural plan contains provisions to maintain contact with the child's community and culture and should be signed by both the adoptive parents and representatives of the child's community. Cultural planning needs to include the following practices:

*Information*
1. Information on birth family should be made available to adoptees as soon as they desire it.
2. Health information from birth families should be preserved for adoptees.
3. Post-adoption registries need to be revised to allow access to other birth family members, such as extended family.
4. Pictures should be mandatory for birth families and adoptees.
5. First Nation adoptees need to know which tribe and First Nation they are from.

*Adoption Practices*
1. Adoption of Indigenous children should be in families with similar cultural backgrounds if possible.
2. Connection to extended family and community needs to be maintained in adoption.
3. If Indigenous children are not placed in an Indigenous family, cultural and racism training needs to be provided to adoptive parents, adoption workers and the children involved.
4. Cultural mentors should be provided to Indigenous adoptees to assist in reconnecting to their cultural heritage.
5. Adoptive families need to continue to be monitored by child and family service agencies.

*Support*
1. Adoptees involved in search and reunion require support services to assist them in these processes.

2. Peer support groups for Indigenous adoptees need to be established.
3. Counselling services should be made available to Indigenous adoptees.

## Moving Forward: Anti-Racist Adoption Practice

For the most part, the story of Indigenous adoption remains in the hearts and minds of adoptees themselves. We need these valuable stories, and we have been privileged to have acquired a glimpse into the experiences of the participants in recent research. An anti-oppressive approach to the adoption of Indigenous children, on a structural level, guides us to examine societal issues of marginalization, racism and poverty as priorities that need to be addressed in Indigenous communities (Mullaly 2002). In the adoption context, this implies uncovering oppressive perspectives, structures and practices, and working towards culturally relevant programming and services, with an anti-racist approach as a foundation. Indigenous adoption is a complex subject that presents several challenges that are, however, easily translated into opportunities for more efficacious policies and practices in the future. As an example, a major challenge with adoption and child welfare for Indigenous peoples in Canada is that adjudication is based on the "best interest of the child" standard, which often conflicts with the Indigenous view that a child is a tribal member of an extended family (Carrière 2005).

Similarly, the complexity of identity as it relates to adoption and Indigenous children is enhanced by various political and legal dynamics. Canadian provinces continue to administer adoption programs for Indigenous children with little or no consideration to the inherent rights of an Indigenous person. The oppressive nature of current policies places the issue of adoption and Indigenous children within the context of cross-cultural adoption without recognizing the contradictions in this practice. At the macro level, the issues are not about race, colour or national origin; they are about the preservation of Indigenous self-determination within a continuing colonial context.

As we indicate in this chapter, Indigenous transracial adoption reveals several key themes that highlight areas of concern for adoptees, including loss of individual and tribal cultural identity, social and intrafamilial racism, and issues around repatriation. Paradoxically, we observe some long-term positive outcomes that belie the negative slant in the existing literature on Indigenous TRA. Many adoptees do recount difficult and traumatic adoption experiences, and turmoil seems to most often manifest in adolescence and young adulthood. Yet, we are beginning to hear stories from the other end of the spectrum. Although their journeys may be difficult, adoptees who choose to reconnect to their birth culture and tribal identity find a needed sense of belonging and validation. Perhaps even more importantly, the repatriation process, which usually includes learning about the adoption within the context of Canadian colonial history, has been a form of Freirian (Freire 1996) conscientization for adoptees. Many are subsequently able to frame those experiences in the socio-political context of Canada's assimilative approaches to Indigenous people, rather than carrying the burden of belief that there was something wrong with them as children that resulted in their experiences. For some adoptees, contextualizing their experiences this way has been a tremendous act of healing.

In the final analysis, we do not contend that Indigenous transracial adoption should not take place. It would be naïve to place the blame for the currently extensive child welfare involvement in the lives of Indigenous peoples solely on government and child welfare authorities. In the context of historical colonial policies such as residential schools, the extensive intrusion of child welfare authorities into Indigenous lives is more clearly understood. Indigenous communities now recognize that the responsibility for child welfare outcomes from this point forward rests with Indigenous communities, who have fought long and hard to have control of child welfare. In an ideal world, all Indigenous children would remain with their families of origin. Until that happens, Indigenous communities, child welfare agencies and families will continue to make decisions to place children for adoption transracially because other options are not readily available.

We are currently in the fortunate position of having the experiences of adoptees to inform our work as we move towards anti-oppressive adoption policies and practices for Indigenous children. By critically analyzing the past and listening carefully to the voices of adoptees we can be adaptive and creative. With core changes in Indigenous transracial adoption ideology, policies and practices through the lens of anti-oppressive social work at structural levels, where policy will take into consideration Indigenous cultural rights, and at personal levels, where everyone involved in the adoption process considers addressing issues of identity and racism as a matter of course, we believe that the adoption milieu can be effectively adapted to meet the needs of Indigenous families, adoptive families and, most importantly, Indigenous children.

All Our Relations!

## Suggestions for Further Reading

Carrière, J. 2008. "Maintaining Identities: The Soul Work of Adoption and Aboriginal Children." *Pimatisiwin: A Journal of Indigenous and Aboriginal Community Health* 6, 1.

_____. 2007. "Maintaining Identities in First Nation Adoption." *First Peoples Child and Family Review* January 3. 1.

Sinclair, R. 2007. "Identity Lost and Found: Lessons from the 60s' Scoop." *First Peoples' Child and Family Review* 3, 1.

Sinclair, R., G. Bruyere and M. Hart (eds.). In press. *Indigenous Social Work in Canada: Perspectives, Practice, Futures.* Halifax and Winnipeg: Fernwood.

## About the Authors

Sohki Aski Esquao [Jeannine Carrière] is Métis originally from the Red River area of southern Manitoba. Jeannine has also lived and worked in Alberta for the last twenty-five years, focusing her career in Indigenous child and family services and teaching in the Access bsw program, which focused on rural remote and Indigenous communities. Her doctoral research focused on the correlation between health and adoption for First

Nation people. Her teaching experience is in areas such as Indigenous child and family services and other Indigenous content courses. Her research interests include Indigenous child and family practice and policy, Indigenous ways of knowing and mental health and decolonization for Indigenous people.

Raven Sinclair is a member of Gordon's First Nation of the Treaty #4 area of southern Saskatchewan. She has a BA in psychology from the University of Saskatchewan, a Certificate and Bachelor's degree in Indian Social Work from the First Nations University of Canada, an MSW from the University of Toronto and a PhD from the Faculty of Social Work at the University of Calgary. Raven's interests include Indigenous knowledge and research methodologies, the synthesis of traditional and contemporary healing theories and modalities, Aboriginal cultural identity issues, colonial theory and concepts in decolonization. Raven is the assistant director of the Indigenous Peoples' Health Research Centre and an assistant professor with the Faculty of Social Work, University of Regina, Saskatoon Centre.

## Note

1.   Names of participants have been changed.

## References

Adams, M. 2002. *Our Son a Stranger: Adoption Breakdown and Its Effects on Parents.* Montréal: McGill-Queen's University Press.

Alfred, T., and J. Corntassel. 2005. "Being Indigenous: Resurgence Against Contemporary Colonialism." Preprint for *Government and Opposition.* Oxford: Blackwell.

Anderson, K. 2000. *A Recognition of Being: Reconstructing Native Womanhood.* Toronto: Sumach.

Arsenault, A. 2006. "The Life Cycle Experiences and Influences of Adoption through Aboriginal Adult Stories." Unpublished masters' thesis, University of British Columbia, Vancouver.

Bennett, M., and J. Cyr. 2001. "Evaluation of the Southern Manitoba First Nation Repatriation Program." Winnipeg: Southern First Nations CFS Directors of Manitoba.

Brendtro, L.K., M. Brokenleg and S.V. Bockern. 1990. *Reclaiming Youth at Risk.* Bloomington, IN: National Education Service.

Cajete, G. 2000. *Native Science Natural Laws of Interdependence.* Santa Fe, NM: Clear Light.

Carrière, J. 2005. "Connectedness and Health for First Nation Adoptees." Unpublished PhD dissertation, Human Ecology, University of Alberta, Edmonton.

Fournier, S., and E. Crey. 1997. *Stolen from our Embrace: The Abduction of First Nations Children and the Restoration of Aboriginal Communities.* Vancouver: Douglas and McIntyre.

Freire, P. 1996. *Pedagogy of the Oppressed.* New York: Continuum.

Frideres, J., and R. Gadacz. 2001. *Aboriginal Peoples in Canada: Contemporary Conflicts.* Toronto: Prentice Hall.

Gilchrist, L. 1995. "Aboriginal Street Youth in Vancouver, Winnipeg and Montréal." Unpublished doctoral dissertation, University of British Columbia, Vancouver.

Jamieson, K. 1978. *Indian Women and the Law in Canada: Citizens Minus.* Ottawa: Supply and Services.

Johnston, P. 1983. *Aboriginal Children and the Child Welfare System.* Toronto: Canadian Council on Social Development.

Kim, D. 1978. "Issues in Transracial and Transcultural Adoption." *Social Casework* 59, 8 (October).

Kimmelman, Justice E.C. 1985. *No Quiet Place: Review Committee on Indian and Métis Adoption and Placements*. Manitoba Community Services.

Kral, M.J. 2003. *Unikaartuit: Meanings of Well-Being, Sadness, Suicide and Change in Two Inuit Communities*. Final report to the National Health Research and Development Programs. Ottawa: Health Canada.

Kulusic, T. 2005. "The Ultimate Betrayal: Claiming and Reclaiming Cultural Identity." *Atlantis: A Women's Study Journal* 29, 2.

Lazarus, K.B. 1997. "Adoption of Native Americans and First Nations Children: Are the United States and Canada Recognizing the Best Interests of Children?" *Arizona Journal of International and Comparative Law* 14, 1.

Mullaly, B. 2002. *Challenging Oppression: A Critical Social Work Approach*. Don Mills, ON: Oxford University Press.

National Archives of Canada. Record Group 10, Volume 6937. "Policy Matters Regarding Care of Children in Private or Forster Homes: 1958–1960." National Archives of Canada.

Nuttgens, S. 2004. "Life Stories of Aboriginal Adults Raised in Non-Aboriginal Families." Unpublished dissertation, University of Alberta, Edmonton.

Robinson, E. 2000. *Adoption and Loss: The Hidden Grief*. Christies Beach, Australia: Clova.

RCAP (Royal Commission Report on Aboriginal Peoples). 1996. *Royal Commission Report on Aboriginal Peoples*. Ottawa.

Rue, M., and L. Rue. 1984. "Reflections on Bicultural Adoption." In P. Bean (ed.), *Adoption: Essays in Social Policy, Law and Sociology*. New York: Tavistock.

Sinclair, R. 2004. "Aboriginal Social Work Education in Canada: Decolonizing Pedagogy for the Seventh Generation." *First Peoples Child and Family Review* 1, 1.

_____. 2007. "All My Relations: Adult Aboriginal Transracial Adoption, A Critical Case Study of Cultural Identity." PhD thesis, University of Calgary.

*Saskatchewan Indian*. 1977. "Indian Children Taken Illegally." 7, 1 (January). Available at <http://www.sicc.sk.ca/saskindian/a77jan11.htm>.

Sindelar, R. 2004. "Negotiating Indian Identity: Native Americans and Transracial Adoption." Unpublished master's thesis, Loyola University, Chicago.

Stolen Generations. 2003. *Book of Voices*. Winnipeg, MB: Stolen Generations, a project of the Aboriginal Healing Foundation.

Swidrovich, C. 2004. "Positive Experiences of First Nations Children in Non-Aboriginal Foster or Adoptive Care: Deconstructing the 'Sixties Scoop.'" Unpublished MA thesis, University of Saskatchewan, Saskatoon.

Timpson, J. 1995. "Four Decades of Literature on Aboriginal Canadian Child Welfare: Changing Themes." *Child Welfare* 74, 3.

Trevethan, S., J. Moore, S. Auger, M. Macdonald and J. Sinclair. 2005. "Childhood Experiences Affect Aboriginal Offenders." Correctional Service of Canada. Available at <http://www.csc-scc.gc.ca/text/pblct/forum/ e143/e143c_e.shtml> accessed May 5, 2008.

Walmsley, C. 2005. *Protecting Aboriginal Children*. Vancouver: UBC Press

# Chapter 16

# Practising from the Heart

*Wa Cheew Wapaguunew Iskew [Carolyn Peacock]*

This chapter addresses the different realities that on reserve social workers face from colleagues who provide similar services off reserve. When you live and work in your community, the stakes are much higher. The children and families become as much a part of your life as you become a part of theirs. This is the challenge that the author and her co-workers keep as a vision to ameliorate conditions in their communities, with the guidance and support of Elders, leaders and community members. The author describes the Yellowhead Tribal Services Agency practice model and provides recommendations for a personal practice model for all social workers.

Questions Addressed in This Chapter

1. What are the differences between First Nations and non-First Nations social work practice?
2. What practice strategies are recommended for child welfare work with on reserve Indigenous families and communities?

Of all the teachings we receive,
This one is the most important: Nothing belongs to you...
Of what there is...
Of what you take
You must share...
Chief Dan George (1989)

As a Cree woman, I am honoured to be asked to share my learning and experiences as a First Nations woman, social worker and director of a First Nations child and family services agency. My name is Wa Cheew Wapaguunew Iskew — Mountain Flower Woman. I am from Enoch Cree Nation. I am from the Wolf Clan. This chapter is a personal story about the experiences of the past twenty years of working with children and families and communities, providing child and family services to the First Nations communities of the Yellowhead Tribal Council in Alberta. This is a story told from the heart, offering insight rather than science.

## Personal Location

Recently, visitors from Ontario asked me if I would share my personal philosophy. Did I believe that prevention approaches and working with families to keep children in the home was a worthwhile thing, or did I believe in the protection approach, to remove kids, then figure it out later? To be truthful I was quite taken aback by the question, and I know they all eagerly awaited my response. I wasn't sure how I was going to answer, as one of the chiefs I had invited to meet them was also present. I thought I owed it first to myself and to everyone present to be honest and speak from my heart. I shared with them a very personal story of who I was, until recently a history I was always ashamed to share.

I shared with them that many, many times the Elders from our five communities would tell us that we did not choose our jobs; we were chosen for this work. I have always had a hard time believing this, especially when the responsibility of being the director weighed heavily on my shoulders. I have thought about quitting. I have questioned my own ethics, values and beliefs. Had I been applying Western standards to our people? Had I sold out to accommodate a particular theory or practice model and try to make it fit the very different realities in our communities? At the end of the day, could we balance everything that we were expected to do for the provincial and federal governments and still be able to do things "our way?" When I look back at all the years, we did! I am pleased to provide an overview of these accomplishments of many people and many hearts.

I told them that my grandparents raised me from a baby. We were very, very poor and they were alcoholics who would leave me alone for days to fend for myself. I could have been apprehended many times. I have early memories of hiding under the bed for hours when the social worker came calling. I witnessed family violence and every kind of abuse when they were drinking, and I didn't even know who my mom and dad were until I was six or so. When my grandparents became sober things were really good. For years I wondered why my aunts were verbally and physically mean to me, whether they were drunk or sober. Today I believe it was because they were jealous of the love and affection that my grandparents gave to me and probably couldn't give to them because they were both raised in residential schools. I was very lucky not to have been apprehended as a child. I had lots of love and caring from extended family members throughout my childhood and was adopted as an adult by my uncle and aunt, who were and are always there for me, my children and my grandchildren. I am a grandmother now, and I can't describe the love I have for my four grandchildren, especially the eldest. She is just like me, the first granddaughter and she has lived with us since birth.

My grandparents had a second chance with me, and I believe people can change. First Nations people can and have changed. It is up to the healthy ones to be there to support others when they decide to do what they need to do to be able to parent. We should be there to walk beside them but not to do the work for them. I became a social worker because of this basic philosophy.

## History of the Yellowhead Tribal Services Agency

In the mid-1980s the chiefs of the Yellowhead Tribal Council (Alexander, Alexis, Enoch, O'Chiese and Sunchild First Nations, located in Central Alberta) were concerned that too many of their children were in care and placed in non-Native foster homes off reserve. They questioned the standard of care when one young man, in a non-Native foster care placement, died under suspicious circumstances and was returned home in a coffin. The chiefs, in consultation with the Elders and community members, envisioned an organization that would be staffed by trained community members who would be able to work towards "keeping our children in their own communities." The Yellowhead Tribal Services Agency (YTSA) was developed based on their vision. The first dual bilateral agreement with the governments of Alberta and Canada was signed on March 1987.

In Alberta, the YTSA was the third agency in Alberta to sign a child and family services agreement. While all the other fifteen First Nations agencies were fully delegated to deliver child protection services when they signed their agreements, the YTSA leadership decided to be a non-delegated agency to start. The YTSA stayed non-delegated for nine years, which enabled the Agency to establish its staffing component, financial structure, governance structure, board of directors, and policies and procedures. As a non-delegated agency, we provided support services and worked collaboratively with the province, which provided the qualified social workers to deliver the statutory services under the legislation. Five community child welfare programs were set up utilizing funding from Indian and Northern Affairs Canada (INAC).[1] The Canada/YTSA agreement included money for family support, foster care support workers, administrative staff, the creation of volunteer child welfare committees, community development initiatives, training and cultural events. The Alberta/YTSA Agreement ensured that the Child and Family Services Ministry was reimbursed for the delivery of statutory services on reserve.

When I became the director of the YTSA in April 1996, there was no policy manual or guidelines that I could get my hands on to show me how to manage a First Nations child and family services agency. I felt ill prepared to do the job even though I had a Bachelor of Social Work, three years front-line experience and five years as the YTSA program supervisor to bring to the position. I had to learn as I went along and to basically write my own job description. I was terrified, yet very excited about the possibilities of creating a different and unique agency. I knew there was a solid foundation to build upon. We had the support of the Elders, community leadership, the Yellowhead Tribal Council, the YTSA board of directors and the child welfare programs of five bands. Collectively we knew we could structure an organization that could make a difference for our children, families and communities, and we could do it our way.

## Challenges as a Director

The YTSA was the third First Nation child and family services agency to be established in Alberta. Agencies that signed their agreements prior to Indian and Northern Affairs Canada developing Directive 20-1, the policy for funding First Nations child and family services (FNCFS) agencies, were referred to as pre-directive agencies. Directive 20-1, which came into effect in 1991, is a national funding formula administered by INAC that restricts funding to "eligible children on reserve." A population threshold (based on children up to eighteen) influences how much funding each First Nations CFS agency receives. Under Directive 20-1, in most provincial jurisdictions, First Nations CFS agencies are incorporated under provincial child welfare legislation that requires them to comply with provincial legislation and standards. Funding to First Nations CFS agencies to provide child welfare services is provided federally through Directive 20-1, except in Ontario, where the First Nations child welfare agencies are funded under a different financial arrangement (Bennett 2004: 3)

In Canada, the five most common jurisdictional models developed by First Nations CFS agencies as a result of the imposed legislation and funding procedures are the delegated model; the pre-mandated model; the band by-law model; the tri-partite model; and the self-assessment model. The delegated model is the most common because of the funding formula from INAC's Directive 20-1, which provides services for on reserve through delegation by the provincial government. The pre-mandated model supports agencies to provide prevention and family support services pursuant to agreements, including licensing agreements, with the provincial/territorial government and is mostly used in Ontario (Blackstock 2003). The YTSA uses these two models in conjunction. The YTSA maintained its pre-directive status until 2000, when we were served with notice to terminate. Negotiating a funding arrangement with INAC and a service delivery agreement with Alberta was very difficult. Both levels of government were pressuring us to agree to financial and service delivery conditions that we could not accept. The YTSA board of directors and executive of chiefs believed that, given the Agency's history and strategic plan for the future, it was in our best interest to negotiate a block funding arrangement or in today's terms, a flexible funding option for maintenance (FFOM).

One of the conditions in the arrangement was that two of our five First Nations communities were non-delegated. At the time, the province delivered all the statutory services, which meant that the YTSA was reimbursing Alberta for all services including staffing. The province presented the Agency with an invoice for an amount that was just about the total amount of funding we received from INAC to operate our whole agency. It took us over a year to sort out a financial protocol that we could all agree to. Over the next three years, we operated on yearly extensions of our Canada/YTSA funding agreement. On three occasions, I was instructed by the board of directors and chiefs to issue lay-off notices to the staff and prepare to shut down the Agency because an agreement with INAC for an adequate funding base could not be reached. It was the most challenging time for everyone involved.

## YTSA Program Development

In spite of all of the obstacles that the YTSA faced, the one constant throughout has been that it was not acceptable for non-Native organizations to decide what was in the best interest of First Nations children. Residential schools, the sixties scoop and a child welfare system that would pay strangers but not family to care for our children are testament to this fact. Carrière (1997: 51) reflects on her work in foster care, where she recalls "saying many times that if we provided birth families with the type of financial and emotional support we provide to strangers or foster parents, it would be one of the best forms of prevention and cost-saving measures for child welfare services." The shift from reactive to proactive planning was a critical and necessary move for us. Richardson and Nelson (2007: 81) identify some important work and changes for First Nations social workers to undertake to improve the lives of our children, families and communities:

> Along with individual and familial capacity, helping interventions can also build community capacity, which is necessary if things are to be different for Aboriginal children. Through "cleaning up" our practice and working in ways that actually preserve and strengthen extended families and communities, we help families to help themselves. With increased wellness and improved White/Aboriginal relations (free of racism, Eurocentrism and economic marginalization) true collaborations may emerge. Under improved conditions, all individuals will begin to care for the young ones, as well as the Earth, in a loving and thoughtful way. On a spiritual level, separation is the cause of much of our planetary grief, solutions will not come from continuing to separate children from their families, from their community and from their lands, traditions and spiritual practice.

It is within this spirit that we began our program development, first going to our Elders following our cultural protocols of offering tobacco and cloth, to ask for their prayers and guidance in this very important undertaking. They gave us the teachings of the Medicine Wheel, which formed the foundation of all of our programs. As Thomas and Green (2007: 92) state,

> The Medicine Wheel is an ancient teaching tool. It has no beginning and no end and teaches us that all things are interrelated. The circularity of the wheel we are utilizing is comprised of quadrants that represent all living things.

The Agency has been a pioneer in the development of First Nations specific programs, such as Custom Care, Open Custom Adoption, Caring for Our Own Community Support Services and our own version of Family Enhancement. Venturing into the realm of program development was a major leap of faith. In order to address practice issues, it is important to begin by describing our programs and services.

## Custom Care Program

In 1988, Elders and members of the First Nations communities of the Yellowhead Tribal Council (YTC) initiated the YTSA Custom Care Program. The Custom Care Program is based upon the traditional practice of utilizing extended family members when parents are unable to care for their children and is designed to keep children who are in need of alternate care connected to their family and community of origin. The Custom Care and Open Custom Adoption programs, their policies and eight training modules have all been developed with the Medicine Wheel as their foundation. We are thankful to those very special Elders who shared their teachings with us.

In developing the Custom Care Program we also produced a video, *Gifts from the Creator*, to be used in orientation training to our community members. We were at a time in the Agency's beginning when we struggled with finding ways to keep our children who needed alternate care in their home communities. It was 1991, and we still had 90 percent of our children in care off reserve in non-First Nations placements. This was haunting us, for as Thomas and Green (2007: 100) point out, "Aboriginal children are precious to us as they represent our collective future."

Our Custom Care Program changed that outcome. In one year, we reversed that number to 90 percent of our children in trained, approved Custom Care placements in their home communities. This was the vision that our Elders and leaders encouraged us toward and was the beginning of believing that we could be the authors of the change needed in our communities. It was focused on our children as "Gifts from the Creator" as "we know and believe that children are the heart of communities and they must be central to how we look at practice" (Thomas and Green 2007: 99). Since the inception of our program we have had a Custom Care Committee, with a representative from each community, which meets on a regular basis to review applications, approve homes, provide training and discuss any new issues concerning program delivery.

It has been an on-going challenge since the inception of the program to recruit, train and maintain our Custom Care Homes. I believe we have been faced with almost every possible obstacle, for example, shortage of homes — many of our placements were/are child specific placements with extended family — and difficulties in completing training of community members — we have provided local day, evening and weekend training conferences, and struggled with mandatory training, new requirements and total hours of training annually. Ongoing recruitment of new homes, updating our training curriculum, updating the Custom Care Policy Manual, implementing new Provincial Home Assessment Reports, training and certifying YTSA staff to do the work, meeting file requirements, meeting provincial safety standards, Alberta First Nation Practice Standards and INAC funding and report requirements, and staff shortages are some of the challenges we continue to work on. It is hard work to keep up with but it is one of our most important programs, and without it we would have to go backwards and place our children who are in need of alternate care off reserve in non-First Nation foster care. So we continue to persevere.

Currently in one of our communities we are training sixteen new families, and I am very excited at the prospect of having these families as resources. They are good, hardworking families who are active in their community through the local school, in recreation and health, and some are respected traditional people. We all share the common vision of providing a caring home to our children in their community, as well as an environment that fosters their culture, language and connection to family. We have made the commitment to our three other member communities to do the same in the next few months, and I look forward to training with them. In total, we have forty-six active Custom Care Homes and are in the process of completing thirty-four Home Assessment Reports and training requirements.

## Open Custom Adoption Program

Historically in Alberta and across Canada, non-First Nations families adopted the majority of First Nations children. Today, many of these children, now adults, are finding their way home to their roots and families. Some are just looking to complete their lives, while others are returning wounded and looking for a place to heal. In February 1997, under direction from the Alberta First Nation Chiefs, Alberta Children's Services issued *The Policy Directive on First Nation Adoption*, which changed the adoption process for First Nation children in Alberta. The directive requires consent from the respective First Nation chief and council for a child's adoption. This measure was implemented to preserve the child's cultural heritage and maintain the very important connection to their family and community. In 1998, representatives from Alberta Children's Services encouraged us to consider the development of an adoption program. We met with our Elders, chiefs and councils, and the YTSA created the internationally recognized Open Custom Adoption Program. We produced a video, *From the Heart*, to utilize in recruitment and training with our Custom Caregivers and families wanting to adopt. The Open Custom Adoption Program's foundation was, like Custom Care, based on the Medicine Wheel concept. We developed a policy manual on our adoption process, as well as a home study and training manual.

We had to follow provincial policy and legislation, fulfilling the court/ legal process but concurrently incorporating our traditional way of the Custom Adoption Ceremony, led by the Elders and traditional spiritual keepers of our five communities. We had to earn the right to be the keeper/facilitator of the Custom Adoption Ceremony. It took us four years for this honour to be bestowed upon us by the Elders. On November 10, 2000, we hosted our first Open Custom Adoption Ceremony at my home community, Enoch Cree Nation. We had three children with permanent guardianship orders (PGO) adopted to three families. It also marked an historical day, being the first and only time in Canadian history that the Alberta Court of Queen's Bench came on reserve to finalize an adoption and witness our sacred ceremony. We were honoured to witness and participate in such a special event. The children's birth families, adoptive families, extended birth and adoptive families, our five chiefs and councils, Elders and community members were present to witness and celebrate the occasion. This event still stands out as the highlight of my social work career. Since then we have hosted four more Open Custom Adoption Ceremonies in our communities and have completed a total of sixty-four adoptions. We are now in the planning stage of our next Open Custom Adoption Ceremony, to be hosted by the Alexis Nakota Sioux Nation.

We have also been fortunate in fulfilling the dream and vision of our Elders by being able to share our program with other First Nations child and family services agencies. On January 17, 2007, we were invited to witness and celebrate with our friends from Lalum'utul'Smun'eem Child and Family Services, Cowichan Tribes in Duncan, B.C., as they hosted their first Custom Adoption Ceremony, where ten of their member children were adopted to their families. It was a beautiful, emotional, happy and historical day for all. As First Nations peoples we celebrate these events as a community in healing. As Carrière (2007) states, "There is a link in knowing who you are, where you come from and how you feel as a whole person" (61).

### Caring for Our Own — Wahsikiw Sakopen — Community Support Services Program

The Caring for Our Own Community Supports Services Program was established to provide intervention and support services required at the community level. The program is designed to provide quality and community-based support services that reflect customary and traditional family values, which emphasize cultural practices and integration of community resources. For example, Elders provide mentoring to children and families and are available to conduct ceremonies and offer healing practices. Our mission is to continue to develop and implement ongoing enhanced and unique community supports for our First Nations children and families. Policy regarding the program has been revamped, and a new and exciting training program has been developed. The mandate, philosophy and vision of the Caring for Our Own Community Supports Services Program have been updated to encompass the importance of support services necessary at the community level.

### Intervention Services

The YTSA continues to fulfill a responsibility, with delegation of authority in accordance to the *Child, Youth and Family Enhancement Act*, to three of our four communities. The YTSA's intervention team continues to strive for best practice in working with our families. In our daily challenges, the delegated staff has continually demonstrated optimum commitment to our children, families, communities and Agency. The casework management and statistical reviews demonstrate how timely, effective and impactful their work has been, which is a true reflection of their compassion and hard work

Regardless of the demand and complexities on the front line, our intervention team is having to learn, adjust and implement a new Casework Practice Model that has been directed from Alberta's Ministry of Children Services. The YTSA has taken on the challenge to be a Casework Practice Model champion site, in that all of our delegated workers have completed mandatory training in the new Casework Practice Model (CPM). Because this work is in progress, we have launched this model in the Enoch community and will slowly integrate the model into the Alexis and O'Chiese First Nations communities. Fortunately, we have a provincial worker through a secondment contract to assist and implement CPM through new intakes. We anticipate more training in electronic imputing (for the new database) and file management, as the Child and Youth Information Module (CYIM) will also be replaced in this new model.

Along with the challenges and changes to Alberta's legislation, policy and practice, we still have to manage our daily responsibilities to our children and families. This includes after hours services as we continue to have on-call workers and a supervisor available for each community. Currently, CYIM has captured approximately 150 open files within our three delegated sites.

## Family Enhancement Services

Family Enhancement Services, established by the Alberta Ministry of Children's Services, has been provided by the YTSA since November 2004. Family Enhancement Services provided to our First Nations communities is approached as a non-intrusive measure to prevent more intensive intervention. The Family Enhancement caseworkers look to community for intervention/prevention programs and resources that are culturally appropriate for our families. The Family Enhancement caseworkers ensure that the views/interests of the children are heard and represented, and that the family unit is preserved.

Services are provided by the YTSA Family Enhancement caseworker only if the family is willing and cooperative. The caseworker meets with the family to discuss issues and how the family may be supported in alleviating the initial concerns in accordance with the *Child, Youth and Family Enhancement Act*. The family then plans what resources/services will support them in their personal growth, healing and empowerment. A YTSA Family Enhancement caseworker continues to be involved with the family/children to ensure positive growth. Family Enhancement Services for the 2006–07 reporting period served an average of eighteen children per month. Approximately 143 children have been served by Family Enhancement Services since 2005.

The connections made within 2006–07 have been strong helping relationships with other support/resource professionals in the four First Nations communities. These professional helping relationships assist our families in attaining their goals on their Family Enhancement plans and alleviate the initial child intervention concerns. These connections also aid our families in their after-care plans once they become no longer involved with Children's Services. Examples of resources/supports within the communities are as follows:

- Alberta Alcohol and Drug Abuse Commission (AADAC) and National Native Alcohol and Drug Abuse Program (NNADAP);
- Sweetgrass Lodge Healthy Parenting Program;
- Enoch Counselling Services/Alexis Counselling/ O'Chiese Counselling;
- Health Centre — Prenatal and Prescription Pill Management;
- School/Guidance Counsellors.

## Annual National CFS Conference

The eighth Annual National First Nations Child and Family Services Conference was held at the new River Cree Resort and Casino, Enoch, Alberta, in 2007 and had over 500 participants. The conference site was well received and the participants were also allowed to debrief with colleagues and get rejuvenated. Each year, the YTSA strives to introduce and bring to light the major social issues affecting First Nations people and communities.

## First Nations Standards and Values

In order to uphold our First Nations values we need to pay attention to our protocols and ethics and how these have guided us from time immemorial. As First Nations social workers, we need to be able to separate our personal standards from Western standards. What we think is best for children can sometimes be the worst thing we can do. Early in my career, I was the acting manager of the Enoch Child Welfare Program. We had to remove two little girls from their single mom's care because she was drinking. We subsequently placed the children in what we thought was an ideal placement off reserve.

The foster mother was a non-First Nations teacher at the community school. She did not have children, owned a beautiful home and showered the girls with clothes, stereos and other material things. We thought we had found the best placement ever because the foster mother loved and treated them so well. When it was time to return them to mom, they refused to go home because they didn't want to give up their beautiful bedrooms and all the things they had acquired. They knew that their mother was living on social assistance and couldn't give them what they had or what they wanted. The mom was devastated because she had done everything we'd asked and then some to get her children back. We unintentionally broke her heart and she attempted suicide. In retrospect, we should have tried harder to place them in a similar environment on reserve.

We learned a valuable lesson; material things cannot replace a mother's love, and we vowed to never do that again. This epiphany was the driving force behind the development of the Custom Care Program. We needed to develop standards that recognized the reality in our communities.

## Working in the Community

Living and working in our home community is a challenge in itself because the stakes are so high. On one hand, we feel a great sense of commitment. We have a vested interest in what happens in the community, and we strive to make things better for children and families. On the other hand, my staff and I are always under a microscope. Our spouses and children are closely watched, and we need to be careful not to do anything that may be viewed as unacceptable behaviour. Our peers and the children and families, many of whom we are related to, hold us accountable for our social work practice. The Elders, chief and council, and federal and provincial governments each have different expectations. It can be a difficult balancing act at times, but we have made the commitment to stick it out through the good times and the bad. These are our people, our communities, and we are not going anywhere. As First Nations social workers we are expected to be model community members in both our personal and professional lives. The Elders of our communities expect us to know, respect, practice and participate in cultural events and respect traditional practices.

When you live and work in your own community, whether you like it or not, you end up being on-call 24-7 (and receiving telephone calls at home or having people come to your home unannounced). Wherever I go in the communities — to the store, band office, hockey rink, community centre, funerals — I am expected to deal with someone's situation immediately or at least hear their side of the story. An example of how it is different, and to me acceptable because this is our way as First Nations, was an encounter I had with a mom from one of our communities. She had her two children apprehended one morning from a women's shelter. Two of our supervisors were involved. It was lunch hour and all of the staff had left me alone in the office with the door unlocked. My eldest son and daughter-in-law from Germany (where he plays professional hockey) had just arrived to take me for lunch.

The woman came in very upset so I took her into an office to talk to her about what had happened. She was yelling and swearing at me in anger, and at that point I knew we could not continue this meeting because she was too upset. She then attempted to shove me and picked up a three-hole paper punch to try and hit me. I immediately directed her to the door, and my son came running to my aid. At the time, my greatest fear was she would hit me, my son would defend me and possibly be charged, which might hurt his hockey career and prevent him being able to go back to Germany. I somehow got the woman out the door and locked it. She continued to yell and bang on the door, but left within a few minutes. My son was very upset, and I explained to him that I understood her anger and it was unfortunate what happened because I knew her and her siblings and I had a good relationship with her mother, who was a respected Elder.

The next day I was at home cooking a traditional meal of moose meat and bannock, at the request of my son, when the woman showed up with her mom, the respected Elder, to apologize to me. It was suppertime so I invited them in and fed them. My son was appalled that I was feeding them after what he had witnessed. I told him, "My boy, that was yesterday. Today she has come to apologize and this is our way — to forgive and to feed our visitors." The Elder I believe made her daughter come to apologize because I was not to blame for her daughter's situation and she should not have behaved the way she did to me. I believe it also happened because of the positive relationship I had with the Elder and because of my own history as the director of the YTSA.

We entered into the child and family services field with our eyes and hearts wide open. We knew the responsibility we were taking on and how we would all be affected on a daily basis. We hurt when we see the impact that substance abuse and family violence has on the children we care about. We worry about their wellbeing. What standard of care are they receiving? Is it better than what we took them from? Are they being held and comforted when they cry because they miss their parents? I don't think that it can ever be said that we care too much. If we don't care, who will?

Our agency could not do all the work we are expected to do without the support and inclusion of our communities. Since the beginning, the YTSA has had Child Welfare Committees led by Elders in each of our four communities. We persevere because of the responsibility they have taken on to care for our children. We relied on our Child Welfare Committees, made up of volunteers from the community, to provide us with guidance and advice on possible placements/family ties, and to share "insider" information and other relevant feedback. To this day, we appreciate the participation of Child Welfare Committees in family group conferencing and all of the other activities they organize to keep our children connected to their culture, family and community.

## First Nations Social Work Practice

It has been very difficult to share my story of social work practice because everything I have shared I have been carrying in my heart. I have seen it, I have lived it and I have experienced it. For many years I struggled with finding a balance between the values, beliefs and traditional Cree knowledge, which have been embedded in me since birth, and what I learned through formal education. I have also wrestled with my decision to choose child welfare as a career because of the negative impact it has had on First Nation people, my community, my family and my personal life.

My social work education began with a community college diploma program that was brought to Yellowhead Tribal Council (YTC) because of the development of the YTSA. My experiences were very positive so I went on to obtain my BSW. The words of Ben Carniol haunted me with truth:

> A major hurdle for Native Students is facing the accusation from family and friends that they're abandoning their people to join the "white man's" world. The bitterness of this accusation becomes more understandable when you consider the historical and current grievances of Natives against white society. Whether it is the hidden or blatant prejudices of white townspeople or urban employer, or whether it is the trivialization of Native Culture by Hollywood movies and TV programs, the institutions of the dominant society have left little room or respect for the expression of authentic Native values. (1990: 79)

I completed my BSW successfully with the support of my family and faced what I knew would a world of challenges and continuous stress, overshadowed by the knowledge that I could not work anywhere else but in my community. This was the choice I made, and I have a practice model that is rich in the values and ancient practices of our people. I relate to Whalmsley (2004: 74) when he states "when a practitioner resides in the community, a different kind of child protection relationship is possible."

Firsthand knowledge of our communities and families, our history, way of life, politics, standards, traditions and customs forms the basis for our practice as First Nations social workers. We are at a different starting point when we begin working with the families. We already know the lives and family circumstances of the children we are involved with. Walmsley (2004: 76) states that "Aboriginal practitioners who live and work in their communities of origin described opportunities for supportive informal intervention outside the office, along with the possibility of bringing their lifelong knowledge of the persons in question to the interaction."

## One of My Teachers

I remember working with a young mom of two little boys. There were some protection concerns, but they were not serious enough to remove the children from her care. I recall sitting in silence with her for a long, long time. I was thinking of how I knew her family, her mother was my birth mother's cousin. I knew how she was raised, and I felt that she was thinking about me — who I was and how I was raised. I believe we evaluated each other's lives during this period of silence. When she was ready, we began the work — planning, problem solving and sharing — in a good way. She was very upfront and didn't give me a hard time like she did our non-First Nations social worker, whom she would either not let into her home or kick out when she started asking too many questions.

I believe there was an unspoken bond between us because we'd had a similar upbringing. We had both grown up in alcoholic homes. I treated her with respect and she reciprocated. We always began our time together by visiting — this is our way. I drank tea with her and she would offer to share her food, which was always bannock right out of the oven — this too is our way. Many times I thought that this informal approach was straying quite far from the social work practice I had been taught. I had learned the theories, preparation for interviews, problem-solving skills, doing a thorough assessment and asking all of the questions that were on the government forms that I was required to complete. I know many times the documents were filled out solely for my benefit and that many of our people would agree to just about anything, even if it was not something they could do within the timelines given. But these were the expectations under the *Child Welfare Act* of 1980 and the provincial policies we were expected to adhere to.

The *Child Welfare Act* was revised in 1984, and it was the first time in First Nations history that the "Indian Child" was recognized in legislation, under section 73 "Matters to be Considered." As a First Nations agency, we thought that we could finally do things a little bit differently and hopefully much better, that we would have more say in the cases that went to court. Unfortunately, that didn't happen for quite a while. At the outset, our peers did not view us as being qualified and competent social workers. The Alberta *Child Welfare Act* was revised again in 2004. As First Nations, we had high hopes as we'd been asked to provide input into the many changes that were to come. Collectively as First Nations we were very disappointed when our written and oral submissions were not included in the changes to the Act. Today, peers and both the federal and provincial governments view our agency as leaders in our field. It only took twenty-some years for the acknowledgement that we were qualified and competent social workers working with our own people.

## What Practice Model Should You Use

I recommend a First Nations practice model similar to the one developed by the First Nation Directors of Alberta, "First Nation Practice Standards in Child, Youth and Family Services in Alberta," in June 2006. These unique practice standards form the heart of our work. They set out our vision, beliefs and principles in the delivery of intervention services in a supportive, respectful, understanding and cultural manner within our communities. The practice standards are designed to serve as a guide and a tool for caseworkers to use in their daily activities with children, youth and families. They reflect the cultural context of our communities and community realities. I am very proud to have been involved in the development of these standards as a steering committee member and as one of the contributing authors. The following is a summary of the standards and how we were able to apply them at the YTSA.

## Theoretical Model of Practice

1. Capacity building for parents and families in implementing the purpose and motivational factors for health and wellbeing of First Nations. Building the capacity of families and their children/youth means protecting and supporting the natural family systems and social networks.

We are able to apply this principle by providing family-group conferencing with our local child welfare committees on a monthly basis or when needed. We also have two programs that assist parents and families in capacity building. The Family Enhancement Program provides culturally appropriate family enhancement services as per the *Child, Youth and Family Enhancement Act* and the Minister of Children's Services Policy Manual. The Caring for Our Own Community Support Services Program also provides support services such as parent aides, homemakers, youth workers and drivers to assist families in keeping the children in the parental home.

2. Strengthening the extended family and kinships systems through contextual value systems provide continuity and sustainable relationships. The raising of

children and youth in healthy and nurturing environments and communities is a collective and collateral responsibility.

Both our Custom Care and our Open Custom Adoption Programs are based on extended family and kinship. Social connections and networks are valued and represent the foundation of these programs.

3.   Traditional healing and problem solving approaches are the strength of First Nations families and communities. Practice standards for safe and sustainable relationships for families and their children/youth are based on their cultural values and heritage.

Traditional healing is offered to the children and families we work, as is counselling by Elders in their communities.

4.   Community and Cultural Competencies of Holistic Healing Practices. The responsibilities and values of First Nations identify community and cultural competencies for the community decision-making processes and interventions.

Holistic healing programs, supports and services through our Family Enhancement Program assist us to utilize a collateral approach to family enhancement and protective services. This means that we can work with a diversity of colleagues to engage in casework practice, family violence, addictions, traditional healing, counselling, therapy, community awareness and parenting programs.

## A Personal Practice Model

I also wish to highlight some recommendations for practice that I have observed as beneficial to First Nation children and families. I have developed these to assist frontline child welfare practitioners entering the field.

### Mentors

It is critical that as a BSW student you find at least two or three mentors in your field of practice (child welfare, education, health, justice). I personally have learned more from my many mentors over the years than anything I ever learned from my professional training. I was very fortunate to be able to work with and learn from some of the best social workers with many years of experience. They taught me the "how" of putting into practice what was in theory, the "how to" in working with clients, work ethics, social work ethics in daily practice and the First Nations practice standards they incorporate into their daily practice. I was able to learn from watching, listening and asking questions (even when I thought they were dumb questions). My mentors were there to guide me through my learning. Many of my mentors have been supervisors, professors and colleagues from different fields of practice and multi-cultural backgrounds. Some I still keep in contact with; others I continue to give credit to for what they taught me. Other mentors came from the academic world — professors and colleagues whom I will always admire for their "academic smarts," their writings and the partnerships of program development. As a First Nations director, I was able to put into practice such programs as our Custom Care model, our Open Custom Adoption Program and Alberta First Nation Standards — none of which would have happened without one special mentor's belief that our agency could take the theories and develop the programs that have changed the way we provide services to our children and families of our communities.

### Networking

I believe in order to do the work we are expected to do in the field of social work we need to have contacts in all kinds of other professions. Part of our responsibility as social workers is to ensure we are referring our clients to competent professionals.

### Continuing Competency

On-going learning, reading current articles of interest, taking workshops, participating in conferences, taking classes, joining your professional association of social workers, and writing papers are all essential parts of continuing your own learning.

### Self-Care

Counselling, traditional healing, attending ceremonies, writing, smudging, praying, going to sweats, keeping a journal and debriefing stressful situations with supervisors and colleagues are some ways you can practise self-care.

### Professional Responsibility

Learn your job description, personnel policy, policies that apply to your job, relevant legislation, regulations, standards, code of ethics, code of conduct and anything else that pertains to the job you are being paid to do. It is your professional responsibility.

### Humour

Many First Nations people have a great sense of humour. Cree people and I would say most First Nations in Canada have mannerisms that we use daily in communicating with each other and we don't even realize we are doing it, such as lip-pointing and saying *chuu, ma, wah-wa, chaa!* We are also great storytellers, and we like to tease each other in fun, joke and laugh with each other. We also love to give nicknames in our language or other names that have a story behind them (P.S. mine is Susie… long story!). Our agency hosts an annual general meeting and we have a fun night where we have a theme and dress-up, pretend to sing like professionals and have lots of fun. The Elders are our greatest fans! We love to play in a safe sober way. I encourage you to laugh, play and have some fun; our work is hard enough!

### Volunteer

Join a committee through your work or professional interest, locally in your community, provincially or nationally. Volunteer at a local woman's shelter, hospital or Elder's home. Your time will be appreciated.

### Self-Evaluation

Question your own practice, ask yourself the tough questions, change what you are not happy with and learn from your past mistakes. Develop work plans, to-do lists, ask for feedback from co-workers, supervisors and mentors.

### Common Sense

Common sense is defined as "sound practical judgment." The use of practical judgment in your everyday practice promotes efficiency in decision-making. It helps find the balance in communication, problem solving, policy, theory and practice. Use it wisely. Without common-sense, nothing makes sense.

### Intuition

This is also referred to as your "gut feeling." If you tune into your intuition, it will help guide you in most situations. Your intuition can give you an advance "warning" when a situation may arise that you may have to act on. Intuition is derived from your personal and professional experiences and can be either a positive or negative feeling. Our Elders encourage the use of intuition in their teachings. In our practice, intuition is an important ingredient in decision-making, and utilizing it wisely, consciously and responsibly will provide you with an effective tool in whatever you do.

### Assessments

The three most important things I learned in university were assessment, assessment and assessment! It is important when working with individuals in all kinds of practice, especially child protection services, to have a good assessment tool in addition to those provided by provincial ministries or First Nations child and family service agencies. Take the time you need to complete your assessment; be thorough. The more information you collect, the more you will be able to assist the individual and family to make good decisions of what change is needed and who needs to do what, as well as what resources in the community could assist in the situation.

I have included the whole person assessment that we use in addition to the assessment that is in the new Casework Practice Model for Alberta (see Appendix 16-1). I like to refer to assessment as the vision and the "work" that comes from it as the transformation. It seems to fit better with our day-to-day realities on reserve and the way we have incorporated our traditional teachings into our practice.

### Relationships

It is critical to work on building healthy relationships with both the people you work with and the professionals you come in connection with. You can accomplish this by treating others the way you would want to be treated — with respect and non-judgment. Be honest, trustworthy, fair and do what you say you are going to; walk your talk. Maintain your relationships in a good way through contact and friendliness; be genuine in what you can commit to.

## Supervision

In any work setting, taking and making quality time for supervision will benefit your social work practice. Find and develop a supervision process that fits your job description. The strength of a supervision model is based on a focused, rational approach to guiding and directing the business of the agency you work for. Formal supervision with a supervisor should occur at least once a month. Go prepared with notes, develop your own supervision file to bring with you and be prepared with goals that are specific, measurable, achievable, realistic and time-related. Be open to constructive feedback, both receiving and giving it; learn and change what you can.

## Practise from Your Heart

Always remember who you are working with and how. When working with children and families from your own community they are not your *cases*; they are your people. Treat them with respect; do not *assume* you know everything about their lives.

## Voices Are Our Strength

Culture to us means a whole way of life, beliefs and language, and how we live with one another and creation; this is the interconnectedness of the elements — culture, spirituality and ethics. I trust in the guidance of our Elders and our traditional ways. I strongly believe that things have worked out for the YTSA because we follow cultural protocols and consult with the Elders. We have learned to listen and really hear what they are trying to tell us through their stories, their vision of what could and should be. I believe the strength to do what we had to do came from their prayers and being entrusted with the responsibility of caring for our most precious gifts: our children. As First Nations social workers, we have the responsibility to acknowledge that many of us have been raised, taught and learned from the teachings and that as we mature in practice we will accept what we know as Indigenous Knowledge.

Michael Hart (2007) speaks to these needs in his paper on Indigenous knowledge and research. He concludes his paper with a quote from Henderson (2000) that is the vision and hopes of our Elders and leadership of the Yellowhead Tribal Council and what we have been workings so hard towards achieving for our children, families and First Nations communities:

> As Aboriginal people, we must reclaim our worldviews, knowledge, languages, and order to find the path ahead. We must sustain our relationship with our environment and follow our Elders' advice. We must rebuild our nations on our worldviews and our good values. We must be patient and thorough, because there are no shortcuts in rebuilding ourselves, our families,

our relationships, our spiritual ceremonies and our solidarity. We must use our abilities to make good choices. (Henderson 2000: 274)

Contained by the many years of practising social work within my home community and for the Yellowhead Tribal Council, I have become very humbled by the teachings of our Elders within the scope of social work practice. I have had the privilege of working directly with the amazing vision that our Elders have set forth as our journey toward integrating culturally embedded practices into provincial standards and legislation. Over the years, our practice has embodied the strengths of our Elders, who have taught us that our history is as much alive today as it was from time immemorial and that of uniting children, family and community is as significant as the delivery of services we provide.

Today, I believe that we have begun the process of change within ourselves as frontline social workers, administrators and First Nations social workers. We have begun to incorporate the "old" traditional teachings into the development of programs, policies and standards of practice. Our voices are our strength. Our voices have become stronger at the provincial, federal and national levels in advocating social policy change for our First Nations.

We are now beginning to have meaningful partnerships that will motivate the process of change and effectiveness in service delivery. It is now evident that our work as social workers is not unseen, nor is it left with no regard. We are doing what social work is based on, "planned change." We are now seeing the benefits of providing First Nations comparable services within our First Nations communities. But most of all, we are *finally* seeing the happiness in our children, the thankfulness in our families and the blessings from our Elders and ancestors. We are helping ourselves heal together with our communities.

## Suggestions for Further Reading

Blackstock, C., and N. Trocmé. 2005. "Community-based Child Welfare for Aboriginal Children: Supporting Resilience through Structural Change." In M. Unger (ed.), *Pathways to Resilience: A Handbook of Theory, Methods and Interventions*. Thousand Oaks, CA: Sage.

MacDonald, R.A.J., and P. Ladd. 2000. *First Nations Child and Family Services Joint National Policy Review: Final Report*. June. Ottawa: Assembly of First Nations.

Trocmé, N., D. Knoke and C. Blackstock. 2004. "Pathways to the Overrepresentation of Aboriginal Children in Canada's Child Welfare System." *Social Services Review* December.

## About the Author

Wa Cheew Wapaguunew Iskew [Carolyn Peacock] is a First Nation woman from the Enoch Cree Nation, who has worked in the field of children services for over twenty years. She has been a social worker in several capacities before assuming her current role as director for Yellowhead Tribal Services Agency (ytsa) in 1995. Wa Cheew Wapaguunew Iskew was influential in the conception of the ytsa Custom Care and Open Custom Adoption programs and has received commendations for outstanding leadership and best practice for Service Delivery in First Nation Child and Family Services at provincial, national and international levels.

## Note

1. Indian and Northern Affairs Canada (INAC) was previously named the Department of Indian and Northern Development (DIAND).

## References

Bennett, M. 2004. "First Nations Fact Sheet: A General Profile on First Nations Child Welfare in Canada." Ottawa: First Nations Child and Family Caring Society of Canada. Available at <www.fncaringsociety.com/docs/FirstNationsFS1.pdf> accessed May 27, 2008.

Blackstock, C. 2003. "Aboriginal Child Welfare: Jurisdictional Models of Service Delivery." Paper presented to the First Nations Child and Family Caring Society of Canada. Ottawa.

Carniol, B. 1990. *Case Critical: Challenging Social Work in Canada* (Second Edition). Toronto: Between the Lines.

Carrière, J, 1997. "Kinship Care in Two First Nation Communities." *Journal of Native Social Work* 1, 1.

_____. 2007. "Promising Practices for Maintaining Identities in First Nation Adoption." *Journal of First Peoples Child and Family Review* 3, 1.

Dobell, L. 2003. *Adoption Piece by Piece.* Vancouver: Ben Simon Press

First Nation Directors of Child and Family Services of Alberta. 2006. "First Nation Practice Standards In Child, Youth And Family Services In Alberta." Edmonton: Alberta Children Services.

George, D. 1989. *My Heart Soars.* Blaine, WA: Hancock House.

Government of Alberta, Ministry of Children's Services. 2006. *First Nation Practice Standards in Child, Youth and Family Services in Alberta.* Edmonton.

Hart, M. 2007. "Indigenous Knowledge and Research: The Mikiwahp as a Symbol for Reclaiming our Knowledge and Ways of Knowing." *First Peoples Child and Family Review* 31.

Henderson, J.Y. 2000. "Ayukpachi: Empowering Aboriginal Thought." In M. Battiste (ed.), *Reclaiming Indigenous Voice and Vision.* Vancouver, BC: University of British Columbia Press.

National Indian Child Welfare Association. 2002. "Whole Person Assessment: Native American Children and Youth Well-Being Indicators: A Strengths Perspective." Portland, OR: National Indian Child Welfare Association.

Richardson, C., and B. Nelson. 2007. "A Change of Residence: Government Schools and Foster Homes as Sites of Forced Aboriginal Assimilation — A Paper Designed to Provoke Though and Systemic Change." *First Peoples Child and Family Review* 3, 2.

Thomas, R., and J. Green. 2007. "A Way of Life: Indigenous Perspective on Anti Oppressive Living." *First Peoples Child and Family Review* 3, 1.

Walmsley, C. 2004. "Talking about the Aboriginal Community: Child Protection Practitioner's Views." *First Peoples Child & Family Review* 1, 1.

## Appendix 16-1 Whole Person Assessment

This Assessment Framework was developed in 2002 by the National Indian Child Welfare Association (First Nation Directors of Child and Family Services of Alberta 2006: 76). It was adapted and developed from a worldview that there is an incredible resilience in First Nations families and communities. A caseworker using this framework would be working from a strengths perspective and not a deficiency model. Some of the titles in the assessment have been changed to place it in the context of Alberta.

Casework practice considerations will be given to the following items in the development of a Whole Person Assessment:

Importance of Spirituality
- Spirituality
- Culture/traditions
- Dreams
- Healing practices
- Inter-community celebrations

Power of the Group
- Extended family resources
- Group orientation (such as community values)
- Relational (Who are your relations)
- Kinship and mutual aid sources
- Doing and helping style
- Interdependency
- Reciprocity
- Personal relationships
- Social connections

Relevance of Identity
- Cultural identity
- First Nation identity
- Bicultural identity
- Non-traditional cultural orientation

The Next Generation
- View of children/youth
- Number of children/youth
- Childcare customs
- Role of parents

Our Values
- Optimism
- Generosity
- Respect

Education
- Schools
- Traditional/cultural

Political Relationships
- First Nation affiliation
- Political involvement

Our Voice
- Language
- Stories

How Do I Do It?
- Use of humuor
- Overcoming trauma
- Other?

## Appendix 16-2 Support Network

The Support Network Grid identifies and assesses significant others in a person's life

| Support Network Grid | | | | | |
|---|---|---|---|---|---|
| Personal | Tasks How they help | How Often? | Professional | Tasks How they help | How Often |
| Friends Who? | | | | | |
| Family Members Who? | | | | | |
| Community Natural Helpers Who? | | | | | |
| Others? Who? | | | | | |

Helps to determine the strengths and relationships for people

*(First Nation Directors of Child and Family Services of Alberta 2006: 78)*